ADOBE ILLUSTRATOR CS4 REVEALED

CHRIS BOTELLO

ADOBE ILLUSTRATOR CS4 REVEALED

CHRIS BOTELLO

DELMAR
CENGAGE Learning™

Australia • Brazil • Japan • Korea • Mexico • Singapore • Spain • United Kingdom • United States

DELMAR
CENGAGE Learning

Adobe Illustrator CS4 Revealed
Chris Botello

Vice President, Career and Professional Editorial: Dave Garza

Director of Learning Solutions: Sandy Clark

Senior Acquisitions Editor: Jim Gish

Managing Editor: Larry Main

Product Managers: Jane Hosie-Bounar, Nicole Calisi

Editorial Assistant: Sarah Timm

Vice President Marketing, Career and Professional: Jennifer McAvey

Executive Marketing Manager: Deborah S. Yarnell

Marketing Manager: Erin Brennan

Marketing Coordinator: Jonathan Sheehan

Production Director: Wendy Troeger

Senior Content Project Manager: Kathryn B. Kucharek

Developmental Editor: Ann Fisher

Technical Editor: Tara Botelho

Art Directors: Bruce Bond, Joy Kocsis

Cover Design: Lisa Kuhn, Curio Press, LLC

Cover Art: Lisa Kuhn, Curio Press, LLC

Text Designer: Ann Small

Proofreader: Harold Johnson

Indexer: Alexandra Nickerson

Technology Project Manager: Christopher Catalina

Production Technology Analyst: Tom Stover

For product information and technology assistance, contact us at
Cengage Learning Customer & Sales Support, 1-800-354-9706

For permission to use material from this text or product, submit all requests online at
www.cengage.com/permissions
Further permissions questions can be e-mailed to
permissionrequest@cengage.com

Adobe® Photoshop®, Adobe® InDesign®, Adobe® Illustrator®, Adobe® Flash®, Adobe® Dreamweaver®, Adobe® Fireworks®, and Adobe® Creative Suite® are trademarks or registered trademarks of Adobe Systems, Inc. in the United States and/or other countries. Third party products, services, company names, logos, design, titles, words, or phrases within these materials may be trademarks of their respective owners.

The Adobe Approved Certification Courseware logo is a proprietary trademark of Adobe. All rights reserved. Cengage Learning and Illustrator CS4–Revealed are independent from ProCert Labs, LLC and Adobe Systems Incorporated, and are not affiliated with ProCert Labs and Adobe in any manner. This publication may assist students to prepare for an Adobe Certified Expert exam, however, neither ProCert Labs nor Adobe warrant that use of this material will ensure success in connection with any exam.

Library of Congress Control Number: 2009922551

Hardcover edition:
ISBN-13: 978-1-4354-8261-6
ISBN-10: 1-4354-8261-1

Soft cover edition:
ISBN-13: 978-1-4354-4188-0
ISBN-10: 1-4354-4188-5

Delmar
5 Maxwell Drive
Clifton Park, NY 12065-2919
USA

Cengage Learning is a leading provider of customized learning solutions with office locations around the globe, including Singapore, the United Kingdom, Australia, Mexico, Brazil, and Japan. Locate your local office at: **international.cengage.com/region**

Cengage Learning products are represented in Canada by Nelson Education, Ltd.

To learn more about Delmar, visit **www.cengage.com/delmar**

Purchase any of our products at your local college store or at our preferred online store **www.ichapters.com**

Notice to the Reader

Printed in the United States of America
1 2 3 4 5 6 7 13 12 11 10 09

Revealed Series Vision

The Revealed Series is your guide to today's hottest multimedia applications. These comprehensive books teach the skills behind the application, showing you how to apply smart design principles to multimedia products such as dynamic graphics, animation, websites, software authoring tools, and digital video.

A team of design professionals including multimedia instructors, students, authors, and editors worked together to create this series. We recognized the unique learning environment of the multimedia classroom and created a series that:

- Gives you comprehensive step-by-step instructions
- Offers in-depth explanation of the "Why" behind a skill
- Includes creative projects for additional practice
- Explains concepts clearly using full-color visuals

It was our goal to create a book that speaks directly to the multimedia and design community—one of the most rapidly growing computer fields today. We think we've done just that, with a sophisticated and instructive book design.

—The Revealed Series

Author's Vision

Hands-on is the best way to explore any software application. You can study every chapter of an instruction manual, but reading about Adobe Illustrator and drawing in Adobe Illustrator are two very different things indeed.

This book is a series of exercises that will take you on a fully guided tour of Illustrator CS4—from basic concepts to advanced techniques—all with a hands-on approach. You will learn by doing, and you'll have fun, which is an essential skill not covered in any instruction manual.

I had fun writing this, and that was possible because of the focus and hard work of my editor and long-time friend Ann Fisher. Ann kept the project on track but left me enough room to bounce around the application and share with you some of my favorite tips and tricks. Her dedication—combined with a great capacity for laughter—brought out the best in both of us. Special thanks also go to Jim Gish, Senior Acquisitions Editor for this series, and Jane Hosie-Bounar, the product manager. I also want to acknowledge the technical editor Tara Botelho for her invaluable input.

—Chris Botello

Introduction to Adobe Illustrator CS4

Welcome to *Adobe Illustrator CS4—Revealed*. This book offers creative projects, concise instructions, and complete coverage of basic to advanced Illustrator skills, helping you to create polished, professional-looking illustrations. Use this book both in the classroom and as your own reference guide.

This text is organized into 13 chapters. In these chapters, you will learn many skills, including how to draw illustrations, transform objects, work with layers, patterns, brushes, and filters, use effects, create graphics for the Web, create graphs, work in 3D, and prepare files for print production.

What You'll Do

A What You'll Do figure begins every lesson. This figure gives you an at-a-glance look at what you'll do in the chapter, either by showing you a page or pages from the current project or a tool you'll be using.

Comprehensive Conceptual Lessons

Before jumping into instructions, in-depth conceptual information tells you "why" skills are applied. This book provides the "how" and "why" through the use of professional examples. Also included in the text are tips and sidebars to help you work more efficiently and creatively, or to teach you a bit about the history or design philosophy behind the skill you are using.

Step-by-Step Instructions

This book combines in-depth conceptual information with concise steps to help you learn Illustrator CS4. Each set of steps guides you through a lesson where you will create, modify, or enhance an Illustrator CS4 file. Step references to large colorful images and quick step summaries round out the lessons. The Data Files for the steps are provided on the CD at the back of this book.

Projects

This book contains a variety of end-of-chapter materials for additional practice and reinforcement. The Skills Review contains hands-on practice exercises that mirror the progressive nature of the lesson material. The chapter concludes with four projects; two Project Builders, one Design Project, and one Portfolio Project. The Project Builders and the Design Project require you to apply the skills you've learned in the chapter. Portfolio Projects encourage to you solve challenges based on the content explored in the chapter and create an Illustrator file worthy of your portfolio.

What Instructor Resources Are Available with This Book?

The Instructor Resources CD-ROM is Delmar's way of putting the resources and information needed to teach and learn effectively into your hands. All the resources are available for both Macintosh and Windows operating systems.

Instructor's Manual

Available as an electronic file, the Instructor's Manual includes chapter overviews and detailed lecture topics for each chapter, with teaching tips. The Instructor's Manual is available on the Instructor Resources CD-ROM.

PowerPoint Presentations

Each chapter has a corresponding PowerPoint presentation that you can use in lectures, distribute to your students, or customize to suit your course.

Data Files for Students

To complete most of the chapters in this book, your students will need Data Files. The Data Files are available on the CD at the back of this text book. Instruct students to use the Data Files List at the end of this book. This list gives instructions on organizing files.

Solutions to Exercises

Solution Files are Data Files completed with comprehensive sample answers. Use these files to evaluate your students' work. Or distribute them electronically so students can verify their work. Sample solutions to all lessons and end-of-chapter material are provided.

Test Bank and Test Engine

ExamView is a powerful testing software package that allows instructors to create and administer printed and computer (LAN-based) exams. ExamView includes hundreds of questions that correspond to the topics covered in this text, enabling students to generate detailed study guides that include page references for further review. The computer-based and LANbased/online testing component allows students to take exams using the EV Player and also saves the instructor time by grading each exam automatically.

Measurements

Text attributes are given in points. Measurements on the artboard and measurements referring to an object are given in inches, not points or picas. In order to follow the exercises, it's important that the General Units Preference in the Preferences dialog box be set to Inches. To set this preference, click Edit (Win) or Illustrator (Mac) on the menu bar, point to Preferences, and then click Units & Display Performance.

You may or may not prefer to work with rulers showing. You can make rulers visible by clicking View on the menu bar, then clicking Show Rulers, or by pressing [Ctrl][R] (Win) or ⌘ [R] (Mac). You can hide visible rulers by clicking View on the menu bar, then clicking Hide Rulers or by pressing [Ctrl][R] (Win) or ⌘ [R] (Mac).

Document Color Mode

Generally, CMYK Color (Cyan, Magenta, Yellow, and Black) is the color mode used for print projects, and RGB Color (Red, Green, and Blue) is the color mode used for projects that will appear on a screen. The New Document Profile menu in the New Document dialog box allows you to specify the type of document you need. You can choose Print, Web, Mobile and Devices, Video and Film, as well as Basic CMYK or Basic RGB. You can also change a document's color mode by clicking File on the menu bar, then clicking Document Color Mode. The color mode for each document is identified in the title bar at the top of the Illustrator window.

Whenever you are asked to create a new document, the color mode will be specified. Many menu commands, such as those under the Effect menu, are available only in RGB mode. If you run into a situation in which a specified menu command is not available, first check the color mode.

Fonts

Whenever fonts are used in Data and Solution Files, they are chosen from a set of very common typefaces that you will most likely have available on your computer. If any of the fonts in use are not available on your computer, please make a substitution.

For variety and typographic appeal, we have used other typefaces in Data and Solution Files that are not standard; however, we have converted those fonts to outlines. When a font is converted to an outline, the letterform is simply a vector graphic, like all other vector graphics.

Quick Keys

Quick keys are keyboard shortcuts that can be used in place of clicking the command on the menu. [Ctrl][X], for example, is the quick key for Cut on the PC platform. Mastering basic quick keys is essential for a smooth work flow in Illustrator. It's a good idea to start with the commands on the Edit and Object menus as candidates for quick keys.

Certification

This book covers the objectives necessary for Adobe Illustrator certification. Use the Certification Grid at the back of the book to find out where an objective is covered.

CHAPTER 2   CREATING TEXT AND GRADIENTS

CHAPTER 4   TRANSFORMING AND DISTORTING OBJECTS

CONTENTS

CHAPTER 9   CREATING GRAPHS IN ILLUSTRATOR

CONTENTS

CHAPTER 10 DRAWING WITH SYMBOLS

CONTENTS

xxi

CHAPTER 12 PREPARING A DOCUMENT FOR PREPRESS AND PRINTING

1

GETTING STARTED
WITH ILLUSTRATOR

1. Create a new document

2. Explore the Illustrator window

3. Create basic shapes

4. Apply fill and stroke colors to objects

5. Select, move, and align objects

6. Transform objects

7. Make direct selections

chapter 1

GETTING STARTED
WITH ILLUSTRATOR

Getting to Know Illustrator

Adobe Illustrator CS4 is a professional illustration software application created by Adobe Systems Incorporated. If this name is familiar to you, it's because Adobe is a leading producer of graphics software for the personal computer. Along with Illustrator, Adobe produces an entire suite of applications, including InDesign, Acrobat, Flash, Dreamweaver, and, of course, the revolutionary and award-winning Photoshop.

With Illustrator, you can create everything from simple graphics, icons, and text to complex and multilayered illustrations, all of which can be used within a page layout, in a multimedia presentation, or on the Web.

Adobe Illustrator offers dozens of essential tools. Using them in combination with various menu commands, you have the potential to create any illustration that your imagination can dream up. With experience, you will find that your ability to create complex graphics rests on your ability to master simple, basic operations.

Tools You'll Use

CREATE A
NEW DOCUMENT

What You'll Do

 In this lesson, you will start Adobe Illustrator and create a new document.

Creating a New Document

When you are ready to create a new document in Illustrator, you begin in the New Document dialog box. In the New document dialog box, you specify the name of the document, which will appear in the document tab of the new file. You also use this dialog box to specify the document size—the width and height of the finished document. In addition, you can choose the number of artboards, the page orientation, landscape or portrait, and the unit of measure you would like the rulers to display. Some designers like to work with inches; others prefer points or picas. Finally, you can choose the appropriate color mode to work in based on the type of document you are creating.

Choosing Color Modes and Document Size

Generally, CMYK Color (Cyan, Magenta, Yellow, and Black) is the color mode used for print projects, and RGB Color (Red, Green, and Blue) is the color mode used for projects that will appear on a screen, such as a monitor, a television or on the Web. The New Document Profile menu in the New Document dialog box allows you to specify the type of document you need. You can choose Print, Web, Mobile and Devices, Video and Film, as well as Basic CMYK or Basic RGB. The dialog box options available depend on which profile you choose. For example, if you choose Mobile and Devices, the Color Mode changes to RGB, the unit of measure changes to pixels, and the Device Central button appears in the dialog box. This button launches Adobe Device Central which allows you to preview how your document will appear on a specific device or mobile phone. If you choose Print, the dialog box will offer all of the appropriate settings for a document that you intend to print.

Another method for specifying the color mode is to click the expand button to the left of the word Advanced, click the Color Mode list arrow, then choose RGB or CMYK.

Once a document is created, you may change color mode settings by clicking File on the Application bar, pointing to Document Color Mode, then clicking CMYK Color or RGB Color. In addition, once a document is created, you can alter the current settings, such as the page size, in the Document Setup dialog box. The Document Setup command is on the File menu.

Choosing a Unit of Measure

Precision is often a key to good design, and many designers choose points and picas as units of measure. A point is ½ of an inch. A pica is 12 points, or ⅙ of an inch. Defining your artboard in points and picas versus inches is a matter of personal preference. As a designer, you're probably familiar with points and picas, but would you really refer to a letter-size page as 612×792 points? On the other hand, when working in inches, using measurements such as ²⁹⁄₃₂ of

an inch would also be a bit ridiculous. Working with a combination of the two is the best bet; many designers work in points for text, rules, and strokes, but they define the page itself in inches.

To set your preferences for units of measure, click Edit (Win) or Illustrator (Mac) on the Application bar, point to **Preferences,** then click Units & Display Performance. Click the General, Stroke, and Type list arrows to choose your preferred unit of measure. The General setting determines the units of measurement for the page and objects on the page.

You'll certainly want to measure your strokes and type in points. Imagine setting type in ¾" Garamond!

QUICKTIP

If you are using a Macintosh, you will find the Preferences command on the Illustrator menu.

Using the Illustrator Options dialog box

Let's say that you have a friend, a co-worker, or a client that you want to send an Illustrator CS4 file to, but you find out that he or she never upgraded to CS4, and therefore cannot open a CS4 file. No problem: Adobe Illustrator CS4 makes it easy to save files that previous versions of Illustrator can open. Simply click the Save As command on the File menu. In the Save As dialog box, choose Adobe Illustrator(*.AI), then click Save. The Illustrator Options dialog box opens. Click the Versions list arrow, then choose the format you need. CS Formats include CS4, CS3, CS2, and CS. Legacy Formats include Illustrator 3, 8, 9, 10, and Japanese Illustrator 3.

Create a new document (Windows)

1. Click the **Start button** 🟩 on the taskbar, point to **All Programs**, click **Adobe Design Premium CS4** (or the name of your Adobe suite), then click **Adobe Illustrator CS4**.

2. Click **File** on the Application bar, then click **New**.

3. Type **The Lay of the Land** in the New Document dialog box.

   | TIP   Note that you have *named* the file in the New Document dialog box, but you have not yet *saved* it.

4. Click the **Size list arrow** to view the available sizes, then click **Letter** (if necessary).

5. Click the **Units list arrow**, then click **Inches** (if necessary).

   The size of your artboard will be 8.5" × 11".

6. Click the **left icon** next to Orientation (Portrait as opposed to Landscape) as the page orientation.

7. Click the **Expand button** ⊗ to the left of the word Advanced, click the **Color Mode list arrow**, then click **CMYK**.

   Your New Document dialog box should resemble Figure 1.

8. Click **OK** to create a new document with these settings.

9. Click **File** on the Application bar, then click **Close**.

You started Illustrator in Windows, then created a new document.

FIGURE 1
New Document dialog box (Windows)

Document name · New Document Profile list arrow · Number of Artboards setting · Size list arrow · Landscape · Portrait · Color Mode list arrow · Expand/Collapse button

Creating Multiple Artboards

With Illustrator CS4, you now have the option to create multiple, different sized artboards in a single document. If you're working with related assets being used for various outputs, you might find it more convenient to work in a single document with multiple artboards than switching between multiple files. It's purely your choice.

Creating multiple artboards happens in the New dialog box using the Number of Artboards setting. Believe it or not, you can create up to 100 artboards in a single Illustrator file. Choose one of the four layout icons (Grid by Row, Grid by Column, Arrange by Row, and Arrange by Column) to determine a default layout for your artboards. You can alter that arrangement of artboards after creating the document. You can also specify the number of rows of artboards and the spacing between them.

The New dialog box is where you've always entered the width and height for the document, and that hasn't changed with multiple artboards. When you're creating a new document, you specify a width and height that will be used for all the artboards in the document. Once the document is created, as shown in Figure 2, you can resize any or all of the artboards independently.

FIGURE 2

Multiple art boards

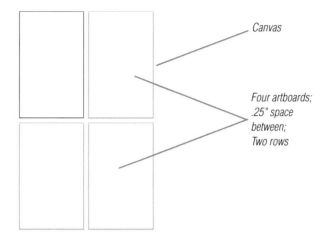

Canvas

Four artboards;
.25" space
between;
Two rows

FIGURE 3

New Document dialog box (Macintosh)

Document name

Number of
Artboards setting

New Document
Profile list arrow

Size list arrow

Landscape

Portrait

Color Mode list
arrow

Expand/Collapse button

1. Double-click the **hard drive icon**, then navigate to and double-click the **Adobe Illustrator CS4 folder**.

2. Double-click the **Adobe Illustrator CS4 program icon**.

3. Click **File** on the Application bar, then click **New**.

4. Type **The Lay of the Land** in the New Document dialog box, as shown in Figure 3.

   | TIP   Note that you have *named* the file in the New Document dialog box, but you have not yet *saved* it.

5. Click the **Size list arrow** to view the available sizes, then click **Letter**.

6. Click the **Units list arrow**, then click **Inches** (if necessary).

   The size of your artboard will be 8.5" × 11".

7. Click the **left icon** next to Orientation (Portrait as opposed to Landscape) as the page orientation.

8. Click the **Expand button** to the left of the word Advanced, click the **Color Mode list arrow**, then click **CMYK**.

   Your New Document window should resemble Figure 3.

9. Click **OK** to create a new document with these settings.

10. Click **File** on the Application bar, then click **Close**.

You started Illustrator in Macintosh, then created a new document.

EXPLORE THE ILLUSTRATOR WINDOW

What You'll Do

 In this lesson, you will learn about the key architecture of the Illustrator window and practice some basic Illustrator skills.

Touring the Illustrator Window

Let's take a few quick minutes to get the lay of the land. It all starts here. The arrangement of windows and panels that you see on your monitor is called the **workspace**. The Illustrator workspace features the following areas: the artboard, the pasteboard, the Application bar, the Tools panel along the left side of the document window, the Control panel beneath the Application bar, the document tab, panels along the right side of the document window, and the status bar. Figure 4 shows the default workspace, which is called Essentials.

Illustrator CS4 offers a number of predefined workspaces that are customized for different types of tasks. Each workspace is designed so that panels with similar functions are grouped together.

If you want to get really good at Illustrator, it's critical that you understand the workspace and learn to how to manage it.

The **document tab** contains the name of your document, magnification level, and color mode.

The **Application bar** includes all of the Illustrator menus. It also includes the Go to Bridge button, the Arrange Documents list arrow, the workspace switcher, and the Minimize, Maximize, and Close buttons.

The **artboard** is the area, bound by a solid line, in which you create your artwork; the size of the artboard can be set as large as 227" × 227".

The **pasteboard** is the area outside the artboard where you can store objects before placing them on the artboard; objects on the pasteboard will not print.

The **Tools panel** contains tools that let you create, select, and manipulate objects in Illustrator. A tiny black triangle beside a tool indicates "hidden" tools behind that tool. Press and hold a tool to expose the panel of hidden tools behind it. Click the Tearoff tab (the tiny black triangle next to

the last tool on the panel) to create a floating toolbar.

QUICKTIP

Click the tiny double arrows at the top left corner of the Tools panel to toggle between a two-column and a single-column Tools panel.

The **Zoom text box** in the lower-left corner of the Illustrator window displays the current magnification level. To the right of the Zoom text box is the Zoom menu, which you access by clicking the Zoom list arrow. The Zoom menu lets you choose another magnification level to work in.

FIGURE 4
Illustrator window

Workspace switcher

Application bar

Control panel

Tools panel

Document tab

Artboard

Pasteboard

Panels

Zoom text box

Zoom list arrow

Artboard Navigation menu   Status bar

Scroll bars

FIGURE 5

Working in Artboard mode

Width & height of selected artboard

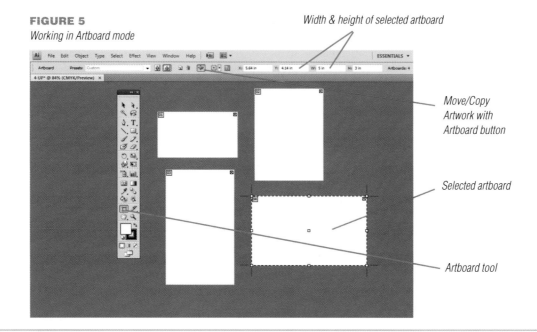

Move/Copy
Artwork with
Artboard button

Selected artboard

Artboard tool

Working in Artboard Mode

There are many ways to work with multiple artboards. You can change the size and location of them and you can also add or delete them.

Click the Artboard tool on the Tools panel to enter "artboard mode," as shown in Figure 5. When you click an individual artboard, handles appear around the selected artboard, indicating that it can be modified. You can click and drag the artboard to move it to a different location. You can also drag any of the resizing handles to modify the size of the artboard on the fly. However, you will likely find it more practical to enter specific new width and height values for the selected artboard on the Control panel.

You can enter artboard mode at any time during your work, not just when setting up a document. When you click and drag an artboard, it will move independently from the art on the artboard. You can override this default by clicking the Move/Copy Artwork with Artboard button, identified in Figure 5.

At any time, you can create a new artboard simply by clicking and dragging in the gray canvas area. It's just as easy to delete an artboard. Simply click it to select it, then press [Delete]. To leave artboard mode, simply click any other tool than the Artboard tool.

When it comes time to print, the Print dialog box offers you controls for determining which of the artboards you want to print. You can print any or all of the artboards in a single printing.

When you save the document as a native Illustrator .ai file, the multiple artboards are saved with the file, as you would expect. If you use the Save As command to save the file for previous versions of Illustrator, like CS3 or CS2, you will be given the option to save the multiple artboards as multiple Illustrator files.

The **status bar** contains the zoom text box, the zoom menu, the Artboard Navigation menu, and Next and Previous buttons.

Scroll bars run along the bottom and right sides of the window; dragging the scroll boxes, clicking in a scroll bar, or clicking the scroll arrows changes the portion of the document displayed in the Illustrator window. **Panels** are windows containing features for modifying and manipulating Illustrator objects. Panels are arranged in groups on the right side of the workspace. Each group is represented by a button. Simply click a button to expand a panel group. To expand all panel groups, click the Expand Panels button at the top of the panels window.

Panels are grouped by function. For example, if you click the Gradient button, you'll see that the Gradient panel is grouped with the Stroke and Transparency panels. If you drag the top of the panel group, all panels in the group move together. You can separate panels from their group by simply dragging the panel

name tab to a new location. You can also merge two panels together by dragging a panel name tab into a new group.

Docking panels allows you to arrange multiple panels or panel groups vertically. Like grouped panels, docked panels move together. To dock a panel or a panel group to another panel group, drag one of the panel name tabs in the group to the bottom edge of another panel then release when the bottom edge is highlighted.

Not all panels are represented by a button in the Illustrator workspace, however, all panels can be accessed using the Window menu.

QUICKTIP
You can temporarily hide all open panels and the Tools panel by pressing [Tab]. Press [Tab] again to show the panels and the Tools panel.

Using Quick Keys in Illustrator

Along with the various tools on the Tools panel, the commands on the Application bar are essential for performing both

basic and complex operations in Illustrator. Many of the menu commands execute operations that you will use over and over again. For that reason, it is a smart idea to memorize the quick keys associated with the basic menu commands. When a quick key is available, it is listed beside the command in the menu.

Many make the mistake of associating quick keys with speed. True, using quick keys will speed up your work, but the real benefit of them is that they help your work flow with fewer disruptions. Leaving your keyboard, moving your mouse, and clicking on a menu command all disrupt the essential flow of your work. Quick keys allow you to quickly execute a command without taking your hands off the keyboard or your eyes off the monitor.

Quick keys are not for 'power users' only; anybody working in Illustrator can use them beneficially. Make learning quick keys a fun part of your work; test yourself along the way. They are so intuitively assigned that you may even find yourself guessing correctly!

In Illustrator, the best place to start memorizing quick keys is with commands on the File, Edit, and Object menus, especially for Open, Close, Save, Copy, Paste, Paste in Front, Paste in Back, Bring to Front, Send to Back, Hide, Show All, Lock, and Unlock All. When you have mastered those commands, keep going. Memorize the keys you use often, and know when to stop. There's no need to memorize the quick key for Clear Guides, unless you find yourself doing it often. Table 1 and Table 2 list essential quick keys for Windows and Macintosh.

Adobe Bridge

Adobe Bridge is a stand-alone software package that ships with the Adobe Creative Suite 4 software package. Bridge, as it is referred to, is a file browser that allows you to locate, browse, and organize files more easily. It also allows you to categorize your files using labels and/or ratings. Using the Sort command on the View menu, you can sort your files in a variety of ways, including, By Date created, By File size, and By Resolution. You can also choose numerous ways to view your files, such as thumbnails, details, or a list. In Bridge, you can assign keywords and metadata to each file, and then search for assets with common metadata attributes, such as files that call for a certain font or a specific Pantone color. You can even embed additional metadata into an asset in Bridge—without opening the file itself. To do so, simply select the file in Bridge, click File on the Application bar, then click File Info. On the left side of the dialog box are many categories such as Camera Data 1, Camera Data 2, and so on. However, if you click the Description category, you can enter custom information about the file, such as the title, author, description, and keywords. This information will then appear on the Metadata and Keywords panels in the Bridge window. To access Bridge, click File on the Application bar, then click Browse in Bridge. Adobe Bridge may be the perfect tool to help you organize your design projects.

TABLE 1: Essential Illustrator Quick Keys (Windows)

command	Windows	command	Windows
Outline	[Ctrl][Y]	Deselect	[Ctrl][Shift][A]
Preview	[Ctrl][Y]	Cut	[Ctrl][X]
Fit Artboard in Window	[Ctrl][0]	Copy	[Ctrl][C]
Zoom In	[Ctrl][+]	Paste	[Ctrl][V]
Zoom Out	[Ctrl][-]	Paste in Front	[Ctrl][F]
Access Hand tool	[Spacebar]	Paste in Back	[Ctrl][B]
Access the Zoom In tool	[Ctrl][Spacebar]	Undo	[Ctrl][Z]
Access the Zoom Out tool	[Ctrl][Spacebar][Alt]	Redo	[Ctrl][Shift][Z]
Select All	[Ctrl][A]		

TABLE 2: Essential Illustrator Quick Keys (Macintosh)

command	Macintosh	command	Macintosh
Outline	⌘ [Y]	Deselect	⌘ [Shift][A]
Preview	⌘ [Y]	Cut	⌘ [X]
Fit Artboard in Window	⌘ [0]	Copy	⌘ [C]
Zoom In	⌘ [+]	Paste	⌘ [V]
Zoom Out	⌘ [-]	Paste in Front	⌘ [F]
Access Hand tool	[Spacebar]	Paste in Back	⌘ [B]
Access the Zoom In tool	⌘ [Spacebar]	Undo	⌘ [Z]
Access the Zoom Out tool	⌘ [Spacebar][option]	Redo	⌘ [Shift][Z]
Select All	⌘ [A]		

Navigate the Illustrator artboard

1. Click **File** on the Application bar, click **Open**, navigate to the drive and folder where your Data Files are stored, click **AI 1-1.ai**, then click **Open**.

2. Click **File** on the Application bar, click **Save As**, type **Window Workout** in the File name text box (Win) or the Save As text box (Mac), navigate to the drive and folder where your Data Files are stored, click **Save**, then click **OK** to close the Illustrator Options dialog box.

3. Click **Window** on the Application bar, point to **Workspace**, then click Essentials.

   The workspace changes to the Essentials workspace.

4. Click **View** on the Application bar, note the quick key for Outline, then click **Outline**.

   As shown in Figure 6, outline mode shows the skeleton of your work—the lines and curves that you have drawn. Outline mode can be useful for making very specific selections.

5. Click **View** on the Application bar, note the quick key for Preview, then click **Preview**.

   Preview mode shows your work complete with the colors and styles you used.

6. Toggle between Outline and Preview modes using the quick key, then return to Preview mode.

7. Click the **Zoom tool** 🔍 on the Tools panel, then click the **circle** four times.

8. Click the **Selection tool** ▶ on the Tools panel.

9. Click **View** on the Application bar, then click **Fit Artboard in Window**.

(continued)

FIGURE 6
Viewing the document in outline mode

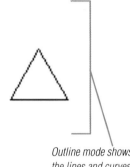

Outline mode shows the lines and curves you have drawn

FIGURE 7

Moving the artboard with the Hand tool

10. Click **View** on the Application bar, note the quick keys for Zoom In and Zoom Out, then release the menu.

11. Use the quick key to zoom in to 200%.

> TIP The current magnification level appears in the document tab and the Zoom text box in the lower-left corner.

12. Use the quick key to zoom out to 66.67%.

13. Press and hold **[Spacebar]**, notice that the pointer changes to the Hand tool , then click and drag the **artboard** with the Hand tool, as shown in Figure 7.

The Hand tool allows you to move the artboard in the window; it's a great alternative to using the scroll arrows. Always press [Spacebar] to access the Hand tool, so as not to interrupt the flow of your work.

You opened an Illustrator document, saved it with a new name, and used menu commands and the Zoom tool to change the view size of the artboard. You then used the Hand tool to move the artboard around.

Exploring the Adobe Illustrator CS4 Welcome Screen

When you start Adobe Illustrator CS4 for the first time, the Welcome Screen appears. The Welcome Screen includes a list of recently opened items on the left and new document templates on the right, such as Print Document and Web Document. The From Template link leads you to pre-designed templates. Templates can really help you jump-start a project if you're running out of time or need some creative guidance. There are six categories of templates: Blank, Film, Japanese, Club, FlexSkins, and Tech. Within those folders are the actual templates, such as Banner Ads, Business Cards, and CD Cases. If you've already installed CS4 and the Welcome Screen doesn't open when you launch the application, fear not! Simply click Help on the Application bar, then click Welcome Screen. If you do not want the Welcome Screen to appear each time, simply click the Don't show again check box in the Welcome Screen dialog box.

Work with objects

1. Click **Select** on the Application bar, then click **All**.

2. Click **View** on the Application bar, then click **Show Bounding Box** (if necessary).

   The bounding box is a box with eight hollow white squares that appears around an object or objects when selected.

   | TIP   If you see Hide Bounding Box on the View menu, the bounding box is already showing.

3. Click **View** on the Application bar, then click **Hide Bounding Box**.

4. Click **Select** on the Application bar, then click **Deselect**.

5. Click the **Selection tool** ▶ on the Tools panel, then move each shape—one at a time—to the bottom of the page.

6. Click **Edit** on the Application bar, then click **Undo Move**.

   The last object you moved returns to its original position, as shown in Figure 8.

7. Undo your last two steps.

8. Click **Edit** on the Application bar, then click **Redo Move**.

9. Redo your last two steps.

10. Click the **artboard** to deselect, click the **red triangle**, click **Edit** on the Application bar, then click **Copy**.

11. Click **Edit** on the Application bar, then click **Paste**.

(continued)

FIGURE 8
Undoing your last step

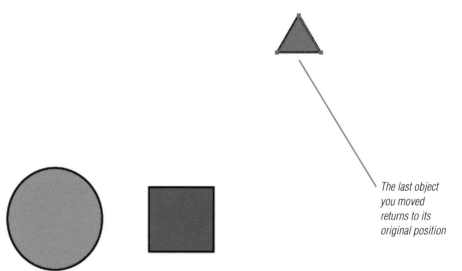

The last object you moved returns to its original position

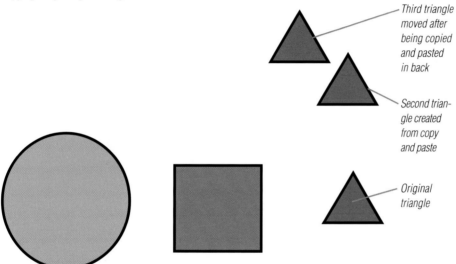

FIGURE 9

Copying and pasting the triangle

Third triangle moved after being copied and pasted in back

Second triangle created from copy and paste

Original triangle

12. Copy the new triangle, click **Edit** on the Application bar, then click **Paste in Back**.

The Paste in Front and Paste in Back commands paste the copied object from the clipboard in front or in back of a selected object. If you select an object, copy it, and then choose Paste in Front; the copy will be pasted above the original in exactly the same location.

13. Move the top red triangle to expose the copied triangle pasted behind it, as shown in Figure 9.

14. Save your work, then close Window Workout.

You moved objects on the artboard and used the Undo and Redo commands on the Edit menu. You selected and copied objects, then applied the Paste in Back command to position a copy precisely in back of its original.

CREATE BASIC SHAPES

What You'll Do

In this lesson, you will examine the differences between bitmap and vector graphics. Then you will use the Rectangle tool to examine Illustrator's various options for creating simple vector graphics.

Getting Ready to Draw

Are you eager to start drawing? Do you want to create complex shapes, special effects, and original art? Perhaps you are a self-taught user of Adobe Illustrator, and your main interest is to graduate to advanced techniques and add a few of those cool special effects to your skill set. Good for you! Enthusiasm is priceless, and no book can teach it. So maintain that enthusiasm for this first exercise, where you'll start by creating a square. That's right . . . a square.

Consider for a moment that Mozart's sublime opera Don Giovanni is based primarily on eight notes, or that the great American novel can be reduced to 26 letters. Illustrator's foundation is basic geometric shapes, so let's start at square one . . . with one square.

Don't rush. As you work, keep in mind that the lessons you will learn here are the foundation of every great illustration.

Understanding Bitmap Images and Vector Graphics

Computer graphics fall into two main categories—bitmap images and vector graphics. To create effective artwork, you need to understand some basic concepts about the two.

Bitmap images are created using a square or rectangular grid of colored squares called **pixels**. Because pixels (a contraction of "picture elements") can render subtle gradations of tone, they are the most common medium for continuous-tone images—what you perceive as a photograph. All scanned images are composed of pixels. All "digital" images are composed of pixels. Adobe Photoshop is the leading graphics application for working with digital "photos." Figure 10 shows an example of a bitmap image. The number of pixels in a given inch is referred to as the image's **resolution**. To be effective, pixels must be small enough to create an image with the illusion of continuous tone. Thus, bitmap images are termed **resolution-dependent**.

The important thing to remember about bitmap images is that any magnification—resizing the image to be bigger—essentially means that fewer pixels are available per inch (the same number of pixels is now spread out over a larger area). This decrease in resolution will have a negative impact on the quality of the image. The greater the magnification, the greater the negative impact.

Graphics that you create in Adobe Illustrator are vector graphics. **Vector graphics** are created with lines and curves and are defined by mathematical objects called vectors. Vectors use geometric characteristics to define the object. Vector graphics consist of **anchor points** and **line segments**, together referred to as **paths**.

For example, if you use Illustrator to render a person's face, the software will identify the iris of the eye using the mathematical definition of a circle with a specific radius and a specific location in respect to other graphics. It will then fill that circle with the color you have specified. Figure 11 shows an example of a vector graphic.

Computer graphics rely on vectors to render bold graphics that must retain clean, crisp lines when scaled to various sizes. Vectors are often used to create logos or "line art," and they are the best choice for typographical work, especially small and italic type.

As mathematical objects, vector graphics can be scaled to any size. Because they are not created with pixels, there is no inherent resolution. Thus, vector graphics are termed **resolution-independent**. This means that any graphic that you create in Illustrator can be output to fit on a postage stamp or on a billboard!

FIGURE 10
Bitmap graphics

FIGURE 11
Vector graphics

Use the Rectangle tool

1. Click **File** on the Application bar, click **New**, create a new document that is 8" wide by 8" in height, name the file **Basic Shapes**, then click **OK**.

2. Click **File** on the Application bar, click **Save As**, navigate to the drive and folder where your Data Files are stored, click **Save,** then click **OK** to close the Illustrator Options dialog box.

3. Click the **Default Fill and Stroke button** on the Tools panel.

4. Click the **Swap Fill and Stroke button** on the Tools panel to reverse the default colors.

   Your fill color should now be black and your stroke color white. The **fill color** is the inside color of an object. The **stroke color** is the color of the object's border or frame.

5. Click the **Rectangle tool** on the Tools panel.

6. Click and drag the **Rectangle tool pointer** on the artboard, then release the mouse pointer to make a rectangle of any size.

7. Press and hold **[Shift]** while you create a second rectangle.

   Pressing and holding [Shift] while you create a rectangle constrains the shape to a perfect square, as shown in Figure 12.

8. Create a third rectangle drawn from its center point by pressing and holding **[Alt]** (Win) or **[option]** (Mac) as you drag the **Rectangle tool pointer**.

   | TIP   Use [Shift] in combination with [Alt] (Win) or [option] (Mac) to draw a perfect shape from its center.

You created a freeform rectangle, then you created a perfect square. Finally you drew a square from its center point.

FIGURE 12
Creating a rectangle and a square

Square created by pressing [Shift] while creating a rectangle

1. Click **Select** on the Application bar, then click **All** to select all of the objects.

2. Click **Edit** on the Application bar, then click **Cut** to remove the objects from the artboard.

3. Click anywhere on the artboard.

   When a shape tool is selected, clicking once on the artboard opens a dialog box, which allows you to enter precise information for creating the object. In this case, it opens the Rectangle dialog box.

4. Type **4** in the Width text box, type **4** in the Height text box, as shown in Figure 13, then click **OK**.

5. Save your work.

Using the Rectangle tool, you clicked the artboard, which opened the Rectangle dialog box. You entered a specific width and height to create a perfect 4" square.

FIGURE 13
Rectangle dialog box

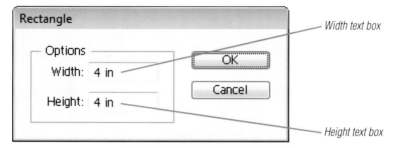

Width text box

Height text box

APPLY FILL AND STROKE
COLORS TO OBJECTS

What You'll Do

▶ *In this lesson you will use the Swatches panel to add a color fill to an object and apply a stroke as a border. Then you will use the Stroke panel to change the size of the default stroke.*

Activating the Fill or Stroke

The Fill and Stroke buttons are on the Tools panel. To apply a fill or stroke color to an object, you must first activate the appropriate button. You activate either button by clicking it, which moves it in front of the other. When the Fill button is in front of the Stroke

button, the fill is activated, as shown in Figure 14. The Stroke button is activated when it is in front of the Fill button.

As you work, you will often switch back and forth, activating the fill and the stroke. Rather than using your mouse to activate the fill or the stroke each time, simply press [X] to switch between the two modes.

FIGURE 14
Fill and Stroke buttons

Swap Fill and Stroke button

Default Fill and Stroke button

Stroke button (not activated)

Fill button (activated)

Applying Color with the Swatches Panel

The Swatches panel as shown in Figure 15, is central to color management in the application and a simple resource for applying fills and strokes to objects.

The panel has 47 preset colors, along with gradients and patterns, and shades of gray.

The swatch with the red line through it is called [None] and used as a fill for a "hollow" object. Any object without a stroke will always have [None] as its stroke color.

When an object is selected, clicking a swatch on the panel will apply that color as a fill or a stroke, depending on which

of the two is activated on the Tools panel. You can also drag and drop swatches onto unselected objects. Dragging a swatch to an unselected object will change the color of its fill or stroke, depending upon which of the two is activated.

FIGURE 15
Swatches panel

Pre-set colors, gradients, patterns, and shades of gray

Apply fill and stroke colors

1. Verify that the new square is still selected.

2. Click the **Swatches button** ⊞ to open the Swatches panel.

    Your Swatches panel may already be available.

3. Click any blue swatch on the Swatches panel to fill the square.

    Note that the Fill button on the Tools panel is now also blue.

    > TIP When you position your pointer over a color swatch on the Swatches panel, a tooltip appears that shows the name of that swatch.

4. Click the **Selection tool** ▶, then click anywhere on the artboard to deselect the blue square.

5. Drag and drop a **yellow swatch** onto the blue square.

    The fill color changes to yellow because the Fill button is activated on the Tools panel. Your colors may vary from the colors shown in the figures.

6. Press **[X]** to activate the Stroke button on the Tools panel.

7. Drag and drop the **red swatch** on the Swatches panel onto the yellow square.

    As shown in Figure 16, a red stroke is added to the square because the Stroke button is activated on the Tools panel.

8. Click the **Stroke button** ☰ to display the Stroke panel.

    Your Stroke panel may already be available.

    (continued)

FIGURE 16
Red stroke is added to the yellow square

FIGURE 17

Yellow square without a stroke

9. Select the square, click the **Weight list arrow** on the Stroke panel, then click **8 pt**.

   TIP Illustrator positions a stroke equally inside and outside an object. Thus, an 8 pt stroke is rendered with 4 pts inside the object and 4 pts outside.

10. Click **[None]** ⊘ on the Swatches panel to remove the stroke from the square.

    Your screen should resemble Figure 17.

11. Save your work.

You filled the square with blue by clicking a blue swatch on the Swatches panel. You then changed the fill and stroke colors to yellow and red by dragging and dropping swatches onto the square. You used the Stroke panel to increase the weight of the stroke, then removed the stroke by choosing [None] from the Swatches panel.

SELECT, MOVE, AND
ALIGN OBJECTS

What You'll Do

▶ *In this lesson, you will use the Selection tool in combination with Smart Guides to move, copy, and align four squares.*

Selecting and Moving Objects

When it comes to accuracy, consider that Illustrator can move objects incrementally by fractions of a point—which itself is a tiny fraction of an inch! That level of precision is key when moving and positioning objects.

Before you can move or modify an Illustrator object, you must identify it by selecting it with a selection tool, menu item, or command key. When working with simple illustrations that contain few objects, selecting is usually simple, but it can become very tricky in complex illustrations, especially those containing a large number of small objects positioned closely together.

Two very basic ways to move objects are by clicking and dragging or by using the arrow keys, which by default move a selected item in 1-pt increments. Pressing [Shift] when dragging an

object constrains the movement to the horizontal, the vertical, and 45° diagonals. Pressing [Alt] (Win) or [option] (Mac) when dragging an object creates a copy of the object.

Grouping Objects

Many of the illustrations you create will be composed of a number of small objects. Once you have established the relationships among those objects, grouping them allows you to select them all with one click of the Selection tool and then move or modify them simultaneously. To group objects, click them, click Object on the Application bar, then click Group.

Making a Marquee Selection with the Selection Tool

By now, you're familiar with using the Selection tool to select objects. You can also use the Selection tool to create a marquee selection, a dotted rectangle that disappears as soon as you release the mouse button. Any object that the marquee touches before you release the mouse button will be selected. Marquee selections are very useful for both quick selections and precise selections. Practice, and make this part of your skill set.

Working with Smart Guides

Smart Guides are temporary guides that can be turned on and off on the View menu. Smart Guides help you move and align objects in relation to other objects or in relation to the artboard. With Smart Guides turned on, you will see words, called Smart Guides, that identify visible or invisible objects, page boundaries, intersections, anchor points, paths, and center points as you move the mouse pointer along the objects on the artboard. When you move an object, Smart Guides give you a visual reference for precise alignment, as shown in Figure 18. For example, if you want to align two objects by their corners, Smart Guides will signal you when the two items come into contact, using the word "intersect."

FIGURE 18
Using Smart Guides

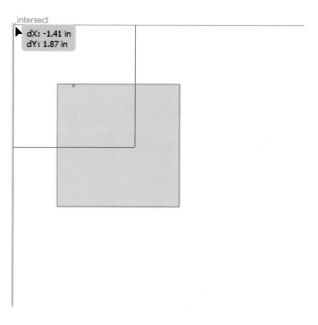

Select and move an object using Smart Guides

1. Click **View** on the Application bar, then click **Fit Artboard In Window**.

2. Click **View** on the Application bar, then verify that both Smart Guides and Snap to Point are checked by verifying that there is a check mark to the left of each menu item.

    > TIP If you do not see a check mark next to Smart Guides or Snap to Point, click View on the Application bar, then click each item, one at a time, to turn these two features on.

    Snap to Point automatically aligns anchor points when they get close together. When dragging an object, you'll see it "snap" to align itself with a nearby object (or guide).

3. Click the **Selection tool** ▶ on the Tools panel, then click the **yellow square**.

4. Identify the anchor points, paths, and center point, as shown in Figure 19.

5. Move the Selection tool pointer over the anchor points, over the paths that connect the points, and over the center point.

6. Position the pointer over the top-left anchor point, click and drag so that the anchor point aligns with the top-left corner of the artboard, as shown in Figure 20, then release the mouse.

    The Smart Guide changes from "anchor" to "intersect" when the two corners are aligned.

You used the Selection tool in combination with Smart Guides to position an object exactly at the top-left corner of the artboard.

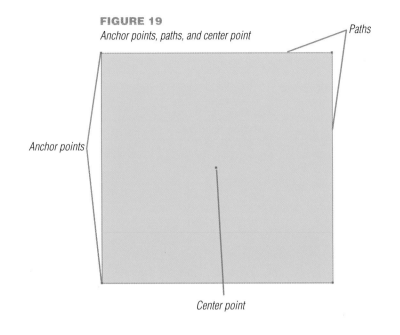

FIGURE 19
Anchor points, paths, and center point

Paths

Anchor points

Center point

FIGURE 20
Intersecting two points

When the top-left anchor point of the square meets the top-left corner of the artboard, the word "intersect" appears

FIGURE 21

Duplicating the square

A copy of the original square

FIGURE 22

Four squares created using drag and drop

1. Click the **top-left anchor point**, press and hold **[Shift][Alt]** (Win) or **[Shift][option]** (Mac), drag straight down until the top-left anchor point touches the bottom-left anchor point (the "intersect" Smart Guide will appear), then release the mouse.

   When moving an object, pressing and holding [Shift] constrains the movement vertically, horizontally, or on 45° diagonals. Pressing [Alt] (Win) or [option] (Mac) while dragging an object creates a copy of the object, as shown in Figure 21.

   > TIP   When you press [Alt] (Win) or [option] (Mac) while dragging an object, the pointer becomes a double-arrow pointer. When two anchor points are directly on top of each other, the Selection tool pointer turns from black to white.

2. With the bottom square still selected, press and hold **[Shift]**, then click the **top square** to select both items.

3. Click the **top-left anchor point** of the top square, press and hold **[Shift][Alt]** (Win) or **[Shift][option]** (Mac), drag to the right until the top-left anchor point touches the top-right anchor point, then release the mouse.

4. Change the fill color of each square to match the colors shown in Figure 22.

5. Save your work.

You moved and duplicated the yellow square using [Shift] to constrain the movement and [Alt] (Win) or [option] (Mac) to duplicate or "drag and drop" copies of the square.

TRANSFORM OBJECTS

What You'll Do

 In this lesson, you will scale, rotate, and reflect objects, using the basic transform tools. You will also create a star and a triangle.

Transforming Objects

The Scale, Rotate, and Reflect tools are the fundamental transform tools. As their names make clear, the Scale and Rotate tools resize and rotate objects, respectively. Double-click a transform tool to open the tool's dialog box. When you use the tool's dialog box, the objects are transformed from their centerpoints. This can be a useful choice, because the object's position essentially doesn't change on the artboard or in relation to other objects.

Use the Reflect tool to "flip" an object over an imaginary axis. The best way to understand the Reflect tool is to imagine positioning a mirror perpendicular to a sheet of paper with a word written on it. The angle at which you position the mirror in relation to the word is the reflection axis. The reflection of the word in the mirror is the end result of what the Reflect tool does. For example, text reflected across a horizontal axis would appear upside down and inverted. Text reflected across a vertical axis would appear to be inverted and running backwards, as shown in Figure 23.

You can transform an object using the desired tool or its dialog box. Each transform tool has a dialog box where you can enter precise numbers to execute the transformation on a selected object. You can access a tool's dialog box by double-clicking the tool. Click the Copy button in the dialog box to create a transformed copy of the selected object. Figure 24 shows the Scale dialog box.

Repeating Transformations

One of the most powerful commands relating to the transform tools is Transform Again, found on the Object menu. Unfortunately, it is a command often overlooked by new users. Whenever you transform an object, selecting Transform Again repeats the transformation. For example, if you scale a circle 50%, the Transform Again command will scale the circle 50% again.

The power of the command comes in combination with copying transformations. For example, if you rotate a square 10° and copy it at the same time, the Transform Again command will create a second square, rotated another 10° from the first copy. Applying Transform Again repeatedly is very handy for creating complex geometric shapes from basic objects.

FIGURE 23
Reflected text

Reflect

Reflect

Reflect ⁞ **Reflect**

FIGURE 24
Scale dialog box

Options for
scaling an
object

Copy
button

Use the Scale and Rotate tools

1. Select the **green square**, double-click the **Scale tool** 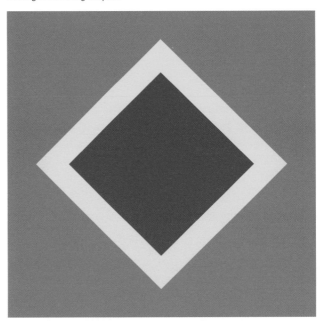, type **50** in the Scale text box, then click **OK**.

2. Click **Edit** on the Application bar, then click **Undo Scale**.

   TIP. You can also undo your last step by pressing [Ctrl][Z] (Win) or ⌘[Z] (Mac).

3. Double-click the **Scale tool** again, type **50** in the Scale text box, then click **Copy**.

   The transformation is executed from the center point; the center points of the original and the copy are aligned.

4. Fill the new square created in Step 3 with blue.

5. Double-click the **Rotate tool**, type **45** in the Angle text box, click **OK**, then click the **Selection tool**.

6. Apply a 22 pt, yellow stroke to the rotated square, deselect, then compare your screen to Figure 25.

You used the Scale tool to create a 50% copy of the square, then filled the copy with blue. You rotated the copy 45°. You then applied a 22 pt, yellow stroke.

FIGURE 25
Scaling and rotating a square

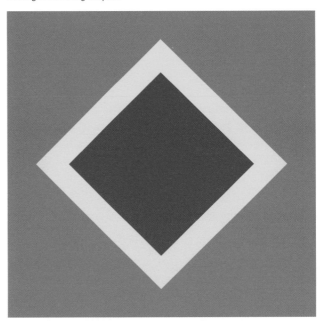

Getting Started with Illustrator

FIGURE 26
Using the Transform Again command

1. Click the **Ellipse tool** ⬭ on the Tools panel.

   TIP   To access the Ellipse tool, press and hold the Rectangle tool until a toolbar of shape tools appears, then click the Ellipse tool.

2. Click the **artboard**, type **3** in the Width text box and **.5** in the Height text box, then click **OK**.

3. Change the fill color to [None], the stroke color to blue, and the stroke weight to 3 pt.

4. Click the **Selection tool** ▶, click the **center point** of the ellipse, then drag it to the center point of the yellow square. (*Hint*: The center Smart Guide appears when the two centers meet.)

5. Double-click the **Rotate tool** ↻, type **45** in the Angle text box, then click **Copy**.

6. Click **Object** on the Application bar, point to **Transform**, then click **Transform Again**.

   TIP   You can also access the Transform Again command by pressing [Ctrl][D] (Win) or ⌘ [D] (Mac).

7. Repeat Step 6 to create a fourth ellipse using the Transform Again command.

   Your screen should resemble Figure 26.

8. Select the four ellipses, click **Object** on the Application bar, then click **Group**.

You created an ellipse, filled and stroked it, and aligned it with the yellow square. You then created a copy rotated at 45°. With the second copy still selected, you used the Transform Again command twice, thus creating two more rotated copies. You then grouped the four ellipses.

Create a star and a triangle, and use the Reflect tool

1. Select the **Star tool** ☆, then click any-where on the artboard.

   The Star tool is hidden beneath the current shape tool.

2. Type **1** in the Radius 1 text box, type **5** in the Radius 2 text box, type **5** in the Points text box, as shown in Figure 27, then click **OK**.

   A star has two radii; the first is from the cen-ter to the inner point, and the second is from the center to the outer point. The **radius** is a measurement from the center point of the star to either point.

3. Double-click the **Scale tool** 🔲, type **25** in the Scale text box, then click **OK**.

   When you create a star using the Star dialog box, the star is drawn upside down.

4. Fill the star with white, then apply a 5 pt blue stroke to it.

5. Click the **Selection tool** ▶, then move the star so that it is completely within the red square.

6. Double-click the **Reflect tool** 🔁, click the **Horizontal option button**, as shown in Figure 28, then click **OK**.

   The star "flips" over an imaginary horizontal axis.

   | TIP   The Reflect tool is hidden beneath the Rotate tool.

   (continued)

FIGURE 27
Star dialog box

Radius 1 text box

Radius 2 text box

FIGURE 28
Reflect dialog box

Horizontal option button

FIGURE 29
Reflecting the star horizontally

FIGURE 30
The finished project

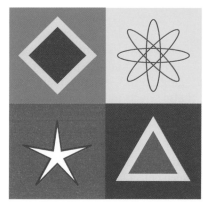

7. Use the Selection tool ▶ or the arrow keys to position the star roughly in the center of the red square.

   Your work should resemble Figure 29.

   TIP Arrow keys move a selected item in 1 pt increments, known as the Keyboard Increment. You can change this amount by clicking Edit (Win) or Illustrator (Mac) on the Application bar, pointing to Preferences, clicking General, then typing a new value in the Keyboard Increment text box.

8. Click the **Polygon tool** ⬡ on the Tools panel.

   The Polygon tool is hidden beneath the current shape tool on the Tools panel.

9. Click anywhere on the blue square.

10. Type **1.5** in the Radius text box, type **3** in the Sides text box, then click **OK**.

11. Fill the triangle with red.

12. Change the stroke color to yellow and the stroke weight to 22 pt.

13. Position the triangle so that it is centered within the blue square.

    Your completed project should resemble Figure 30.

14. Save your work, then close Basic Shapes.

You used the shape tools to create a star and a triangle and used the Reflect tool to "flip" the star over an imaginary horizontal axis.

Selecting

The Select menu offers some powerful selection commands under the Same submenu. There you have commands to select by the same fill, stroke, fill and stroke, stroke color, and stroke weight. You can even select objects with the same opacity and blending mode applied. When it comes to selecting multiple objects, using the Select menu is much faster than Shift-clicking!

MAKE DIRECT SELECTIONS

What You'll Do

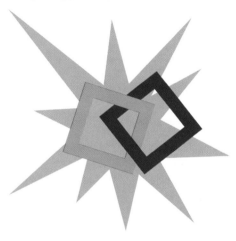

In this lesson, you will use the Direct Selection tool and a combination of menu commands, such as Add Anchor Points and Paste in Front, to convert existing shapes into new designs.

Using the Direct Selection Tool

The Direct Selection tool selects individual anchor points or single paths of an object. Using [Shift], you can select multiple anchor points or multiple paths. You can also select multiple points or paths by dragging a direct selection marquee. The tool also selects individual objects within a group, which can be very useful for modifying just one object in a complex group. Figure 31 demonstrates the Direct Selection tool selecting one piece of a grouped object.

Clicking the center of an object with the Direct Selection tool selects the entire object. Clicking the edge selects the path only. You will know you have made this direct selection successfully if the anchor points on the object all appear white. A white anchor point is not selected.

The Direct Selection tool gives you the power to distort simple objects such as squares and circles into unique shapes. Don't underestimate its significance. While the Selection tool is no more than a means

to an end for selecting and moving objects, the Direct Selection tool is in itself a drawing tool. You will use it over and over again to modify and perfect your artwork.

Adding Anchor Points

As you distort basic shapes with the Direct Selection tool, you will often find that to create more complex shapes, you will need additional anchor points to work with.

The Add Anchor Points command creates new anchor points without distorting the object. To add anchor points to an object, click the Object menu, point to Path, then click Add Anchor Points. The new points are automatically positioned exactly between the original anchor points. You can create as many additional points as you wish to use.

Turning Objects into Guides

Guides are one of Illustrator's many features that help you to work with precision. Any object you create can be turned into a guide. With the object selected, click the View menu, point to Guides, then click Make Guides. Guides can be locked or unlocked in the same location. It is a good idea to work with locked guides so that they don't interfere with your artwork. Unlock guides only when you want to select them or delete them.

When an object is turned into a guide, it loses its attributes, such as its fill, stroke, and stroke weight. However, Illustrator remembers the original attributes for each

guide. To transform a guide back to its original object, first unlock, then select the guide. Click the View menu, point to Guides, then click Release Guides.

FIGURE 31
Using the Direct Selection tool

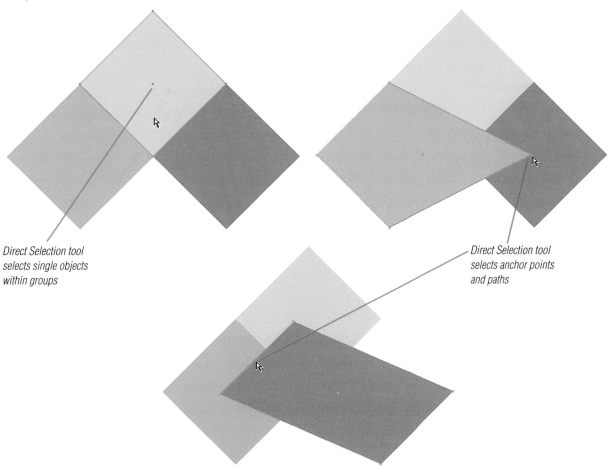

Direct Selection tool selects single objects within groups

Direct Selection tool selects anchor points and paths

Make guides and direct selections

1. Open AI 1-2.ai, then save it as **Direct Selections**.

   TIP Each time you save a Data File, click OK to close the Illustrator Options dialog box.

2. Click **View** on the Application bar, then click **Smart Guides** to turn this feature off.

3. Select the **green polygon**.

4. Click **View** on the Application bar, point to **Guides**, then click **Make Guides**.

   The polygon is converted to a guide.

   TIP If you do not see the polygon-shaped guide, click View on the Application bar, point to Guides, then click Show Guides.

5. Convert the purple starburst to a guide.

6. Click **View** on the Application bar, point to **Guides**, verify that there is a check mark to the left of Lock Guides, then release the mouse.

7. Click the **Direct Selection tool** ⬙., then click the edge of the red square.

   The four anchor points turn white, as shown in Figure 32.

8. Click and drag the anchor points to the four corners of the guide to distort the square.

   Your work should resemble Figure 33.

You converted two objects into guides. You then used the Direct Selection tool to create a new shape from a square by moving anchor points independently.

FIGURE 32
Red square selected with the Direct Selection tool

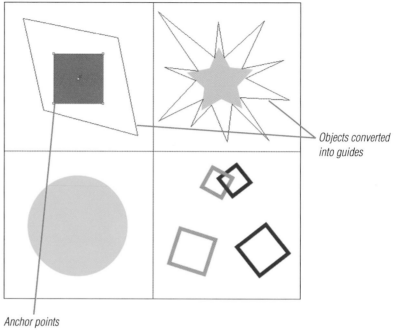

Objects converted into guides

Anchor points are hollow

FIGURE 33
Red square distorted

FIGURE 34
Star selected with Direct Selection tool

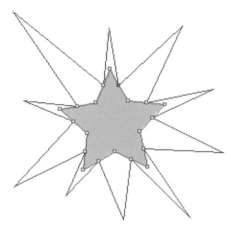

FIGURE 35
Completed starburst

Add anchor points

1. Using the **Direct Selection tool** ⊳. click the center of the light blue star, and note the anchor points used to define the shape.

2. Click **Object** on the Application bar, point to **Path**, then click **Add Anchor Points**.

3. Click the **artboard** to deselect the star, then click the edge of the star.

   All the anchor points turn white and are available to be selected independently, as shown in Figure 34.

4. Move the top anchor point on the star to align with the top point of the guide that you made earlier.

5. Working clockwise, move every other anchor point outward to align with the guide, creating a ten-point starburst.

   Your work should resemble Figure 35.

6. Select and move any of the inner anchor points to modify the starburst to your liking.

You used the Add Anchor Points command and the Direct Selection tool to create an original ten-point starburst from a generic five-point star.

Making a direct selection marquee

When you create a marquee selection with the Selection tool, any object the marquee touches is selected in its entirety. You can also use the Direct Selection tool to create selection marquees. A Direct Selection tool marquee selects only the anchor points and the paths that it touches. A Direct Selection tool marquee is very useful for selecting multiple points or paths in one step.

Select paths

1. Click the edge of the yellow circle with the Direct Selection tool.

   The yellow circle is comprised of four anchor points and four line segments, as shown in Figure 36. Clicking the edge selects one of the four segments.

2. Copy the segment.

3. Click **Edit** on the Application bar, then click **Paste in Front**.

   A copy is pasted directly on top of the selected segment.

4. Change the fill color to [None].

5. Change the stroke color to dark blue and the stroke weight to 14 pt.

6. Moving clockwise, repeat Steps 1, 2, 3, and 4 for the next three line segments, choosing different colors for each.

   Your finished circle should resemble Figure 37.

You selected individual segments of a circle, copied them, and then pasted them in front. You then created a special effect by stroking the four new segments with different colors.

FIGURE 36
Viewing the path of the circle

Clicking the edge of an object with the Direct Selection tool selects one line segment of the entire path

FIGURE 37
Completed circle

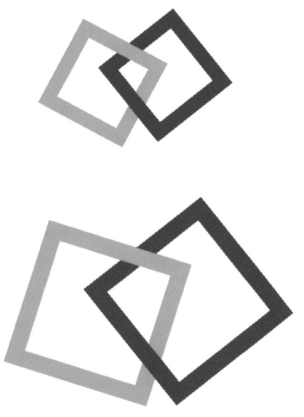

FIGURE 38
Completed linked squares

Create a simple special effect utilizing a direct selection

1. Click the Selection tool ▶, then overlap the large orange and blue squares so that they resemble the small orange and blue squares, then deselect.

2. Click the Direct Selection tool ▶, then select the top path of the orange square.

3. Copy the path.

4. Select the intersecting path on the blue square.

5. Paste in front, then save your work.

   Your work should resemble Figure 38.

6. Close the document.

   TIP Remember this technique; it's one you'll probably use over and over again when you create artwork in Illustrator.

You learned a classic Illustrator trick. Selecting only a path, you copied it and pasted it in front of an intersecting object to create the illusion that the two objects were linked.

Create a new document.

1. Create a new document and name it **Flag**.
2. Make the size of the document 6" × 4".
3. Select Inches for the type of units, and CMYK Color for the color mode, then click OK.
4. Click File on the Application bar, click Save As, navigate to the drive and folder where you store your Data Files, then click Save.
5. Create a circle at the center of the artboard.
6. Click the Selection tool.

Explore the Illustrator window.

1. Click Window on the Application bar, point to Workspace, then click Essentials.
2. Click View on the Application bar, then click Outline.
3. Click View on the Application bar, then click Preview.
4. Click View on the Application bar, then click Zoom In.
5. Click View on the Application bar, then click Zoom Out.
6. Press and hold [Spacebar] to access the Hand tool, then move the artboard.
7. Click View on the Application bar, then click Fit Artboard in Window.
8. Select the circle, click Edit on the Application bar, then click Copy.

9. Click Edit on the Application bar, then click Paste in Front.
10. Move the new circle to the bottom of theartboard.
11. Click Edit on the Application bar, then click Undo Move.
12. Click Edit on the Application bar, then click Redo Move.
13. Click Select on the Application bar, then click All.
14. Click Select on the Application bar, then click Deselect.
15. Select all of the objects, click Edit on the Application bar, then click Cut.
16. Save your work.

Create basic shapes and apply fill and stroke colors.

1. Set the Fill and Stroke buttons on the Tools panel to black and [None], respectively.
2. Create a rectangle that is 3" × 1".
3. Show the Swatches panel (if necessary).
4. Fill the rectangle with a light yellow.

Select, move, and align objects.

1. Click View on the Application bar, then click Smart Guides (if necessary).
2. Move the rectangle so that its top-left anchor point intersects with the top-left corner of the artboard.
3. Click the top-left anchor point, press and hold [Shift][Alt] (Win) or [Shift][option] (Mac), drag straight down until the top-left

anchor point touches the bottom-left anchor point (the "intersect" Smart Guide appears), then release the mouse.
4. Click Object on the Application bar, point to Transform, then click Transform Again.
5. Repeat Step 4.
6. Change the fill color of the second and fourth rectangles to a darker yellow.
7. Save your work.

Transform objects.

1. Select the four rectangles.
2. Double-click the Reflect tool, click the Horizontal option button, then click Copy. The four rectangles are copied on top of the original rectangles.
3. Move the four new rectangles to the right so that they align with the right side of the artboard.
4. Click the Rectangle tool, click the artboard, and create a square that is .75" × .75".
5. Apply a 1-point black stroke to the square and no fill.
6. Click the Selection tool, click the edge of the square, then position it at the center of the artboard.
7. Use the Rotate dialog box to create a copy of the square rotated at 10°.
8. Apply the Transform Again command seven times.
9. Save your work.

Make direct selections.

1. Use [Shift] to select each of the nine black squares.
2. Click Object on the Application bar, then click Group.
3. Scale the group of squares 200%.
4. Create a 3.75" × 3.75" circle, fill it with orange, add a 1-point black stroke, then position it at the center of the artboard.
5. Cut the circle from the artboard, click the group of black squares, click Edit on the Application bar, then click Paste in Back.
6. Adjust the location of the circle, as needed.
7. Click Object on the Application bar, point to Path, then click Add Anchor Points.
8. Deselect the circle by clicking anywhere on the artboard.
9. Click the Direct Selection tool, then click the edge of the circle.
10. One at a time, move each of the four new anchor points to the center of the circle.
11. Switch to the Selection tool, then select the orange-filled shape.
12. Double-click the Rotate tool, type **22** in the Angle text box, then click Copy.
13. Apply the Transform Again command two times.
14. Save your work, then compare your illustration to Figure 39.
15. Close the Flag document.

FIGURE 39
Completed Skills Review

The lady who owns the breakfast shop that you frequent knows that you are a designer and asks for your help. Her nephew has designed a sign for her store window, but she confides in you that she doesn't like it. She thinks that it's "boring" and "flat." She wants to redesign the sign with something that is "original" and feels "more like a starburst."

1. Open AI 1-3.ai, then save it as **Window Sign**.
2. Click the Direct Selection tool, then click the edge of the star.
3. Move two of the outer anchor points of the star farther from its center.
4. Move four of the inner points toward the center.
5. Select the entire star.
6. Reflect a copy of the star across the horizontal axis.
7. Fill the new star with an orange swatch and reposition it to your liking.
8. Group the two stars.
9. Copy the group, then paste in back.
10. Fill the copies with black.
11. Using your arrow keys, move the black copies five points to the right and five points down.

12. Select only the orange star using the Direct Selection tool.
13. Copy the orange star, then paste in back.
14. Fill the new copy with black.
15. Rotate the black copy 8°.

FIGURE 40
Completed Project Builder 1

16. Apply a yellow fill to the orange star, then apply a 1-point black stroke to both yellow stars.
17. Save your work, then compare your illustration to Figure 40.
18. Close Window Sign.

Iris Vision Labs has contracted with your design firm to bid on a design for their logo. Researching the company, you learn that they are a biotech firm whose mission is to develop cures for genetic blindness and vision problems. You decide to build your design around the idea of an iris.

1. Create a new document that is 6" × 6".
2. Save the document as **Iris Vision Design**.
3. Create an ellipse that is 1" wide × 4" in height, and position it at the center of the artboard.
4. Fill the ellipse with [None], and add a 1-point blue stroke.
5. Create a copy of the ellipse rotated at 15°.
6. Apply the Transform Again command 10 times.
7. Select all and group the ellipses.
8. Create a copy of the group rotated at 5°.
9. Apply a red stroke to the new group.
10. Transform again.
11. Apply a bright blue stroke to the new group.
12. Select all.
13. Rotate a copy of the ellipses 2.5°.
14. Create a circle that is 2" × 2".
15. Fill the circle with a shade of gray.
16. Remove the stroke from the circle.
17. Position the gray-filled circle in the center of the ellipses.

18. Cut the circle.
19. Select all.
20. Paste in back.

21. Save your work, then compare your illustration to Figure 41.
22. Close Iris Vision Design.

FIGURE 41
Completed Project Builder 2

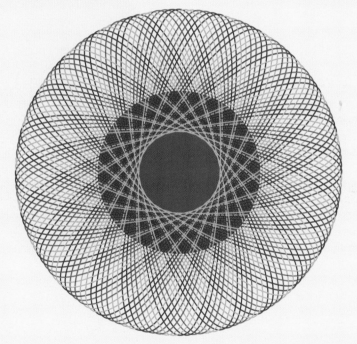

The owner of Emerald Design Studios has hired you to design an original logo for her new company. She's a beginner with Illustrator, but she's created a simple illustration of what she has in mind. She tells you to create something "more sophisticated." The only other information that she offers about her company is that they plan to specialize in precise, geometric design.

1. Open AI 1-4.ai, then save it as **Emerald Logo**.
2. Select all four diamonds and group them.
3. Select the group of diamonds on the artboard, then create a 75% copy.
4. Use the Transform Again command five times.
5. Use Smart Guides or Outline mode to help you identify each of the seven groups.
6. Rotate one of the groups 75°.
7. Select two other groups of your choice and repeat the last transformation, using the Transform Again command.
8. Apply a dark green stroke to all groups. Figure 42 shows one possible result of multiple transformations. Your illustration may differ.
9. Save your work, then close Emerald Logo.

FIGURE 42
Completed Design Project

You attend a design school, and you're part of a team that is responsible for the artwork placed throughout the common areas of the school. One of the most admired professors brings you a file that he created in Illustrator, admitting that he's a beginner. You open the file and notice that the file is poorly built—everything is misaligned and uneven. After consulting with the professor, you decide that the file needs to be rebuilt from scratch.

1. Open AI 1-5.ai, then save it as **Rings**.
2. Identify the areas of the file that are misaligned and poorly constructed.
3. Pull apart the file, object by object, to see how the effect was achieved.
4. Create a "game plan" for reproducing the artwork with precision. Where's the best place to start? What's the best methodology for recreating the professor's design?
5. Work to rebuild the file, using precise methods.
6. Save your work, then compare your illustration to Figure 43.
7. Close the Rings document.

FIGURE 43
Completed Portfolio Project

2

CREATING TEXT AND
GRADIENTS

1. Create and format text

2. Flow text into an object

3. Position text on a path

4. Create colors and gradients

5. Apply colors and gradients to text

6. Adjust a gradient and create a drop shadow

2 CREATING TEXT AND
GRADIENTS

Working with Text

When it comes to creating compelling and dramatic display text, no other software package offers the graphic sophistication that you'll find with Adobe Illustrator. You can quickly change fonts, font size, leading, and other text attributes with the Character panel. You can make tracking and kerning measurements with a level of precision that would satisfy even the most meticulous typographer. For the designer, Illustrator is the preeminent choice for typography. Powerful type tools offer the ability to fill objects with text, position text on lines—curved or straight—and set type vertically, one letter on top of the next. Once the text is positioned, the Create Outlines command changes the fonts to vector graphics that you can manipulate as you would any other object. For

example, you can apply a gradient fill to letter outlines for stunning effects.

Creating and Applying Gradient Fills

A **gradient** is a graduated blend between two or more colors used to fill an object or multiple objects. Illustrator's sophistication for creating gradients and its ease of use for applying them to objects are a dream come true for today's designers. You can create linear or radial gradients between multiple colors, then control the way they fill an object. Moreover, a single gradient can be used to fill multiple objects simultaneously! The unique gradient fills that you create can be saved with descriptive names, then imported into other Illustrator documents to be used again.

Tools You'll Use

CREATE AND
FORMAT TEXT

What You'll Do

BERRY

In this lesson, you will use the Type tool to create the word BERRY as display text. You will use the Character panel to format the text and perfect its appearance. You will also create a vertical version of the text.

Creating Text

You can create text anywhere on the artboard simply by selecting the Type tool then clicking the artboard to start typing. You can enter text horizontally or vertically. The ability to type vertically is rather unusual; most text-based applications don't offer this option.

Text generated by the Type tool is positioned on a path called the **baseline**. You can select text simply by clicking anywhere on the text. This feature is a preference that you can turn on or off: Click Edit on the Application bar, point to Preferences, click Type, then remove the check mark in the Type Object Selection by Path Only check box, if necessary. When this feature is checked, you must click the baseline to select text.

Formatting Text

The Character and Paragraph panels neatly contain all of the classic commands for formatting text. Use the Character panel to modify text attributes such as font and type size, tracking, and kerning. You can adjust the **leading**, which is the vertical space between baselines, or apply a horizontal or vertical scale, which compresses or expands selected type. The Paragraph panel applies itself to more global concerns, such as text alignment, paragraph indents, and vertical spaces between paragraphs. Figure 1 shows examples of formatting that you can apply to text.

Tracking and kerning are essential (and often overlooked) typographic operations. **Tracking** inserts uniform spaces between characters to affect the width of selected words or entire blocks of text. **Kerning** is used to affect the space between any two characters; it is particularly useful for improving the appearance of headlines and other display text. Positive tracking or kerning values move characters farther apart; negative values move them closer together.

Illustrator can track and kern type down to $1/1000$ of a standard em space. The width of an em space is dependent on the current type size. In a 1-point font, the em space is 1 point. In a 10-point font, the em space is 10 points. With kerning units that are $1/1000$ of an em, Illustrator can manipulate a 10-point font at increments of $1/1000$ of 1 point! Figure 2 shows examples of kerning and tracking values.

Hiding Objects

Two factors contribute to difficulty in selecting text and other objects: the number of objects in the document and proximity of objects. Multiple objects positioned closely together can make selections difficult and impede productivity.

Hiding an object is one simple solution. Hidden objects are safe; they won't be deleted from the document when you quit.

Also, they won't print. Just don't forget that they're there!

The Hide Selection command is under the Object menu, as is Show All, which reveals all hidden objects. When hidden objects are revealed, they are all selected; you can use this to your advantage. Simply press [Shift] as you click to deselect the object you want to see, then hide the remaining objects.

FIGURE 1
Examples of text formatting

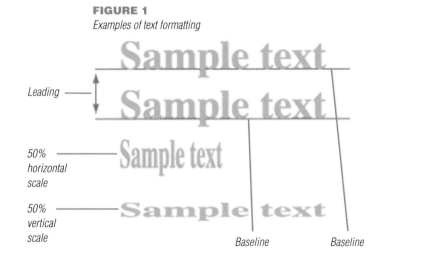

Leading

50% horizontal scale

50% vertical scale

Baseline

Baseline

FIGURE 2
Examples of kerning and tracking

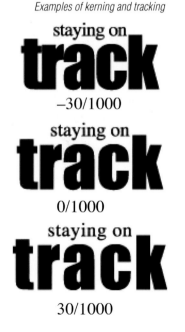

−30/1000   −30/1000

0/1000   0/1000

30/1000   30/1000

Create text

1. Open AI 2-1.ai, then save it as **Berry Symposium**.

2. Click **View** on the Application bar, then click **Hide Bounding Box**, if necessary.

3. Click the **Type tool** T., then click anywhere on the artboard.

4. Type **BERRY** using all capital letters.

   TIP By default, new text is generated with a black fill and no stroke.

5. Click the **Selection tool** , then drag the **text** to the center of the artboard.

   TIP Hide Smart Guides, if necessary.

6. Click **Window** on the Application bar, point to **Type**, then click **Character** to show the Character panel.

7. Click the **Character panel list arrow**, then click **Show Options** to view the entire panel as shown in Figure 3.

You used the Type tool to create the word BERRY, showed the Character panel then expanded the view of the Character panel.

FIGURE 3
Character panel

Character panel list arrow

DESIGNTIP Tracking and kerning

Typography, the art of designing letterforms, has a long and rich history that extends back to the Middle Ages. With the advent of desktop publishing in the mid-1980s, many conventional typographers and typesetters declared "the death of typography." Cooler minds have since prevailed. The personal computer and software such as Adobe Illustrator have made vast libraries of typefaces available as never before. Imagine the days when the typewriter ruled—its single typeface and two point sizes the standard for literally millions of documents—and you get a sense of the typographic revolution that has occurred in the last 20 years.

Many designers are so eager to tackle the "artwork" that they often overlook the type design in an illustration. Tracking and kerning—the manipulation of space between words and letters—are essential elements to good type design and are often woefully ignored.

Illustrator's precise tracking and kerning abilities are of no use if they are ignored. One good way of maintaining awareness of your tracking and kerning duties is to take note of others' oversights. Make it a point to notice tracking and kerning—or lack thereof—when you look at magazines, or posters, or especially billboards. You'll be amazed at what you'll see.

FIGURE 4
Character panel

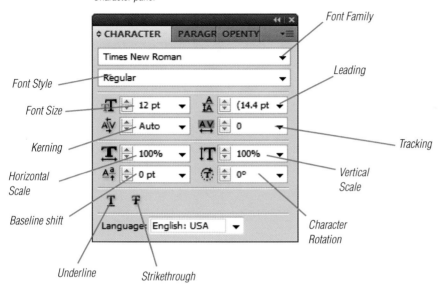

Font Family

Font Style

Font Size

Kerning

Horizontal
Scale

Baseline shift

Underline

Strikethrough

Leading

Tracking

Vertical
Scale

Character
Rotation

Format text

1. Click the **Font family** (Win) or **Font menu** (Mac) **list arrow**, then click **Times New Roman**, or a similar font, as shown in Figure 4.

2. Click the **Font size text box**, type **142**, then press **[Enter]** (Win) or **[return]** (Mac).

3. Click the **Horizontal Scale text box**, type **90**, then press **[Enter]** (Win) or **[return]** (Mac).

4. Deselect all.

5. Compare your text to Figure 5.

You used the Character panel to modify the font, the font size, and the horizontal scaling of the word BERRY.

FIGURE 5
Formatted text

BERRY

Track and kern text

1. Select the text, if necessary.

2. Using the Character panel, click the **Tracking text box**, then type **-30**.

   TIP Click the Character panel list arrow, then click Show Options, if necessary.

3. Click the **Type tool** T, then click the cursor between the B and the E.

4. Using the Character panel, click the **up and down arrows** in the Kerning text box to experiment with higher and lower kerning values, then change the kerning value to -40.

5. Using Figure 6 as a guide, change the kerning to -20, 0, and -120 between the next three letter pairs.

6. Click the **Selection tool** , click the **Paragraph panel name tab**, then click the **Align center button** , as shown in Figure 7.

   When text is center-aligned, its anchor point doubles as its center point, which is handy for aligning it with other objects.

   TIP If you do not see the Paragraph panel, click Window on the Application bar, point to Type, then click Paragraph.

7. Click **Object** on the Application bar, point to **Hide**, then click **Selection**.

You used the Character panel to change the tracking of the word BERRY, then you entered different kerning values to affect the spacing between the four letter pairs. You center-aligned the text, then hid the text.

FIGURE 6
Kerning and tracking applied to text

-30 pt. tracking

-40 pt. kern   -20 pt. kern   0 pt. kern   -120 pt. kern

FIGURE 7
Paragraph panel

Align buttons

Left indent text box

Right indent text box

First-line left indent text box

Space before paragraph

Space after paragraph

FIGURE 8
Vertical text

B
E
R
R
Y

Using the Glyphs panel

The Glyphs panel contains various type characters that aren't necessarily available on your keyboard. Examples of these characters include trademarks, copyright marks, accented letters, and numbers expressed as fractions. Click Window on the Application bar, point to Type, then click Glyphs to display the Glyphs panel. To access a glyph, click the Type tool, click the artboard as you would to type any character, then double-click the glyph on the Glyph panel that you wish to use.

1. Click the **Vertical Type tool** T , then click anywhere on the artboard.

   TIP   The Vertical Type tool is hidden beneath the Type tool.

2. Type the word **BERRY** using all capital letters.

   TIP   The Type tools retain the formatting attributes that were previously chosen.

3. Click the **Selection tool** , select the text, then move it to the center of the artboard.

   TIP   When any tool other than the Selection tool is selected on the Tools panel you can press [Ctrl] (Win) or ⌘ (Mac) to switch to the Selection tool. When you release [Ctrl] (Win) or ⌘ (Mac), the last chosen tool will be active again.

4. Using the Character panel, change the font size to 84 pt.

5. Change the Tracking value to -160.

6. Set both the Horizontal and Vertical Scales to 100%, then deselect the text.

   Your screen should resemble Figure 8.

7. Delete the vertical text, then save your work.

You used the Vertical Type tool to create a vertical alternative to the first word you typed. You adjusted the tracking and kerning to better suit a vertical orientation, and then deleted the text.

FLOW TEXT INTO
AN OBJECT

What You'll Do

rasp
straw blue
cran straw tea
straw checker cran
blue boysen black tea straw
blue boysen checker cran tea rasp
boysen blue black straw tea boysen
checker cran rasp boysen blue black rasp straw
blue black straw tea boysen checker cran rasp straw
blue tea black rasp straw blue black straw tea
boysen checker cran rasp straw blue black
rasp straw blue cran straw tea straw
checker cran straw boysen
black tea straw blue
boysen checker
cran tea
rasp

 In this lesson, you will use the Area Type tool to flow text into an object.

Filling an Object with Text

Using the Area Type tool and the Vertical Area Type tool, you can flow text into any shape you can create, from circles to birds to bumblebees! Text in an object can be formatted as usual. You can change fonts, font size, alignment, etc., and the text will be reflowed in the object as you format it.

When text is flowed into an object, you can manipulate the object as you would any other object. Apply fills and strokes and transformations; use the Rotate tool, or the Scale or Reflect tools. You can even use the Direct Selection tool to distort the shape. Best of all, you can apply those operations to the text or to the text object independently! Figure 9 shows an example of an object, in this case a star, filled with text.

> **QUICK**TIP
>
> You can underline text and strike through text using the Underline and Strikethrough buttons on the Character panel.

Locking Objects

Working in tandem with the Hide command, the Lock Selection command on the Object menu allows you to exempt an object from selections and affix its position on the artboard. The Lock Selection command is useful simply as a device to protect objects from accidental modifications.

Locked objects can be selected only after they are unlocked by choosing the Unlock All command on the Object menu. The Unlock All command unlocks every locked object on the artboard. When locked objects are unlocked, they are all selected. Simply press [Shift] while you click to deselect the object you want to work with, and relock the remaining objects.

Using Rulers, Guides, and the Grid

Illustrator has two built-in rulers that run along the top and left side of the document window. You can create ruler guides and place them on the artboard by positioning the mouse pointer in the top or left ruler, then dragging the mouse pointer onto the artboard. As you drag, you'll see a guide emerge and when you release the mouse pointer, the guide will be positioned at that point. To view rulers, click View on the Application bar, then click Show Rulers. You can lock guides and hide guides temporarily as you work in Illustrator. Click View on the

Application bar, point to Guides and you will see all of the Guide menu commands.

Another tool for aligning objects on the artboard is to use the grid. Grid settings are defined in the Guides & Grid section of the Preferences dialog box. You can choose a color and style for the grid, choose the distance between gridlines and how many subdivisions between gridlines. To hide and show the grid, click View on the Application bar, then click Hide Grid or Show Grid.

Making Guides

Guides are one of Illustrator's many features that help you to work with precision. You can select any object and make it into a guide with the Make Guides command on the View menu. You can also create guides by clicking and dragging the mouse pointer from each ruler to the artboard.

FIGURE 9
An object filled with text

To be, or not to be. That is the question. Whether 'tis nobler in the mind to suffer the slings and arrows of outrageous fortune, or to take arms against a sea of troubles — and by opposing — end them. To die. To sleep. To sleep. Perchance to dream? Ay, there's the rub.

Fill an object with text

1. Open AI 2-2.ai, then save it as **Diamond Text**.

2. Select the yellow square, double-click the **Rotate tool** 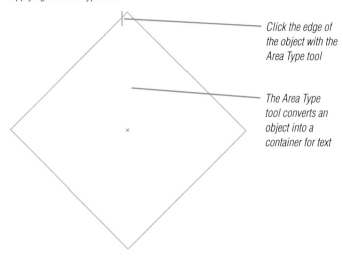, type **45** in the Angle text box, then click **OK**.

3. Click the **Area Type tool** , then click the block of text.

   TIP The Area Type tool is hidden beneath the current type tool.

4. Click **Select** on the Application bar, then click **All**.

   TIP When you click a Type tool cursor on text and apply the Select All command, all the text is selected—not the object that contains the text, and not any other text or objects on the page.

5. Copy the text.

6. Click the **Selection tool** , then select the yellow square.

   TIP When you are working with a Type tool, you can press [Ctrl] (Win) or [⌘] (Mac) to access the Selection tool temporarily and remain in Area Type tool mode.

7. Click the **Area Type tool** , if necessary, then click the edge of the yellow square.

   A flashing cursor appears, and the square loses its fill color, as shown in Figure 10.

8. Paste the copied text into the square.

   Your work should resemble Figure 11.

You rotated the yellow square, then filled it with text by first copying text from another object, then clicking the edge of the square with the Area Type tool before you pasted the text into the square.

FIGURE 10
Applying the Area Type tool

Click the edge of the object with the Area Type tool

The Area Type tool converts an object into a container for text

FIGURE 11
Text pasted into an object

Object loses its fill color

Indicates overflow text

rasp
straw blue
cran straw tea
straw checker cran
blue boysen black tea
straw blue boysen checker cran
tea rasp boysen blue black straw tea
boysen checker cran rasp boysen blue
black rasp straw blue black straw
tea boysen checker cran rasp
straw blue tea black
rasp straw blue
black straw
tea
b

Creating Text and Gradients

FIGURE 12

Centered text in an object

```
                    rasp
                straw blue
              cran straw tea
          straw checker cran  blue
        boysen black tea  straw blue
      boysen checker cran tea rasp boysen
     blue black straw tea boysen checker cran
   rasp boysen blue black rasp straw blue black
 straw tea boysen checker cran rasp straw blue tea black
   rasp straw blue black straw tea boysen checker
     cran rasp straw blue black rasp straw blue
        cran straw tea straw checker cran
          straw boysen black tea  straw
            blue boysen checker cran
              tea rasp boysen blue
                 black straw
                     tea
```

Using Character and Paragraph Styles

A style is a group of formatting attributes, such as font, font size, color, and tracking, that is applied to text. You use the Character Styles panel to create and apply styles for individual words or characters, such as a footnote. You use the Paragraph Styles panel to apply a style to a paragraph. Paragraph styles include formatting options such as indents and drop caps. Using styles saves you time, and keeps your work consistent. If you create styles for an Illustrator document, the styles are saved with the document and are available to be loaded for use in other documents.

Format text in an object

1. Select all of the text in the rotated square.

2. Click the **Align center button** ≡ on the Paragraph panel.

   TIP   When filling an object other than a square or a rectangle with text, centering the text is often the best solution.

3. Click the **Character panel name tab** next to the Paragraph panel name tab, then change the font size to 9 pt.

4. Click the **Leading text box**, type **11**, click the **artboard** to deselect the text, then compare your work to Figure 12.

   It's OK if the line breaks in your document differ from the text in the figure.

5. Click the **Selection tool** ▶, then click the **diamond-shaped text**.

   Both the text and the object that contains the text are selected.

6. Copy the text object.

   Both the text and the object are copied.

7. Click **Window** on the Application bar, then click the **Berry Symposium document tab**.

   TIP   All open Illustrator documents are tabbed.

8. Paste the text object into the Berry Symposium document.

You used the Paragraph and Character panels to format text in the object. You used the Selection tool to select the text object, and then you copied and pasted it into the Berry Symposium document.

Make guides and use the Lock command

1. Click **View** on the Application bar, then click **Show Rulers**, if necessary.

2. Using Figure 13 as a reference, position your pointer in the top horizontal ruler, click and drag the pointer straight down to the 5" mark on the vertical ruler, then release the mouse to create a guide.

   TIP You may need to move the Tools panel out of the way to see the vertical ruler.

3. Position a vertical guide at the 5" mark on the horizontal ruler.

   TIP To change the color or style of guides, click Edit (Win) or Illustrator (Mac) on the Application bar, point to Preferences, then click Guides & Grid. The Guides & Grid Preferences dialog box is shown in Figure 14.

4. Click **View** on the Application bar, point to **Guides**, then verify that Lock Guides is checked.

5. Click the **Selection tool** , if necessary.

(continued)

FIGURE 13
Making guides

Use opposite ruler to position guide

Click and drag pointer to create guide

Start by positioning pointer in the ruler area

Creating Text and Gradients

FIGURE 14

Guides & Grid Preferences settings

6. Select the text object, then align the center point of the text object with the intersection of the guides.

> TIP   Use the arrow keys to nudge the selection right, left, up, or down.

7. Click **Object** on the Application bar, point to **Lock**, then click **Selection**.

> TIP   Locking objects is standard practice. You can also lock a selection by first selecting an object, then pressing [Ctrl][2] (Win) or ⌘ [2] (Mac). Make it a point to remember the quick key.

8. Save your work.

You created a horizontal and a vertical guide that intersect at the center of the artboard. You then aligned the center of the diamond text object with the intersection of the guides, and locked the diamond text object.

POSITION TEXT
ON A PATH

What You'll Do

rasp
straw blue
cran straw tea
straw checker cran
blue boysen black tea straw
blue boysen checker cran tea rasp
boysen blue black straw tea boysen
checker cran rasp boysen blue black rasp straw
blue black straw tea boysen checker cran rasp straw
blue tea black rasp straw blue black straw tea
boysen checker cran rasp straw blue black
rasp straw blue cran straw tea straw
checker cran straw boysen
black tea straw blue
boysen checker
cran tea
rasp

▶ *In this lesson, you will explore the many options for positioning text on a path.*

Using the Path Type Tools

Using the Type on a Path tool or the Vertical Type on a Path tool, you can type along a straight or curved path. This is the most compelling of Illustrator's text effects, and it opens up a world of possibilities for the designer and typographer.

You can move text along a path to position it where you want. You can "flip" the text to make it run in the opposite direction—on the opposite side of the path. You can

also change the baseline shift to modify the distance of the text's baseline in relation to the path. A positive value "floats" the text above the path, and a negative value moves the text below the path. You can modify text on a path in the same way you would modify any other text element. Figure 15 shows an example of text on a path, whereas Figure 16 shows an example of text flipped across a path.

FIGURE 15
Text on a path

FIGURE 16
Text flipped across a path

*Text flowed along
a sharply curved
path often presents
kerning challenges*

Flow text on a path

1. Click the **Ellipse tool** ⬭, press **[Alt]** (Win) or **[option]** (Mac), then click the center of the artboard.

   Pressing [Alt] (Win) or [option] (Mac) while you click a shape tool on the artboard ensures that the center of the shape will be drawn from the point that you clicked.

2. Enter **2.9** in for the width and the height of the circle in the Ellipse dialog box, then click **OK**.

3. Click the **Type on a Path tool** ⬚, then click anywhere on the edge of the circle.

   | TIP   The Type on a Path tool may be hidden beneath the current Type tool.

   A flashing cursor appears, and the circle loses its fill color.

4. Type **three rivers** in lowercase, using Times New Roman PS MT for the font.

   | TIP   If you do not have Times New Roman PS MT, substitute a similar font.

5. Click the **Selection tool** � to select the text by its baseline, then change the font size to 47 pt.

   You will see three brackets—one at the beginning of the path, one at the end of the path, and one at the midpoint between the two brackets. These brackets allow you to move text along a path.

   | TIP   Text flowed on a circle will often require kerning, especially when it is set at a large point size.

6. Compare your screen to Figure 17.

You created a 2.9" circle from its center, then typed along the circle's path using the Type on a Path tool. You changed the font and font size using the Character panel.

FIGURE 17
Text on a circular path

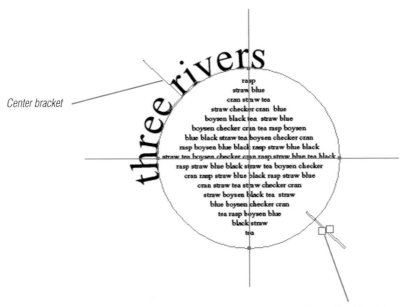

Center bracket

Start and end brackets
(overlapped because a
circle path begins and
ends at the same point)

FIGURE 18

Moving text on a path

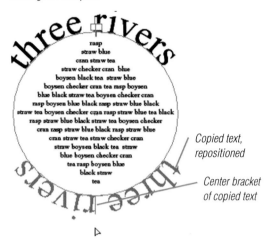

Copied text,
repositioned

Center bracket
of copied text

FIGURE 20

Modifying a baseline shift

Baseline shift

FIGURE 19

Flipping text across a path

Center bracket of copied text

FIGURE 21

Flipped text positioned below the path

Move text along a path

1. Click **View** on the Application bar, point to **Guides**, then click **Hide Guides**.

2. Using the Selection tool ▶, drag the **center bracket** until the text is centered at the top of the circle.

3. Click **Edit** on the Application bar, click **Copy**, click **Edit** on the Application bar, then click **Paste in Front**.

4. Drag the **center bracket** of the copied text clockwise to move the copied text to the position shown in Figure 18.

5. Drag the **center bracket** of the copied text straight up to flip the text across the path, as shown in Figure 19.

   TIP Enlarge your view of the artboard if you have trouble dragging the bracket.

6. Click the **Baseline text box** on the Character panel, type **-21**, as shown in Figure 20, then press **[Enter]** (Win) or **[return]** (Mac).

7. Click the **Type tool** T, highlight **three rivers** at the bottom of the circle, then type **symposium**.

8. Click the **Selection tool** ▶, then drag the **center bracket** to center the text at the bottom of the circle, if necessary.

9. Lock the two text objects, save your work, then compare your image to Figure 21.

You moved and copied text along a path, flipped its direction, changed the baseline shift, then locked both text objects.

CREATE COLORS AND GRADIENTS

What You'll Do

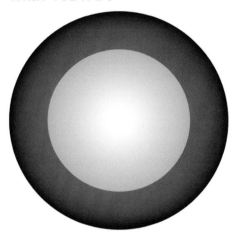

▶ *In this lesson, you will use the Color panel, the Gradient panel, and the Swatches panel to create, name, and save colors and gradients.*

Using the Gradient Panel

A **gradient** is a graduated blend between colors. The Gradient panel is the command center for creating and adjusting gradients. In the panel you will see a slider that represents the gradient you are creating or working with. The slider has at least two colors. The leftmost color is the starting color, and the rightmost color is the ending color.

The colors used in a gradient are represented on the Gradient panel by small house-shaped icons called **stops**. The Gradient panel shown in Figure 22 shows a two-color gradient.

The point at which two colors meet in equal measure is called the **midpoint** of the gradient. The midpoint is represented by the diamond above the slider. The midpoint does not necessarily need to be positioned evenly between the starting and ending colors. You can change the appearance of a gradient by moving the midpoint.

The Swatches panel contains standard gradients that come with the software. To create your own original gradients, start by clicking an object filled with an existing gradient. You can then modify that existing gradient on the Gradient panel. You can change either or both the beginning and ending colors. You can change the location of the midpoint. You can also add additional colors into the gradient, or remove existing colors.

> **QUICK**TIP
>
> As you work to perfect a gradient, you can see how your changes will affect the gradient automatically, by filling an object with the gradient that you are working on. As you make changes on the Gradient panel, the changes will be reflected in the object.

You can define a gradient as linear or radial. A linear gradient can be positioned left to right, up and down, or on any angle. You can change the angle of the gradient by entering a new value in the Angle text box on the Gradient panel.

Think of a radial gradient as a series of concentric circles. With a radial gradient, the starting color appears at the center of the gradient. The blend radiates out to the ending color. By definition, a radial gradient has no angle ascribed to it.

Using the Color Panel

The Color panel, as shown in Figure 23, is where you move sliders to mix new colors for fills, strokes, and gradients. You can also use the panel to adjust the color in a filled object. The panel has five color modes: CMYK, RGB, Grayscale, HSB, and Web Safe RGB. The panel will default to CMYK or RGB, depending on the color mode you choose when creating a new document. Grayscale mode allows you to create shades

of gray in percentages of black. If you select a filled object and choose the HSB mode, you can adjust its basic color (hue), the intensity of the color (saturation), and the range of the color from light to dark (brightness). If you are designing illustrations for the Internet, you might consider using Web Safe RGB mode to create colors that are in accordance with colors defined in HTML.

Rather than use the sliders, you can also type values directly into the text boxes. For example, in CMYK mode, a standard red color is composed of 100% Magenta and 100% Yellow. The notation for this callout would be 100M/100Y. Note that you don't list the zero values for Cyan (C) and Black (K). In RGB mode (0-255), a standard orange color would be noted as 255R/128G.

Adding Colors and Gradients to the Swatches Panel

Once you have defined a color or a gradient to your liking, it's a smart idea to save it by dragging it into the Swatches panel. Once a color or gradient is moved into the Swatches panel, you can name it by double-clicking it, then typing a name in the Swatch Options dialog box. You can't, however, modify it. For example, if you click a saved gradient and adjust it on the Gradient panel, you can apply the new gradient to an object, but the original gradient on the Swatches panel remains unaffected. You can save the new gradient to the Swatches panel for future use.

FIGURE 22
Gradient panel

Custom gradients

Type list arrow

Rotation text box

Gradient Ramp

Stops

Opacity text box

Location text box

FIGURE 23
Color panel

Current fill and stroke colors

CMYK values

Sliders

CMYK Spectrum

Create a gradient and a color

1. Show the guides.

2. Create a 4" circle at the center of the artboard, then apply a yellow fill to the circle.

   The most recently drawn object is automatically placed above the other objects on the artboard.

3. Hide the guides, click **Window** on the Application bar, then click **Gradient** to open the Gradient panel, if necessary.

4. Click the **Blended Rainbow swatch** on the Swatches panel.

   The yellow fill changes to the Blended Rainbow fill.

5. Click the **Gradient panel list arrow**, then click **Show Options**, if necessary.

6. Click the **yellow stop** on the Gradient Slider, and drag it straight down off the panel to delete it.

7. Delete all the stops except for the first and last stops.

   | TIP The changes you make to the Gradient Slider are reflected in the circle.

8. Click the bottom edge of the Gradient Ramp to add a new color stop, then drag the stop along the slider until you see 50% in the Location text box on the Gradient panel as shown in Figure 24.

9. Drag each of the diamond sliders to the 50% mark in the Location text box.

10. Verify that the new stop is selected, press and hold **[Alt]** (Win) or **[option]** (Mac), click **Squash** on the Swatches panel, then compare your circle to Figure 25.

(continued)

FIGURE 24
Adding and deleting stops

Click list arrow to choose a custom gradient

Drag stop along the slider to position it at a new location

Location text box

Click bottom edge of ramp to add a new stop

FIGURE 25
Adding the new Squash swatch to the gradient

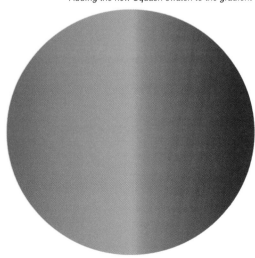

Creating Text and Gradients

FIGURE 26

Changing the first and last colors of the gradient

FIGURE 27

Changing the middle color and the midpoint locations

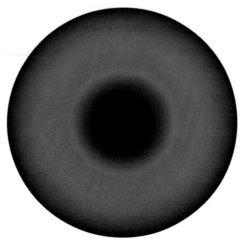

You must select a stop in order to change its color.

> TIP   If you don't press [Alt] (Win) or [option] (Mac), as you choose a swatch for your gradient, you will change the selected object's fill to a solid color.

11. Click the **first stop** on the Gradient Ramp, press **[Alt]** (Win) or **[option]** (Mac), then click **Black** on the Swatches panel.

12. Repeat the previous step to apply Black to the third stop, then compare your circle to Figure 26.

13. Double-click the **Squash stop** to select it and open the Color panel, then drag each slider on the Color panel until the new CMYK values are 5C/95M/95Y/3K.

14. Click the **Type list arrow** on the Gradient panel, then click **Radial**.

15. Click the **diamond** at the top of the Gradient Ramp between the first two stops, then drag it to the 87% location on the ramp.

16. Compare your circle to Figure 27.

You applied the Blended Rainbow gradient to the yellow circle. You modified the gradient by deleting stops and adding a new stop. You changed the color of the new stop, then adjusted the midpoint of the blend between the starting color and the middle color.

Add gradients and colors to the Swatches panel

1. Double-click the **Scale tool** 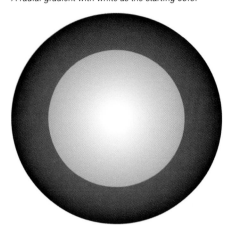, type **65** in the Scale text box, then click **Copy**.

2. Keeping the smaller circle selected, delete the red stop from the ramp on the Gradient panel.

3. Change the first stop to White, then change the ending stop to **0C/40M/50Y/0K**.

   ⏐ TIP   Press [Alt] (Win) or [option] (Mac). When a stop is selected on the Gradient Slider, the color of that stop appears in the Gradient Stop Color box on the Color panel.

4. Position the midpoint at 65%.

   Your screen should resemble Figure 28.

5. Drag the **Gradient Fill box** from the Gradient panel to the Swatches panel, as shown in Figure 29.

6. Double-click **New Gradient Swatch 1** (the gradient you just added) on the Swatches panel to open the Swatch Options dialog box.

7. Type **Pinky** in the Swatch Name text box, then click **OK**.

8. Click the **last color stop** on the Gradient Slider.

(continued)

FIGURE 28
A radial gradient with white as the starting color

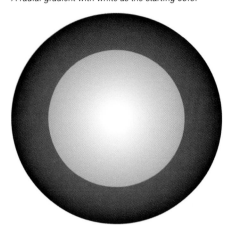

FIGURE 29
Adding a gradient to the Swatches panel

Adding a gradient
to the Swatches
panel

Drag the **Gradient Stop Color box** from the Color panel to the Swatches panel to add this color to the Swatches panel, as shown in Figure 30, then name it **Pinky Ending**.

10. Click the **Selection tool** .

11. Click the **artboard** to deselect the smaller circle.

12. Click the **large circle**, drag the **Gradient Fill box** on the Gradient panel to the Swatches panel, then name the new gradient **Crimson Gradient**.

13. Save your work.

You used the Gradient panel to create a new gradient. You added the gradient fills from the two circles to the Swatches panel and gave them descriptive names. You added a color named Pinky Ending to the Swatches panel then saved the Crimson Gradient to the Swatches panel.

FIGURE 30
Adding a color to the Swatches panel

Adding a color
from the Color
panel to the
Swatches panel

Gradient Stop Color box

When a stop is selected,
the color appears in the
Gradient Stop Color box
on the Color panel

APPLY COLORS AND
GRADIENTS TO TEXT

What You'll Do

▶ *In this lesson, you will apply colors to text, convert text into objects, and fill the objects with a gradient.*

Applying Fills and Strokes to Text

Regardless of the fill and stroke colors shown on the Tools panel new text is generated by default with a black fill and no stroke. To change the color of text, you must either select the text by highlighting it with a type tool, or switch to a selection tool. When you switch to a selection tool, the text is selected as a single object (a blue baseline and anchor point are revealed). Any color changes you make will affect the text globally. If you want to change the fill or the stroke of an individual character, you must select that character with a type tool.

Converting Text to Outlines

About the only thing you can't do to Illustrator text is fill it with a gradient. To create the effect, you first need to convert the text into objects. You can do this by selecting the text, then using the Create Outlines command on the Type menu. The letterforms, or outlines, become standard Illustrator objects with anchor points and

Working with the stacking order

The stacking order defines how objects will be displayed when they overlap. Illustrator stacks each object. Beginning with the first object, each successive object you create overlaps the previously drawn objects. You can change the stacking order by moving objects forward and backward through the stack, one object at a time. You can also move an object to the very top or the very bottom of the stack with one command. Grouped objects are stacked together behind the top object in the group. If you group two objects that are separated in the stack, the objects in between will be positioned behind the new group.

paths able to be modified like any other object—and able to be filled with a gradient. Figure 31 shows an example of text converted to outlines.

Create Outlines is a powerful feature. Beyond allowing you to fill text with a gradient, it makes it possible to create a document with text and without fonts. This can save you time in document management when sending files to your printer, and will circumvent potential problems with missing fonts or font conflicts.

Once text is converted to outlines, you can no longer change the typeface. Also, the type loses its font information, including sizing "hints" that optimize letter shape at different sizes. Therefore, if you plan to scale type, change its font size on the Character panel before converting to outlines.

FIGURE 31
Text converted to outlines

Apply color to text

1. Select the two circles, click **Object** on the Application bar, point to **Arrange**, then click **Send to Back**.

   The two circles move behind the locked text objects.

2. Click **Object** on the Application bar, then click **Unlock All**.

   The three text objects you created and locked are now unlocked and selected.

3. Apply the Pinky Ending color as a fill for the three unlocked text objects.

4. Deselect all, then lock the diamond text object.

   Your work should resemble Figure 32.

You unlocked the three text objects, filled them with the Pinky Ending color, then locked the diamond text object.

FIGURE 32
Text with a new fill color

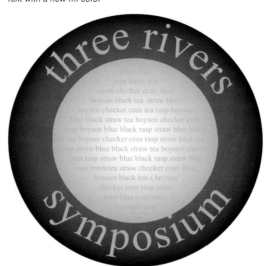

Importing a swatch library

Swatches and gradients that you create are saved with the document they were created in. You can, however, import swatches from one document into another. Click Window on the Application bar, point to Swatch Libraries, then click Other Library. A dialog box opens allowing you to choose the document whose swatches you want to import. Click Open, and that document's Swatches panel will appear in your current document. When you import a Swatches panel, the panel automatically appears with the name of the document from which it came. The imported Swatches panel is not editable—you cannot add new swatches to it or delete existing ones from it.

FIGURE 33

Outlines filled with a gradient

1. Show the guides.

2. Click **Object** on the Application bar, then click **Show All**.

3. Select the **BERRY** text, click **Object** on the Application bar, point to **Arrange**, then click **Bring to Front**.

4. Click **Type** on the Application bar, then click **Create Outlines**.

5. Apply the Steel gradient swatch on the Swatches panel to fill the text outlines, then deselect the outlines.

6. Using Figure 33 as a guide, position the BERRY text outlines so that they are centered within the entire illustration, then hide the guides.

7. Save your work.

You showed the BERRY text, moved it to the front, converted it to outlines, then filled the outlines with a gradient.

ADJUST A GRADIENT AND
CREATE A DROP SHADOW

What You'll Do

In this lesson, you will use the Gradient tool to modify how the gradient fills the outlines. You will then explore the effectiveness of a simple drop shadow as a design element.

Using the Gradient tool with Linear Gradient fills

The Gradient tool on the Tools panel is used to manipulate gradient fills that are already applied to objects; it affects only the way a gradient fills an object.

To use the Gradient tool, you first select an object with a gradient fill. When you click the Gradient tool, the **gradient control bar** appears in the object itself, as shown in Figure 34. For linear gradients, by default,

the gradient control bar begins at the left edge and ends at the right edge.

You can change the length, angle, and direction of the gradient control bar by simply dragging the Gradient tool.

Figure 35 shows the gradient control bar starting outside the object at the top and ending below it. Where you begin dragging and where you end dragging determines the length of the gradient from the beginning color to the ending

FIGURE 34
Gradient control bar

FIGURE 35
Changing the position of the gradient control bar

color – even if it's outside the perimeter of the object.

You can further modify how the gradient fills the object by modifying the gradient control bar itself. Click and drag the diamond-shaped endpoint of the bar to lengthen or shorten the gradient. You can also click and drag the circle-shaped starting point to move then entire bar to a different location.

When you click the gradient control bar, the color stops that compose the gradient appear, as shown in Figure 36. You can

click and drag the stops right there, on the object, for precise control of how the gradient fills the object. You can change the color of the stops on the gradient control bar and even add or delete stops. To change the color of a stop, simply double-click it and the Color panel will appear.

Perhaps the best method for working with the gradient control bar is to first click and drag the Gradient tool as close as possible to where you want it to begin and end. Then, use the gradient control bar for tweaking the position of the

gradient and the position of the color stops within the object.

When you float your cursor near the endpoint of the gradient control bar, the rotate icon appears, as shown in Figure 37. Click and drag to rotate the bar and the gradient within the object.

Applying gradient fills to multiple objects

If you select multiple objects then click a gradient swatch on the Swatches panel, the gradient will fill each object individually.

FIGURE 36
Color stops on the gradient control bar

FIGURE 37
Rotating the gradient control bar

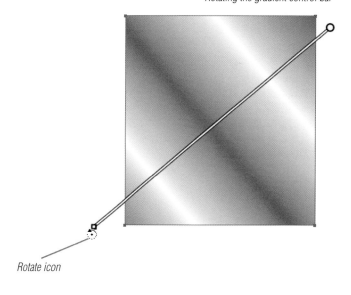

Rotate icon

However, with all the objects selected, you can use the Gradient tool to extend a single gradient across all of them.

When you convert text to outlines and apply a gradient fill, the gradient automatically fills each letter individually. In other words, if you fill a five-letter word with a rainbow gradient, each of the five letters will contain the entire spectrum. To extend the gradient across all the letters, drag the Gradient tool from the left edge of the word to the right edge, or vice versa. Figure 38 shows examples of different angles and lengths of a gradient fill created with the Gradient tool.

Using the Gradient tool with radial gradient fills

With radial gradients the gradient control bar shows the length of the gradient from the center to the circle to the outermost circle. Figure 39 shows the gradient control bar for three radial gradients.

When you click the gradient control bar on a radial gradient, a dotted-line appears showing you the perimeter of the gradient, whether that's within or outside the actual object. In Figure 40, the dotted line indicates that more of the gradient is

FIGURE 38
Using the Gradient tool

FIGURE 39
Three radial gradients

actually outside of the object than visible within the object.

In Illustrator CS4, radial gradients are not limited to being concentric circles: you can also create radial gradients with concentric ellipses. To do so, click and drag the black circle on the dotted line of the radial gradient. As shown in Figure 41, doing so will distort the concentric circles into ellipses.

Adding a Drop Shadow

Applying a shadow behind text is an effective design tool to distinguish the text from other objects and add dimension to the illustration. To apply a drop shadow to text, copy the text, then paste the copy behind it. Fill the copy with a darker color, then use the keyboard arrows to move it so that it is offset from the original text.

FIGURE 40

Dotted line shows the perimeter of the radial gradient

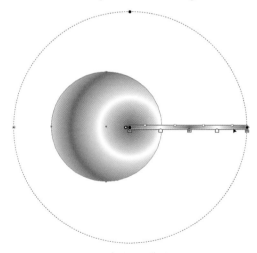

FIGURE 41

Distorting the gradient

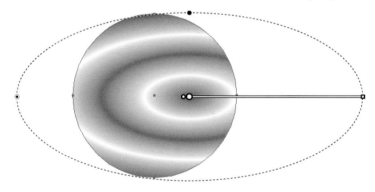

Use the Gradient tool

1. Select the **BERRY text outlines**, if necessary.

2. Click the **Gradient tool** ▣, then position the pointer at the top of the B.

3. Drag straight down to the bottom of the B, release the mouse, then deselect.

   TIP Pressing and holding [Shift] while you drag the Gradient tool pointer allows you to drag in a perfectly straight line.

4. Switch to the **Selection tool** ▸, then click the large circle filled with the Crimson gradient fill behind the text.

5. Click the **Gradient tool** ▣.

6. Position the color stops and the midpoints as shown in Figure 42 so that the red gradient is behind the "three rivers symposium" letters.

You used the Gradient tool to flow the gradient from top to bottom in the word BERRY. You adjusted the stops and the midpoints on the gradient control bar to perfect the gradient behind the text.

FIGURE 42
A highlight behind the text

FIGURE 43
Drop shadow with a 3 pt offset

FIGURE 44
Drop shadows add dimension

FIGURE 45
Finished illustration

Add a drop shadow to text

1. Select the word **BERRY**.

2. Apply a 1 pt Black stroke to the outlines.

3. Copy the word, then paste in back.

4. Change the fill of the copied object to Black.

   TIP Even though you can't see the copy of the text in back, it is still selected.

5. Press ↓ three times and ← three times to move the copied text 3 pts down and 3 pts to the left, as shown in Figure 43.

6. Copy the word symposium, then paste in back.

7. Change the fill of the copied text to Black.

   TIP Since the copy is still selected, you only need to click Black on the Swatches panel.

8. Using the arrow keys, move the copied text 2 pts down and 2 pts to the left, as shown in Figure 44.

9. Apply the same drop shadow to the three rivers text.

   TIP You might find it easier to select the three rivers text if you first lock the symposium text and the symposium shadow text.

10. Unlock all, select everything on the artboard, then rotate the illustration 15°.

11. Click the **Selection tool** ▶, then click the **artboard** to deselect all.

   Your work should resemble Figure 45.

12. Save your work, then close and save each document.

You applied a black stroke to the display text and then pasted a copy behind. You filled the copy with black, then offset the copy to create a drop shadow effect. You then applied a drop shadow to symposium and three rivers. Finally, you rotated the entire illustration.

Create and format text.

1. Open AI 2-3.ai, then save it as **Restaurant Logo.**
2. Using a bold font, type **NOW OPEN** on two lines, using all capital letters. (*Hint*: The font used in Figure 46 is Impact.)
3. Change the font size to 29 pt and the leading to 25 pt.
4. Change the Baseline Shift to 0.
5. Change the alignment to Center and the Horizontal Scale to 75%.
6. Position the text in the center of the white circle.
7. Hide the text.
8. Save your work.

Flow text into an object.

1. Copy the beige circle.
2. Paste the copy in front of it.
3. Click the Type tool, then select all of the green text at the bottom of the artboard, with the Type tool.
4. Copy the green text.
5. Click the Selection tool, then click the top beige circle.
6. Click the Area Type tool, click the edge of the top beige circle, then paste.
7. Center-align the text in the circle.
8. Change the Baseline Shift to -4 pts.
9. Fill the selected text with the same fill color as the beige circle (50% Orange).

10. In the Color panel, drag the Magenta slider to 40% to darken the text.
11. Hide the text.
12. Save your work.

Position text on a path.

1. Select the dark gray circle.
2. Click the Type on a Path tool, then click the top of the circle.
3. Using a bold font, type **THE HOLE-IN-ONE** in all capital letters across the top of the circle. (*Hint*: The font in Figure 41 is Techno Regular. If your type appears at the bottom of the circle, drag the start or end bracket to position the type at the top of the circle. Zoom in so that you can clearly see the brackets. If you move the circle instead of the type, undo your last step and try again.)
4. Change the font size to 34 pt and the fill color to white. (*Hint*: You may need to use a smaller font size, depending on the font you choose.)
5. Click the Selection tool, click Edit on the Application bar, click Copy, click Edit on the Application bar, click Paste in Front, then move the center bracket clockwise to position the copied text across the bottom of the circle.
6. Highlight the copied text, then type **RESTAURANT & BAR** with the Type tool.

7. Drag the RESTAURANT & BAR text across the path to flip its direction.
8. Apply a negative baseline shift to move the text below the path. (*Hint*: The baseline shift used in Figure 46 is -27 pts.)
9. Copy both text objects, then paste them in back.
10. Fill the back copies of the text with black, then move them 2 pts up and 2 pts to the right.
11. Save your work.

Create and apply gradients

1. Apply the White, Black Radial gradient to the small white circle.
2. Change the ending color stop on the Gradient Ramp to Smoke. (*Hint*: Press [Alt] (Win) or [option] (Mac) while you select Smoke from the Swatches panel.)
3. Save the new gradient to the Swatches panel.
4. Name it **Golf Ball**.
5. Fill the large green circle with the Golf Ball gradient.
6. Change the starting color stop to Pure Yellow.
7. Change the ending color stop to Little Sprout Green.

8. Move the midpoint to the 80% location on the Gradient Slider.

9. Save the new gradient as **The Rough**.

10. Save your work.

Adjust a gradient and create a drop shadow.

1. Click Object on the Application bar, then click Show All.

2. Deselect all by clicking the artboard.

3. Select NOW OPEN and convert the text to outlines. (*Hint*: Use the Type menu.)

4. Fill the text with the White, Black gradient.

5. Change the starting color stop to black.

6. Create an intermediary white color stop at the 50% mark on the Gradient Ramp.

7. Drag the Gradient tool starting at the top of the word NOW to the bottom of the word OPEN.

8. Change the middle color stop of the gradient to Latte.

9. Save the new gradient as **Flash**.

10. Deselect the text.

11. Delete the green text from the bottom of the artboard.

12. Convert the remaining text objects into outlines.

13. Select all, then lock all objects.

14. Save your work, compare your illustration to Figure 46, then close Restaurant Logo.

FIGURE 46
Completed Skills Review

An eccentric California real-estate mogul hires your design firm to "create an identity" for La Mirage, his development of high-tech executive condominiums in Palm Springs. Since he's curious about what you'll come up with on your own, the only creative direction he'll give you is to tell you that the concept is "a desert oasis."

1. Create a new 6" × 6" CMYK Color document, then save it as **Desert Oasis**.
2. Using a bold font and 80 pt for a font size, type **LA MIRAGE** in all capitals. (*Hint*: The font shown in Figure 47 is Impact.)
3. Change the horizontal scale to 80%.
4. Change the baseline shift to 0.
5. Apply a -100 kerning value between the two words.
6. Convert the text to outlines, then click the Linear Gradient 1 gradient on the Swatches panel.
7. Using the Color panel, change the first color stop to 66M/100Y/10K (*Hint*: Press and hold [Alt] (Win) or [option] (Mac) when creating the new color.)
8. Create an intermediary color stop that is 25M/100Y.
9. Position the intermediary color stop at 70% on the slider.
10. Save the gradient on the Swatches panel, and name it **Desert Sun**.
11. Drag the Gradient tool from the exact top to the exact bottom of the text.
12. Create a rectangle around the text and fill it with the Desert Sun gradient.
13. Drag the Gradient tool from the bottom to the top of the rectangle.
14. Send the rectangle to the back of the stack.
15. Apply a 1-point black stroke to LA MIRAGE.
16. Type the tagline: **a desert oasis** in 14 pt lowercase letters.
17. Apply a tracking value of 500 or more to the tagline, then convert it to outlines.
18. Save your work, then close Desert Oasis.

FIGURE 47
Completed Project Builder 1

Your friend owns Loon's Balloons. She stops by your studio with a display ad that she's put together for a local magazine and asks if you can make all the elements work together better. Her only direction is that the balloon must remain pink, the same color as her logo.

1. Open AI 2-4.ai, then save it as **Balloons**.
2. Save the pink fill on the balloon to the Swatches panel, and name it **Hot Pink**.
3. Fill the balloon shape with the White, Black Radial gradient from the Swatches panel.
4. Change the black stop on the Gradient Slider to Hot Pink.
5. Using the Gradient tool, change the highlight point on the balloon shape so that it is no longer centered in the balloon shape.
6. Copy the balloon, then paste it in front.
7. Click the Selection tool on the block of text that says "specializing in etc.," then cut the text.
8. Click the top balloon with the Selection tool, then switch to the Area Type tool.
9. Click the top edge of the top balloon, then paste.
10. Center the text and apply a -4 baseline shift.
11. Adjust the layout of the text as necessary. (*Hint*: You can force a line of text to the next line by clicking before the first word in the line you want to move, then pressing [Shift][Enter] (Win) or [Shift][return] (Mac).)

12. Move the headline LOON'S BALLOONS so that each word is on a different side of the balloon string.

FIGURE 48
Completed Project Builder 2

13. Apply a 320 kerning value between the two words.
14. Save your work, compare your screen to Figure 48, then close Balloons.

Creating Text and Gradients

You work in the marketing department of a major movie studio, where you design movie posters and newspaper campaigns. You are respected for your proficiency with typography. Your boss asks you to come up with a "teaser" campaign for the movie *Vanishing Point*, a spy thriller. The campaign will run on billboards in 10 major cities and will feature only the movie title, nothing else.

1. Create a new 6" × 6" CMYK Color document, then save it as **Vanish**.
2. Type **VANISHING POINT**, using 100 pt and a bold font. (*Hint*: The font used in Figure 44 is Impact.)
3. Change the horizontal scale to 55%.
4. Convert the text to outlines.
5. On the Swatches panel, click the Linear Gradient 1 gradient.
6. Drag the Gradient tool from the exact bottom to the exact top of the letters.
7. Copy the letters, then paste them in front.
8. Fill the copied letters in front with white.
9. Using your arrow keys, move the white letters 2 pts to the left and 8 pts up.
10. Save your work, then compare your text with Figure 49.
11. Close Vanish.

FIGURE 49
Completed Design Project

Creating Text and Gradients

Firehouse Chili Pepper Company, a local specialty food manufacturer, has hired you to design a label for its new line of hot sauces. Since this is a new product line, they have no existing materials for you to start from.

1. Create a new 6" × 6" CMYK Color document, then save it as **Firehouse Chili**.
2. Search the Internet to get design ideas. Use keywords such as chili, pepper, hot sauce, barbecue, and salsa. What have other designers created to convey these concepts? Is there a broad range of ideas, or are they all pretty much different versions of the same idea? If so, can you think of something original that works?
3. Go to the grocery store and return with some samples of other products in this niche. Be sure to purchase both products that you've heard of before and products you've never heard of before. Are the known products' design concepts better than the unknown products'? Look for any correlation between the successful products and better design, if it is evident.

4. Begin brainstorming and sketching out ideas. Although there are no existing materials, the product line's name is very evocative. You should create design ideas that spring from the concepts of "firehouse" and "chili pepper," as well as from more broad-based concepts such as salsa, Mexico, and fire.

5. Use the skills that you learned in this chapter to create the label. (*Hint*: Fill text outlines with a gradient that conveys "hot." Use reds, oranges, and blacks. Use a bold font for the text so that the gradient will be clearly visible. Position the stops on the slider so that the "hot" colors are prominent in the letterforms.)
6. Save your work, then compare your results with Figure 50.
7. Close Firehouse Chili.

FIGURE 50
Completed Portfolio Project

chapter

3

DRAWING AND COMPOSING
AN ILLUSTRATION

1. Draw straight lines

2. Draw curved lines

3. Draw elements of an illustration

4. Apply attributes to objects

5. Assemble an illustration

6. Stroke objects for artistic effect

7. Use Live Trace and the Live Paint Bucket tool

Drawing in Illustrator

You can create any shape using the Pen tool, which is why it's often called "the drawing tool." More precisely, the pen is a tool for drawing straight lines, curved lines, polygons, and irregularly shaped objects. It is, however, no *more* of a drawing tool than the shape tools—it's just more versatile.

The challenges of the Pen tool are finite and able to be grasped with no more than 30 minutes' study. As with many aspects of graphic design (and of life!), mastery comes with practice. So make it a point to learn Pen tool techniques. Don't get frustrated. And use the Pen tool often, even if it's just to play around making odd shapes.

To master Illustrator, you must master the Pen tool.

All artists learn techniques for using tools—brushes, chalk, palette knives, etc.

Once learned, those techniques become second nature—subconscious and unique to the artist. Ask yourself, was Van Gogh's mastery of the palette knife a triumph of his hands or of his imagination?

When you draw, you aren't conscious of how you're holding the crayon or how much pressure you're applying to the paper. Much the same goes for Illustrator's Pen tool. When you are comfortable and confident, you will find yourself effectively translating design ideas from your imagination straight to the artboard—without even thinking about the tool!

When you work with the Pen tool, you'll want complete control over your artboard. Using the Zoom tool and the New View feature, you can create custom views of areas of your artboard, making it easy to jump to specific elements of your illustration for editing purposes.

Tools You'll Use

DRAW STRAIGHT
LINES

What You'll Do

▶ *In this lesson, you will create three new views, then explore basic techniques for using the Pen tool as you prepare to draw a complex illustration.*

Viewing Objects on the Artboard

If you are drawing on paper and you want to see your work up close, you move your nose closer to the paper. Computers offer more effective options. As you have already seen, the Zoom tool is used to enlarge areas of the artboard for easier viewing. When you are working with the Pen tool, your view of the board becomes more critical, as anchor points are tiny, and you will often move them in 1 point increments.

Instead of clicking the Zoom tool to enlarge an area, you can click and drag it over the area you want to zoom in on, creating a **marquee**, a rectangular, dotted line that surrounds the area you drag over. When you release the Zoom tool, the marquee disappears, and whatever was in the marquee is magnified as much as possible while still fitting in the window.

The New View command allows you to save any view of the artboard. Let's say you zoom in on an object. You can save that view and give it a descriptive name, using the New View command. The name of the view is then listed at the bottom of the View menu, so you can return to it at any time by selecting it. Saving views is an effective way to increase your productivity.

Drawing Straight Segments with the Pen Tool

You can use the Pen tool to make lines, also known as paths; you can also use it to create a closed shape such as a triangle or a pentagon. When you click the Pen tool to make anchor points on the artboard, straight segments are automatically placed between the points. When the endpoints of two straight segments are united by a point that point is called a **corner point**. Figure 1 shows a simple path drawn with five anchor points and four segments.

Perfection is an unnecessary goal when you are using the Pen tool. Anchor points and segments can be moved and repositioned. New points can be added and deleted. Use the Pen tool to create the general shape that you have in your mind. Once the object is complete, use the Direct Selection tool to perfect—or tweak—the points and segments. "Tweaking" a finished object—making small, specific improvements—is always part of the drawing process.

Aligning and Joining Anchor Points

Often, you will want to align anchor points precisely. For example, if you have drawn a diamond-shaped object with the Pen tool, you may want to align the top and bottom points on the same vertical axis and then align the left and right points on the same horizontal axis to perfect the shape.

The **Average** command is a simple and effective choice for aligning points. With two or more points selected, you can use the Average command to align them on the horizontal axis, on the vertical axis, or on both the horizontal and vertical axes. Two points aligned on both the horizontal and vertical axes are positioned one on top of the other.

Why is the command named Average? The name is appropriate, because when the command moves two points to line them up on a given axis, that axis is positioned at the average distance between the two points. Thus, each moves the same distance.

The **Join** command unites two anchor points. When two points are positioned in different locations on the artboard, the Join command creates a segment between them. When two points are aligned on both the horizontal and vertical axes and are joined, the two points become one.

You will often use the Average and Join commands in tandem. Figure 2 shows two pairs of points that have each been aligned on the horizontal axis, then joined with the Join command.

FIGURE 1

Elements of a path composed of straight segments

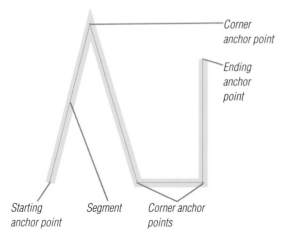

Corner anchor point

Ending anchor point

Starting anchor point

Segment

Corner anchor points

FIGURE 2

Join command unites open points

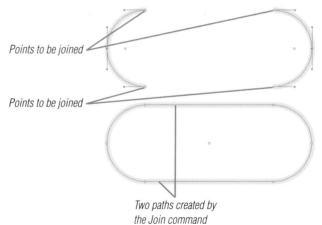

Points to be joined

Points to be joined

Two paths created by the Join command

Create new views

1. Open AI 3-1.ai, then save it as **Straight Lines**.

2. Choose the Essentials workspace, click the **Zoom tool** 🔍, then position it at the upper-left corner of the artboard.

3. Click and drag a **selection box** that encompasses the entire yellow section, as shown in Figure 3.

   The area within the selection box is now magnified.

4. Click **View** on the Application bar, then click **New View**.

5. Name the new view **yellow**, then click **OK**.

6. Press and hold **[Spacebar]** to access the Hand tool 🖐, then drag the **artboard** upward until you have a view of the entire pink area.

7. Create a new view of the pink area, and name it **pink**.

   TIP If you need to adjust your view, you can quickly switch to a view of the entire artboard by pressing [Ctrl][0] (Win) or ⌘[0] (Mac), then create a new selection box with the Zoom tool.

8. Create a new view of the green area, named **mint**.

9. Click **View** on the Application bar, then click **yellow** at the bottom of the menu.

   The Illustrator window changes to the yellow view.

   TIP You can change the name of a view by clicking View on the Application bar, then clicking Edit Views.

You used the Zoom tool to magnify an area of the artboard. You then named and saved the new view of the artboard. You named and saved two other views.

FIGURE 3
Drag the Zoom tool to select what will be magnified

Selection box

FIGURE 4
Four anchor points and three segments

FIGURE 5
Click the path with the Pen tool to add a new point

Add Anchor
Point tool

FIGURE 6
Move an anchor point with the Direct Selection tool

Draw straight lines

1. Verify that you are still in the yellow view, then click the **Pen tool** ✎.

2. Open the Swatches panel, set the fill color to [None], the stroke color to Black, and the stroke weight to 1 pt.

3. Using Figure 4 as a reference, click **position 1 (start)**.

4. Click **position 2**, then notice the segment that is automatically drawn between the two anchor points.

5. Click **position 3**, then click **position 4**.

   TIP   If you become disconnected from the current path you are drawing, undo your last step, then click the last anchor point with the Pen tool and continue.

6. Press and hold **[Ctrl]** (Win) or ⌘ (Mac) to switch to the Selection tool ▶, then click the artboard to stop drawing the path and to deselect it.

   You need to deselect one path before you can start drawing a new one.

7. Release [Ctrl] (Win) or ⌘ (Mac), then click **position 1 (start)** on the next path, then click **position 2**.

8. Skip over position 3 and click **position 4**.

9. Using Figure 5 as a guide, position the Pen tool anywhere on the segment between points 2 and 4, then click to add a new anchor point.

   TIP   When the Pen tool is positioned over a selected path, the Add Anchor Point tool appears.

10. Click the **Direct Selection tool** ▶., then drag the **new anchor point** to position 3, as shown in Figure 6.

Using the Pen tool, you created two straight paths.

Close a path and align the anchor points

1. Click **View** on the Application bar, then click **pink**.

2. Click the **Pen tool** ✎, click the **start/end position** at the top of the polygon, then click **positions 2 through 6**.

3. Position the Pen tool over the first point you created, then click to close the path, as shown in Figure 7.

4. Switch to the **Direct Selection tool** ▶, click **point 3**, press and hold **[Shift]**, then click **point 6**.

   TIP Use the [Shift] key to select multiple points.

   Anchor points that are selected appear as solid blue squares; anchor points that are not selected are white or hollow squares.

5. Click **Object** on the Application bar, point to **Path**, then click **Average**.

6. Click the **Horizontal option button** in the Average dialog box, then click **OK**.

   The two selected anchor points align on the horizontal axis, as shown in Figure 8.

7. Select both the start/end point and point 4.

8. Use the Average command to align the points on the vertical axis.

9. Select both point 2 and point 5, then use the Average command to align the points on both axes, as shown in Figure 9.

You drew a closed path, then used the Average command to align three sets of points. You aligned the first set on the horizontal axis, the second on the vertical axis. You aligned the third set of points on both axes, which positioned them one on top of the other.

FIGURE 7
Close a path at its starting point

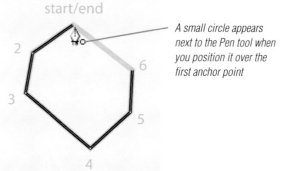

A small circle appears next to the Pen tool when you position it over the first anchor point

FIGURE 8
Two points aligned on the horizontal axis

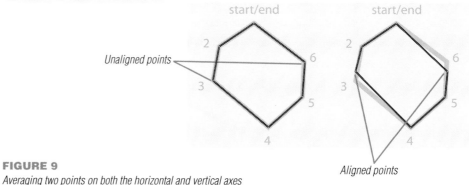

Unaligned points

Aligned points

FIGURE 9
Averaging two points on both the horizontal and vertical axes

FIGURE 10

Cutting points also deletes the segments attached to them

FIGURE 11

Join command unites two distant points with a straight segment

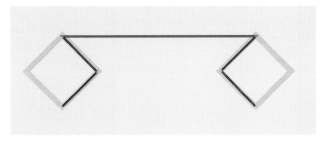

FIGURE 12

Joining the two open anchor points on an open path closes the path

Join anchor points

1. Switch to the mint view of the artboard.

2. Use the Pen tool ♦. to trace the two diamond shapes.

    TIP   Remember to deselect the first diamond path with the Selection tool before you begin tracing the second diamond.

3. Click the **left anchor point** of the first diamond with the Direct Selection tool ▶., click **Edit** on the Application bar, then click **Cut**.

    Cutting points also deletes the segments attached to them.

4. Cut the right point on the second diamond.

    Your work should resemble Figure 10.

5. Select the top point on each path.

6. Click **Object** on the Application bar, point to **Path**, then click **Join**.

    The points are joined by a straight segment, as shown in Figure 11.

    TIP   The similarity of the quick keys for Average and Join makes them easy to work with in tandem.

7. Join the two bottom points.

8. Apply a yellow fill to the object, then save your work.

    Your work should resemble Figure 12.

9. Close the Straight Lines document.

You drew two closed paths. You cut a point from each path, which deleted the points and the segments attached to them, creating two open paths. You used the Join command, which drew a new segment between the two top points and the two bottom points on each path. You then applied a yellow fill to the new object.

CURVED LINES

What You'll Do

In this lesson, you will use the Pen tool to draw and define curved paths, and learn techniques to draw lines that abruptly change direction.

Defining Properties of Curved Lines

When you click to create anchor points with the Pen tool, the points are connected by straight segments. You can "draw" a curved path between two anchor points by *clicking and dragging* the Pen tool to create the points, instead of just clicking. Anchor points created by clicking and dragging the Pen tool are known as **smooth points**.

When you use the Direct Selection tool to select a point connected to a curved segment, you will expose the point's **direction lines**, as shown in Figure 13. The angle and length of the direction lines determine the arc of the curved segment. Direction lines are editable. You can click

Drawing and Composing an Illustration

and drag the **direction points**, or handles, at the end of the direction lines to reshape the curve. Direction lines function only to define curves and do not appear when you print your document.

A smooth point always has two direction lines that move together as a unit. The two curved segments attached to the smooth point are both defined by the direction lines. When you manipulate the direction lines on a smooth point, you change the curve of both segments attached to the point, always maintaining a *smooth* transition through the anchor point.

When two paths are joined at a corner point, the two paths can be manipulated independently. A corner point can join two straight segments, one straight segment and one curved segment, or two curved segments. That corner point would have zero, one, or two direction lines, respectively. Figure 14 shows examples of smooth points and corner points.

FIGURE 13
Direction lines define a curve

Direction point

Direction line

Smooth anchor point

FIGURE 14
Smooth points and corner points

A corner point joining two straight segments

A corner point joining one straight and one curved segment

A smooth point

A corner point joining two curved paths (note the direction lines)

When a corner point joins one or two curved segments, the direction lines are unrelated and are often referred to as "broken." When you manipulate one, the other doesn't move.

Converting Anchor Points

The Convert Anchor Point tool changes corner points to smooth points and smooth points to corner points.

To convert a corner point to a smooth point, you click and drag the Convert

Anchor Point tool on the anchor point to *pull out* direction lines. See Figure 15.

The Convert Anchor Point tool works two ways to convert a smooth point to a corner point, and both are very useful when drawing.

FIGURE 15
Converting a corner point to a smooth point

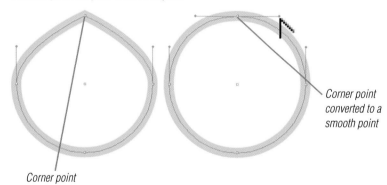

Corner point converted to a smooth point

Corner point

When you click directly on a smooth point with the Convert Anchor Point tool, the direction lines disappear. The two attached segments lose whatever curve defined them and become straight segments, as shown in Figure 16.

You can also use the Convert Anchor Point tool on one of the two direction lines of a smooth point. The tool "breaks" the direction lines and allows you to move one independently of the other. The smooth point is converted to a corner point that now joins two unrelated curved segments.

Once the direction lines are broken, they remain broken. You can manipulate them independently with the Direct Selection tool; you no longer need the Convert Anchor Point tool to do so.

FIGURE 16
Converting smooth points to corner points

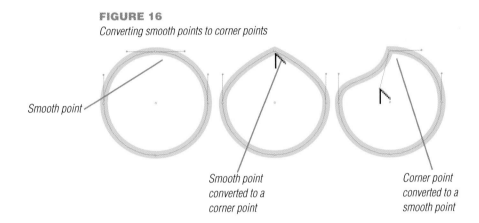

Smooth point

Smooth point
converted to a
corner point

Corner point
converted to a
smooth point

Toggling between the Pen tool and the selection tools
Drawing points and selecting points go hand in hand, and you will often switch back and forth between the Pen tool and one of the selection tools. Clicking from one tool to the other on the Tools panel is unnecessary and will impede your productivity. To master the Pen tool, you *must* incorporate the keyboard command for "toggling" between the Pen tool and the selection tools. With the Pen tool selected, press [Ctrl] (Win) or ⌘ (Mac), which will switch the Pen tool to the Selection tool or the Direct Selection tool, depending on which tool you used last.

Draw and edit a curved line

1. Open AI 3-2.ai, then save it as **Curved Lines 1**.
2. Click the **Pen tool** , then position it over the first point position on the line.
3. Click and drag upward until the pointer is at the center of the purple star.
4. Position the Pen tool over the second point position.
5. Click and drag down to the red star.
6. Using the same method, trace the remainder of the blue line, as shown in Figure 17.
7. Click the **Direct Selection tool** .
8. Select the second anchor point.
9. Click and drag the **direction handle** of the *top* direction line to the second purple star, as shown in Figure 18.

   The move changes the shape of *both* segments attached to the anchor point.
10. Select the third anchor point.
11. Drag the **bottom direction handle** to the second red star, as shown in Figure 19.
12. Manipulate the direction lines to restore the curves to their appearance in Figure 17.
13. Save your work, then close the Curved Lines 1 document.

You traced a curved line by making smooth points with the Pen tool. You used the Direct Selection tool to manipulate the direction lines of the smooth points and adjust the curves. You then used the direction lines to restore the line to its original curves.

FIGURE 17
Smooth points draw continuous curves

FIGURE 18
Moving one direction line changes two curves

Click the Direct Selection tool on any smooth point to expose its direction lines

FIGURE 19
Round curves are distorted by moving direction lines

FIGURE 20
Smooth points are converted to corner points

Convert anchor points

1. Open AI 3-3.ai, then save it as **Curved Lines 2**.

2. Click **View** on the Application bar, then click **View #1**.

3. Click the **Direct Selection tool** � anywhere on the black line.

   Six anchor points become visible.

4. Click **Object** on the Application bar, point to **Path**, then click **Add Anchor Points**.

   Five anchor points are added that do not change the shape of the line.

5. Click the **Convert Anchor Point tool** ↖, then click each of the five new anchor points.

   | TIP The Convert Anchor Point tool is hidden beneath the Pen tool.

   The smooth points are converted to corner points, as shown in Figure 20.

6. Click the six original anchor points with the Convert Anchor Point tool.

7. Starting from the left side of the line, position the Convert Anchor Point tool over the sixth anchor point.

8. Click and drag the **anchor point** to the purple star.

   The corner point is converted to a smooth point.

9. Using Figure 21 as a guide, convert the corner points to the left and right of the new curve.

You added five new anchor points to the line, then used the Convert Anchor Point tool to convert all 11 points from smooth to corner points. You then used the Convert Anchor Point tool to convert three corner points to smooth points.

FIGURE 21
Smooth points restored from corner points

Draw a line with curved and straight segments

1. Click **View** on the Application bar, then click **View #2**.

2. Click the **Pen tool** 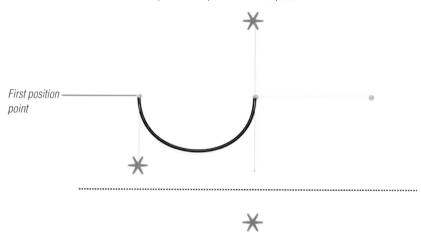, position it over the first point position, then click and drag down to the green star.

3. Position the Pen tool over the second point position, then click and drag up to the purple star, as shown in the top section of Figure 22.

4. Click the **second anchor point**.

   The direction line you dragged is deleted, as shown in the lower section of Figure 22.

5. Click the **third point position** to create the third anchor point.

6. Position the Pen tool over the third anchor point, then click and drag a direction line up to the green star.

7. Position the Pen tool over the **fourth point position**, then click and drag down to the purple star.

8. Click the **fourth anchor point**.

9. Position the Pen tool over the fifth position, then click.

10. While the Pen tool is still positioned over the fifth anchor point, click and drag a direction line down to the green star.

11. Finish tracing the line, then deselect the path.

You traced a line that has three curves joined by two straight segments. You used the technique of clicking the previous smooth point to convert it to a corner point, allowing you to change the direction of the path.

FIGURE 22
Click to convert an open smooth point to a corner point

First position point

Direction line is deleted

Clicking the last smooth point you drew converts it to a corner point

FIGURE 23

Use the Convert Anchor Point tool to "break" the direction lines and redirect the path

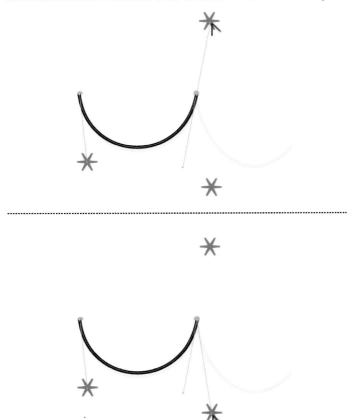

1. Click **View** on the Application bar, then click **View #3**.

2. Click the **Pen tool** ✒. position it over the first point position, then click and drag down to the purple star.

3. Position the Pen tool ✒. over the second point position, then click and drag up to the red star, as shown in the top section of Figure 23.

4. Press and hold **[Alt]** (Win) or **[option]** (Mac) to switch to the Convert Anchor Point tool ⌐, then click and drag the **direction handle** on the red star down to the second purple star, as shown in the lower section of Figure 23.

   TIP Press [Alt] (Win) or [option] (Mac) to toggle between the Pen and the Convert Anchor Point tools.

5. Release [Alt] (Win) or [option] (Mac), then continue to trace the line using the same method.

   TIP If you switch between the Pen tool and the Convert Anchor Point tool using the Tools panel, instead of using [Alt] (Win) or [option] (Mac), you will disconnect from the current path.

6. Save your work, then close the Curved Lines 2 document.

You used the Convert Anchor Point tool to "break" the direction lines of a smooth point, converting it to a corner point in the process. You used the redirected direction line to define the next curve in the sequence.

DRAW ELEMENTS OF
AN ILLUSTRATION

What You'll Do

In this lesson, you will draw 14 elements of an illustration. By tracing previously drawn elements, you will develop a sense of where to place anchor points when drawing a real-world illustration.

Starting an Illustration

Getting started with drawing an illustration is often the hardest part. Sometimes the illustration will be an image of a well-known object or a supplied sketch or a picture. At other times, the illustration to be created will exist only in your imagination. In either case, the challenge is the same: How do you translate the concept from its source to the Illustrator artboard?

Drawing from Scratch

Drawing from scratch means that you start with a new Illustrator document and create the illustration, using only the Illustrator tools. This approach is common, especially when the goal is to draw familiar items such as a daisy, a fish, or the sun, for example.

Illustrator's shape tools (such as the Ellipse tool) combined with the transform tools (such as the Rotate tool) make the program very powerful for creating geometric designs from scratch. The Undo and Redo commands allow you to experiment, and

you will often find yourself surprised by the design you end up with!

Typographic illustrations—even complex ones—are often created from scratch.

Many talented illustrators and designers are able to create complex graphics off the cuff. It can be an astounding experience to watch an illustrator start with a blank artboard and, with no reference material, produce sophisticated graphics—graphics with attitude and expression and emotion, with unexpected shapes and subtle relationships between objects.

Tracing a Scanned Image

Using the Place command, it is easy to import a scanned image into Illustrator. For complex illustrations—especially those of people or objects with delicate relationships, such as maps or blueprints—many designers find it easier to scan a sketch or a photo and import it into Illustrator as a guide or a point of reference.

Tracing a scanned image is not "cheating." An original drawing is an original drawing, whether it is first created on a computer or on a piece of paper. Rather than being a negative, the ability to use a computer to render a sketch is a fine example of the revolutionary techniques that illustration software has brought to the art of drawing. Figure 24 shows an illustration created from scratch in Illustrator, and Figure 25 shows a scanned sketch that will be the basis for the illustration you will create throughout this chapter.

FIGURE 24
An illustration created from scratch

FIGURE 25
Place a scanned sketch in Illustrator, and you can trace it or use it as a visual reference

Draw a closed path using smooth points

1. Open AI 3-4.ai, then save it as **Snowball Parts**.

2. Click **View** on the Application bar, then click **Arm**.

3. Verify that the fill color is set to [None] and the stroke color is set to Black.

4. Click the **Pen tool** ✒️ , position it over point 1, then click and drag a **direction line** to the green star on the right side of the 1.

5. Go to position 2, then click and drag a **direction line** to the next green star.

   | TIP   Watch the blue preview of the new segment fall into place as you drag the Pen tool. This will help you understand when to stop dragging the direction line.

6. Using the same method, continue to draw points 3 through 6, then compare your screen to Figure 26.

7. Position the Pen tool over point 1.

8. Press and hold **[Alt]** (Win) or **[option]** (Mac), then click and drag to position the ending segment and close the path.

You drew a curved path. To close the path, you used a corner point, which allowed you to position the ending segment without affecting the starting segment.

FIGURE 26
Points 1 through 6 are smooth points

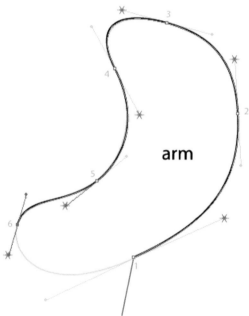

When closing a path, pressing [Alt] (Win) or [option] (Mac) converts the end/start anchor point to a corner point

FIGURE 27
Point 5 is a corner point

Corner point

hatband

1. Click **View** on the Application bar, then click **Hatband**.

2. Verify that the fill color is set to [None] and the stroke color is set to Black.

3. Click the **Pen tool** 🖋 , then click **position 1** to create a corner point.

4. Draw the next two curved segments for positions 2 and 3, using the green stars as guides.

5. Position the Pen tool over position 4, then click and drag to the green star.

6. Click **position 5** to create a corner point, as shown in Figure 27.

7. Position the Pen tool over position 6, then click and drag to the green star.

8. Click **position 1** to close the path with a corner point.

9. Click the **Selection tool** ▶ , then deselect the path.

You began a path with a corner point. When it was time to close the path, you simply clicked the starting point. Since the point was created without direction lines, there were no direction lines to contend with when closing the path.

Redirect a path while drawing

1. Click **View** on the Application bar, then click **Nose**.

   The Nose view includes the nose, mouth, eyebrow, and teeth.

2. Click the **Pen tool** 🖊, then click **point 1** on the nose to start the path with a corner point.

3. Create smooth points at positions 2 and 3.

   The direction of the nose that you are tracing abruptly changes at point 3.

4. Press and hold **[Alt]** (Win) or **[option]** (Mac) to switch to the Convert Anchor Point tool ⌐, then move the top direction handle of point 3 down to the red star, as shown in Figure 28.

5. Release [Alt] (Win) or [option] (Mac) to switch back to the Pen tool, click and drag **position 4** to finish drawing the path, click the Selection tool ▶, then deselect the path.

   The nose element, as shown in Figure 29, is an open path.

Tracing the nose, you encountered an abrupt change in direction, followed by a curve. You used the Convert Anchor Point tool to redirect the direction lines on point 3, simultaneously converting point 3 from smooth to corner and defining the shape of the curved segment that follows.

FIGURE 28
Use the Convert Anchor Point tool to redirect the path

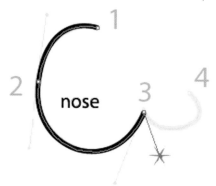

FIGURE 29
Nose element is an open path

FIGURE 30

Use a scanned sketch as a reference or for tracing

1. Click **View** on the Application bar, then click **Fit All in Window**.

2. Click **File** on the Application bar, then click **Place**.

3. Navigate to the drive and folder where your Data Files are stored.

4. Click **Snowball Sketch.tif**, then click **Place**.

   A scan of the Snowball Sketch illustration is placed in a bounding box at the center of the artboard.

5. Use the Scale tool ▨ to scale the placed file 115%.

   | TIP   You can apply all of the transform tools to placed files.

6. Click the **Selection tool** ▶, move the placed file into the scratch area, then lock it.

7. Draw the remaining elements of the illustration, referring to the sketch in the scratch area or to Figure 30 for help.

   | TIP   The mouth, eyebrow, and teeth are located in the Nose view.

8. Save your work after you complete each element.

You placed a file of a scanned sketch to use as a reference guide. You scaled the object, dragged it to the scratch area, locked it, then drew the remaining elements of the illustration.

APPLY ATTRIBUTES
TO OBJECTS

What You'll Do

▶ *You will create four new colors on the Color panel and apply each to one of the illustration elements. Using the Eyedropper tool, you will paint the remaining items quickly and easily.*

Using the Eyedropper Tool

Illustrator uses the word **attributes** to refer to that which has been applied to an object that affects its appearance. Typographic attributes, for example, would include font, leading, horizontal scale, etc. Artistic attributes include the fill color, stroke color, and stroke weight.

The Eyedropper tool is handy for applying *all* of an object's attributes to another object. Its icon is particularly apt: The Eyedropper tool "picks up" an object's attributes, such as fill color, stroke color, and stroke weight.

> **QUICK**TIP
>
> You can think of the Eyedropper tool as taking a sample of an object's attributes.

The Eyedropper tool is particularly useful when you want to apply one object's attrib-utes to another. For example, if you have appplied a blue fill with a 3.5 pt orange stroke to an object, you can easily apply those attributes to new or already-existing objects. Simply select the object that you want to format, then click the formatted object with the Eyedropper tool.

This is a simple example, but don't under-estimate the power of the Eyedropper tool. As you explore more of Illustrator, you will find that you are able to apply a variety of increasingly complex attributes to objects. The more – and more complex – the attrib-utes, the more the Eyedropper tool reveals its usefulness.

You can also use the Eyedropper tool to copy type formatting and effects between text elements. This can be especially useful when designing display type for headlines.

Adding a Fill to an Open Path

You can think of the letter O as an example of a closed path and the letter U as an example of an open path. Although it seems a bit strange, you are able to add a fill to an open path just as you would to a closed path. The program draws an imaginary straight line between the endpoints of an open path to define where the fill ends. Figure 31 shows an open path in the shape of a U with a red fill. Note where the fill ends. For the most part, avoid applying fills to open paths. Though Illustrator will apply the fill, an open path's primary role is to feature a stroke. Any effect that you can create by filling an open path you can also create with a more effective method by filling a closed path.

FIGURE 31
A fill color applied to an open path

Apply new attributes to open and closed paths

1. Verify that nothing is selected on the artboard.

2. Open the Color panel, create a royal blue color on the Color panel.

3. Fill the arm with the royal blue color, then change its stroke weight to 6 pt.

   TIP Use the views at the bottom of the View menu to see and select each element you need to work with. The mouth, eyebrow, and teeth are located in the Nose view.

4. Deselect the arm, then create a deep red color on the Color panel.

5. Fill the hatband with the deep red color, then change its stroke weight to 3 pt.

6. Deselect the hatband, then create a flesh-toned color on the Color panel that is 20% magenta and 56% yellow.

7. Fill the head with the flesh tone; don't change the stroke weight.

8. Fill the pompom with White; don't change the stroke weight.

9. Fill the mouth with Black; don't change the stroke weight.

10. Compare your work with Figure 32.

You applied new attributes to five closed paths by creating three new colors, using them as fills, then changing the stroke weight on two of the objects.

FIGURE 32
New attributes applied to five elements

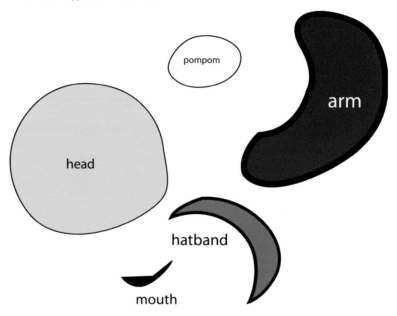

FIGURE 33

Use the Eyedropper tool to apply the attributes of one object to another . . . with one click!

Selected

Click

FIGURE 34

All elements ready to be assembled

Copy attributes with the Eyedropper tool

1. Select the torso.
2. Click the **Eyedropper tool** 🖊, then click the **blue arm**.

   As shown in Figure 33, the torso takes on the same fill and stroke attributes as the arm.
3. Switch to the Selection tool ▸, select the hat, click the **Eyedropper tool** 🖊 then click the **hatband**.
4. Using any method you like, fill and stroke the remaining objects using the colors shown in Figure 34.

You applied the same attributes from one object to another by first selecting the object you wanted to apply the attributes to, then clicking the object with the desired attributes, using the Eyedropper tool.

ASSEMBLE AN ILLUSTRATION

What You'll Do

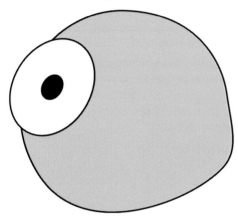

▶ In this lesson, you will arrange the elements that you drew in Lesson 4 to create a composed illustration.

Assembling an Illustration

Illustrator's basic stacking order design is sophisticated enough to compose any illustration. Assembling an illustration with multiple objects will test your fluency with the stacking order commands: Bring to Front, Send to Back, Bring Forward, Send Backward, Paste in Front, Paste in Back, Group, Lock, Unlock All, Hide, and

Show All. The sequence in which you draw the elements determines the stacking order (newer elements are in front of older ones), so you'll almost certainly need to adjust the stacking order when assembling the elements. Locking and hiding placed elements will help you to protect the elements when they are positioned correctly.

FIGURE 35
Eye positioned on the head

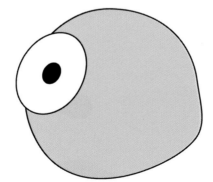

FIGURE 36
Second eye is a copy of the first

Drawing and Composing an Illustration

FIGURE 37
Nose pasted in front of the left eye

The nose behind
the left eye

The nose in front
of the left eye

FIGURE 38
Eyebrow positioned over the right eye

FIGURE 39
All elements in position

Assemble the illustration

1. Select and copy all the elements on the artboard.

2. Create a new CMYK Color document that is 9" × 9", then save it as **Snowball Assembled**.

3. Paste the copied elements into the Snowball Assembled document.

4. Deselect all objects, select the head, click **Object** on the Application bar, point to **Arrange**, then click **Send to Back**.

5. Group the eye and the iris, then position the eye on the head as shown in Figure 35.

6. Click the **eye**, press **[Alt]** (Win) or **[option]** (Mac), then drag to create a copy of it, as shown in Figure 36.

7. Position the nose on the face, cut the nose, select the left eye, then paste in front.

   The nose is pasted in the same position, but now it is in front of the eye, as shown in Figure 37.

8. Select the teeth, then bring them to the front.

9. Position the teeth over the mouth, then group them.

10. Position the mouth and the teeth on the head, and the eyebrow over the right eye, as shown in Figure 38.

11. Finish assembling the illustration, using Figure 39 as a guide, then save your work.

   TIP   Use the Object menu and the Arrange menu command to change the stacking order of objects, as necessary.

You assembled the illustration, utilizing various commands to change the stacking order of the individual elements.

STROKE OBJECTS FOR
ARTISTIC EFFECT

What You'll Do

In this lesson, you will experiment with strokes of varying weight and attributes, using options on the Stroke panel. You will then apply pseudo-strokes to all of the objects to create dramatic stroke effects.

Defining Joins and Caps

In addition to applying a stroke weight, you use the Stroke panel to define other stroke attributes, including joins and caps, and whether a stroke is solid or dashed. Figure 40 shows the Dashed Line utility on the Stroke panel.

Caps are applied to the ends of stroked paths. The Stroke panel offers three choices: Butt Cap, Round Cap, and Projecting Cap. Choose Butt Cap for squared ends and Round Cap for rounded ends. Generally, round caps are more appealing to the eye.

The projecting cap applies a squared edge that extends the anchor point at a distance that is one-half the weight of the stroke. With a projecting cap, the weight of the stroke is equal in all directions around the line. The projecting cap is useful when you align two anchor points at a right angle, as shown in Figure 41.

FIGURE 40
Stroke panel

Dash width text box
Gap width text box
Miter Limit text box

FIGURE 41
Projecting caps are useful when segments meet at right angles

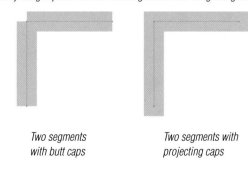

Two segments with butt caps

Two segments with projecting caps

Drawing and Composing an Illustration

When two stroked paths form a corner point, **joins** define the appearance of the corner. The default is a miter join, which produces stroked lines with pointed corners. The round join produces stroked lines with rounded corners, and the bevel join produces stroked lines with squared corners. The greater the weight of the stroke, the more apparent the join will be, as shown in Figure 42.

Defining the Miter Limit

The miter limit determines when a miter join will be squared off to a beveled edge.

The miter is the length of the point, from the inside to the outside. The length of the miter is not the same as the stroke weight. When two stroked paths are at an acute angle, the length of the miter will greatly exceed the weight of the stroke, which results in an extreme point that can be very distracting.

QUICKTIP

You can align a stroke to the center, inside, or outside of a path using the Align Stroke buttons on the Stroke panel.

The default miter limit is 4, which means that when the length of the miter reaches 4 times the stroke weight, the program will automatically square it off to a beveled edge. Generally, you will find the default miter limit satisfactory, but remain conscious of it when you draw objects with acute angles, such as stars and triangles. Figure 43 shows the impact of a miter limit on a stroked star with acute angles.

FIGURE 42

Three types of joins

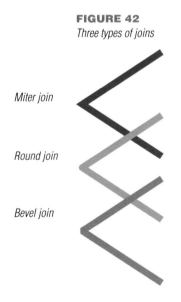

Miter join

Round join

Bevel join

FIGURE 43

Miter limit affects the length of stroked corner points

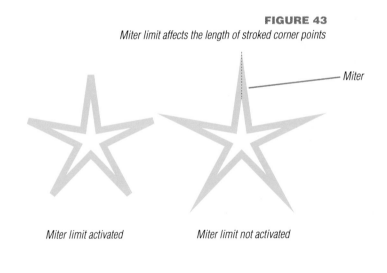

Miter

Miter limit activated

Miter limit not activated

Creating a Dashed Stroke

A dashed stroke is like any other stroked path in Illustrator, except that its stroke has been broken up into a sequence of dashes separated by gaps. The Stroke panel offers you the freedom to customize dashed or dotted lines; enter the lengths of the dashes and the gaps between them in the six dash and gap text boxes. You can create a maximum of three different sizes of dashes separated by three different sizes of gaps. The pattern you establish will be repeated across the length of the stroke.

When creating dashed strokes, remain conscious of the cap choice on the Stroke panel. Butt caps create familiar square dashes, and round caps create rounded dashes. Creating a dotted line requires round caps. Figure 44 shows two dashed lines using the same pattern but with different caps applied.

Creating Pseudo-Stroke Effects

Strokes around objects—especially black strokes—often contribute much to an illustration in terms of contrast, dimension, and dramatic effect. To that end, you may find the Stroke panel to be limited.

Sometimes, the most effective stroke is no stroke at all. A classic technique that designers have used since the early versions of Illustrator is the "pseudo-stroke," or false stroke. Basically, you place a black-filled copy behind an illustration element, then distort the black element with the Direct Selection tool so that it "peeks" out from behind the element in varying degrees.

This technique, as shown in Figure 45, is relatively simple to execute and can be used for dramatic effect in an illustration.

FIGURE 44

Caps are an important factor in determining the appearance of a dashed line

Round caps

Butt caps

Align Stroke to Center button

Align Stroke to Outside button

Align Stroke to Inside button

FIGURE 45

The "pseudo-stroke" effect

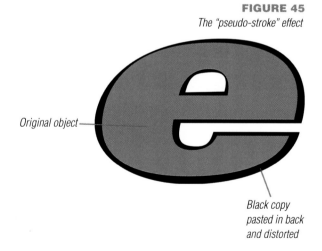

Original object

Black copy pasted in back and distorted

FIGURE 46
Bevel joins applied to paths

Miter joins on mouth
and nose change to
bevel joins

FIGURE 47
Round joins applied to paths

Bevel joins on mouth
and nose change to
round joins

Modify stroke attributes

1. Select the eyebrow, the nose, and the mouth.

2. Click **Select** on the Application bar, then click **Inverse**.

   The selected items are now deselected, and the deselected items are selected.

3. Hide the selected items, then open the Stroke panel.

4. Select all, then change the stroke weight to 3 pt.

5. Click the **Stroke panel list arrow**, click **Show Options** (if necessary), then click the **Round Cap button** ⊑.

   The caps on open paths are rounded.

6. Click the **Bevel Join button** 🔲.

   The miter joins on the mouth and nose change to a bevel join, as shown in Figure 46.

7. Click the **Round Join button** 🔲.

   The bevel joins on the mouth and nose change to round joins, as shown in Figure 47.

8. Remove the stroke from the teeth.

   TIP   Use the Direct Selection tool to select the teeth, since they are grouped to the mouth.

You hid elements so you could focus on the eyebrow, nose, and mouth. You applied round caps to the open paths and round joins to the corner points.

Create a dashed stroke

1. Show all objects, then select all.

2. Deselect the snowball, then hide the selected items.

   The snowball should be the only element showing.

3. Select the snowball, then change the stroke weight to 4 pt.

4. Click the **Dashed Line check box** on the Stroke panel.

5. Experiment with different dash and gap sizes.

6. Toggle between butt and round caps.

   The dashes change from rectangles to ovals.

7. Enter 1 pt dashes and 4 pt gaps.

8. Click the **Round Cap button** , compare your snowball to the one shown in Figure 48, then show all of the objects that are currently hidden.

You applied a dashed stroke to the snowball object and noted how a change in caps affected the dashes.

FIGURE 48
Creating a dashed stroke using the Stroke panel

FIGURE 49

A black copy peeking out beneath the front object

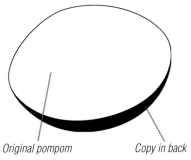

Original pompom   Copy in back

FIGURE 50

Pompom with the pseudo-stroke effect

FIGURE 51

Completed illustration

Create pseudo-strokes

1. Copy the pompom, then paste in back.

2. Apply a black fill to the copy.

   TIP   The copy is still selected behind the original white pompom, making it easy to apply the black fill.

3. Click the **white pompom**, then remove the stroke.

4. Lock the white pompom.

5. Using the Direct Selection tool ▶, select the bottom anchor point on the black copy.

6. Use the arrow keys to move the anchor point 5 pts down, away from the white pompom, using Figure 49 as a reference.

   The black copy is increasingly revealed as its size is increased beneath the locked white pompom.

7. Move the left anchor point 4 pts to the left.

8. Move the top anchor point 2 pts up, then deselect.

   Your work should resemble Figure 50.

9. Using the same methods, and Figure 51 as a reference, create distorted black copies behind all the remaining elements except the torso, the mouth, and the eyebrow.

10. Save your work, then close Snowball Assembled.

You created black copies behind each element, then distorted them, using the Direct Selection tool and the arrow keys, to create the illusion of uneven black strokes around the object.

USE LIVE TRACE AND THE
LIVE PAINT BUCKET TOOL

What You'll Do

In this lesson, you will use the Live Trace and Live Paint features.

Introducing Live Trace

Have you ever roughed out a sketch on paper, only to have to recreate it from scratch on your computer? Or, have you ever wished that you could convert a scanned photograph into editable vector graphics to use as the basis of an illustration? With Live Trace, you can have Illustrator trace a graphic for you.

Live Trace offers a number of built-in tracing presets that help you fine-tune your tracing results from the start. Additional presets, such as Hand Drawn Sketch, Comic Art, and Detailed Illustration, help create even extra special effects.

So what is the "live" in Live Trace, you ask? The live aspects of Live Trace occur in the Tracing Options dialog box, shown in Figure 52. Here, you can click the Preset list arrow to choose which type of preset you want to use to trace the bitmap (in the figure, Hand Drawn Sketch is the chosen

FIGURE 52
Tracing Options dialog box

Hand Drawn
Sketch preset

Drawing and Composing an Illustration

preset). To see the resulting artwork before you close the dialog box, click the Preview check box. You can also continue to manipulate the graphic by changing the many settings in the Adjustments and Trace Settings sections of the dialog box. Illustrator will continually retrace the graphic to preview the final effect. That's the live part of Live Trace!

Tracing a Line-Art Sketch

Figure 53 shows a magic marker sketch of a dog that has been scanned into Photoshop and placed in Illustrator. Figure 54 shows the artwork after it has been traced using the default Live Trace settings. Not much difference,

you say? Well, that's a good thing, a testament to how accurately Live Trace does its job.

As you were undoubtedly taught years ago, appearances can be deceiving. Though the artwork in 53 and 54 appears similar, they couldn't be more different, because the artwork in 54 is a vector graphic that has been traced from the bitmap graphic shown in 54.

Expanding a Traced Graphic

When a bitmap image is selected in Illustrator, the Live Trace button becomes available on the Control panel. After Live

Trace has been executed, the Expand button becomes available on the Control panel. In order to select and modify the paths and points that make up the new vector graphic, you must first click the Expand button. Once done, the illustration is able to be selected and modified, as shown in Figure 55.

QUICKTIP
Figure 55 shows the artwork in Outline mode so that you can better see the paths and points.

FIGURE 53
Bitmap graphic placed in Illustrator

FIGURE 54
Traced graphic

FIGURE 55
Expanded traced graphic, in Outline mode

Tracing a Photograph

You use Live Trace to trace a bitmap photo the same way you trace a sketch. With photographic images, however, the settings in the Tracing Options dialog box can be used to create some very interesting illustration effects.

Figure 56 shows a scanned photograph that has been placed in Illustrator. Clicking the Live Trace button instructs Illustrator to trace the photo using the default Black & White setting. The result is shown in Figure 57.

QUICKTIP
The default Black & White setting is 128 Threshold.

The resulting graphic is not the only result possible—not by a long shot. Rather than use the default setting, you can click the Tracing presets and options list arrow on the Control panel and choose from a variety of styles, such as Comic Art or Technical Drawing. The Tracing presets and options list arrow is also available in the Tracing Options dialog box.

FIGURE 56

Scanned photograph placed in Illustrator

FIGURE 57

Photograph traced at default Black & White setting

Introducing Live Paint

Adobe is touting the Live Paint Bucket tool as being "revolutionary," and it's not an overstatement. The Live Paint Bucket tool breaks all the fundamental rules of Illustrator, and creates some new ones. For that reason, when you are working with the Live Paint Bucket tool, it's a good idea to think of yourself as working in Live Paint *mode*, because Illustrator will function differently with this tool than it will with any other.

Essentially, the Live Paint Bucket tool is designed to make painting easier and more intuitive. It does this by changing the basic rules of Illustrator objects. In Live Paint mode, the concept of layers no longer applies—selected objects are all on the same level. The Live Paint Bucket tool uses two new Illustrator object types called regions and edges. Regions and edges are comparable to fills and strokes, but they are "live." As shown in Figure 58, where two regions overlap, a third region is created and can be painted with its own color. Where two edges overlap, a third edge is created. It too can be painted its own color.

Adobe likes to say that Live Paint is intuitive—something that looks like it should be able to be filled with its own color can indeed be filled with its own color. As long as you have the Live Paint Bucket tool selected, selected objects can be filled using the new rules of Live Paint mode. Once you leave Live Paint mode, the paint that you have applied to the graphic remains part of the illustration.

FIGURE 58
Identifying regions and edges in an illustration

Edge

Region

Edge with new color applied

Region with new color applied

Live Painting Regions

To paint objects with the Live Paint Bucket tool, you must first select the objects you wish to paint. Figure 59 shows three selected rectangles that overlap each other. The selection marks show various shapes created by the overlapping. As stated earlier, these overlapping areas or shapes are called regions. To fill the regions, click the Live Paint Bucket tool, click a color on the Swatches panel, then click a region that you want to fill. As shown in Figure 60, when you position the Live Paint Bucket tool pointer over a region,

that region is highlighted. Click the Live Paint Bucket tool and the region is filled, as shown in Figure 61.

As shown in Figure 62, each region can be filled with new colors. But that's not all that the Live Paint Bucket tool has to offer. The "live" part of Live Paint is that these regions are now part of a **live paint group**, and they maintain a dynamic relationship with each other. This means that when any of the objects is moved, the overlapping area changes shape—and fill—accordingly. For

example, in Figure 63, the tall thin rectangle has been moved to the left—note how the overlapping regions have been redrawn and how their fills have updated with the move.

FIGURE 59
Three overlapping selected rectangles

FIGURE 60
Positioning the Live Paint Bucket tool pointer

FIGURE 61
Filling a region with a new color

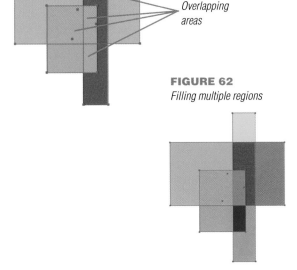

Overlapping areas

Region is highlighted

Region is filled with new color

FIGURE 62
Filling multiple regions

FIGURE 63
Moving an object in a Live Paint group

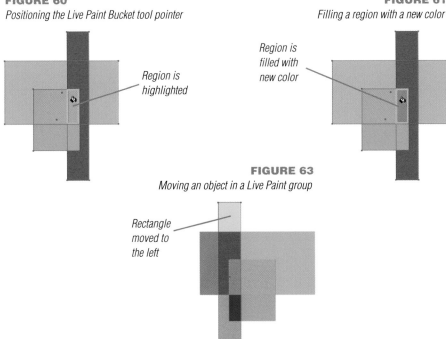

Rectangle moved to the left

Painting Virtual Regions

The intuitive aspect of Live Paint mode goes one step further with virtual regions. Figure 64 shows six Illustrator paths. Each has a 1-point black stroke and no fill—and each is selected. With the Live Paint Bucket tool, the regions that are created by the intersection of the paths are able to be filled—as though they were objects. Figure 65 shows four regions that have been filled with the Live Paint Bucket tool.

In this case, as in the case of the overlapping rectangles, the dynamic relationship is maintained. Figure 66 shows the same six regions having been moved, and the filled regions have been redrawn and their fills updated.

FIGURE 64
Six paths

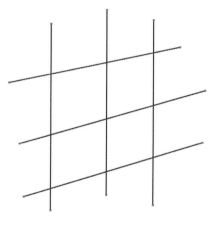

FIGURE 65
Four regions between paths filled

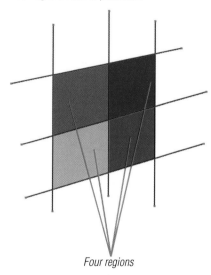

Four regions

FIGURE 66
Moving paths in a live paint group

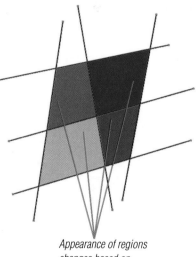

Appearance of regions changes based on paths being moved

Inserting an Object into a Live Paint Group

New objects can be inserted into a live paint group. To do so, switch to the Selection tool, then double-click inside any of the regions of the group. As shown in Figure 67, a gray rectangle appears around the group, indicating that you are in **insertion mode**. Once in insertion mode, you can then add an object or objects to the group.

As shown in Figure 68, another tall rectangle has been added to the group. It can now be painted with the Live Paint Bucket tool as part of the live paint group. Once you've added all that you want to the live paint group, exit insertion mode by double-clicking the Selection tool outside of the live paint group.

FIGURE 67
Viewing the art in insertion mode

FIGURE 68
Adding an object to the live paint group

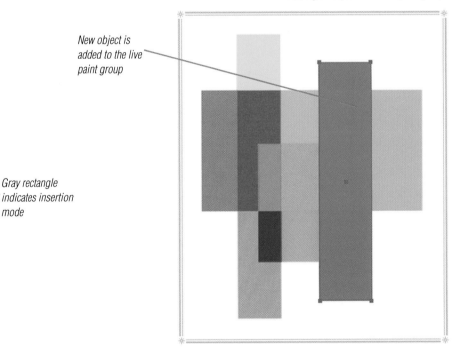

New object is added to the live paint group

Gray rectangle indicates insertion mode

Expanding a Live Paint Group

When you deselect a live paint group, the deselected group does not change its appearance. Additionally, you have the option of using the Expand command to release the Live Paint group into its component regions. Simply select the live paint group, then click the Expand button on the Control panel. Each region will be converted to an ordinary Illustrator object.

Live Painting Edges

In Live Paint mode, if regions are akin to fills, then edges are akin to strokes. With the Live Paint Bucket tool, you can paint edges as well as regions.

Figure 69 shows two overlapping objects, each with a 6-point stroke. To paint edges (strokes), double-click the Live Paint Bucket tool, then click the Paint Strokes check box in the Live Paint Bucket Options dialog box, as shown in Figure 70.

When you position the Live Paint Bucket tool over an edge, its icon changes to a paint brush icon. The edge is highlighted and able to be painted as though it were its own object, as shown in 71.

FIGURE 69
Two overlapping rectangles

FIGURE 70
Specifying the Live Paint Bucket tool to paint strokes (edges)

FIGURE 71
Painting edges

Use Live Trace to trace a sketch

1. Open AI 3-5.ai, then save it as **Live Trace Sketch**.

   The file contains a placed marker sketch that was scanned in Photoshop.

2. Click **Window** on the Application bar, then click **Control** (if necessary).

3. Click the **Selection tool** ▶ then click the **placed graphic**.

   When the placed graphic is selected, the Live Trace button on the Control panel becomes visible.

4. Click the **Live Trace button** on the Control panel.

5. Click the **Expand button** on the Control panel.

   As shown in Figure 72, the traced graphic is expanded into vector objects.

6. Deselect all, then using the Direct Selection tool ▶., select and fill the illustration with whatever colors you like.

   Figure 73 shows one example.

7. Save your work, then close the Live Trace Sketch document.

You used the default settings of the Live Trace utility to convert a placed sketch into Illustrator objects.

FIGURE 72
Expanding the traced graphic

FIGURE 73
One example of the painted illustration

FIGURE 74
Photo traced with default Black and White

1. Open AI 3-6.ai, then save it as **Live Trace Photo**.

   The file contains three copies of a placed photo that was scanned in Photoshop.

2. Zoom in on the top photo, click the **Selection tool** , click the **top photo**, then click the **Live Trace button** on the Control panel.

   > TIP   If you do not see the Live Trace button, click the Edit Contents button ☆ on the Control panel.

   Using default black and white settings, Live Trace creates the trace shown in Figure 74.

3. Deselect the image, then zoom in on the middle photo.

4. Click the **Selection tool** click the **middle photo**, click the **Tracing presets and options list arrow** to the right of the Live Trace button, then click **Tracing Options**.

   (continued)

5. Click the **Preview check box** (if necessary), to place a check mark.

6. In the Adjustments section, click the **arrow** to the right of current Threshold value, then drag the **Threshold slider** until the Threshold value reads 200.

   Live Trace redraws the graphic.

7. Drag the **Threshold slider** until the Threshold value reads 160, wait for Live Trace to redraw the graphic, then click **Trace**.

8. Drag the **middle graphic** to the right of the top graphic, then compare the two graphics to Figure 75.

   (continued)

FIGURE 75
Comparing a Black and White trace using different threshold values

Drawing and Composing an Illustration

FIGURE 76
Applying fills to the traced photo

9. Deselect all, zoom in on the bottom photo, select it, click the **Tracing presets and options list arrow**, then click **Color 6**.

   Color 6 is a tracing preset.

10. Click the **Expand button** on the Control panel, then deselect all.

11. Click the **Direct Selection tool**, then select and fill the objects that make up the illustration.

   Figure 76 shows one example.

12. Save your work, then close the Live Trace Photo.

You used Live Trace to trace a photo three different ways. First, you simply clicked the Live Trace button, which executed the Default preset. Next, you opened the Trace Options dialog box and specified the threshold value for the Black and White trace. Finally, you traced with the Color 6 preset.

Use the Live Paint Bucket tool

1. Open AI 3-7.ai, then save it as **Live Paint Circles.**

2. Open the Swatches panel, fill the top circle with red, fill the left circle with green, then fill the right circle with blue.

3. Select all, double-click the **Live Paint Bucket tool** to open the Live Paint Bucket Options dialog box, verify that both the Paint Fills and Paint Strokes check boxes are checked, then click **OK.**

4. Click any of the orange swatches on the Swatches panel.

   Note that because you are in Live Paint mode, none of the selected objects changes to orange when you click the orange swatch.

5. Position the Live Paint Bucket tool pointer over the red fill of the red circle, then click.

6. Click any pink swatch on the Swatches panel, position the Live Paint Bucket tool pointer over the area where the orange circle overlaps the blue circle, then click.

   As shown in Figure 77, the region of overlap between the two circles is filled with pink.

(continued)

FIGURE 77
Painting the region that is the overlap between two circles

Drawing and Composing an Illustration

FIGURE 78
Viewing seven painted regions

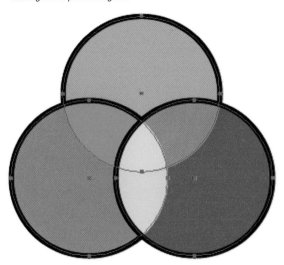

7. Using any colors you like, fill all seven regions so that your artwork resembles Figure 78.

8. Change the Stroke button on the Tools panel to any purple, position the Live Paint Bucket tool pointer ✎ over any of the black strokes in the artwork, then click.

   When positioned over a stroke, the Live Paint Bucket tool pointer changes to a paint-brush icon.

9. Using any color you like, change the color of all twelve edges then deselect all so that your artwork resembles Figure 79.

   (continued)

FIGURE 79
Viewing twelve painted edges

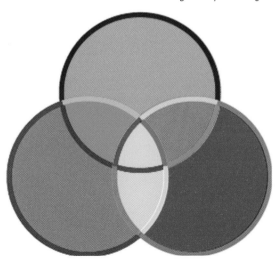

Lesson 7 Use Live Trace and the Live Paint Bucket Tool

10. Click the **Direct Selection tool** ▶, then, without pulling them apart, drag the circles in different directions noticing that they stay grouped, as shown in Figure 80.

    The components of the live paint group maintain a dynamic relationship.

11. Select all, click **Expand** on the Control panel, deselect all, then pull out all of the regions so that your artwork resembles Figure 81.

    The illustration has been expanded into multiple objects.

12. Save your work, then close the Live Paint Circles document.

You used the Live Paint Bucket tool to fill various regions and edges of three overlapping circles. You then moved various components of the live paint group, noting that they maintain a dynamic relationship. Finally, you expanded the live paint group, which changed your original circles into multiple objects.

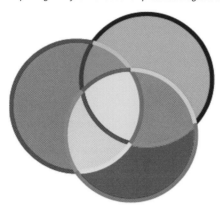

FIGURE 81
Dissecting the expanded live paint group

FIGURE 82

Using the Live Paint Selection tool

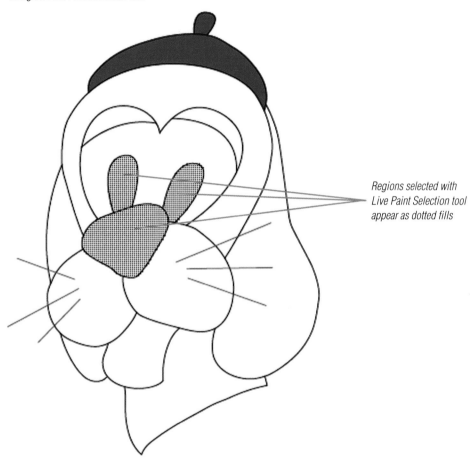

Regions selected with
Live Paint Selection tool
appear as dotted fills

Use the Live Paint Bucket tool to paint an illustration

1. Open AI 3-8.ai, then save it as **Live Paint Dog.**

2. Click the **Selection tool** , then click the different colored strokes so that you understand how the illustration has been drawn.

   The illustration has been created with a series of open paths. The only closed path is the nose.

3. Select all, then change the stroke color of all the paths to Black.

4. Click the **Live Paint Bucket tool** , then click a **red swatch** on the Swatches panel.

   Note that because you are in Live Paint mode, none of the selected objects changes to red when you click the red swatch.

5. Fill the hat and the knot at the top of the hat with red, then click **Black** on the Swatches panel.

6. Click the **Live Paint Selection tool** , click the **nose,** press and hold **[Shift],** click the **left eye,** then click the **right eye.**

   Your illustration should resemble Figure 82.

   TIP When you select multiple areas with the Live Paint Selection tool, the areas are filled with a dot pattern until you apply a color.

7. Click **Black** on the Swatches panel.

8. Using the same method, select both eyelids, then fill them with a lavender swatch.

   (continued)

9. Click the **Live Paint Bucket tool** , click a **yellow swatch** on the Swatches panel, then paint the illustration so that your illustration resembles Figure 83.

Note the small areas between the whiskers that must be painted yellow.

10. Using the Live Paint Bucket tool , paint the right jowl light brown, paint the left jowl a darker brown, then paint the tongue pink.

11. Click the **Stroke button** on the Tools panel to activate the stroke, then click a **gray swatch** on the Swatches panel.

12. Double-click the **Live Paint Bucket tool** , click the **Paint Stroke check box** in the Live Paint Bucket Options dialog box if it is not already checked, then click **OK**.

(continued)

FIGURE 83
Painting the yellow regions

Drawing and Composing an Illustration

FIGURE 84

Viewing the finished artwork

13. Paint the edges that draw the whiskers.

> TIP   You will need to click 14 times to paint the six whiskers.

14. Deselect, compare your work to Figure 84, save your work, then close the Live Paint Dog document.

You used the Live Paint Bucket tool to fill regions created by the intersection of a collection of open paths. You also used the tool to paint edges.

Draw straight lines.

1. Open AI 3-9.ai, then save it as **Mighty Montag**.
2. Place the Montag Sketch.tif from the drive and folder where your Data Files are stored into the Montag document.
3. Position the sketch in the center of the artboard, then lock it.
4. Set the fill color to [None] and the stroke to 1 pt black.
5. Use the Pen tool to create a four-sided polygon for the neck. (*Hint*: Refer to Figure 53 as a guide.)
6. Draw six whiskers.
7. Save your work.

Draw curved lines.

1. Using the Pen tool, draw an oval for the eye.
2. Draw a crescent moon shape for the eyelid.
3. Draw an oval for the iris.
4. Save your work.

Draw elements of an illustration.

1. Trace the left ear.
2. Trace the hat.
3. Trace the nose.
4. Trace the left jowl.
5. Trace the right jowl.
6. Trace the tongue.
7. Trace the right ear.
8. Trace the head.
9. Save your work.

Apply attributes to objects.

1. Unlock the placed sketch and hide it.
2. Fill the hat with a red swatch.
3. Fill the right ear with 9C/18M/62Y.
4. Fill the nose with black.
5. Fill the eye with white.
6. Fill the tongue with salmon.
7. Using Figure 85 as a guide, use the colors on the Swatches panel to finish the illustration.
8. Save your work.

Assemble an illustration.

1. Send the neck to the back of the stacking order, then lock it.
2. Send the head to the back, then lock it.
3. Send the left ear to the back, then lock it.
4. Bring the hat to the front.
5. Bring the right ear to the front.
6. Select the whiskers, group them, then bring them to the front.
7. Select the tongue, then cut it.
8. Select the right jowl, then apply the Paste in Back command.
9. Bring the nose to the front.
10. Select the eye, the eyelid, and the iris, then group them.
11. Drag and drop a copy of the eye group. (*Hint*: Press and hold [Alt] (Win) or [option] (Mac) as you drag the eye group.)
12. Select the right jowl.
13. On the Color panel add 10% K to darken the jowl.
14. Use the Color panel to change the fills on other objects to your liking.
15. Save your work.

Stroke objects for artistic effect.

1. Make the caps on the whiskers round.
2. Change the whiskers' stroke weight to .5 pt.
3. Unlock all.
4. Select the neck and change the joins to round.
5. Apply pseudo-strokes to the illustration. (*Hint*: Copy and paste the elements behind themselves, fill them with black, lock the top objects, then use the Direct Selection tool to select anchor points on the black-filled copies. Use the arrow keys on the keyboard to move the anchor points. The black copies will peek out from behind the elements in front.)
6. Click Object on the Application bar, then click Unlock All.
7. Delete the Montag Sketch file behind your illustration.
8. Save your work, compare your illustration to Figure 85, then close Mighty Montag.

FIGURE 85
Completed Skills Review, Part 1

Use Live Trace and the Live Paint Bucket tool

1. Open AI 3-10.ai, then save it as **Skills Trace Photo**.

2. Zoom in on the top photo, click the Selection tool, click the top photo, then click the Live Trace button on the Control panel. (*Hint*: If you do not see the Live Trace button, click the Edit Contents button on the Control panel.)

3. Deselect the image, then zoom in on the middle photo.

4. Click the Selection tool, click the middle photo, click the Edit Contents button on the Control panel (if necessary), click the Tracing presets and options list arrow to the right of the Live Trace button, then click Tracing Options.

5. Click the Preview check box, (if necessary), to place a check mark.

6. In the Adjustments section, click the arrow to the right of the current Threshold value, then drag the Threshold slider until the Threshold value reads 200.

7. Drag the Threshold slider until the Threshold value reads 166, wait for Live Trace to redraw the graphic, then click Trace.

8. Deselect all, zoom in on the bottom photo, select it, click the Edit Contents button, click the Tracing presets and options list arrow, then click Color 6.

9. Click the Expand button on the Control panel, then deselect all.

10. Click the Direct Selection tool, then select and fill the objects that make up the illustration so that your artwork resembles Figure 86.

FIGURE 86
Completed Skills Review, Part 2

Drawing and Composing an Illustration

1. Open AI 3-11.ai, then save it as **Live Paint Skills.**

2. Open the Swatches panel, fill the top circle with Orange, fill the left circle with blue, then fill the right circle with purple.

3. Select all, then double-click the Live Paint Bucket tool to open the Live Paint Bucket Options dialog box, verify that both the Paint Fills and Paint Strokes check boxes are checked, then click OK.

4. Click any yellow swatch on the Swatches panel.

5. Position the Live Paint Bucket tool pointer over the orange fill of the orange circle, then click.

6. Click any pink swatch on the Swatches panel, position the Live Paint Bucket tool pointer over the area where the yellow circle overlaps the purple circle, then click.

7. Using any colors you like, fill the remaining five regions with different colors.

8. Click the Stroke button on the Tools panel, click any blue swatch on the Swatches panel, position the Live Paint Bucket tool pointer over any of the black strokes in the artwork, then click.

9. Using any color you like, change the color of all twelve edges then deselect all.

10. Click the Direct Selection tool, then, without pulling them completely apart, drag the circles in different directions noticing that they stay grouped, as shown in Figure 87.

11. Save your work, then close Live Paint Skills.indd.

FIGURE 87
Completed Skills Review, Part 3

The owner of The Blue Peppermill Restaurant has hired your design firm to take over all of their marketing and advertising, saying they need to expand their efforts. You request all of their existing materials—slides, prints, digital files, brochures, business cards, etc. Upon examination, you realize that they have no vector graphic version of their logo. Deciding that this is an indispensable element for future design and production, you scan in a photo of their signature peppermill, trace it, and apply a blue fill to it.

1. Create a new 6" × 6" CMYK Color document, then save it as **Peppermill**.
2. Place the Peppermill.tif file into the Peppermill Vector document. (*Hint*: The Peppermill.tif file is in the Chapter 3 Data Files folder.)
3. Scale the placed image 150%, then lock it.
4. Set your fill color to [None], and your stroke to 2 pt black.
5. Using the Zoom tool, create a selection box around the round element at the top of the peppermill to zoom in on it.
6. Using the Pen tool, trace the peppermill, then fill it with a blue swatch.
7. When you finish tracing, tweak the path (if necessary), then save your work.

8. Unlock the placed image and cut it from the document.
9. Save your work, compare your illustration to Figure 88, then close Peppermill.

FIGURE 88
Completed Project Builder 1

Drawing and Composing an Illustration

Bostonchefs.com, your client of three years, contacts you with bad news. They have accidentally deleted their Illustrator "chef logo" from the backup server. They need the vector graphic to produce many of their materials. Their first designer has all the original files, but he has retired to a small island in the Caribbean and cannot be contacted. They want to know if there's anything you can do to recreate the vector graphic.

1. Connect to the Internet, then go to www.bostonchefs.com.
2. Right-click (Win) or [control] click (Mac) the logo of the chef, click Save Picture As (Win) or Save to the Desktop (Mac), then save it in your Chapter 3 Solution Files folder, keeping the same name.
3. Create a new 6" × 6" CMYK Color document, then save it as **Boston chefs**.
4. Place the chef logo file into the document and lock it.
5. Zoom in on the chef logo so that you are at a comfortable view for tracing. (*Hint*: Use the Zoom tool to create a selection box around the logo.)
6. Set your fill color to [None] and your stroke to 1 pt red.
7. Use the Ellipse tool to trace the head.

8. Use the Pen tool to trace the hat and the perimeter of the body.
9. Trace the two triangles that define the chef's inner arms.
10. Unlock the placed image and cut it from the document.
11. Fill the head, the hat, and the body with White.

FIGURE 89
Completed Project Builder 2

12. Fill the triangles with a shade of blue.
13. Remove the strokes from the objects.
14. Create a rectangle that encompasses the chef objects, then fill it with the same shade of blue.
15. Send the rectangle to the back of the stacking order.
16. Save your work, compare your illustration to Figure 89, then close Boston chefs.

Your design firm is contacted by a company called Stratagem with a request for a proposal. They manufacture molds for plastic products. The terms of the request are as follows: You are to submit a design for the shape of the bottle for a new dishwashing liquid. You are to submit a single image that shows a black line defining the shape. The line art should also include the nozzle. The size of the bottle is immaterial. The design is to be "sophisticated, so as to be in visual harmony with the modern home kitchen." The name of the product is "Sleek."

1. Go to the grocery store and purchase bottles of dishwashing liquid whose shape you find interesting.
2. Use the purchases for ideas and inspiration.
3. Sketch your idea for the bottle's shape on a piece of paper.
4. Scan the sketch and save it as a TIFF file.
5. Create a new Illustrator document, then save it as **Sleek Design**.
6. Place the scan in the document, then lock it.
7. Trace your sketch, using the Pen tool.
8. When you are done tracing, delete the sketch from the document.
9. Tweak the line to define the shape to your specifications.
10. Use the Average dialog box to align points to perfect the shape.
11. Save your work, compare your illustration to Figure 90, then close Sleek Design.

FIGURE 90
Completed Design Project

Note to Instructors: The central point of this exercise—a discussion of shapes and their role in the history of mankind—can be had with or without screening *2001: A Space Odyssey*. Should you choose to not show the film, simply omit questions 1 and 2. Rephrase Question 8 so that individuals are instructed to draw any abstract shape from their own imaginations.

The classic sci-fi movie, *2001: A Space Odyssey,* includes a 20-minute "Dawn of Man" includes a sequence that begins millions of years ago with a group of apes, presumably on the African plains. One day, *impossibly*, a tall, black, perfectly rectangular slab appears out of nowhere on the landscape. At first the apes are afraid of it, afraid to touch it. Eventually, they accept its presence.

Later, one ape looks upon a femur bone from a dead animal. With a dawning understanding, he uses the bone as a tool, first to kill for food, and then to kill another ape from an enemy group. Victorious in battle, the ape hurls the bone into the air. The camera follows it up, up, up, and—in one of the most famous cuts in film history—the image switches from the white bone in the sky to the similar shape of a white spaceship floating in space.

1. How do you feel upon first seeing the "monolith" (the black rectangular slab). Were you frightened? Do you sense that the monolith is good, evil, or neutral?
2. How would you describe the sudden appearance of the straight-edged, right-angled monolith against the landscape. What words describe the shapes of the landscape in contrast to the monolith?
3. Do you think perfect shapes exist in nature, or are they created entirely out of the imagination of human beings?
4. If perfect shapes exist—if they are *real*— can you name one example? If they are not real, how is it that humankind has proven so many concepts in mathematics that are based on shapes, such as the Pythagorean theorem?
5. What advancements and achievements of humankind have their basis in peoples' ability to conceive of abstract shapes?
6. Can it be said legitimately that the ability to conceive abstract shapes is an essential factor that distinguishes humankind from all the other species on the planet?
7. Create a new document, then save it as **Shape**.
8. In Adobe Illustrator, draw any shape that you remember from the opening sequence, *except* the monolith. Did you render a shape based on the bone?
9. Save your work, compare your results to Figure 91, then close Shape.

FIGURE 91
Completed Portfolio Project

TRANSFORMING AND
DISTORTING OBJECTS

1. Transform objects

2. Offset and outline paths

3. Create compound paths

4. Work with the Pathfinder panel

5. Create clipping masks

Putting It All Together

Think about a conventional toolbox. You've got a hammer, nails, a few different types of screwdrivers, screws, nuts, bolts, a wrench, and probably some type of measuring device. That set of tools could be used to build anything from a birdhouse to a dollhouse to a townhouse to the White House.

A carpenter uses tools in conjunction with one another to create something, and that something is defined far less by the tools than by the imagination of the carpenter. But even the most ambitious imagination is tempered by the demands of knowing which tool to use, and when.

Illustrator offers a number of sophisticated transform "tools" on the Tools panel, and the metaphor is apt. Each "tool" provides a basic function: a rotation, a scale, a precise move, a precise offset, or a reflection. It is you, the designer, who uses those tools in combination with each other, with menu commands, and with other features, to realize your vision. And like the carpenter's, your imagination will be tempered by your ability to choose the right tool at the right time.

This is one of the most exciting aspects of working in Illustrator. After you learn the basics, there's no map, no blueprint for building an illustration. It's your skills, your experience, your smarts, and your ingenuity that lead you toward your goal. No other designer will use Illustrator's tools quite the same way you do. People who appreciate digital imagery understand this salient point: Although the tools are the same for everyone, the result is *personal*. It's *original*.

Tools You'll Use

TRANSFORM OBJECTS

What You'll Do

▶ *In this lesson, you will explore options for transforming objects with the transform tools.*

Defining the Transform Tools

When you change an object's size, shape, or position on the artboard, Illustrator defines that operation as a transformation. Transforming objects is a fundamental operation in Illustrator, one you will perform countless times.

Because transformations are so essential, Illustrator provides a number of methods for doing them. As you gain experience, you will naturally adopt the method that you find most comfortable or logical.

The tools panel contains five transform tools: the Rotate, Scale, Reflect, Shear, and Free Transform tools. The essential functions of the Rotate and Scale tools are self-explanatory. The Reflect tool "flips" an object across an imagined axis, usually the horizontal or the vertical axis. However, you can define any diagonal as the axis for a reflection. In Figure 1, the illustration has been flipped to create the illusion of a reflection in a mirror.

QUICKTIP

The Reflect tool comes in very handy when you are drawing or tracing a symmetrical object, like a spoon. Simply draw or trace half of the drawing, then create a flipped copy—a mirror image. Join the two halves, and you have a perfectly symmetrical shape . . . in half the time!

The Shear tool slants—or skews—an object on an axis that you specify. By definition, the Shear tool distorts an object. Of the five transform tools, you will probably use the Shear tool the least, although it is useful for creating a cast shadow or the illusion of depth.

Finally, the Free Transform tool offers you the ability to perform quick transformations and distort objects in perspective.

Defining the Point of Origin

All transformations are executed in relation to a fixed point; in Illustrator, that point is called the **point of origin**. For each transform tool, the default point of origin is the selected object's center point. However, you can change that point to another point on the object or to a point elsewhere on the artboard. For example, when a majorette twirls a baton, that baton is essentially rotating on its own center. By contrast, the petals of a daisy rotate around a central point that is not positioned on any of the petals themselves, as shown in Figure 2.

There are four basic methods for making transformations with the transform tools. First, select an object, then do one of the following:

- Click a transform tool, then click and drag anywhere on the artboard. The

object will be transformed using its center point as the default point of origin.

- Double-click the transform tool, which opens the tool's dialog box. Enter the values by which you want to execute the transformation, then click OK. You may also click Copy to create a transformed copy of the selected object. The point of origin for the transformation will be the center point of the selected object.
- Click a transform tool, then click the artboard. Where you click the artboard defines the point of origin for the transformation. Click and drag anywhere on the artboard, and the selected

object will be transformed from the point of origin that you clicked.

- Click a transform tool, Press [Alt] (Win) or [option] (Mac), then click the artboard. The tool's dialog box opens, allowing you to enter precise values for the transformation. When you click OK or Copy, the selected object will be transformed from the point of origin that you clicked.

FIGURE 1

The Reflect tool flips an image horizontally or vertically

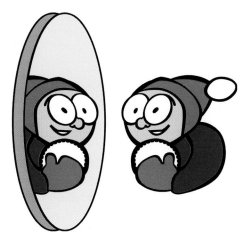

FIGURE 2

All transformations are executed from a point of origin

A baton rotating around its own center

Petals of a daisy rotate around a central point

Working with the Transform Again Command

An essential command related to transformations is Transform Again. Whenever you execute a transformation, such as scale or rotate, you can repeat the transformation quickly by using the Transform Again command. This is also true for moving an object. Using the Transform Again command will move an object the same distance and angle entered in the last step. The quickest way to use the Transform Again command is to press [Ctrl][D] (Win) or ⌘[D] (Mac). To remember this quick key command, think D for *duplicate*.

A fine example of the usefulness of the Transform Again command is its ability to make transforming in small increments easy. For example, let's say you have created an object to be used in an illustration, but you haven't decided how large the object should be. Simply scale the object by a small percentage—say 5%—then press the quick key for Transform Again repeatedly until you are happy with the results. The object gradually gets bigger, and you can choose the size that pleases your eye. If you transform again too many times, and the object gets too big, simply undo repeatedly to decrease the object's size in the same small increments.

Using the Transform Each Command

The Transform Each command allows you to transform multiple objects individually, as shown in Figure 3. The Transform Each dialog box offers options to move, scale, rotate, or reflect an object, among others. All of them will affect an object independent of the other selected objects.

Without the Transform Each command, applying a transformation to multiple objects simultaneously will often yield an undesired effect. This happens because the selected objects are transformed as a group—in relation to a single point of origin—and are repositioned on the artboard.

FIGURE 3
Multiple objects rotated individually

Before   *After*

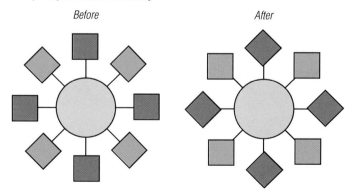

The eight squares are rotated on their own center points

Using the Free Transform Tool

The Free Transform tool applies an eight-handled bounding box to a selected image. You can move those handles to scale and shear the object. You can click and drag outside the object to rotate the object.

With the Free Transform tool, transformations always use the selected object's center point as the point of origin. In general, the role of the Free Transform tool is to make quick, inexact transformations. However, the tool has a powerful, hidden ability. Moving the handles in conjunction with certain keyboard commands allows you to distort the object or distort the object in perspective, as shown in Figure 4. Press and hold [Shift][Ctrl] (Win) or [Shift]⌘ (Mac) to distort the image. Press and hold [Shift][Alt][Ctrl] (Win) while dragging to distort in perspective. On a Macintosh, press and hold [Shift][option]⌘ to execute the same transformation.

Using the Transform Panel

The Transform panel displays information about the size, orientation, and location of one or more selected objects. You can type new values directly into the Transform panel to modify selected objects. All values on the panel refer to the bounding boxes of the objects, whether the bounding box is visible or not. You can also identify—on the Transform panel—the reference point on the bounding box from which the object will be transformed. To reflect an object vertically or horizontally using the Transform panel, click the Transform panel list arrow, then choose the appropriate menu item, as shown in Figure 5.

FIGURE 4

Use the Free Transform tool to distort objects in perspective

FIGURE 5

Transform panel

Transform panel
list arrow

Width text box

Rotate text box

Height text box

Shear text box

Transform panel menu

Rotate an object around a defined point

1. Open AI 4-1.ai, then save it as **Mod Clock**.

2. Click the **Selection tool** , click the **brown line**, then click the **Rotate tool** .

3. Press and hold **[Alt]** (Win) or **[option]** (Mac), then click the **bottom anchor point** of the line to set the point of origin for the rotation.

   With a transform tool selected, pressing [Alt] (Win) or [option] (Mac) and clicking the artboard defines the point of origin and opens the tool's dialog box.

4. Enter **30** in the Angle text box, then click **Copy**.

5. Press **[Ctrl][D]** (Win) or $\mathcal{H}$**[D]** (Mac) ten times so that your screen resembles Figure 6.

   [Ctrl][D] (Win) or $\mathcal{H}$[D] (Mac) is the quick key for the Transform Again command.

6. Select all twelve lines, group them, send them to the back, then hide them.

7. Select the small orange circle, click **View** on the Application bar, then click **Outline**.

(continued)

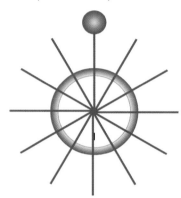

FIGURE 6
Twelve paths rotated at a point

X and Y coordinates

The X and Y coordinates of an object indicate the object's horizontal (X) and vertical (Y) locations on the artboard. These numbers, which appear on the Transform panel and the Control panel, represent the horizontal and vertical distance from the bottom-left corner of the artboard. The current X and Y coordinates also depend on the specified reference point. Nine reference points are listed to the left of the X and Y Value text boxes on the Transform panel. Reference points are those points of a selected object that represent the four corners of the object's bounding box, the horizontal and vertical centers of the bounding box, and the center point of the bounding box. (You do not need to have the bounding box option turned on to view any of the reference point coordinates.)

FIGURE 7
Twelve circles rotated around a central point of origin

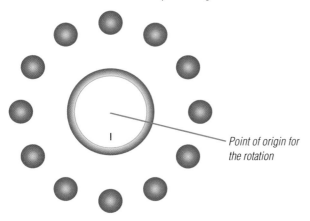

Point of origin for
the rotation

FIGURE 8
Completed illustration

8. Click the **Rotate tool** ⟳, press and hold
   [Alt] (Win) or **[option]** (Mac), then click the
   center point of the larger circle to set the
   point of origin for the next rotation.

   The small circle will rotate around the
   center point of the larger circle.

   | TIP   Outline mode is especially useful for
   rotations; center points are visible and easy
   to target as points of origin.

9. Enter **30** (if necessary), click **Copy**, apply the
   Transform Again command ten times, then
   switch to Preview mode.

   Your screen should resemble Figure 7.

10. Select the small black vertical dash, then
    transform again eleven times.

    The dash is also rotated around the center
    point of the larger circle, since a new point
    of origin has not been set.

11. Unlock the hands in the scratch area, then
    move them onto the clock face.

12. Show all, then deselect all to reveal the
    twelve segments, as shown in Figure 8.

13. Save your work, then close the Mod
    Clock document.

*You selected a point on the brown line, then
rotated eleven copies of the object around that
point. Second, you defined the point of origin for a
rotation by clicking the center point of the larger
circle, then rotated eleven copies of the smaller
circle and the dash around that point.*

Use the Shear tool

1. Open AI 4-2.ai, then save it as **Shear**.

2. Select all, copy, paste in front, then fill the copy with the swatch named Graphite.

3. Click the **Shear tool** .

    TIP The Shear tool is hidden behind the Scale tool.

4. Press and hold **[Alt]** (Win) or **[option]** (Mac), then click the **bottom-right anchor point** of the letter R to set the origin point of the shear and open the Shear dialog box.

5. Enter **45** in the Shear Angle text box, verify that the Horizontal option button is checked, then click **OK**.

    Your screen should resemble Figure 9.

6. Click the **Scale tool** .

7. Press **[Alt]** (Win) or **[option]** (Mac), then click any bottom anchor point or segment on the sheared objects to set the point of origin for the scale and open the Scale dialog box.

8. Click the **Non-Uniform option button**, enter **100** in the Horizontal text box, enter **50** in the Vertical text box, then click **OK**.

9. Send the sheared objects to the back.

10. Apply a 1 pt black stroke to the orange letters, deselect, then compare your screen to Figure 10.

11. Save your work, then close the Shear document.

You created a shadow effect using the Shear tool.

FIGURE 9
Letterforms sheared on a 45° axis

The objects are sheared on a 45° angle in relation to a horizontal axis

FIGURE 10
Shearing is useful for creating a cast-shadow effect

The shadow is "cast" from the letters in the foreground

Transforming and Distorting Objects

FIGURE 11
Use the Reflect tool for illustrations that demand exact symmetry

FIGURE 12
Selecting two anchor points with the Direct Selection tool

Selection box

Selected anchor points

Use the Reflect tool

1. Open AI 4-3.ai, then save it as **Reflect**.
2. Select all, then zoom in on the top anchor point.
3. Click the **Reflect tool** [icon].

   The Reflect tool is hidden behind the Rotate tool.
4. Press **[Alt]** (Win) or **[option]** (Mac), then click the **top anchor point** to set the point of origin for the reflection.
5. Click the **Vertical option button**, then click **Copy**.

   A copy is positioned, reflected across the axis that you defined, as shown in Figure 11.
6. Deselect all, then click the **Direct Selection tool** [icon].
7. Using Figure 12 as a guide, drag a selection box around the top two anchor points to select them.
8. Click **Object** on the Application bar, point to **Path**, click **Average**, click the **Both option button**, then click **OK**.
9. Click **Object** on the Application bar, point to **Path**, click **Join**, click the **Smooth option button**, then click **OK**.
10. Select the bottom two anchor points, average them on both axes, then join them in a smooth point to close the path.
11. Save your work, then close the Reflect document.

You created a reflected copy of a path, then averaged and joined two pairs of open points.

OFFSET AND
OUTLINE PATHS

What You'll Do

 In this lesson, you will use the Offset Path command to create concentric squares and the Outline Stroke command to convert a stroked path into a closed path.

Using the Offset Path Command

Simply put, the Offset Path command creates a copy of a selected path set off by a specified distance. The Offset Path command is useful when working with closed paths—making concentric shapes or making many copies of a path at a regular distance from the original.

Figure 13 shows two sets of concentric circles. By definition, the word **concentric** refers to objects that share the same centerpoint, as the circles in both sets do. The set on the left was made with the Scale tool, applying an 85% scale and copy to the outer circle, then repeating the transformation ten times. Note that with each successive copy, the distance from the copy to the previous circle decreases. The set on the right was made by offsetting the outside circle -.125", then applying the same offset to each successive copy. Note the different effect.

When you offset a closed path, a positive value creates a larger copy outside the original; a negative value creates a smaller copy inside the original.

Using the Outline Stroke Command

The Outline Stroke command converts a stroked path into a closed path that is the same width as the original stroked path.

This operation is useful if you want to apply a gradient to a stroke. It is also a useful design tool, allowing you to modify the outline of an object more than if it were just a stroke. Also, it is often easier to create an object with a single heavy stroke—for example the letter S—and then convert it to a closed path than it would be to try to draw a closed path directly, as shown in Figure 14.

FIGURE 13

Two sets of concentric circles

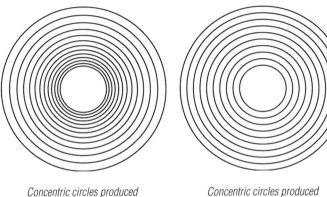

Concentric circles produced by the Scale tool

Concentric circles produced by the Offset Path command

FIGURE 14

The Outline Stroke command converts a stroked path to a closed object

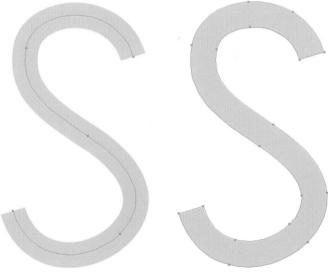

Offset a path

1. Open AI 4-4.ai, then save it as **Squares**.

2. Select the square.

3. Click **Object** on the Application bar, point to **Path**, then click **Offset Path**.

4. Enter **-.125** in the Offset text box, then click **OK**.

   | TIP   Be sure that your Units preference is set to Inches in the General section of the Units & Display Performance Preferences.

   A negative value reduces the area of a closed path; a positive value increases the area.

5. Apply the Offset Path command four more times, using the same value.

   | TIP   The Transform Again command does not apply to the Offset Path command because it is not one of the transform tools.

6. Deselect all, save your work, compare your screen to Figure 15, then close the Squares document.

You used the Offset Path command to create concentric squares.

FIGURE 15
Concentric squares created with the Offset Path command

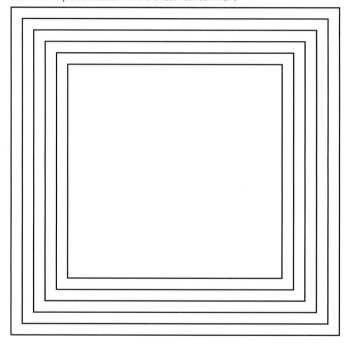

Transforming and Distorting Objects

FIGURE 16

The Outline Stroke command converts any stroked path into a closed path

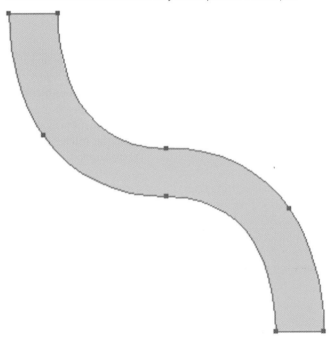

1. Open AI 4-5.ai, then save it as **Outlined Stroke**.

2. Select the path, then change the weight to 36 pt.

3. Click **Object** on the Application bar, point to **Path**, then click **Outline Stroke**.

   The full weight of the stroke is converted to a closed path, as shown in Figure 16.

4. Save your work, then close the Outlined Stroke document.

You applied a heavy weight to a stroked path, then converted the stroke to a closed path, using the Outline Stroke command.

CREATE COMPOUND PATHS

What You'll Do

In this lesson, you will explore the role of compound paths for practical use and for artistic effects.

Defining a Compound Path

Practically speaking, you make a compound path to create a "hole" or "holes" in an object. As shown in Figure 17, if you were drawing the letter "D," you would need to create a hole in the outlined shape, through which you could see the background. To do so, select the object in back (in this case, the black outline that defines the letter) and the object in front (the yellow object that defines the hole) and apply the Make Compound Path command. When compounded, a "hole" appears where the two objects overlap.

The overlapping object still exists, however. It is simply *functioning* as a transparent hole in conjunction with the object behind it. If you move the front object independently, as shown in Figure 18, it yields an interesting result. Designers have seized upon this effect and have run with it, creating complex and eye-catching graphics, which Illustrator calls compound shapes.

It is important to understand that when two or more objects are compounded, Illustrator defines them as *one* object. This sounds strange at first, but the concept is as familiar to you as the letter D. You identify the letter D as one object. Although it is drawn with two paths—one defining the outside edge, the other defining the inside edge—it is nevertheless a single object.

Compound paths function as groups. You can select and manipulate an individual element with the Direct Selection tool, but you cannot change its appearance attributes independently. Compound paths can

be released and returned to their original component objects by applying the Release Compound Path command.

FIGURE 17

The letter D is an example of a compound path

FIGURE 18

Manipulating compound paths can yield interesting effects

Create compound paths

1. Open AI 4-6.ai, then save it as **Simple Compound**.

2. Cut the red circle in the middle of the illustration, then undo the cut.

   The red circle creates the illusion that there's a hole in the life-preserver ring.

3. Select the red background object, then change its fill to the Ocean Blue gradient on the Swatches panel.

   The illusion is lost; the red circle no longer appears as a hole in the life preserver.

4. Select both the white "life preserver" circle and the red circle in the center.

5. Click **Object** on the Application bar, point to **Compound Path**, then click **Make**.

   As shown in Figure 19, the two circles are compounded, with the top circle functioning as a "hole" in the larger circle behind it.

6. Move the background object left and right, and up and down behind the circles.

   The repositioned background remains visible through the compounded circles.

7. Deselect all, save your work, then close the Simple Compound document.

You selected two concentric circles and made them into one compound path, which allowed you to see through to the gradient behind the circles.

FIGURE 19
A compound path creates the effect of a hole where two or more objects overlap

FIGURE 20

A simple compound path

FIGURE 21

A more complex compound path

FIGURE 22

Simple compound paths can yield stunning visual effects

Each of the five small circles is scaled, using its own center point as the point of origin

Create special effects with compound paths

1. Open AI 4-7.ai, then save it as **Compound Path Effects**.

2. Select all.

   The light blue square is locked and does not become part of the selection.

3. Click **Object** on the Application bar, point to **Compound Path**, then click **Make**.

4. Deselect, click the **Direct Selection tool**, then click the **edge** of the large blue circle.

5. Click the **center point** of the circle, then scale the circle 50% so that your work resembles Figure 20.

6. Click **Select** on the Application bar, then click **Inverse**.

7. Click **Object** on the Application bar, point to **Transform**, then click **Transform Each**.

8. Enter **225** in the Horizontal and Vertical text boxes in the Scale section of the Transform Each dialog box, click **OK,** then deselect all.

   Your work should resemble Figure 21.

9. Using the Direct Selection tool, click the edge of the center circle, click its center point to select the entire circle, then scale the circle 120%.

10. Apply the Transform Again command twice, then compare your screen to Figure 22.

11. Deselect all, save your work, then close Compound Path Effects.

You made a compound path out of five small circles and one large circle. You then manipulated the size and location of the individual circles to create interesting designs.

WORK WITH THE PATHFINDER PANEL

What You'll Do

▶ In this lesson, you will use shape modes and pathfinders to create compound shapes from simple shapes.

Defining a Compound Shape

Like a compound path, a **compound shape** is two or more paths that are combined in such a way that "holes" appear wherever paths overlap.

The term compound shape is used to distinguish a complex compound path from a simple one. Compound shapes generally assume an artistic rather than a practical role. To achieve the effect, compound shapes tend to be composed of multiple objects. You can think of a compound shape as an illustration composed of multiple compound paths.

Understanding Essential Shape Modes and Pathfinders

Shape modes and **pathfinders** are preset operations that help you combine paths in a variety of ways. They are very useful operations for creating complex or irregular shapes from basic shapes. In some cases, they are a means to an end in creating an object; in others, the operation they provide will be the end result you want to achieve. Shape modes and pathfinders can be applied to overlapping objects using the Effect menu or the Pathfinder panel.

For the purposes of drawing and creating new objects, the following five shape modes and pathfinders are essential; compare each with Figure 23.

- **Unite shape mode**: Converts two or more overlapping objects into a single, merged object.

- **Minus Front shape mode**: Where objects overlap, deletes the frontmost object(s) from the backmost object in a selection of overlapped objects.
- **Intersect shape mode**: Creates a single, merged object from the area where two or more objects overlap.

- **Minus Back pathfinder**: The opposite of Subtract; deletes the backmost object(s) from the frontmost object in a selection of overlapped objects.
- **Divide pathfinder**: Divides an object into its component filled faces. Illustrator defines a "face" as an area undivided by a line segment.

FIGURE 23

Five essential shape modes and pathfinders

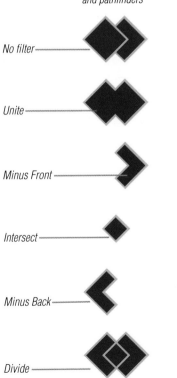

No filter

Unite

Minus Front

Intersect

Minus Back

Divide

Using the Pathfinder Panel

The Pathfinder panel contains ten buttons for creating compound shapes, as shown in Figure 24. As you learned earlier, a compound shape is a complex compound path. You can create a compound shape by overlapping two or more objects, then clicking one of the four shape mode buttons in the top row of the Pathfinder panel, or clicking the Pathfinder panel list arrow, then clicking Make Compound Shape. The four shape mode buttons are Unite, Minus Front, Intersect, and Exclude. When you apply a shape mode button, the two overlapping objects are combined into one object with the same formatting as the topmost object in the group before the shape mode button was applied. After applying a shape mode button, the resulting objects in the compound shape can be selected and formatted using the Direct Selection tool. You can also press [Alt] (Win) or [option] (Mac) when you click a shape mode button. Doing so results in a compound shape whose original objects can be selected and formatted using the Direct Selection tool.

FIGURE 24
Pathfinder panel

Applying Shape Modes

Figure 25 shows a square overlapped by a circle.

If you apply the Minus Front shape mode button, the resulting object is a compound shape, as shown in Figure 26. Notice the overlapped area is deleted from the square. The circle, too, is deleted, as shown in Figure 26. The result is a simple reshaped object.

If you took the same two overlapping shapes shown in Figure 25, but this time pressed [Alt] (Win) or [option] (Mac) when applying the Subtract shape mode button, the circle would not be deleted; it would function as a hole or a "knockout" wherever it overlaps the square, as shown in Figure 27. The relationship is dynamic: You can move the circle independently with the Direct Selection tool to change its effect on the square and the resulting visual effect.

Figure 28 shows a group of objects converted into a compound shape using the Make Compound Shape command on the Pathfinder panel.

Releasing and Expanding Compound Shapes

You can release a compound shape, which separates it back into individual objects. To release a compound shape, click the Pathfinder panel list arrow, then click Release Compound Shape. Expanding a compound shape is similar to releasing it, except that it maintains the shape of the compound object. You cannot select the original individual objects. You can expand a compound shape by selecting it, and then clicking the Expand button on the Pathfinder panel.

FIGURE 25
Two overlapping objects

FIGURE 26
Applying the Minus Front shape mode without [Alt] (Win) or [option] (Mac)

FIGURE 27
Applying the Minus Front shape mode with [Alt] (Win) or [option] (Mac)

FIGURE 28
A compound shape

Apply the Unite shape mode

1. Open AI 4-8.ai, then save it as **Heart Parts**.

2. Click **Window** on the Application bar, then click **Pathfinder**.

3. Select both circles, then click the **Unite button** on the Pathfinder panel.

   The two objects are united.

4. Move the diamond shape up so that it overlaps the united circles, as shown in Figure 29.

5. Click the **Delete Anchor Point tool**, then delete the top anchor point of the diamond.

6. Select all, press and hold **[Alt]** (Win) or **[option]** (Mac), then click the **Unite button** so that your screen resembles Figure 30.

7. Remove the black stroke, then apply a red fill to the new object.

8. Draw a rectangle that covers the "hole" in the heart, then fill it with black, as shown in Figure 31.

9. Select all, press **[Alt]** (Win) or **[option]** (Mac), then click the **Unite button**.

10. Double-click the **Scale tool**, then apply a non-uniform scale of 90% on the horizontal axis and 100% on the vertical axis.

You created a single heart-shaped object from two circles and a diamond shape using the Unite button.

FIGURE 29
A diamond shape in position

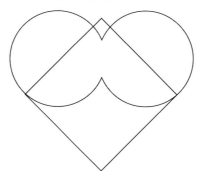

FIGURE 30
The diamond shape and the object behind it are united

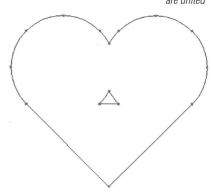

FIGURE 31
A heart shape created by applying the Unite shape mode to three objects

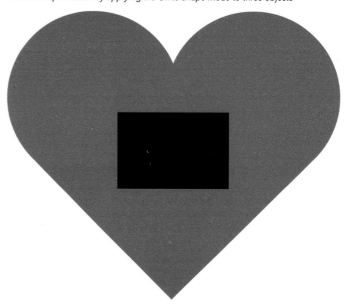

FIGURE 32
Circle overlaps the square

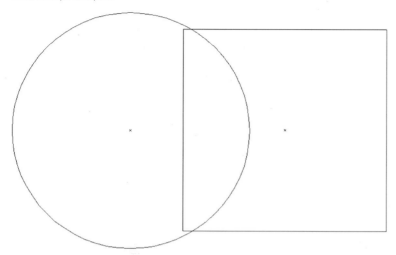

Apply the Minus Back shape mode

1. Rotate the black heart shape 180°, then hide it.
2. Create a square that is 1.5" × 1.5" without a fill color and with a 1 pt black stroke.
3. Create a circle that is 1.75" in width and height.
4. Switch to Outline mode.
5. Move the circle so that it overlaps the square, as shown in Figure 32.
6. Verify that the circle is still selected, click the **Reflect tool** ⟡, press **[Alt]** (Win) or **[option]** (Mac), then click the **center point** of the square.
7. Click the **Vertical option button**, click **Copy**, then arrange the three objects so that your work resembles Figure 33.

FIGURE 33
Right circle is a reflected copy of the left one

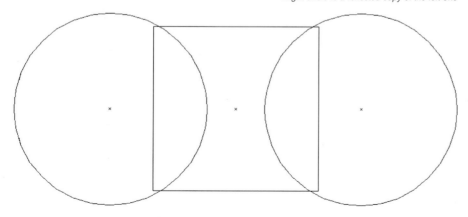

8. Select all, then click the **Minus Front button** 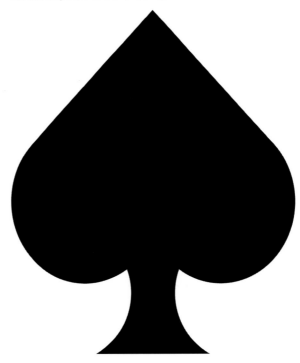 on the Pathfinder panel.

9. Switch to Preview mode, then apply a black fill to the new object.

10. Show all, then overlap the new shape with the black heart shape to make a spade shape.

11. Select all, click the **Unite button** then deselect.

Your work should resemble Figure 34.

You overlapped a square with two circles, then applied the Minus Front shape mode to delete the overlapped areas from the square. You used the Unite button to unite the new shape with a heart-shaped object to create a spade shape.

FIGURE 34
The final shape, with all elements united

Transforming and Distorting Objects

FIGURE 35

Use the Align panel to align objects precisely

FIGURE 36

Yellow shape is the intersection of the star and the spade

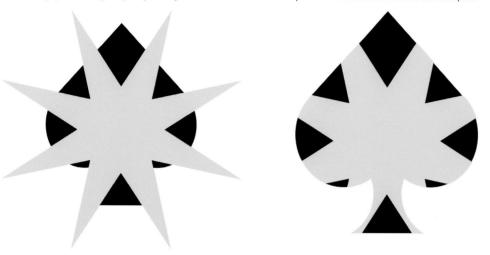

1. Click the **Star tool** ⭐, then click the **artboard**.

2. Enter **1** in the Radius 1 text box, **3** in the Radius 2 text box, and **8** in the Points text box, then click **OK**.

3. Apply a yellow fill to the star and remove any stroke (if necessary).

4. Use the Align panel to align the center points of the two objects, so that they resemble Figure 35.

5. Copy the black spade, then paste in front.

   Two black spades are now behind the yellow star; the top one is selected.

6. Press and hold **[Shift]**, then click to add the star to the selection.

7. Click the **Intersect shape areas button** 🔲 on the Pathfinder panel.

   The intersection of the star and the copied spade is now a single closed path. Your work should resemble Figure 36.

8. Save your work, then close Heart Parts.

You created a star and then created a copy of the black spade-shaped object. You used the Intersect shape mode button to capture the intersection of the two objects as a new object.

Working with the Align panel

The Align panel offers a quick and simple solution for aligning selected objects along the axis you specify. Along the vertical axis, you can align selected objects by their rightmost point, leftmost point, or center point. On the horizontal axis, you can align objects by their topmost point, center point, or bottommost point. You can also use the panel to distribute objects evenly along a horizontal or vertical axis. In contrasting the Align panel with the Average command, think of the Average command as a method for aligning anchor points and the Align panel as a method for aligning entire objects.

When you align and distribute objects, you have the choice of aligning them to a selection, a key object, or the artboard. If you want to align or distribute objects using the artboard, you must first define the artboard area using the Artboard tool on the Tools panel. Click the Align To list arrow on the Align panel, then click Align to Artboard. Resize the artboard as desired. Finally, choose the alignment setting you need on the Align panel.

Apply the Divide pathfinder

1. Open AI 4-9.ai, then save it as **Divide**.

2. Select the red line, then double-click the **Rotate tool** 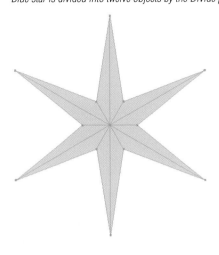.

3. Enter **30** in the Angle text box, then click **Copy**.

4. Repeat the transformation four times.

5. Select all, then click the **Divide button** on the Pathfinder panel.

   The blue star is divided into twelve separate objects, as defined by the red lines, which have been deleted. See Figure 37.

6. Deselect, click the **Direct Selection tool**, select the left half of the top point, press **[Shift]**, then select every other object, for a total of six objects.

7. Apply an orange fill to the selected objects.

8. Select the inverse, then apply a yellow fill so that your work resembles Figure 38.

9. Save your work, then close the Divide document.

You used six lines to define a score pattern, then used those lines and the Divide pathfinder to break the star into twelve separate objects.

FIGURE 37
Blue star is divided into twelve objects by the Divide pathfinder

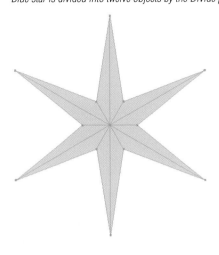

FIGURE 38
Divide pathfinder is useful for adding dimension

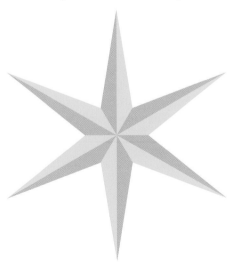

Transforming and Distorting Objects

FIGURE 39
An example of the Exclude shape mode

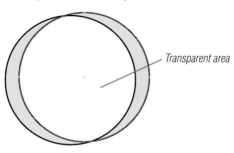

Transparent area

Create compound shapes using the Pathfinder panel

1. Open AI 4-10.ai, then save it as **Compound Shapes**.

2. Click **View** on the Application bar, then click **Yellow**.

3. Select the two yellow circles, press **[Alt]** (Win) or **[option]** (Mac), then click the **Exclude button** on the Pathfinder panel.

   The area that the top object overlaps becomes transparent.

4. Deselect, click the **Direct Selection tool**, then move either circle to change the shape and size of the filled areas.

   Figure 39 shows one effect that can be achieved.

5. Select **Green** from the View menu, select the two green circles, press **[Alt]** (Win) or **[option]** (Mac), then click the **Intersect button** on the Pathfinder panel.

   The area not overlapped by the top circle becomes transparent.

6. Deselect, then use the Direct Selection tool to move either circle to change the shape and size of the filled area.

   Figure 40 shows one effect that can be achieved.

7. Save your work, then close the Compound Shapes document.

You applied shape modes to two pairs of circles, then moved the circles to create different shapes and effects.

FIGURE 40
An example of the Intersect shape mode

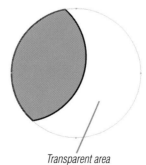

Transparent area

Create special effects with compound shapes

1. Open AI 4-11.ai, then save it as **Compound Shape Effects**.

2. Select all, press **[Alt]** (Win) or **[option]** (Mac), then click the **Exclude button** on the Pathfinder panel.

   Your work should resemble Figure 41.

3. Deselect all, click the **Direct Selection tool**, select the three squares, then move them to the right, as shown in Figure 42.

4. Drag and drop a copy of the three squares, as shown in Figure 43.

   TIP Use [Shift][Alt] (Win) or [Shift][option] (Mac) to drag and drop a copy at a 45-degree angle or in straight lines vertically or horizontally.

5. Scale each circle 150% using the Transform Each command.

6. Scale the center circle 200%, then bring it to the front of the stacking order.

7. Press **[Alt]** (Win) or **[option]** (Mac), then click the **Intersect button** on the Pathfinder panel.

   Figure 44 shows the results of the intersection. Your final illustration may vary slightly.

   TIP The topmost object affects all the objects behind it in a compound shape.

8. Save your work, then close Compound Shape Effects.

You made three squares and three circles into a compound shape by excluding overlapping shape areas. You then manipulated the size and location of individual elements to create different effects. Finally, you enlarged a circle, brought it to the front, then changed its mode to Intersect. Only the objects that were overlapped by the circle remained visible.

FIGURE 41
A compound shape

FIGURE 42
A compound shape

FIGURE 43
A compound shape

FIGURE 44
A compound shape

CREATE CLIPPING
MASKS

What You'll Do

 In this lesson, you will explore the role of clipping masks for practical use and for artistic effects.

Defining a Clipping Mask

As with compound paths, clipping masks are used to yield a practical result. And as with compound paths, that practical result can be manipulated to create interesting graphic effects.

Practically speaking, you use a clipping mask as a "window" through which you view some or all of the objects behind the mask in the stacking order. When you select any two or more objects and apply the Make Clipping Mask command, the *top object* becomes the mask and the object behind it becomes "masked." You will be able to see only the parts of the masked object that are visible *through* the mask, as shown in Figure 45. The mask crops the object behind it.

Using Multiple Objects as a Clipping Mask

When multiple objects are selected and the Make Clipping Mask command is applied, the top object becomes the mask. Since every object has its own position in the stacking order, it stands to reason that there can be only one top object.

If you want to use multiple objects as a mask, you can do so by first making them into a compound path. Illustrator regards compound paths as a single object. Therefore, a compound path containing multiple objects can be used as a single mask.

Creating Masked Effects

Special effects with clipping masks are, quite simply, fun! You can position as many objects as you like behind the mask, and position them in such a way that the mask crops them in visually interesting (and eye-popping!) ways. See Figure 46 for an example.

FIGURE 45
Clipping mask crops the object behind it

—Object to be used as a mask

—Object to be masked

—The result after applying the Make Clipping Mask command

FIGURE 46
Masks can be used for stunning visual effects

FIGURE 47

Masking objects must be in front of objects to be masked

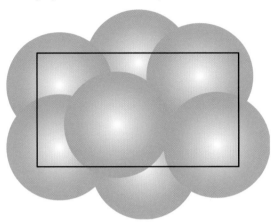

FIGURE 48

The rectangle masks the gold spheres

FIGURE 49

A compound path used as a mask

A black stroke applied to a mask

Create a clipping mask

1. Open AI 4-12.ai, then save it as **Simple Masks**.
2. Click **View** on the Application bar, then click **Mask 1**.
3. Move the rectangle so that it overlaps the gold spheres, as shown in Figure 47.
4. Apply the Bring to Front command to verify that the rectangle is in front of all the spheres.
5. Select the seven spheres and the rectangle.
6. Click **Object** on the Application bar, point to **Clipping Mask**, then click **Make**.
7. Deselect, then compare your screen to Figure 48.
8. Click **View** on the Application bar, then click **Mask 2**.
9. Select the three circles, then move them over the "gumballs."

   The three circles are a compound path.
10. Select the group of gumballs and the three circles, then apply the Make Clipping Mask command.
11. Deselect, click **Select** on the Application bar, point to **Object**, then click **Clipping Masks**.
12. Apply a 1 pt black stroke to the masks.

    Your work should resemble Figure 49.
13. Save your work, then close the Simple Masks document.

You used a rectangle as a clipping mask. Then, you used three circles to mask a group of small spheres, and applied a black stroke to the mask.

Apply a fill to a clipping mask

1. Open AI 4-13.ai, then save it as **Magnify**.

2. Move the large outlined text over the small outlined text so that the *g*s align as shown in Figure 50.

3. Select the smaller text, then hide it.

4. Select the magnifying glass and the handle, then drag them over the letter *g*, as shown in Figure 51.

5. Deselect all, select only the circle and the text, click **Object** on the Application bar, point to **Clipping Mask**, then click **Make**.

   The circle is the masking object.

6. Deselect, click **Select** on the Application bar, point to **Object**, then click **Clipping Masks**.

7. Use the Swatches panel to apply a light blue fill and a gray stroke to the mask.

FIGURE 50
Lining up the letter g

FIGURE 51
Positioning the magnifying glass

The two objects that make up the magnifying glass are not grouped

Transforming and Distorting Objects

FIGURE 52
A fill and stroke are applied to a mask

The mask

By default, a fill is positioned behind the masked elements, and the stroke is in front of the mask

FIGURE 53
Large text is masked by the magnifying glass

When a fill is applied to a mask, the fill is positioned behind all the objects that are masked

As the mask moves, different areas of the large text become visible, creating the illusion of a magnifying glass moving over a word

8. Change the weight of the stroke to 8 pt, so that your work resembles Figure 52.

9. Show all, deselect, then compare your screen to Figure 53.

10. Select the mask only, press and hold **[Shift]**, then click the **magnifying glass handle**.

11. Press the **arrow keys** to move the magnifying glass.

12. Save your work, then close the Magnify document.

You used the circle in the illustration as a clipping mask in combination with the large text. You added a fill and a stroke to the mask, creating the illusion that the small text is magnified in the magnifying glass.

Use text as a clipping mask

1. Open AI 4-14.ai, then save it as **Mask Effects**.

2. Select the four letters that make the word MASK.

   The word MASK was converted to outlines and ungrouped.

3. Make the four letters into a compound path.

4. Select the compound path and the rectangle behind it.

5. Apply the Make Clipping Mask command, then deselect.

6. Save your work, then compare your text to Figure 54.

You converted outlines to a compound path, then used the compound path as a mask.

FIGURE 54
Outlined text used as a mask

FIGURE 55

Curvy object in position to be masked by the letters

FIGURE 56

Object behind the mask is selected

The rectangle behind
the mask is selected

FIGURE 57

Curvy object is masked by the letters

FIGURE 58

Pasting multiple objects behind a mask yields interesting effects

Use a clipping mask for special effects

1. Position the curvy object with the gradient fill over the mask, as shown in Figure 55.

2. Cut the curvy object.

3. Use the **Direct Selection tool** to select the original rectangle behind the mask.

   TIP   Click slightly above the mask until you see the rectangle selected, as shown in Figure 56.

4. Paste in front, then deselect so that your screen resembles Figure 57.

   The object is pasted in front of the masked rectangle and behind the mask.

5. Click the **Selection tool**, select the purple dotted line, position it over the letter K, then cut the purple dotted line.

6. Select the mask (rectangle) with the Direct Selection tool, click **Edit** on the Application bar, then click **Paste in Front**.

7. Using the same technique, mask the other objects on the artboard in any way that you choose.

   When finished, your mask should contain all of the objects, as shown in Figure 58.

   TIP   Add a stroke to the mask if desired.

8. Save and close Mask Effects.

You created visual effects by pasting objects behind a mask.

Transform objects.

1. Open AI 4-15.ai, then save it as **Transform Skills.**
2. Select "DIVIDE."
3. Scale the text objects non-uniformly: Horizontal = 110% and Vertical = 120%.
4. Rotate the text objects 7°.
5. Shear the text objects 25° on the horizontal axis.
6. Save your work.

Offset and outline paths.

1. Ungroup the text outlines.
2. Using the Offset Path command, offset each letter -.05".
3. Save your work.

Work with the Pathfinder panel.

1. Select all.
2. Apply the Divide pathfinder.

3. Fill the divided elements with different colors, using the Direct Selection tool.
4. Select all, then apply a 2-point white stroke. Figure 59 is an example of the effect. (*Hint*: Enlarge the view of your document window, if necessary.)
5. Save your work, compare your image to Figure 59, then close the Transform Skills document.

FIGURE 59
Completed Skills Review, Part 1

Create compound paths.

1. Open AI 4-16.ai, then save it as **Compounded**.
2. Select all, press [Alt] (Win) or [option] (Mac), then click the Exclude button.
3. Deselect, then click the center of the small square with the Direct Selection tool.
4. Rotate a copy of the small square 45°.
5. Save your work, compare your image to Figure 60, then close the Compounded document.

Create Clipping Masks

1. Open AI 4-17.ai, then save it as **Masked Paths**.
2. Position any three of the letters on the right side of the canvas over the artwork on the left.
3. Hide the three letters you didn't choose.
4. Select the three letters over the artwork, click Object on the Application bar, point to Compound Path, then click Make.
5. Select everything on the canvas.
6. Click Object on the Application bar, point to Clipping Mask, then click Make.
7. Deselect all.
8. Click Select on the Application bar, point to Object, then click Clipping Masks.
9. Add a 1.5 pt black stroke to the selection.
10. Compare your results to Figure 61, which shows one potential result.
11. Save your work, then close Masked Paths.ai.

FIGURE 60
Completed Skills Review, Part 2

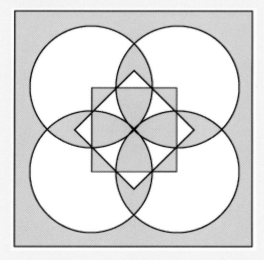

FIGURE 61
Completed Skills Review, Part 3

You are entering a contest to design a new stamp. You have decided to use a picture of Mona Lisa, which you have placed in an Illustrator document. You have positioned text over the image. Now, to complete the effect, you want to mimic the perforated edges of a stamp.

1. Open AI 4-18.ai, then save it as **Mona Lisa**.
2. Select all the circles, then make them into a compound path.
3. Add the rectangle to the selection.
4. Apply the Minus Front shape mode, then deselect all.
5. Save your work, compare your image to Figure 62, then close Mona Lisa.

FIGURE 62
Completed Project Builder 1

You're contracted to design the logo for Wired Gifts, an online gift site. Your concept is of a geometric red bow. You feel that your idea will simultaneously convey the concepts of gifts and technology.

1. Open AI 4-19.ai, then save it as **Wired**.
2. Switch to Outline mode.
3. Select the small square, click the Rotate tool, press and hold [Alt] (Win) or [option] (Mac), then click the center of the large square.
4. Type **15** in the Angle text box, then click Copy.
5. Repeat the transformation 22 times.
6. Delete the large square at the center.
7. Switch to Preview mode.
8. Select all, then fill all the squares with Caribbean Blue.
9. Apply the Divide pathfinder to the selection.
10. Fill the objects with the Red Bow gradient.
11. Delete the object in the center of the bow. (*Hint*: Use the Direct Selection tool to select the object.)
12. Select all, then remove the black stroke from the objects.
13. Save your work, compare your illustration with Figure 63, then close Wired.

FIGURE 63
Completed Project Builder 2

You are a fabric designer for a line of men's clothing. The line is known for its conservative patterns and styles. You are asked to supervise a team that will design new patterns for men's ties. You will present your recommended new patterns using Illustrator.

1. Create a new CMYK Color document and name it **New Tie.**
2. Create a square, rotate it 45°, then reshape it using the Direct Selection tool by dragging the top anchor point straight up to create the shape of a tie.
3. Use a square and the Minus Front button to square off the top of the diamond.
4. Draw a second polygon to represent the tie's knot.
5. Lock the two polygons.
6. Create a small circle, then copy it using the Move dialog box to create a polka dot pattern that exceeds the perimeter of both polygons.
7. Unlock the polygons, then bring them to the front.
8. Create a compound path out of the two polygons.
9. Select all, then use the polygons to mask the polka-dot pattern.
10. Apply a fill to the mask, save your work, compare your image to Figure 64, then close the New Tie document.

FIGURE 64
Completed Design Project

You are the design department manager for a toy company, and your next project will be to design a dartboard that will be part of a package of "Safe Games" for kids. The target market is boys and girls ages six to adult. You will design only the board, not the darts.

1. Create a new CMYK Color document and name it **Dartboard**.
2. Search the Internet for pictures of dartboards.
3. Research the sport of throwing darts. What are the official dimensions of a dartboard? Is there an official design? Are there official colors?
4. Decide which colors should be used for the board, keeping in mind that the sales department plans to position it as a toy for both girls and boys.
5. Using the skills you learned in this chapter and Figure 64 as a guide, design a dartboard.
6. Save your work, compare your image to Figure 65, then close Dartboard.

FIGURE 65
Completed Portfolio Project

WORKING WITH
LAYERS

1. Create and modify layers

2. Manipulate layered artwork

3. Work with layered artwork

4. Create a clipping set

Designing with Layers

When you're creating complex artwork, keeping track of all the items on the artboard can become quite a challenge. Small items hide behind larger items, and it may become difficult to find them, select them, and work with them. The Layers panel solves this problem. Using the Layers panel, you organize your work by placing objects or groups of objects on separate layers. Artwork on layers can be manipulated and modified independently from artwork on other layers. The Layers panel also provides effective options to select, hide, lock, and change the appearance of your work. In addition, layers are an effective solution for storing multiple versions of your work in one file.

Tools You'll Use

Layers panel

LAYERS

				Foreground	○
		▷		Sculpture	○
		▷		End Table	○
		▷		Sofa	○
		▷		Chair	○
		▷		Rug	○
	🔒	▷		Empty room	○

4 Layers

CREATE AND
MODIFY LAYERS

What You'll Do

In this lesson, you will create new layers and explore options on the Layers panel for viewing, locking, hiding, and selecting layers and layered artwork.

Creating Layers and Sublayers

Layers are a smart solution for organizing and managing a complex illustration. For example, if you were drawing a map of your home state, you might put all the interstate freeways on one layer, the local freeways on a second layer, secondary roads on a third layer, and all the text elements on a fourth layer.

As the name suggests, the Layers panel consists of a series of layers. The number of layers that a document can have is limited only by your computer's memory. By default, every Illustrator document is created with one layer, called Layer 1. As you work, you can create new layers and move objects into them, thereby segregating and organizing your work. The first object that is placed on Layer 1 is placed on a sublayer called <Path>. Each additional object placed on the same layer is placed on a separate <Path> sublayer.

Importing an Adobe Photoshop file with layers

When you use the Open command to import a layered Photoshop file into Illustrator CS4, you have the option to open that file with its layers intact. In the Photoshop Import Options dialog box that appears, click the Convert Layers to Objects option button, then click OK. Display the Illustrator Layers panel and you will see that Illustrator has preserved as much of the Photoshop layer structure as possible.

Each layer has a thumbnail, or miniature picture of the objects on that layer, to the left of the layer name. Thumbnails display the artwork that is positioned on all of the sublayers in the layer. You can change the size of the rows on the Layers panel by choosing a new size in the Layer Panel Options dialog box. Click the Layers panel list arrow, then click Panel Options. Layers and sublayers can also be given descriptive names to help identify their contents.

The stacking order of objects on the artboard corresponds to the hierarchy of layers on the Layers panel. Artwork in the top layer is at the front of the stacking order, while artwork in the bottom layer is in the back. The hierarchy of sublayers corresponds to the stacking order of the objects within a single layer.

Illustrator offers two basic ways to create new layers and sublayers. You can click the New Layer or New Sublayer command on the Layers panel menu, or you can click the Create New Layer or Create New Sublayer button on the Layers panel. Figure 1 shows a simple illustration and its corresponding layers on the Layers panel.

Duplicating Layers

In addition to creating new layers, you can duplicate existing layers by clicking the Duplicate command on the Layers panel menu, or by dragging a layer or sublayer onto the Create New Layer button on the Layers panel. When you duplicate a layer, all of the artwork on the layer is duplicated as well. Note the difference between this and copying and pasting artwork. When you copy and paste artwork, the copied artwork is pasted on the same layer.

FIGURE 1
Layers panel

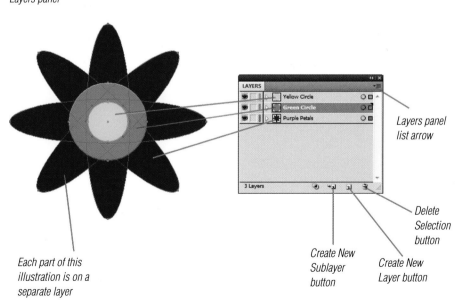

Each part of this illustration is on a separate layer

Create New Sublayer button

Create New Layer button

Delete Selection button

Layers panel list arrow

Setting Layer Options

The Layer Options dialog box offers a wealth of options for working with layered artwork, many of which are not available to you unless you are working with layers. You can name a layer, and you can also set a selection color for the layer. When an object is selected, its selection marks will be the same color as specified for the layer, making it easy to differentiate layers of artwork on the artboard.

Also in the Layer Options dialog box are options for locking, unlocking, showing, and hiding artwork on the layer. When you lock a layer, all the objects on the layer are locked and protected. When the Show check box is checked, all the artwork that is contained in the layer is displayed on the artboard. When the Show check box is not checked, the artwork is hidden.

The Preview option displays all the artwork on a layer in Preview mode. When the Preview option is not activated, the artwork is displayed in Outline mode. Thus, with layers, some elements on the artboard can be in Preview mode, while others are in Outline mode.

The Print option allows you to choose whether or not to print a layer. This feature is useful for printing different versions of the same illustration. The Dim Images to option reduces the intensity of bitmap images that are placed on the artboard. Dimming a bitmap often makes it easier to trace an image.

Use the Template option when you want to use the artwork on a layer as the basis for a new illustration—for example, if you want to trace the artwork. By default, a template layer is locked and cannot be printed.

Buttons on the Layers panel represent ways to lock, unlock, hide, and show artwork on each layer, making it unnecessary to use the Layer Options dialog box to activate these functions. The Toggles Visibility button (the eye) lets you hide and show layers, and the Toggles Lock button (the padlock) lets you lock and unlock layers.

Selecting Artwork on Layers and Sublayers

When you select an object on the artboard, its layer is selected (highlighted) on the Layers panel, and the Indicates Selected Art button appears, as shown in Figure 2. Selecting a layer or sublayer on the Layers panel does not select the artwork on that layer.

Changes that you make to layers on the Layers panel affect the artwork on those layers. For example, if you delete a layer, the artwork on the layer will be deleted. The artwork on a layer will be duplicated if the layer is duplicated. Changing a layer's

position in the layers hierarchy will move the artwork forward or backward in the stacking order.

Duplicating the artwork on the artboard does not duplicate the layer that the artwork is on. If you delete all the artwork on a layer, you are left with an empty layer. *A layer is never automatically created, copied, or deleted, regardless of what you do to the artwork on the layer.*

The same is *not* true for sublayers. If you delete or copy artwork that is on a sublayer, the *sublayer* is deleted or copied, respectively.

Selecting All Artwork on a Layer

The Select All command makes it easy to select every object on the artboard in one step. At times, however, you will want to select every object on a layer or sublayer, not every object on the artboard. To select all the artwork on a single layer or sublayer, select the Click to target, drag to move appearance button to the left of the Indicates Selected Art button, shown in Figure 2, or [Alt] (Win) or [option] (Mac) click the layer. All objects on that layer will become selected on the artboard.

FIGURE 2
The chair on the artboard and on the Layers panel

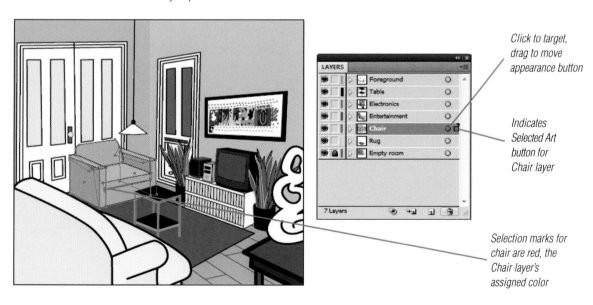

Click to target, drag to move appearance button

Indicates Selected Art button for Chair layer

Selection marks for chair are red, the Chair layer's assigned color

Create a new layer

1. Open AI 5-1.ai, then save it as **Living Room**.

2. Open AI 5-2.ai, then save it as **Showroom**.

   You will work with two documents during this lesson.

3. Click the **Selection tool** ▶, select the chair, then copy it.

4. Click the **Living Room.ai document tab** to activate the Living Room document.

   | TIP Using the Window menu is an easy way to switch between open documents.

5. Click the **Layers button** ◈ to open the Layers panel.

   The Layers panel shows two layers. The Empty room layer contains the artwork you see on the artboard. The objects on the Foreground layer are hidden.

6. Click the **Create New Layer button** ▣ on the Layers panel.

   A new layer named Layer 3 appears above the Foreground layer.

7. Click **Edit** on the Application bar, then click **Paste**.

   The chair artwork is pasted into Layer 3.

8. Position the chair on the artboard as shown in Figure 3.

You created a new layer using the Create New Layer button on the Layers panel, then pasted an object onto that new layer.

FIGURE 3
Chair positioned on its own layer

Thumbnail of chair artwork on Layer 3

FIGURE 4

Layer Options dialog box

Color list arrow

1. Double-click **Layer 3**.

2. Name the layer **Chair**, then click **OK**.

   The Layers panel reflects the name change.

3. Double-click the **Chair layer**.

4. Click the **Color list arrow**, click **Red**, as shown in Figure 4, then click **OK**.

   Note that the selection marks on the chair are now red, reflecting the new selection color for the Chair layer.

5. Deselect the chair.

You used the Layer Options dialog box to rename Layer 3 and assign it a new selection color.

Select items on a layer and lock a layer

1. Click the **chair** with the Selection tool ⮕.

   Note that the Indicates Selected Art button appears when the chair is selected, as shown in Figure 5.

   | TIP The Indicates Selected Art button is the same color as its layer.

2. Deselect the chair.

   The Indicates Selected Art button disappears.

3. Press **[Alt]** (Win) or **[option]** (Mac), then click the **Chair layer** on the Layers panel.

   The chair artwork is selected.

4. Click either of the two mauve walls in the illustration.

   When an object is selected on the artboard, the layer on which the selected object is placed is highlighted on the Layers panel.

5. Double-click the **Empty room layer**, click the **Lock check box**, then click **OK**.

   The Toggles Lock button 🔒 appears on the Empty room layer, indicating that all the objects on the Empty room layer are locked. See Figure 6.

You noted the relationship between a selected item and its corresponding layer on the Layers panel. You activated the Indicates Selected Art button and selected the artwork on the Chair layer. You then locked the Empty room layer.

Indicates Selected Art button

FIGURE 6
Toggles Lock button identifies a locked layer

Toggles lock button

FIGURE 7

Foreground layer is locked and hidden

The absence of the Toggles Visibility button indicates that this layer is hidden

The Toggles Lock button indicates that this layer is locked

Show and hide layers

1. Double-click the **Foreground layer**.

2. Click the **Color list arrow**, then click **Grass Green**.

3. Click the **Show check box**, then click **OK**.

   The objects on the Foreground layer become visible, and the Toggles Visibility button ![eye] appears on the Foreground layer.

4. Click the **Toggles Visibility button** ![eye] on the Foreground layer to hide the objects.

5. Click the **Toggles Visibility button** (in its off state) ![blank] on the Foreground layer to show the objects.

   TIP   The Toggles Visibility and Toggles Lock buttons appear as empty gray squares in their off state.

6. Click the **Toggles Lock button** (in its off state) ![blank] on the Foreground layer.

   The **Toggles Lock button** ![lock] appears.

7. Click the **Toggles Visibility button** ![eye] on the Foreground layer to hide the objects.

   Your Layers panel should resemble Figure 7.

8. Save your work.

You used the Toggles Visibility button on the Layers panel to toggle between showing and hiding the artwork on two layers. You also locked the Foreground layer.

MANIPULATE LAYERED ARTWORK

What You'll Do

In this lesson, you will learn methods for manipulating layers to change the display of layered artwork. You will change the order of layers on the panel, merge layers, work with sublayers, and move objects between layers.

Changing the Order of Layers and Sublayers

The hierarchy of the layers on the Layers panel determines how objects on the artboard overlap. All the objects on a given layer are behind the objects on the layer above it and in front of the objects on the layer beneath it. Multiple objects within a given layer overlap according to their stacking order and can be repositioned with the standard stacking order commands.

To change the position of a layer or sublayer in the hierarchy, simply drag it up or down on the panel. Small black triangles and a heavy horizontal line identify where the layer will be repositioned, as shown in Figure 8. When you reposition a layer, its sublayers move with it.

Merging Layers

When you have positioned artwork to your liking using multiple layers and sublayers, you will often want to consolidate those layers to simplify the panel. First, you must

select the layers that you want to merge. Press [Ctrl] (Win) or ⌘ (Mac) to select multiple layers. Once you have selected the layers that you want to merge, apply the Merge Selected command on the Layers panel menu. When you merge layers, all the artwork from one or more layers moves onto the layer that was last selected before the merge.

Be careful not to confuse merging layers with condensing layers. Condensing layers is simply the process of dragging one layer into another. The repositioned layer becomes a sublayer of the layer it was dragged into.

Defining Sublayers

Whenever you have one or more objects on a layer, you by definition have **sublayers**. For example, if you draw a circle and a square on Layer 1, it will automatically have two sublayers—one for the square, one for the circle. The layer is the sum total of its sublayers.

As soon as the first object is placed on a layer, a triangle appears to the left of the layer name, indicating that the layer contains sublayers. Click the triangle to expand the layer and see the sublayers, then click it again to collapse the layer and hide the sublayers.

Working with Sublayers

When you place grouped artwork into a layer, a sublayer is automatically created with the name <Group>. A triangle appears on the <Group> sublayer, which, when clicked, exposes the sublayers—one for every object in the group, as shown in Figure 9.

Dragging Objects Between Layers

Sublayers are the easiest objects to move between layers: You can simply drag and drop a sublayer from one layer to another.

You can drag artwork from one layer to another by dragging the Indicates Selected Art button. Select the artwork on the artboard that you want to move; the layer is selected, and the Indicates Selected Art button appears. Drag the button to the destination layer or sublayer, as shown in Figure 10. If you drag the Indicates Selected Art button to a layer, the artwork becomes the top sublayer in the layer. If you drag the Indicates Selected Art button to a

sublayer, the artwork is grouped with the object already on the sublayer.

If you don't feel comfortable dragging artwork between layers, you have two other options for moving objects between layers. You can simply cut and paste artwork from one layer to another by selecting the object that you want to move, cutting it from the artboard, selecting the layer you wish to place it on, then pasting. You can also use the Send to Current Layer command. Select the artwork you want to move, click the name of the destination layer to make it the active layer, click Object on the Application bar, point to Arrange, then click Send to Current Layer.

FIGURE 8

Changing the order of layers

Moving a layer on the Layers panel

FIGURE 9

A <Group> sublayer

Each object in a group is placed on its own sublayer

FIGURE 10

Dragging a sublayer to another layer

Drag the Indicates Selected Art button to another layer

Change the hierarchy of layers

1. Use the Window menu to switch to the Showroom document, copy the rug, then return to the Living Room document.

2. Press **[Ctrl]** (Win) or ⌘ (Mac), then click the **Create New Layer button** 🔲 on the Layers panel.

   Pressing [Ctrl] (Win) or ⌘ (Mac) creates a new layer at the top of the layer list.

3. Click **Edit** on the Application bar, then click **Paste**.

   The rug is pasted into the new layer because it is the active—or "targeted"—layer.

4. Name the new layer **Rug**, set its color to yellow, then position the rug artwork with a corner of it hanging slightly off the artboard, as shown in Figure 11.

5. Click and drag the **Rug layer** and position it below the Chair layer until you see a double black line with small triangles beneath the Chair layer, as shown in Figure 12, then release the mouse.

   The rug artwork is now positioned below the chair artwork.

You created a new layer at the top of the Layers panel. You pasted artwork into that layer, then moved the layer below another layer in the hierarchy so that the artwork on the two layers overlapped properly on the artboard.

FIGURE 11
The Rug layer is at the top of the layers hierarchy

FIGURE 12
Changing the hierarchy of layers

Tiny black triangles appear

Double black line appears beneath the Chair layer

FIGURE 13
Sculpture artwork positioned on top of the end table

FIGURE 14

Foreground and Sculpture layers merged

Merged layer

Merge layers

1. Switch to the Showroom document, copy the sculpture, then return to the Living Room document.

2. Press **[Ctrl]** (Win) or ⌘ (Mac), then click the **Create New Layer button** 🔳.

3. Paste the sculpture into the new layer, then name the layer **Sculpture**.

   For the remainder of the lesson, assign it a color that is different from the other layers.

4. Show the Foreground layer, then position the sculpture artwork on the brown end table, as shown in Figure 13.

5. Deselect the sculpture, then drag the **Foreground layer** above the Sculpture layer on the Layers panel.

6. Unlock the Foreground layer.

7. Click the **Sculpture layer** to select it, press **[Ctrl]** (Win) or ⌘ (Mac), then click the **Foreground layer**.

   When merging layers, the last layer selected becomes the merged layer.

8. Click the **Layers panel list arrow**, then click **Merge Selected**.

   The objects from both layers are merged into the Foreground layer; the Sculpture layer is deleted.

   TIP Layers must be showing and unlocked in order to be merged.

9. Compare your screen to Figure 14.

   Don't worry that your sculpture is temporarily behind the table.

You merged the Sculpture and the Foreground layers.

Work with sublayers

1. Expand the Foreground layer by clicking the **triangle** ▷ to the left of the layer.

   Three sublayers, all named <Group>, are revealed.

2. Expand the sofa <Group> sublayer by clicking the **triangle** ▷ to the left of it.

   The five paths that compose the sofa are revealed.

3. Select the sofa artwork on the artboard.

   The Indicates Selected Art buttons appear for each of the selected paths, as shown in Figure 15.

4. Click the **triangle** ▽ to the left of the sofa <Group> sublayer to collapse it, then deselect the sofa.

5. Double-click the **sofa <Group> sublayer**, name it **Sofa**, then click **OK**.

6. Name the sculpture sublayer **Sculpture**, then name the end table sublayer **End Table**.

7. Move the Sculpture sublayer above the End Table sublayer so that your Layers panel resembles Figure 16.

   Notice that the sculpture artwork is on top of the end table.

8. Click the **triangle** ▽ to the left of the Foreground layer to hide the three sublayers.

9. Hide the Foreground layer.

You viewed sublayers in the Foreground layer. You then renamed the three sublayers in the Foreground layer and rearranged the order of the Sculpture and the End Table sublayers.

FIGURE 15
Each path in the sofa <Group> sublayer is selected

Indicates Selected
Art buttons

FIGURE 16
Sculpture layer moved above the End Table sublayer

FIGURE 17

Cabinet and plant are on the same layer

FIGURE 18

Moving the Plant 2 sublayer

Plant 2 sublayer

FIGURE 19

The reflected copy of the plant in position

The new plant is positioned behind the cabinet

FIGURE 20

The reflected copy of the plant, scaled and pruned

Create new sublayers

1. Switch to the Showroom document, copy the cabinet, then return to the Living Room document.

2. Press **[Ctrl]** (Win) or ⌘ (Mac), then click the **Create New Layer button** ⬓.

3. Name the new layer **Entertainment**, select Violet as the layer color, then click **OK**.

4. Paste the cabinet artwork into the new layer.

5. Copy the plant from the Showroom document, then paste the plant artwork into the Entertainment layer.

6. Position the cabinet artwork and the plant artwork as shown in Figure 17.

7. Deselect all, expand the Entertainment layer, then select the plant artwork on the artboard.

8. Double-click the **Reflect tool** 🔁, click the **Vertical option button**, then click **Copy**.

   The reflected copy of the plant is placed on a new sublayer above the original plant sublayer.

9. Rename the new sublayer **Plant 2**.

10. Move the Plant 2 sublayer to the bottom of the Entertainment sublayer hierarchy, as shown in Figure 18.

11. Click the **Selection tool** ▶, then move the new plant artwork into the position shown in Figure 19.

12. Scale the new plant artwork 85%, delete or move some leaves on it so that it's not an obvious copy of the original plant, then compare your screen to Figure 20.

You created and moved new sublayers.

Move objects between layers

1. Switch to the Showroom document, copy the electronics images, then return to the Living Room document.

2. Create a new layer at the top of the hierarchy, name it **Electronics**, choose Magenta as its color, then click **OK**.

3. Paste the electronics on the Electronics layer, then position the electronics artwork on the cabinet.

   The plant on the right needs to be positioned in front of the electronics for the visual to be realistic.

4. Name the top sublayer in the Entertainment layer **Plant 1**, then select the Plant 1 artwork on the artboard.

   The Indicates Selected Art button appears in the Plant 1 sublayer.

5. Drag the **Indicates Selected Art button** from the Plant 1 sublayer to the Electronics layer, as shown in Figure 21.

   The Plant 1 sublayer moves into the Electronics layer. The Plant 1 sublayer automatically becomes the top sublayer in the Electronics layer.

6. Switch to the Showroom document, copy the Matisse, return to the Living Room document, then create a new layer at the top of the hierarchy, named **Matisse**.

7. Paste the Matisse artwork into the new layer, then position it as shown in Figure 22.

(continued)

FIGURE 21
Moving a sublayer from one layer to another

Drag the Indicates Selected Art button to the Electronics layer

FIGURE 22
The Matisse in position on its own layer

Working with Layers

FIGURE 23

Moving the Matisse layer into the Electronics layer

The Matisse layer becomes a
sublayer of the Electronics layer

Large black triangles

FIGURE 24

The lamp and table in position

New Table and Lamp layers

8. Drag the Matisse layer on top of the Electronics layer.

   Two large, black triangles appear on the Electronics layer when the Matisse layer is on top of it, as shown in Figure 23. The Matisse layer is moved into the Electronics layer as the topmost sublayer.

9. Create new layers for the lamp and the table, copy and paste the lamp and table artwork from the Showroom document to the new layers, then position the artwork so that your illustration resembles Figure 24.

10. Save your work.

You created a new layer named Electronics, dragged the Plant 1 sublayer into the Electronics layer by dragging its Indicates Selected Art button to the Electronics layer. You then moved the Matisse layer into the Electronics layer by dragging it on top of the Electronics layer and created new layers for the table and the lamp.

WORK WITH LAYERED
ARTWORK

What You'll Do

In this lesson, you will explore options for managing your work using the Layers panel.

Using the View Buttons on the Layers Panel

The view options available on the Layers panel make working with layers a smart choice for complex illustrations. The options are targeted: You can apply specific viewing options to each layer in the document. Without layers, your options for viewing your work are limited to the Hide and Show All commands on the Object menu.

The Toggles Visibility button makes it easy to quickly change what can be seen on the artboard. Clicking this button once hides all the artwork on a layer, and the button disappears. Clicking the empty gray square where the button was shows all of the artwork on the layer, and the button reappears. Pressing [Alt] (Win) or [option] (Mac) and clicking the button once shows all layers; clicking a second time hides all layers except for the layer you clicked.

Pressing [Ctrl] (Win) or ⌘ (Mac) and clicking the button toggles between Outline and Preview modes; all the artwork on the layer will switch between outlined and filled objects. Pressing [Alt][Ctrl] (Win) or [option] ⌘ (Mac) and clicking the button switches all other layers between Outline and Preview modes.

Locating an Object on the Layers Panel

With complex illustrations, layers and sublayers tend to multiply—so much so that you will often find it easiest to work with collapsed layers, those in which you hide the sublayers. Sometimes it can be difficult to identify an object's layer or sublayer, especially if there are multiple copies of the object in the illustration. The Locate Object command offers a simple solution. Select an object on the artboard, click the Layers panel list arrow, then click Locate Object. The layers expand, revealing their sublayers, and the selected object's layer or sublayer is selected.

Reversing the Order of Layers

Another option that the Layers panel offers for managing your artwork is the ability to reverse the order of layers. Select the layers whose order you want to reverse. Press [Shift] to select multiple contiguous (those next to each other on the panel) layers. Press [Ctrl] (Win) or ⌘ (Mac) to select multiple noncontiguous layers. Click the Layers panel list arrow, then click Reverse Order.

Making Layers Nonprintable

The ability to choose whether or not the artwork on a specific layer will print is a useful function, especially during the middle stages of producing an illustration. For example, you could print just the text elements and give them to a copy editor for proofing. You could print just the elements of the illustration that are ready to be shown to the client, holding back the elements that still need work.

Another value of the print option is the ability to print different versions of a document. Let's say you're working on the design of a poster for a client, and you've finalized the artwork but you're still undecided about the typeface for the headline, after narrowing down the choices to five typefaces. You could create five layers, one for the headline formatted in each typeface. Then you would print the illustration five times, each time printing only one of the five different headline layers. This is a smart and simple way to produce comps quickly.

QUICKTIP

You can export Illustrator layers to Photoshop by clicking File on the Application bar, clicking Export, clicking the Save as type list arrow (Win) or the Format list arrow (Mac), clicking Photoshop (*.PSD) (Win) or Photoshop (psd) (Mac), then clicking Save (Win) or Export (Mac). The Photoshop Export Options dialog box opens. Verify that the Write Layers option button is selected. Click OK to export the layers to a Photoshop document.

Explore view options on the Layers panel

1. Collapse the Electronics and Entertainment layers, then hide them.

2. Press and hold **[Alt]** (Win) or **[option]** (Mac), then click the **Toggles Visibility button** on the Chair layer.

   All of the layers are displayed.

3. Using the same keyboard commands, click the **Toggles Visibility button** on the Chair layer again.

   All layers, except for the Chair layer, are hidden.

4. Using the same keyboard commands, click the **Toggles Visibility button** on the Chair layer again so that all of the layers are displayed.

5. Move the Foreground layer to the top of the hierarchy.

6. Press **[Ctrl]** (Win) or ⌘ (Mac), then click the **Toggles Visibility button** on the Chair layer.

   The artwork on the Chair layer switches to Outline mode.

7. Using the same keyboard commands, click the **Toggles Visibility button** on the Chair layer again.

8. Press **[Alt][Ctrl]** (Win) or **[option]** ⌘ (Mac), then click the same **Toggles Visibility button** .

   The artwork on every layer, except for the Chair layer, switches to Outline mode, as shown in Figure 25.

9. Using the same keyboard commands, click the **Toggles Visibility button** again.

You learned keyboard commands to explore view options on the Layers panel.

FIGURE 25

The Chair layer shown in Preview mode and all other layers shown in Outline mode

FIGURE 26

Duplicating the Lamp layer

*To duplicate a layer and its
contents, drag it on top of the
Create New Layer button*

FIGURE 27

Positioning the second lamp

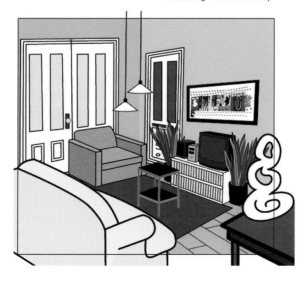

Locate, duplicate, and delete layers

1. Select the Plant 2 artwork on the artboard.

2. Click the **Layers panel list arrow**, then click **Locate Object**.

   The Entertainment layer expands, as does the Plant 2 sublayer.

   > TIP   The Locate Object command is useful when you are working with collapsed layers or with many layers and sublayers.

3. Collapse the Entertainment layer.

4. Select the Lamp layer, then drag it on top of the Create New Layer button 🔳 , as shown in Figure 26.

   The Lamp layer and its contents are duplicated onto a new layer that is created above the original lamp layer. The copied lamp artwork is positioned directly on top of the original lamp artwork.

5. Position the duplicated lamp artwork on the artboard, as shown in Figure 27.

6. Drag the **Lamp copy layer** to the Delete Selection button 🗑 on the Layers panel.

You used the Locate Object command to identify a selected object's position on the Layers panel. You duplicated a layer, then deleted it.

Dim placed images

1. Hide all layers, then create a new layer at the top of the hierarchy, named **Photo**.

2. Click **File** on the Application bar, then click **Place**.

3. Navigate to the drive and folder where your Data Files are stored, click **Living Room Original.tif**, then click **Place**.

   The source for the illustration is placed on its own layer.

4. Align the photo with the top-left corner of the artboard, as shown in Figure 28.

5. Double-click the **Photo layer**, click the **Dim Images to check box**, type **50** in the Dim Images to text box, then click **OK**.

   The placed image is less vivid.

   TIP Dimming a placed image is useful for tracing.

You created a new layer, placed a photo on the new layer, then used the Layer Options dialog box to dim the photo 50%.

FIGURE 28
The source of the illustration, placed on its own layer

FIGURE 29
Using a layer for a message to the printer

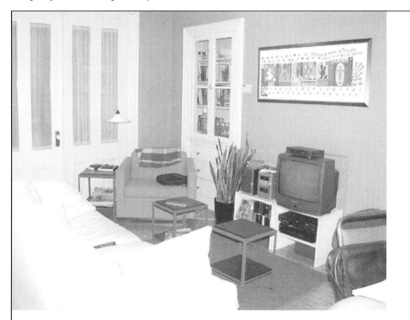

**Printer: Use photo for reference if necessary. Thank you!
Call me at 555-1234 if any problems.**

1. Create a new layer at the top of the hierarchy, named **Message**.

2. Using any font you like, type a message for the printer, as shown in Figure 29.

3. Convert the message text to outlines. Double-click the **Message layer**, remove the check mark from the Print check box, then click **OK**.

   The Message layer will not print to any output device.

   TIP When a layer is set to not print, its name is italicized on the Layers panel.

4. Make the Photo layer nonprintable.

5. Hide the Message and Photo layers.

6. Make all the other layers visible.

7. Save your work.

You created a new layer called Message, typed a message for the printer, then designated the Message and Photo layers as nonprintable. You then displayed all of the layers except for the Message and Photo layers.

CREATE A
CLIPPING SET

What You'll Do

In this lesson, you will create a clipping mask on a sublayer that will mask the other sublayers in the layer.

Working with Clipping Sets

Adobe uses the terms "clipping mask" and "clipping path" interchangeably. The term **clipping set** is used to distinguish clipping paths used in layers from clipping paths used to mask nonlayered artwork. There's no difference; it's just terminology. Essentially, the term "clipping set" refers to the clipping mask *and* the masked sublayers as a unit.

The following rules apply to clipping sets:
- The clipping mask and the objects to be masked must be in the same layer.
- You cannot use a sublayer as a clipping mask, unless it is a <Group> sublayer. However, the top sublayer in a layer becomes the clipping mask if you first select the layer that the sublayer is in, then create the clipping mask.
- The top object in the clipping set becomes the mask for every object below it in the layer.
- A <Group> sublayer can be a clipping set. The top object in the group will function as the mask.
- Dotted lines between sublayers indicate that they are included in a clipping set.

Flattening Artwork

When you apply the Flatten Artwork command, all visible objects in the artwork are consolidated in a single layer. Before applying the command, select the layer into which you want to consolidate the artwork. If you have a layer that is hidden, you will be asked whether to make the artwork visible so that it can be flattened into the layer, or whether to delete the layer and the artwork on it.

FIGURE 30
The new <Path> sublayer

The rectangle is placed on a new sublayer called <Path>, on top of the other sublayers in the Foreground layer

FIGURE 31
Clipping path masks only the objects on its own layer

Clipping path

Create clipping sets

1. Select the Foreground layer, click the **Rectangle tool** , then create a rectangle that is 6.5" wide × 6" tall.

2. Position the rectangle so that it aligns exactly with the edges of the artboard.

3. Apply a black stroke to the rectangle and no fill color.

4. Expand the Foreground layer.

   The rectangle, identified as <Path>, is at the top of the sublayers, as shown in Figure 30.

5. Click the **Make/Release Clipping Mask button** on the Layers panel.

   Any path on the Foreground layer that is positioned off the artboard is masked. The part of the rug that extends beyond the artboard is not masked, because it is not in the same layer as the clipping path. The lamp, too, extends beyond the artboard and is not masked, as shown in Figure 31.

You created a rectangle, then used it as a clipping path to mask the sublayers below it in its layer.

Copy a clipping mask and flatten artwork

1. Click the **<Clipping Path> layer** to select it.

2. Click **Edit** on the Application bar, click **Copy**, click **Edit** on the Application bar again, then click **Paste in Front**.

   A new sublayer named <Path> is created. The rectangle on the <Clipping Path> sublayer is duplicated on the new <Path> sublayer and can be used to mask other layers.

3. Drag the **Indicates Selected Art button** on the <Path> sublayer down to the Rug layer, as shown in Figure 32.

4. Expand the Rug layer to see the new <Path> sublayer, select the Rug layer, then click the **Make/Release Clipping Mask button** 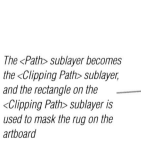.

   Compare your Layers panel to Figure 33. The <Path> sublayer becomes the <Clipping Path> sublayer, and the rectangle on the <Clipping Path> sublayer is used to mask the rug on the artboard.

   (continued)

FIGURE 32
Moving the copy of the rectangle to the Rug layer

Drag the Indicates Selected
Art button to the Rug layer

FIGURE 33
Using the duplicate rectangle to mask the rug

The <Path> sublayer becomes
the <Clipping Path> sublayer,
and the rectangle on the
<Clipping Path> sublayer is
used to mask the rug on the
artboard

FIGURE 34
Completed illustration

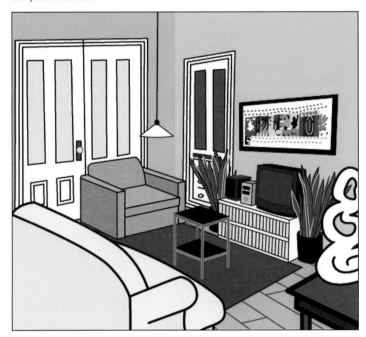

5. Select the lamp artwork on the artboard, drag the **Indicates Selected Art button** on the Lamp layer to the Sculpture sublayer of the Foreground layer, then deselect all.

The lamp artwork moves to the Sculpture sublayer and is therefore masked. Deselect the lamp and your illustration should resemble Figure 34.

TIP   When you drag the Indicates Selected Art button from one layer to another, the selected artwork moves to the new layer, but the layer does not move.

6. Select the empty Lamp layer, then click the **Delete Selection button** 🗑 on the Layers panel.

7. Click **File** on the Application bar, then click **Save**.

8. Select the Foreground layer, click the **Layers panel list arrow**, click **Flatten Artwork**, then click **Yes** when you are asked whether or not you want to discard the hidden art on the hidden layers.

9. Click **File** on the Application bar, click **Save As**, then save the file as **Living Room Flat**.

Note that we saved the flattened version as a separate file and saved the original Livingroom.ai file with all layers intact. Whenever you flatten a layered document, always save the flattened version as a copy so that you can preserve your original layered file.

You made a copy of the rectangle, moved the copied rectangle to the Rug layer, then made it into a clipping path to mask the rug artwork. You then moved the lamp artwork into the Sculpture sub-layer, which masked the lamp. You deleted the empty Lamp layer and flattened all of the artwork on the Foreground layer.

Create and modify layers.

1. Open AI 5-3.ai, then save it as **Gary**.
2. Create a new layer at the top of the layer hierarchy, named **Text**.
3. Create a new layer at the top of the layer hierarchy, named **Gary Garlic**.
4. Rename Layer 2 **Body Parts**.
5. Save your work.

Manipulate layered artwork.

1. Move the garlic artwork into the Gary Garlic layer.
2. Move the three text groups onto the Text layer.
3. Merge the Background layer with the Box Shapes layer so that the Box Shapes layer is the name of the resulting merged layer. (*Hint*: Click the Background layer, press [Ctrl] (Win) or ⌘ (Mac), click the Box Shapes layer, click the Layers panel list arrow, then click Merge Selected.)
4. Move the Body Parts layer to the top of the layer hierarchy.
5. Save your work.

Work with layered artwork.

1. View each layer separately to identify the artwork on each.
2. Using Figure 35 as a guide, assemble Gary Garlic.
3. Merge the Gary Garlic and Body Parts layers so that the resulting merged layer will be named Body Parts.
4. Select all the artwork on the Body Parts layer, then group the artwork.
5. Save your work.

Create a clipping set.

1. Target the Box Shapes layer.
2. Create a rectangle that is 5" wide by 8" in height.
3. Position the rectangle so that it is centered on the artboard.
4. With the rectangle still selected, expand the Box Shapes layer on the Layers panel.
5. Click the Make/Release Clipping Mask button on the Layers panel.
6. Reposition the masked elements (text and box parts) so that your illustration resembles Figure 35.
7. Save your work, then close Gary.

FIGURE 35
Completed Skills Review

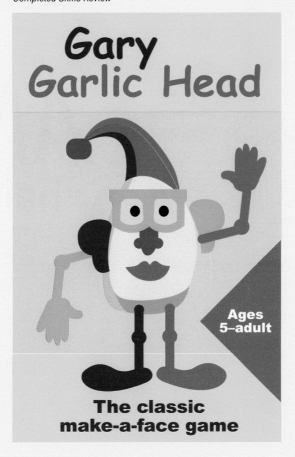

You are designing an outdoor sign for Xanadu Haircutters, a salon that recently opened in your town. You are pleased with your concept of using scissors to represent the X in Xanadu, and decide to design the logo with different typefaces so that the client will feel she has some input into the final design.

1. Open AI 5-4.ai, then save it as **Xanadu**.
2. Create a new layer, then move the ANADU headline into that layer.
3. Make four duplicates of the new layer.
4. Change the typeface on four of the layers, for a total of five versions of the logo type.
5. Rename each type layer, using the name of the typeface you chose.
6. Rename Layer 1 Xanadu Art.
7. View the Xanadu Art layer five times, each time with one of the typeface layers, so that you can see five versions of the logo.
8. Save your work, compare your illustration with Figure 36, then close Xanadu.

FIGURE 36
Completed Project Builder 1

You are the Creative Director for a Los Angeles design firm that specializes in identity packages for television networks. One of your most important projects this week is delivering the first round of comps for a new cable channel, Milty TV. Your art directors have come up with two concepts—one dark, one light. You decide to bring each to the client with two options for typography, for a total of four comps.

1. Open AI 5-5.ai, then save it as **Milty Cable**.
2. Select the four pieces of artwork at the top of the artboard, then group them.
3. Group the four pieces of artwork at the bottom of the artboard, then cut them.
4. Create a new layer, name it **Orange**, then paste the artwork.
5. Position the orange artwork exactly on top of the blue artwork on the artboard so that it is covered.
6. Rename Layer 1 **Blue**, then duplicate the layer and name it **Blue Two**.
7. Duplicate the Orange layer, then name it **Orange Two**.
8. Deselect all, use the Direct Selection tool to select the large M, change its typeface to Algerian, then hide the two Orange layers. (*Hint*: If you do not have Algerian as a typeface, choose another one.)

9. Select the Blue Two layer, change the M to Algerian, then hide it.
10. View each of the four layers separately.
11. Save your work, compare your illustration to Figure 37, then close Milty Cable.

FIGURE 37
Completed Project Builder 2

You are a freelance designer, working out of your house. The owner of the town's largest plumbing company, Straight Flush, has hired you to redesign his logo. He gives you an Illustrator file with a design created by his son. You study the logo, then decide that it lacks cohesion and focus.

1. Open **AI 5-6.ai**, then save it as **Straight Flush**.
2. Group the elements of each playing card together.
3. Create four new layers.
4. Move each card to the layer with the corresponding number in the layer name.
5. Select all the layers, click the Layers panel list arrow, then click Reverse Order.
6. Reposition the cards on each layer so that they are in order, directly behind the ace.
7. Adjust the layout of the cards to your liking to create a new layout for the logo.
8. Save your work, compare your illustration with Figure 38, then close Straight Flush.

FIGURE 38
Completed Design Project

Working with Layers

You are a fabric designer for a line of men's clothing. You are asked to supervise a team that will design new patterns for men's ties. Now that you have studied working with layers, how would you approach building a file that shows three patterns for a tie?

1. Open AI 5-7.ai, then save it as **Tie Pattern**.
2. Select various objects to see how the file has been built.
3. Ask yourself how the document would be more practical if it were built with layers.
4. How many masks would be required to show the three patterns?
5. How many layers would be required?
6. Redesign the document with layers so that the three patterns are all in one clipping set with one tie shape functioning as the mask.
7. Save your work, compare your Layers panel with Figure 39, then close Tie Pattern.

FIGURE 39
Completed Portfolio Project

chapter

6

WORKING WITH PATTERNS
AND BRUSHES

1. Use the Move command

2. Create a pattern

3. Design a repeating pattern

4. Work with the Brushes panel

5. Work with scatter brushes

6. Compare the Paintbrush tool to the Blob Brush tool

Working with Patterns and Brushes

Artwork that you create in Illustrator is, of course, an end in and of itself—the result of your efforts in conceiving an image and rendering it, using your skills and talents. As you become more familiar with Illustrator, you will learn to use completed artwork as a component of new illustrations.

Using patterns and brushes is a fine example of this working method. You can design artwork and then use it as a pattern to fill and stroke new artwork. This would be very useful if you were drawing a field of flowers, or stars in the night sky, or trees on a mountainside.

The powerful options in Illustrator's Brushes panel extend this concept even further. Using brushes, you can use completed artwork as a stroke, a pattern, or a freestanding illustration of greater complexity. For example, you could create a custom brush stroke, such as a leaf, and then use the Paintbrush tool to paint with the leaf as a brush stroke. Instead of being limited to filling or stroking an object with leaves, you could paint leaves wherever you wanted on the artboard.

Tools You'll Use

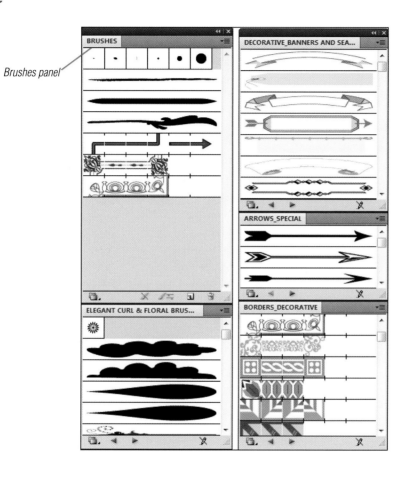

Brushes panel

USE THE MOVE
COMMAND

What You'll Do

 In this lesson, you will use the Move command to copy an object at precise offsets and create a simple pattern.

Using the Move Command

The word **offset** comes up when you explore the Move command. Quite simply, the term refers to the distance that an object is moved or copied from a starting location to an ending location. In a simple drop shadow, for example, you can describe the effect by saying, "The black copy behind the original has been offset three points to the left and three points down."

The Move command provides the most effective method for moving an object—or a copy of an object—at precise offsets. In the Move dialog box, you enter the horizontal distance and the vertical distance that you want a selected object to move. A positive value moves the object horizontally to the right, and a negative value moves it to the left. A positive value moves the object vertically up, and a negative value moves it down.

An alternate (and seldom used) method for using the Move dialog box is to enter a value for the distance you want the object to move and a value for the angle it should move on. Entering a distance and an angle is the same as specifying the move in horizontal and vertical values. When you enter values in the Distance and Angle text boxes, the Horizontal and Vertical text boxes update to reflect the move. Conversely, when you enter values in the Horizontal and Vertical text boxes, the Distance and Angle text boxes update to reflect the move. The Move dialog box is shown in Figure 1.

FIGURE 1
Move dialog box

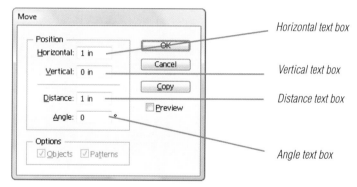

Horizontal text box

Vertical text box

Distance text box

Angle text box

Using the Document Info panel

The Document Info panel, listed on the Window menu, offers you useful information about the document and about objects in the document. Along with general file information such as filename, ruler units and color space, the panel lists specific information like the number and names of graphic styles, custom colors, patterns, gradients, fonts, and placed art. To view information about a selected object, choose Selection Only from the panel menu. Leaving this option deselected lists information about the entire document. To view artboard dimensions, click the Artboard tool, choose Document from the panel menu, and then click to select the artboard you want to view.

Copy and move objects using the Move dialog box

1. Create a new 4" × 4" CMYK Color document, then save it as **Checkerboard**.

2. Click **Edit** (Win) or **Illustrator** (Mac) on the Application bar, point to **Preferences**, then click **Units & Display Performance**.

3. Verify that the General units of measure are Inches, then click **OK**.

4. Create a ½" square, apply a red fill and no stroke, then position it at the upper-left corner of the artboard.

5. Click **Object** on the Application bar, point to **Transform**, then click **Move**.

6. Enter **.5** in the Horizontal text box, press **[Tab]**, enter **0** in the Vertical text box, then press **[Tab]** again.

   TIP Values in the Distance and Angle text boxes automatically appear, based on the values entered in the Horizontal and Vertical text boxes.

7. Click **Copy**.

   A copy of the square is positioned immediately to the right of the original.

8. Change the fill on the second square to black, select both squares, click **Object** on the Application bar, point to **Transform**, then click **Move**.

9. Enter **1** in the Horizontal text box, then click **Copy**.

10. Click **Object** on the Application bar, point to **Transform**, click **Transform Again**, then repeat this step.

    Your work should resemble Figure 2.

    (continued)

FIGURE 2
A simple pattern created using the Move command

FIGURE 3
A checkerboard created with a single starting square and the Move dialog box

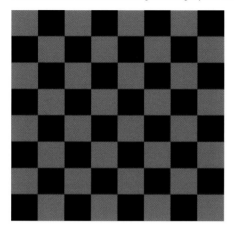

11. Select all, open the Move dialog box, enter **0** in the Horizontal text box, enter **-.5** in the Vertical text box, then click **Copy**.

    TIP Apply a negative value to move an object down.

12. Double-click the **Rotate tool** ⟳, enter **180** in the Angle text box, then click **OK**.

13. Select all, open the Move dialog box, enter **-1** in the Vertical text box, then click **Copy**.

14. Apply the Transform Again command twice, then save your work.

    Your screen should resemble Figure 3.

15. Close the Checkerboard document.

Starting with a single square, you used the Move command to make multiple copies at precise distances, to create a checkerboard pattern.

Saving and exporting Illustrator CS4 files

You can export your Illustrator files in a variety of formats. For example, you can export your artwork as a JPEG, which is a Web file format, or as a Photoshop (*.PSD) file. To export, click File on the Application bar, point to Export, type a new name for the exported file in the File name text box, then choose the file type from the Save as type list arrow. Depending on the file format that you choose, you may have another Options dialog box appear offering you more settings for your exported file. For example, if you export your illustration as Flash (*.SWF), you'll be able to choose a background color, a lossy or lossless compression, and whether you want the Illustrator layers to be converted to Flash layers or to individual Flash files. These are only a few of the many options in the Flash (*.SWF) Format Options dialog box. When you plan to use your artwork on the Web, you should export it as a JPEG if it contains photographic images or continuous tones. You can save your Illustrator document as a PDF, which creates a file that can be opened and read on computers that have Adobe Reader installed. This is a handy way to share your work with someone who may not have Illustrator installed. If you export your file as a Photoshop PSD, you can choose to retain the file's original layer structure, complete with layer names. Finally, the SVG (Scalable Vector Graphics) format is a language for describing two-dimensional graphics in XML.

CREATE A PATTERN

What You'll Do

 In this lesson, you will create a pattern from a simple illustration, add it to the Swatches panel, name it, and then fill an object with it.

Creating Patterns

In Illustrator you can design patterns that can be used to fill objects or that can be applied as outlines for objects. You can design patterns that are simple or complex, abstract or specific, and you can save them for future use and applications. The Swatches panel comes pre-loaded with two patterns—Waves and Polka Dot—which you can modify to create your own versions.

To create a pattern, you first create artwork for the pattern, then drag that artwork into the Swatches panel, where it is automatically defined as a pattern swatch. You can use paths, compound paths, or text in patterns. The following cannot be used as artwork for a pattern: gradients, blends, brush strokes, meshes, bitmap images, graphs, masks, or other patterns.

Designing a Pattern

Patterns repeat. A pattern fills an object by repeating the original pattern, a process called **tiling**. The word is used intentionally as a reference to floor tiles. Illustrator creates pattern fills in much the same way that you would use multiple tiles to cover a floor. Think of the pattern as the floor tile and the object to be filled as the floor.

You design fill patterns by designing one tile. For efficiency with previewing and printing, a pattern tile should be a ½" to 1" square. When saved as a pattern and applied as a fill, the tile will repeat as many times as necessary to fill the object, as shown in Figure 4.

Many times, you will create a pattern that contains no rectangular objects, such as a polka dot pattern, or a pattern of lines. In these cases, you create a **bounding box** to define the perimeter of the pattern tile. Position an unfilled, unstroked rectangular object at the back of the stacking order of the pattern tile. Illustrator will regard this as the bounding box. All of the objects within the bounding box will be repeated as part of the pattern.

The pattern in Figure 5 is composed of lines only. The square is used as a bounding box. It defines the perimeter of the tile, and the pattern is created by repeating only the elements that fall within the bounding box. Again, a bounding box must have no fill and no stroke, it must be a rectangle or a square, and it must be the backmost object of the pattern tile.

Controlling How a Pattern Fills an Object

The way a pattern fills an object is tricky to understand. The pattern begins from the origin of the ruler, which is by default at the bottom-left corner of the artboard. In other words, by default, the pattern begins at the bottom-left of the artboard, not the bottom-left corner of the object.

When an object is filled with a pattern, if you move the object, the pattern changes within the object. If you understand the concept of a clipping mask, the pattern fill is easier to understand. Think of it this way: The pattern covers the *entire* artboard; the object that is filled with the pattern functions like a clipping mask—you can see the pattern only through the object.

FIGURE 4
The tile repeats to fill the object

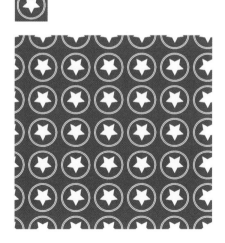

FIGURE 5
Bounding box determines the perimeter of the pattern tile

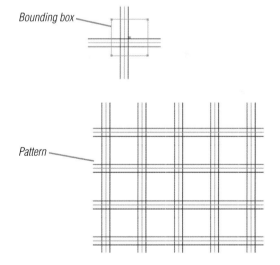

Bounding box

Pattern

The best method for controlling how a pattern appears within an object is to align the ruler origin with the bottom-left corner of the object. To do this, display the rulers, then position your cursor at the top-left corner of the window, where the two rulers meet. The cross hairs are the ruler origin. Drag the cross hairs to the bottom-left corner of the filled object, as shown in Figure 6. Because the ruler origin and the bottom-left corner of the square are the same point, the first tile is positioned evenly in the corner. The pattern fills the object left to right, bottom to top.

Transforming Patterns

When an object is filled with a pattern, you can choose to transform only the object, only the pattern, or both the object and the pattern. For example, the Scale tool dialog box, shown in Figure 7, contains options for determining whether or not the transformation will affect a pattern fill.

QUICKTIP

The options that you choose in one transform tool dialog box will be applied to all transform tool dialog boxes.

When you transform a pattern, all subsequent objects that you create will be filled with the transformed pattern. To return a pattern fill to its nontransformed appearance, fill an object with a different swatch, then reapply the pattern swatch.

FIGURE 6
Aligning the ruler origin with the bottom-left corner of the filled object

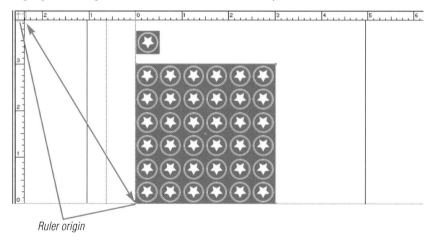

Ruler origin

FIGURE 7
Options for patterns in the Scale dialog box

Scale Strokes & Effects check box

Objects check box

Patterns check box

FIGURE 8
Artwork to be used as a pattern tile

FIGURE 9

Artwork applied as a pattern fill

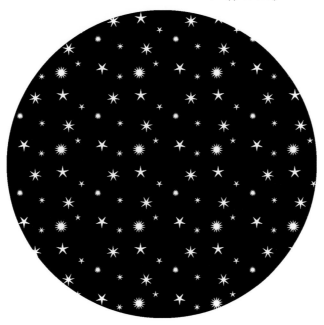

Create a pattern swatch

1. Open AI 6-1.ai, then save it as **Starry Night**.
2. Position the ten stars randomly over the black box.

   | TIP   Enlarge your view of the artboard.
3. Change the fill color of the stars to White.

   Compare your screen to Figure 8.
4. Group the white stars.
5. Select all, then drag the **artwork** into the Swatches panel.

   The Swatches panel automatically identifies and defines the new swatch as a pattern swatch.
6. Double-click the **new swatch** called New Pattern Swatch 1, name it **Starry Night** in the Swatch Options dialog box, then click **OK**.
7. Delete all the artwork on the artboard.
8. Create a circle that is 4" in diameter.
9. Apply the Starry Night swatch to fill the circle.

   | TIP   The Starry Night swatch may have automatically been applied to your circle when you created it because it is still selected on the Swatches panel.

   Your screen should resemble Figure 9.

You created a 1" × 1" collection of objects, selected all of them, then dragged them into the Swatches panel. You named the new pattern swatch, then applied it as a fill for a circle.

Transform pattern-filled objects

1. Select the circle, then double-click the **Scale tool** 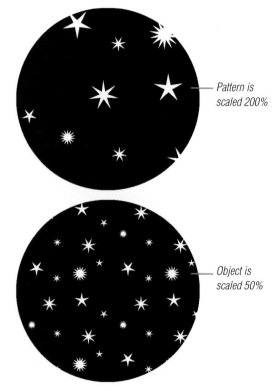.

2. Type **50** in the Scale text box, verify that only the Objects check box is checked in the Options section of the dialog box, then click **OK**.

   The object is scaled 50%; the pattern is not scaled.

3. Drag and drop a copy above the original circle.

4. Double-click the **Scale tool**.

5. Type **200** in the Scale text box, verify that only the Patterns check box is checked, then click **OK**.

   The pattern is scaled 200%; the object is not scaled. Your screen should resemble Figure 10.

6. Save your work, then close the Starry Night document.

You experimented with options for scaling a pattern fill and an object independently using the Scale dialog box.

FIGURE 10
Patterns can be transformed independently of the objects that they fill

Pattern is scaled 200%

Object is scaled 50%

FIGURE 11

Position a bounding box to define a pattern

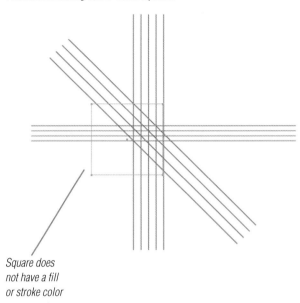

*Square does
not have a fill
or stroke color*

FIGURE 12

A yellow square behind a line pattern

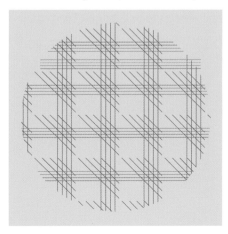

Create a pattern using open paths

1. Open AI 6-2.ai, then save it as **Line Pattern**.

2. Create a 1" square.

3. Position the square over the lines, then remove both the fill and the stroke colors, as shown in Figure 11.

   Note that the rightmost purple line is not within the perimeter of the square.

4. Send the square to the back.

   TIP If you deselect the square, switch to Outline mode so that you can see the outline of the square to select it, then switch back to Preview mode.

5. Select all, then drag the **objects** into the Swatches panel.

6. Hide the objects on the artboard.

7. Create a 4" circle, then fill it with the new pattern.

8. Create a 5" square, fill it with yellow, remove the stroke color if necessary, send it to the back, then position it behind the circle, as shown in Figure 12.

   The yellow square is visible behind the pattern because the pattern is composed of lines only.

9. Save your work, then close the Line Pattern document.

You placed a 1" square with no fill or stroke behind a group of straight paths. You used all the objects to create a pattern swatch, with the square defining the perimeter of the pattern tile. You filled a circle with the pattern, then positioned a yellow square behind the circle, creating the effect of a circle pattern within a square.

DESIGN A REPEATING
PATTERN

What You'll Do

▶ *In this lesson, you will design a visually repetitive pattern. You will then explore options for modifying the pattern after it has been applied as a fill.*

Designing Patterns

Simple patterns can be tricky to design. Understanding how patterns tile is important for achieving a desired effect. You will often be surprised to find that the tile you design does not create the pattern that you had in mind.

In Figure 13, it at first seems logical that the tile on the left could produce the pattern below. However, it requires the more complex tile on the right to produce what appears to be a "simple" pattern.

Another consideration when designing patterns is whether or not you want the pattern to be apparent. If you were designing a plaid pattern, you would by definition want the pattern to be noticed. However, if you were designing artwork for a field of flowers, you might want the pattern to be subtle, if not invisible. An invisible pattern is difficult to create, especially when it's based on a 1" tile!

In every case, precision is important when creating a pattern. If two objects are meant to align, be certain that they do align; don't rely on just your eye. Use dialog boxes to move and transform objects; don't try to do it by hand.

Modifying Patterns

You modify a pattern by editing the artwork in the pattern tile, then replacing the old pattern on the Swatches panel with the new pattern. When you replace the old pattern, any existing objects on the artboard that were filled with the old pattern will automatically update with the new pattern. Of course, you can always leave the original pattern as is and save the edited pattern as a new swatch. This is often a wise move, because you may want to use that original pattern again sometime.

FIGURE 13
Only the top-right tile could create the pattern

This tile could not create the pattern

Note the four quarter circles in each corner

Create a repeating pattern with precision

1. Open AI 6-3.ai, then save it as **Repeating Pattern**.

2. Select the lavender circle, click **Object** on the Application bar, point to **Transform**, then click **Move**.

3. Enter **1** in the Horizontal text box, enter **0** in the Vertical text box, then click **Copy**.

   A copy of the lavender circle is created at the upper-right corner of the square.

4. Select both lavender circles, open the Move dialog box, enter **0** in the Horizontal text box and **-1** in the Vertical text box, then click **Copy**.

   Your screen should resemble Figure 14.

5. Select the blue diamond, then apply the Transform Again command.

   A copy of the blue diamond is created at the bottom edge of the square.

6. Select both blue diamonds, double-click the **Rotate tool** ⟳, enter **90** in the Angle text box, then click **Copy**.

   Your work should resemble Figure 15.

(continued)

FIGURE 14
Work precisely when designing pattern tiles

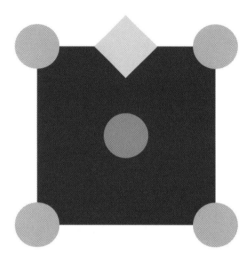

FIGURE 15
Use dialog boxes to make transformations when designing pattern tiles

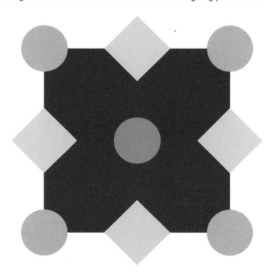

Working with Patterns and Brushes

FIGURE 16
Designing pattern tiles can be tricky work

FIGURE 17
A "simple" pattern

7. Select all, then click the **Divide button** on the Pathfinder panel.

8. Deselect, click the **Direct Selection tool**, click the **artboard**, then delete the areas of the diamonds and circles that are outside the perimeter of the square, so that your design resembles Figure 16.

9. Click the **Selection tool**, select all, drag the **artwork** into the Swatches panel, then name the new pattern **Alpha Shapes**.

10. Delete the artwork on the artboard.

11. Create a 6" × 6" square, fill it with the Alpha Shapes pattern, then center it on the artboard.

12. Compare your screen to Figure 17.

You used the Move command to position multiple objects in a symmetrical pattern over a 1" square. You then used the Divide pathfinder, which allowed you to select and then delete the areas of objects that were positioned outside the square. You dragged the pattern into the Swatches panel. You named the pattern, then created a square with the pattern as its fill.

Modify a pattern

1. Drag the **Alpha Shapes pattern** from the Swatches panel to the scratch area at the upper-right corner of the artboard.

2. Click the **Direct Selection tool** , click the **artboard** to deselect the pattern, then click the **royal blue section** on the pattern.

3. Change the royal blue fill to a purple fill.

4. Switch to the **Selection tool**, then select the entire pattern.

5. Press and hold [**Alt**] (Win) or [**option**] (Mac), then drag the **modified pattern** on top of the Alpha Shapes pattern on the Swatches panel.

   The Alpha Shapes pattern is replaced on the Swatches panel, and the fill of the square is updated, as shown in Figure 18.

   (continued)

FIGURE 18
Changing the background color of the pattern

Working with Patterns and Brushes

FIGURE 19

Updated pattern without the purple background

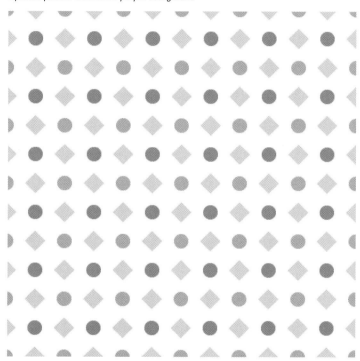

6. Using the Direct Selection tool ![cursor], select all of the pattern pieces in the scratch area, except for the purple section.

7. Press and hold [**Alt**] (Win) or [**option**] (Mac), then drag the **selected objects** on top of the Alpha Shapes swatch on the Swatches panel.

   Your screen should resemble Figure 19.

8. Save and close the Repeating Pattern file.

You dragged the Alpha Shapes pattern swatch out of the Swatches panel and onto the scratch area in order to modify it. You changed a color in the pattern, then replaced the old pattern swatch with the new pattern. The object filled with the original pattern was updated to reflect the changes to the pattern. You modified the pattern again by dragging only parts of it to the Swatches panel.

WORK WITH THE
BRUSHES PANEL

What You'll Do

▶ In this lesson, you will create a calli-graphic brush, a scatter brush, an art brush, and a pattern brush.

Working with the Brushes Panel

The Brushes panel, shown in Figure 20, houses all of the brush artwork that you will work with in Illustrator. The term **brush** refers to any artwork that you can apply to paths or paint with using the Paintbrush tool.

The Brushes panel comes with standard brushes, but you can use your own Illustrator artwork as a brush. For example, you could create a star shape then use it as brush artwork. In that case, you'd be able to paint with the star using the Paintbrush tool, or you could apply the star artwork to an open path or a closed object.

Click the Brushes panel list arrow, point to Open Brush Library, and you'll see a list of pre-loaded brush libraries that you can work with. It is very much worth your time to explore these pre-loaded brushes. Figure 20 shows a number of brush libraries opened and available to be used in artwork.

FIGURE 20
Brushes panel with pre-loaded brush libraries

Working with Patterns and Brushes

The Brushes panel houses four types of brushes:

Calligraphic brushes apply strokes that resemble those drawn with a calligraphic pen. Figure 21 is an example.

Scatter brushes disperse copies of an object along a path, as shown in Figure 22.

You can apply artwork—such as an arrow or a feather—to a path with an art brush.

Art brushes stretch an object along the length of a path, as shown in Figure 23.

Pattern brushes repeat a pattern along a path. Pattern brushes are made with tiles that you create. You can define up to five tiles as components of the pattern: one tile for the side, one for the inner corner, one for the outer corner, and one each for the beginning and ending of the path. Figure 24 shows

five tiles and a pattern that was created with them.

You can create any of the four types of brushes. Artwork for brushes must be composed of simple paths—no gradients, blends, mesh objects, bitmap images, masks, or other brush strokes can be used. Art and pattern brushes cannot include text. You must convert text to outlines before it can be used as artwork for these types of brushes.

FIGURE 21
A calligraphic brush applied to a path

FIGURE 22
A scatter brush applied to a path

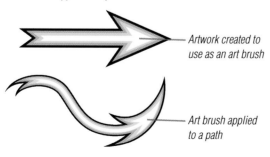

FIGURE 23
An art brush applied to a path

Artwork created to use as an art brush

Art brush applied to a path

FIGURE 24
Five tiles used for a pattern brush

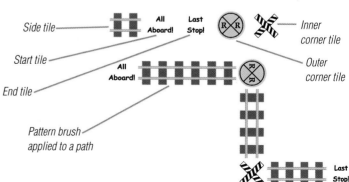

Side tile
Start tile
End tile
Pattern brush applied to a path

Inner corner tile
Outer corner tile

Create a calligraphic brush

1. Open AI 6-4.ai, then save it as **Four Brushes**.

2. Click the **Brushes button** to display the Brushes panel.

3. Click the **Brushes panel list arrow**, then click **New Brush**.

4. Click the **New Calligraphic Brush option button** in the New Brush dialog box, then click **OK**.

5. Type **Twelve Points** in the Name text box, **45** in the Angle text box, and **12** in the Diameter text box, as shown in Figure 25, then click **OK**.

   The Twelve Points brush is added to the calligraphy brush section and is selected on the Brushes panel.

6. Click the **Selection tool** , select the first curved line on the artboard, then click the **Twelve Points brush** on the Brushes panel.

(continued)

FIGURE 25
Calligraphic Brush Options dialog box

Calligraphic Brush Options

Name: Calligraphic Brush 1

OK

Cancel

Name text box

Angle: 0°   Fixed   Variation: 0°

Angle text box

Roundness: 100%   Fixed   Variation: 0%

Diameter: 9 pt   Fixed   Variation: 0 pt

Diameter text box

Using the Paintbrush tool

You can apply any brush on the Brushes panel to any path simply by selecting the path then clicking the brush swatch. Many designers draw a shape with the Pen tool, then apply their brush of choice. Other designers, however, prefer a more "freehand" approach and use the Paintbrush tool. The Paintbrush tool creates paths that are painted with a brush that you preselect on the Brushes panel. In addition to drawing freehand with the tool, you can set options in the tool's dialog box that determine the smoothness of the stroke or the curve and how far the artwork can stray or scatter from the path you draw.

FIGURE 26

Applying a calligraphic brush to paths

7. Double-click the **Twelve Points brush** on the Brushes panel.

8. Click the **Preview check box** in the Calligraphic Brush Options dialog box, change the Roundness to **20%**, then click **OK**.

9. Click **Apply to Strokes** in the Brush Change Alert dialog box.

   The curved line updates to reflect the changes.

10. Apply the Twelve Points brush to the circle, then deselect all.

    Your screen should resemble Figure 26.

You created and set the parameters for a new calligraphic brush, which you applied to a curved path and to a circle.

The Pencil, Smooth, and Path Eraser tools

When drawing paths, be sure to experiment with the Pencil, Smooth, and Path Eraser tools, which are grouped together on the Tools panel. You can draw freehand paths with the Pencil tool and then manipulate them using the Direct Selection tool, the Smooth tool, and the Path Eraser tool. The Smooth tool is used to smooth over line segments that are too bumpy or too sharp. The Path Eraser tool looks and acts just like an eraser found at the end of a traditional pencil; dragging it over a line segment erases that part of the segment from the artboard.

Create a scatter brush

1. Select the star target in the lower-right corner of the artboard, click the **Brushes panel list arrow**, click **New Brush**, click the **New Scatter Brush option button**, then click **OK**.

2. Name the brush **Star Target**, type **20** in the Size text box, type **60** in the Spacing text box, then click **OK**.

   The Star Target brush is selected on the Brushes panel.

3. Hide the star target artwork on the artboard.

4. Apply the Star Target brush to the second curved line, then apply it to the circle.

   | TIP   To remove a brush stroke from a path, select the path, then click the Remove Brush Stroke button ✕ on the Brushes panel.

5. Double-click the **Star Target brush**, change the spacing to **20%**, click **OK**, then click **Apply to Strokes** in the Brush Change Alert dialog box.

6. Save your work, then compare your screen to Figure 27.

You used a group of simple objects as the artwork for a scatter brush, which you applied to a curved path and to a circle.

FIGURE 27
Applying a scatter brush to paths

Working with Patterns and Brushes

FIGURE 28

Applying an art brush to paths

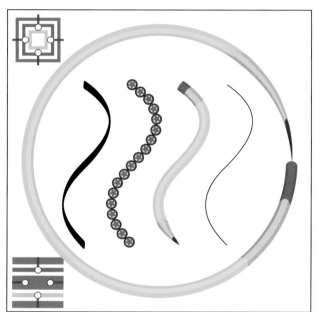

Create an art brush

1. Select the pencil artwork, click the **Brushes panel list arrow**, click **New Brush**, click the **New Art Brush option button**, then click **OK**.

2. Click the **Stroke From Right To Left arrow** in the Art Brush Options dialog box.

   The direction arrow in the preview window updates and points in the same direction as the point of the pencil.

3. Enter **75** in the Width text box, then click **OK**.

   The pencil brush is selected on the Brushes panel.

4. Hide the pencil artwork on the artboard.

5. Apply the pencil brush to the third curved line, then apply it to the circle.

6. Save your work, then compare your screen to Figure 28.

You used an illustration of a pencil as the art for an art brush. You defined the parameters of the art brush—its direction and its size—then applied the brush to a curved path and to a circle.

Create a pattern brush

1. Verify that your Swatches panel is visible.

2. Select the artwork in the lower-left corner of the artboard, drag it into the Swatches panel, then name it **Green Side**.

3. Hide the artwork used for the Green Side swatch on the artboard.

4. Select the artwork in the top-left corner, drag it into the Swatches panel, then name it **Green Corner**.

5. Hide the artwork used for the Green Corner swatch on the artboard.

6. Click the **Brushes panel list arrow**, click **New Brush**, click the **New Pattern Brush option button**, then click **OK**.

7. Name the new brush **Tomato Worm**.

8. Click the **Side Tile box**, then click **Green Side** in the list of patterns.

9. Click the **Outer Corner Tile box**, then click **Green Corner** in the list of patterns, as shown in Figure 29.

10. Type **40** in the Scale text box, then click **OK**.

    The Tomato Worm brush is selected on the Brushes panel.

You dragged the two pieces of artwork into the Swatches panel and named them. You then created a new pattern brush and, in the dialog box, defined the first piece of artwork as the side tile of the brush, and the second as a corner tile.

FIGURE 29
Pattern Brush Options dialog box

Side Tile box

Outer Corner Tile box

List of available patterns

Working with Patterns and Brushes

FIGURE 30
Applying the pattern brush to paths

Modify a pattern brush

1. Apply the Tomato Worm brush to the fourth curved line, then apply it to the square.

   Your screen should resemble Figure 30.

2. Double-click the **Tomato Worm brush** on the Brushes panel.

3. Click the **Start Tile box**, then click **Green Corner** in the list of patterns.

4. Click the **End Tile box**, click **Green Corner** in the list of patterns, click **OK**, then click **Apply to Strokes** in the Brush Change Alert dialog box.

   The curved line now begins and ends with the corner artwork, as shown in Figure 31.

5. Save your work.

6. Close the Four Brushes document.

You applied the pattern brush to a curved path and to a square. You then modified the brush, adding artwork for a start tile and an end tile.

FIGURE 31
Modifying the pattern brush

The curved line
now begins and
ends with the
corner artwork

WORK WITH
SCATTER BRUSHES

What You'll Do

▶ *In this lesson, you will work with scatter brushes, enter fixed and random values in the Scatter Brush Options dialog box, and view how those values affect your artwork.*

Working with Scatter Brushes

The role of brushes in creating artwork is easy to underestimate. Many designers identify them as a method for creating really cool strokes and leave it at that. What they are missing is that brushes can themselves be the best option for creating an illustration.

Of the four types of brushes, the scatter brush best illustrates this point. For example, if you were drawing a pearl necklace, a scatter brush would be your smartest choice for creating the illustration, as opposed to dragging and dropping copies of a single pearl illustration along a path, or creating a blend between two pearls.

Why? The reason is that with the scatter brush, you can manipulate the path endlessly, with precise control of the size, spacing, and rotation of the elements along the path. In addition, you can input a scatter value, which determines how far the objects can be positioned from the path, an option that blending does not offer.

The scatter brush is even more powerful for creating the effect of "randomness." Figure 32 shows a fine example of this effect using a flying beetle as the artwork for the scatter brush. In the Scatter Brush Options dialog box, you can apply a random range for size, spacing, scatter, and rotation and create the effect of a three-dimensional swarm of beetles flying in different directions—some of them closer to you and larger, some of them farther away and smaller.

For each setting in the Brush Options dialog box, you can choose fixed or random values. When you apply random settings to a scatter brush, the positioning of the objects on the path will be different every time you apply the brush.

QUICKTIP
Click the Brush Libraries Menu button on the Brushes panel to display a list of brush libraries. Each brush library opens in a new panel. For example, the Artistic_Watercolor brush library includes 12 watercolor brush styles that offer the look and feel of real water color paint strokes.

FIGURE 32
A swarm of beetles created with a flying beetle scatter brush

Modify a scatter brush

1. Open AI 6-5.ai, then save it as **Random Flies**.

2. Select the circle, then apply the Flying Beetle scatter brush.

3. Double-click the **Flying Beetle brush** on the Brushes panel, click the **Preview check box** to add a check mark (if necessary), then move the Scatter Brush Options dialog box so that you can see as much of the artboard as possible.

4. Click the **Size list arrow**, then click **Fixed**.

   The beetles become the same size.

   > TIP Press [Tab] to see changes made to the artwork after you change a value in the dialog box.

5. Type **50** In the Size text box.

   The beetles are 50% the size of the original flying beetle artwork.

6. Click the **Scatter list arrow**, click **Fixed**, then type **0** in the Scatter text box.

   The beetles are positioned on the path.

7. Click the **Spacing list arrow**, click **Fixed**, then type **50** in the Spacing text box.

   The beetles are evenly spaced along the path.

8. Click the **Rotation list arrow**, click **Fixed**, then type **0** in the Rotation text box, as shown in Figure 33.

   The beetles rotate 360° as they move from the beginning to the end of the path.

   (continued)

FIGURE 33
Scatter Brush Options dialog box

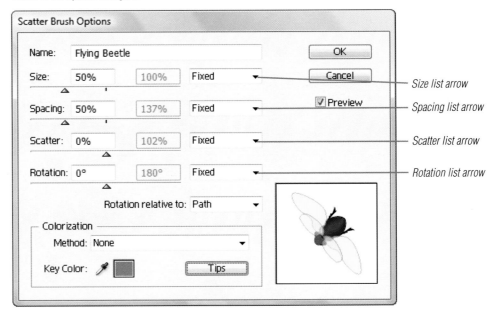

Size list arrow

Spacing list arrow

Scatter list arrow

Rotation list arrow

Working with Patterns and Brushes

FIGURE 34

The Flying Beetle scatter brush, using fixed values

9. Click the **Rotation relative to list arrow**, then click **Page**.

    The beetles no longer rotate along the path.

10. Click the **eyedropper button** 🖋 in the dialog box, then click the **black leg** of the beetle artwork in the preview window of the dialog box.

    The Key Color box turns black.

11. Click the **Method list arrow**, then click **Tints**.

    The beetles are tinted with the new key color. Your work should resemble Figure 34.

12. Click **OK**, then click **Apply to Strokes** in the Brush Change Alert dialog box.

You explored the parameters that define a scatter brush. You started with scatter brush artwork that was random in size, spacing, scatter, and rotation. By removing the parameters that defined the randomness of the artwork, you gained an understanding of how those parameters created the random effects in the original artwork.

Manipulate random values in a scatter brush

1. Double-click the **Flying Beetle brush** on the Brushes panel.

2. Click the **Size list arrow**, click **Random**, then type **20** in the first Size text box and **100** in the second.

   The beetles will be randomly assigned a size anywhere between 20% and 100% of the original artwork.

3. Click the **Spacing list arrow**, click **Random**, then type **50** in the first Spacing text box and **200** in the second, as shown in Figure 35.

   The beetles are spaced randomly along the path within the set range of values.

4. Click the **Scatter list arrow**, click **Random**, then type **-100** in the first Scatter text box and **100** in the second.

   These values define the distance from each side of the path that the artwork can be positioned. In the case of a circular path, the first value determines how far into the circle the artwork can be positioned, and the second value determines how far outside the circle.

   (continued)

FIGURE 35
Scatter Brush Options dialog box

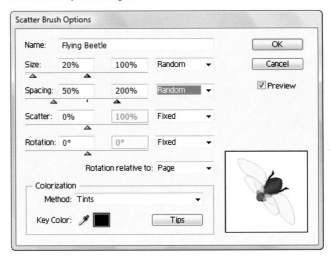

Working with Patterns and Brushes

FIGURE 36
Scatter artwork using random values

5. Click the **Rotation list arrow**, click **Random**, then type **-180** in the first Rotation text box and **180** in the second.

   The artwork can be rotated to any position within a full 360°.

6. Click the **Method list arrow**, click **None**, click **OK**, then click **Apply to Strokes**.

   Figure 36 is an example of this brush setting.

7. Click the **Remove Brush Stroke button** ✕ on the Brushes panel, then reapply the Flying Beetle brush.

   The artwork will be different each time you reapply the brush, because the values are determined randomly with each application.

8. Save and close the Random Flies document.

Starting with symmetrical, evenly spaced scatter brush artwork, you manipulated parameters to create artwork that was random in size, spacing, scatter, and rotation values.

COMPARE THE PAINTBRUSH TOOL TO
THE BLOB BRUSH TOOL

What You'll Do

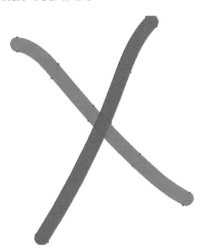

▶ *In this lesson you will make strokes with the Paintbrush tool and the Blob Brush tool and compare and contrast the results.*

Working with the Paintbrush Tool

"Drawing" in Illustrator can be accomplished in many different ways. As you saw earlier in the book, one of the main methods of drawing is to use the Pen tool to draw paths. As you saw earlier in this chapter, you can then apply brush strokes to paths. The Paintbrush tool accomplishes both tasks simultaneously. Working with the Paintbrush tool, you choose a brush from the Brushes panel, then simply "paint" on the artboard. The Paintbrush tool creates a path with the selected brush applied as a stroke. As with any path, you can change the brush style applied to the path at any time.

The main difference between using the Paintbrush tool and the Pen tool to create artwork is largely a measure of control.

The Pen tool offers precision: as you draw, you can manipulate handles and anchor points to draw and position the path exactly where you want it to be and exactly how you want it to look. The Paintbrush tool, on the other hand, offers more of a "freehand" approach to drawing. You can use the Paintbrush tool to sketch out a drawing and create artwork that is more spontaneous and "hand-drawn."

Because both tools produce paths, you can manipulate the paths after you've drawn them. That's a big plus for the Paintbrush tool. Though you might use the tool to create more spontaneous strokes, you can always go back and manipulate anchor points and paths and perfect any paths that you make with the Paintbrush tool.

Comparing the Paintbrush Tool with the Blob Brush Tool

The essential difference between the Paintbrush tool and the Blob Brush tool is that the Paintbrush tool creates a stroked path and the Blob Brush tool creates a closed filled object. Figure 37 shows two simple pieces of artwork: the top piece is made with the Paintbrush tool. The bottom piece is made with the Blob Brush tool. Figure 38 shows the same artwork in Outline mode. Note that the Blob Brush tool created the bottom artwork as a closed, filled object.

Paintbrush tool

Blob Brush tool

Paintbrush tool

Blob Brush tool

Both the Paintbrush tool and the Blob Brush tool paint with color. The Paintbrush tool always creates individual, non-connected paths with every stroke of the tool. The Blob Brush tool behaves differently. With the Blob Brush tool, if you overlap one stroke with a second stroke of the same color, the two strokes will be united as one object. Figure 39 shows a horizontal stroke and a vertical stroke created with the Blob Brush tool. Figure 40 shows the artwork in Outline mode, revealed as one closed object.

FIGURE 39

An "X" created with the Blob Brush tool

FIGURE 40

The "X" revealed as a single object

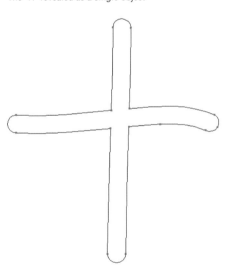

The Blob Brush tool is sensitive to color. Figure 41 shows a pink stroke crossed by a blue stroke, both created by the Blob Brush tool. Note that they are two separate filled objects. Because the second object was created with a different fill color, the Blob Brush tool does not unite the two objects.

This is an important feature of the Blob Brush tool. Let's say you were using the Blob Brush tool to paint a tree against a sky. You wouldn't want the "tree" to unite with the "sky." You'd want to keep them as separate objects. That's exactly what would happen if you painted the sky blue and the tree green: the Blob Brush tool would create them as two separate objects.

FIGURE 41
Two intersecting objects created with the Blob Brush tool

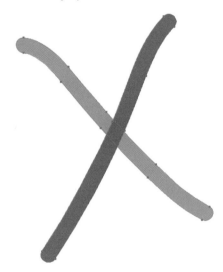

Use the Paintbrush tool

1. Open AI 6-6.ai, then save it as **Brush and Blob**.

2. Zoom in on the top half of the artboard, then click the **Paintbrush tool** ✐ on the Tools panel.

3. Verify that the Fill color is set to None and the Stroke color is set to black, then click the brush on the Brushes panel named **45 pt Oval**.

4. Use the Paintbrush tool to trace the single black dash in the top section.

5. Make two strokes to trace the black "plus" sign.

6. Change the stroke color to red, then trace the red component of the X.

7. Change the stroke color to blue, then trace the blue component of the X.

8. Switch to Outline mode to see the results of your work.

   As shown in Figure 42, the Paintbrush tool created one open path for each stroke.

9. Switch back to Preview mode, then save your work.

You painted strokes with the Paintbrush tool then switched to Outline mode to reveal that the tool creates simple paths.

FIGURE 42
Paths created with the Paintbrush tool

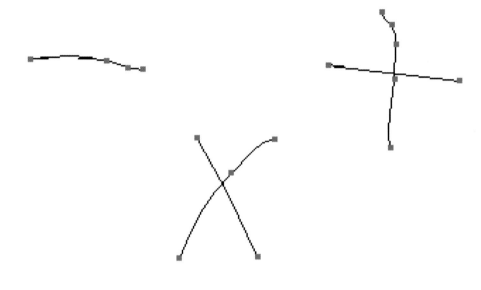

FIGURE 43
Paths created with the Blob Brush tool

1. Zoom in on the bottom half of the artboard, then click the **Blob Brush tool** ☑ on the Tools panel.

2. Verify that the Fill color is set to None and the Stroke color is set to black, then verify that the 45 pt Oval brush on the Brushes panel is selected.

3. Use the Blob Brush tool to trace the single black dash in the bottom section.

4. Make two strokes to trace the black "plus" sign.

5. Change the stroke color to red, then trace the red component of the X.

6. Change the stroke color to blue, then trace the blue component of the X.

7. Click **Object** on the Application bar, then click **Unlock All**.

   The placed image is unlocked and selected.

8. Click **Object** on the Application bar, point to **Hide**, then click **Selection**.

9. Select all, then switch to Outline mode to see the results of your work.

   Your artboard should resemble Figure 43.

10. Switch back to Preview mode, save your work, then close the file.

You painted the same strokes, this time using the Blob Brush tool. Then you switched to Outline mode to compare the results of the Blob Brush tool to that of the Paintbrush tool.

Use the Move command.

1. Create a new 6" × 6" CMYK Color document, then save it as **Polka Dot Pattern**.
2. Create a 2" square, then fill it with a green fill, and remove any stroke if necessary.
3. Create a .25" circle, then fill it with white.
4. Align the circle and the square by their center points. (*Hint*: Select both the circle and the square, then click the Horizontal Align Center button and the Vertical Align Center button on the Align panel.)
5. Deselect all, select the white circle, click Object on the Application bar, point to Transform, then click Move.
6. Type **-.5** in the Horizontal text box, type **.5** in the Vertical text box, then click Copy.
7. Keeping the new circle selected, click Object on the Application bar, point to Transform, then click Move.
8. Type **1** in the Horizontal text box, type **0** in the Vertical text box, then click Copy.

9. Select the two new circles, then move a copy of them 1 inch below by typing **0** in the Horizontal text box, **-1** in the Vertical text box, then clicking Copy.
10. Fill the center circle with any blue swatch that you like.
11. Save your work.

Create a pattern.

1. Select all the artwork, then drag it into the Swatches panel.
2. Name the new swatch **Green Polka Dot**.
3. Delete the artwork on the artboard.
4. Create a 4" square, then fill it with the Green Polka Dot pattern.
5. Double-click the Scale tool, then scale only the pattern 25%.
6. Save your work.

Design a repeating pattern.

1. Hide the 4" square.
2. Drag the Green Polka Dot pattern swatch from the Swatches panel onto the artboard.

3. Deselect the pattern swatch, draw a diagonal 1 point black line from the bottom-left corner to the top-right corner of the green square.
4. Change the stroke color of the line to a shade of green.
5. Deselect, select the line with the Selection tool, then rotate a copy of the line 90°. (*Hint*: Be sure to click the Objects check box in the Rotate dialog box.)
6. Click the Direct Selection tool, select the five circles, then cut them.
7. Click the Selection tool, select the two green lines, then paste in front.
8. Select the green square, click Object on the Application bar, point to Path, click Offset Path, type **-.5** in the Offset text box, then click OK.
9. Cut the new green square, then paste it in back of the blue circle.
10. Select all the artwork, press and hold [Alt] (Win) or [option] (Mac), then drag the artwork on top of the Green Polka Dot swatch to replace the old pattern with the new one.
11. Delete the artwork from the artboard.

12. Show all, then save your work. Your square should resemble Figure 43.
13. Close Polka Dot Pattern.ai.

Work with the Brushes panel.

1. Open AI 6-7.ai, then save it as **Brushes Review**.
2. Select the snowflake artwork on the artboard, click the Brushes panel list arrow, then click New Brush.
3. Click the New Scatter Brush option button, then click OK.
4. Name the new brush **Snowflake**.
5. Set the size to 30%.
6. Set the spacing to 40%, then click OK.
7. Hide the snowflake artwork on the artboard.
8. Create a circle that is 4" in diameter, then apply the Snowflake brush to the circle.
9. Save your work.

Work with scatter brushes.

1. Double-click the Snowflake brush on the Brushes panel.
2. Set all the Scatter and Rotation options to Random.
3. Set the scatter range between 10% and 20%.
4. Set the rotation range between 45° and 25°.
5. Click OK, then click Apply to Strokes.
6. Save your work, deselect all, compare your screen with Figure 44, then close the Brushes Review document.

Compare the Paintbrush tool to the Blob Brush tool.

1. Open AI 6-8.ai, then save it as **Brush Skills**.
2. Click the Paintbrush tool on the Tools panel.
3. Verify that the Fill color is set to None and the Stroke color is set to red, then verify that the 15 pt Round brush on the Brushes panel is selected.
4. Using the Paintbrush tool, make four strokes to trace the left object.
5. Click the Blob Brush tool on the Tools panel, then make four strokes to trace the right object.

6. Click Object on the Application bar, then click Unlock All.
7. Click Object on the Application bar, point to Hide, then click Selection.
8. Select all, then switch to Outline mode to see the results of your work.
9. Switch back to Preview mode, save your work, then close the file.

FIGURE 44
Completed Skills Review, Part 1

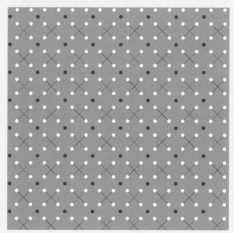

FIGURE 45
Completed Skills Review, Part 2

Working with Patterns and Brushes

You work in the textile industry as a pattern designer. Your boss asks you to design a pattern for a new line of shower curtains. Her only direction is that the pattern must feature triangles and at least eight colors.

1. Create a new 6" × 6" CMYK Color document, then save it as **New Curtain**.
2. Create a 1" square with a blue fill and no stroke.
3. Copy the square, paste in front, then fill the new square with green.
4. Click Object on the Application bar, point to Path, click Add Anchor Points, then click the Delete Anchor Point tool. (*Hint*: The Delete Anchor Point tool is hidden beneath the Pen tool.)
5. Delete the top-left corner, top-right corner, left side, and right side anchor points, so that the square is converted to a triangle.
6. Use the Move command to create a copy of the two shapes to the right, then two copies below, so that, together, the area of the four tiles is 2" × 2".
7. Change the colors in each tile.
8. Scale the four tiles 15%.
9. Make a new pattern swatch out of the four tiles, name it **Triangle Pattern**, then apply the pattern to a 4" square.
10. Save your work, then compare your pattern to Figure 45.
11. Close the New Curtain document.

FIGURE 46
Completed Project Builder 1

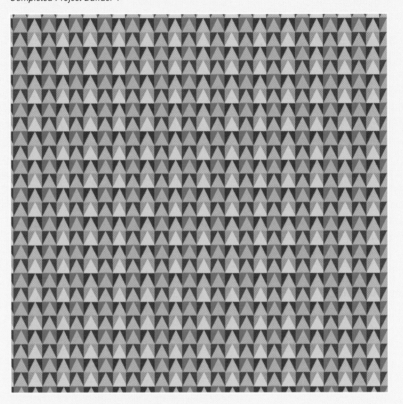

You are a jewelry designer, and you've been hired to create the original design for a new line of necklaces that will be targeted to teenage girls. The necklaces will be made with flat, tinted metals, and you are asked to use bright colors. One catch: Your client tells you that he's "unsure" of what he's looking for and hints that he may make many changes to your design before he's satisfied.

1. Open AI 6-9.ai, then save it as **Jewelry**.
2. Create a new scatter brush with the artwork provided.
3. Name the new brush **Smile**.
4. Set the size to 20%.
5. Set the spacing to 25%.
6. Set the rotation to Random.
7. Set the rotation range from -92° to 92°, make it relative to the page, then click OK.
8. Hide the original artwork.
9. Draw a path resembling the arc of a necklace, then apply the Smile scatter brush to the path.
10. Save your work, then compare your pattern to Figure 46.
11. Close the Jewelry document.

FIGURE 47
Completed Project Builder 2

You own a gallery in Key West called Funky Frames. You are known for designing unusual and festive frames of various sizes. The process of designing the frames is complex, as you use many different kinds of materials. However, they all begin with a brush pattern that you create in Illustrator.

1. Open AI 6-10.ai, then save it as **Funky Frames**.
2. Select the left tile, drag it into the Swatches panel, then name it **Side Tile**.
3. Select the right tile, drag it into the Swatches panel, then name it **Corner Tile**.
4. Hide the artwork on the artboard.
5. Create a new pattern brush.
6. Name the new brush **Funky**.
7. Apply the Side Tile swatch as the side tile and the Corner Tile swatch as the outer corner tile.
8. Set the scale value to 70%, then click OK.
9. Apply the Funky pattern brush as a stroke to a 6" white square.
10. Save your work, then compare your pattern to Figure 47.
11. Close Funky Frames.ai.

FIGURE 48
Completed Design Project

You have been commissioned to design an original plaid pattern, which will be used to produce kilts for the wedding of a famous singer and her Scottish groom. Your only direction is that it must be an original pattern, and it must have at least three colors.

1. Create a new CMYK Color document, then save it as **Wedding Plaid**.
2. Research the history of plaid patterns and their association with specific groups, families, and organizations.
3. Search the Internet for plaid patterns.
4. Research the Burberry pattern, one of the most famous patterns ever created.
5. Create color swatches to compare and choose colors that work together, then design the pattern.
6. Fill a 6" × 6" square with the new pattern.
7. Save your work, then compare your pattern to Figure 48.
8. Close the Wedding Plaid document.

FIGURE 49
Completed Portfolio Project

WORKING WITH DISTORTIONS, GRADIENT MESHES, ENVELOPES, AND BLENDS

1. Edit colors and distort objects

2. Work with gradient meshes

3. Work with envelopes

4. Create blends

chapter 7 WORKING WITH DISTORTIONS, GRADIENT MESHES, ENVELOPES, AND BLENDS

Illustrator software comes programmed with built-in operations—mathematical algorithms—that create specific effects when applied to objects. These include effects, gradient meshes, envelopes, and blends. There are also color editing commands that affect the color of objects and create color blends between objects. Distort effects twist, pucker, and bloat objects, among other operations. The Create Gradient Mesh command produces a multicolored object on which colors can transition smoothly and flow in different directions. Envelopes are objects that you use to distort other objects. Blends create a series of intermediate objects and colors between two or more selected objects.

When you are working with effects, meshes, envelopes, and blends, you are working at the intermediate level in Illustrator. All are challenging—less in learning how to use them than in activating your imagination for ideas of how to *best* use them. Of the four, meshes and blends are the broadest in scope, offering powerful options for adding color, shape, depth, and perspective to an illustration.

Tools You'll Use

Mesh
tool

Blend
tool

EDIT COLORS AND
DISTORT OBJECTS

What You'll Do

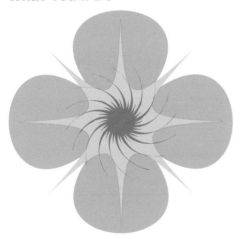

In this lesson, you will explore options for manipulating colors and basic shapes with effects.

Introducing Effects

Illustrator provides a number of effects that you can use to alter the shape of an object. These effects provide simple operations that you can use for a final look or that you can tweak to create a unique effect. Of the many effects that modify shapes, some are essential operations that you will want to have in your skills set.

The Pucker & Bloat effect adjusts the segments between an object's anchor points.

FIGURE 1
Pucker effect applied

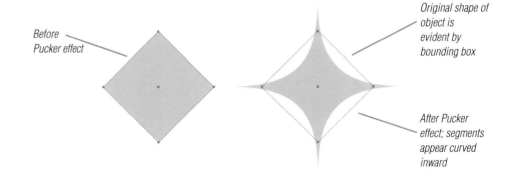

Before Pucker effect

Original shape of object is evident by bounding box

After Pucker effect; segments appear curved inward

With a pucker effect, the segments are moved inward, toward the center of the object, while the anchor points are moved outward, as shown in Figure 1. The bloat effect is achieved by moving the segments outward and the anchor points inward, as shown in Figure 2.

The Twist effect rotates an object more sharply in the center than it does at the edges, creating a whirlpool effect, as shown in Figure 3. With the Twist effect, it's often a good idea to use the Add Anchor Points command to add more anchor points to the object; thus the twist effect will be smoother with more anchor points to work with. The Pucker & Bloat and Twist exercises in this chapter are intended to familiarize you with these types of transformations, which are very useful for designing artwork. In addition, these steps will serve as an introduction to effects.

When you apply the Pucker & Bloat and the Twist commands, they will be applied as **effects**. Effects change only the appearance of the object. Note how in Figures 1, 2 & 3, the selected object does not change, even after the effect has been applied. This is evident by the bounding box.

Effects are controlled on the Appearance panel. You will study effects and the Appearance panel in-depth in Chapter 8. In this chapter, focus more on the Pucker & Bloat and Twist effects from a design perspective and how you might use them in your artwork.

Modifying Color with the Edit Colors Command

The Edit Colors commands on the Edit menu are very useful for quickly applying color changes to objects. With the Edit Colors commands, the changes are applied directly to the objects; they are not effects.

You can saturate an illustration, which makes colors more intense. Conversely, you can reduce the saturation of an illustration, making its colors duller, with a washed-out appearance. Use the Convert to Grayscale command to completely desaturate an illustration and create the effect of a black-and-white image.

You can also use the Edit Colors commands to make color blends between objects. The Blend Front to Back command creates a color blend through all the objects in the stacking order, using the frontmost object as the starting color and the backmost object as the ending color. This command can be very useful for adding the effect of color depth to an illustration.

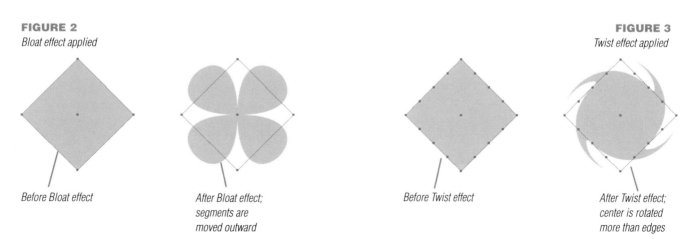

FIGURE 2
Bloat effect applied

Before Bloat effect

After Bloat effect; segments are moved outward

FIGURE 3
Twist effect applied

Before Twist effect

After Twist effect; center is rotated more than edges

Create a front to back blend

1. Open AI 7-1.ai, then save it as **Edit Colors**.
2. Select all, click **Object** on the Application bar, point to **Path**, then click **Outline Stroke**.

   The strokes are converted to closed paths.
3. Deselect, then fill the smallest object with yellow.
4. Select all, click **Edit** on the Application bar, point to **Edit Colors**, then click **Blend Front to Back**.

   A color blend is created from the frontmost to the backmost object in the stacking order. Deselect and your work should resemble Figure 4.

   | TIP   The Blend Front to Back command does not work on open paths.
5. Save your work, then close Edit Colors.ai.

You converted stroked paths to outlines, and then used the Blend Front to Back command to create the effect that the objects lighten as they move from left to right.

FIGURE 4
Blending colors front to back

Managing assets with the Link panel
Whenever you link to or embed artwork from another file - for example a tiff file from Photoshop - that file will be listed on the Links panel along with any metadata that has been saved with the file. The Links panel shows a thumbnail of the artwork and the filename to help you identify the file. The Links panel also uses icons to indicate the artwork's status, for example, whether the link is up to date, whether the file is missing or whether the file has been modified since you placed it. You can use the Links panel to see and manage all linked or embedded artwork. To select and view a linked graphic, select a link and then click the Go To Link button, or choose Go To Link on the Links panel menu. The file will appear centered in the window.

FIGURE 5
Illustration with saturated colors

Saturate and desaturate an illustration

1. Open AI 7-2.ai, then save it as **Saturation**.

2. Select all, click **View** on the Application bar, then click **Hide Edges**.

3. Click **Edit** on the Application bar, point to **Edit Colors**, then click **Saturate**.

4. Click the **Preview check box**, drag the **Intensity slider** all the way to the right, then click **OK**.

   Your work should resemble Figure 5.

5. Click **Edit** on the Application bar, point to **Edit Colors**, then click **Convert to Grayscale**.

   Every object is filled with a shade of gray, as shown in Figure 6.

6. Click **View** on the Application bar, then click **Show Edges**.

7. Deselect all by clicking the artboard.

8. Save your work, then close the Saturation document.

You used the Saturate command to intensify the color of an image. You then used the Convert to Grayscale command to remove all chromatic color from the illustration, thereby creating a black and white illustration.

FIGURE 6
Illustration with the Convert to Grayscale command applied

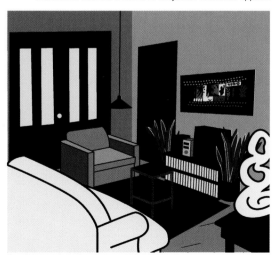

Apply the Pucker & Bloat and Twist effects

1. Open AI 7-3.ai, then save it as **Pucker and Bloat**.

2. Select the large orange square, click **Effect** on the Application bar, point to **Distort & Transform**, then click **Pucker & Bloat**.

3. Type **85** in the text box, then click **OK**.

   | TIP   A positive value produces a bloat effect; a negative value produces a pucker effect.

4. Select the gray circle, click **Object** on the Application bar, point to **Path**, then click **Add Anchor Points**.

5. Click **Effect** on the Application bar, point to **Distort & Transform**, then click **Pucker & Bloat**.

   The Pucker & Bloat dialog box opens with the settings last used.

6. Type **-75**, then click **OK**.

   Your work should resemble Figure 7.

7. Select the blue circle, then apply the Add Anchor Points command twice.

8. Open the Pucker & Bloat dialog box, type **180** in the text box, then click **OK**.

9. Click **Effect** on the Application bar, point to **Distort & Transform**, then click **Twist**.

10. Type **90** in the Angle text box, then click **OK**.

    Deselect and your work should resemble Figure 8.

11. Save your work, then close the Pucker and Bloat document.

You applied the Pucker & Bloat effect in varying degrees to each object, producing three distinctly different effects. You also applied the Twist effect.

FIGURE 7
The orange shape is bloated, the gray is puckered

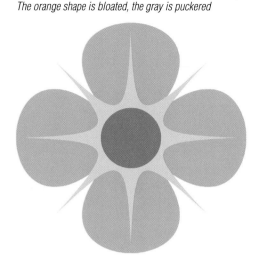

FIGURE 8
The blue circle with added anchor points and the Bloat and Twist effects applied

Bloat

Pucker

Bloat & Twist

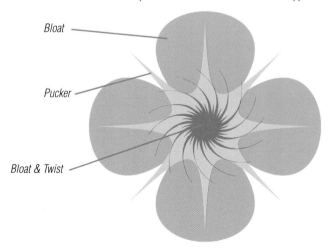

Working with Distortions, Gradient Meshes, Envelopes, and Blends

WORK WITH
GRADIENT MESHES

What You'll Do

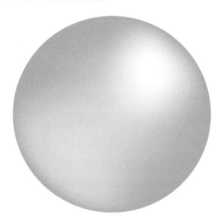

In this lesson, you will create and manipulate a gradient mesh to add dimension to basic shapes.

Working with a Mesh Object

The Mesh tool and the Create Gradient Mesh command can be used to transform a basic object into a mesh object. A **mesh object** is a single, multicolored object in which colors can flow in different directions, and colors transition gradually from point to point. Meshes exceed the ability of simple radial and linear gradients for applying color blends to objects and are very effective for adding contrast and dimension.

When you create a mesh object, multiple **mesh lines** crisscross the object, joined at their intersections by mesh points. **Mesh points** are diamond-shaped and work just like anchor points, with the added functionality of being able to be assigned a color. When you assign a color to a mesh point, the color gradates outward from the point.

The area between four mesh points is a **mesh patch**. You can apply color to all four mesh points simultaneously by applying the color to the patch. Work with this method to apply broad color changes to the object.

Mesh points can be added, deleted, and moved along the mesh line without altering the shape of the mesh.

Anchor points are also part of the mesh, and they function as they do on simple paths. Just as with simple paths, you can manipulate the anchor points' direction lines to alter the shape of the mesh. Figure 9 shows an example of a mesh object.

Creating a Mesh Object

You can create a mesh object from any path. You cannot create a mesh object from compound paths or text objects. You can create a mesh object with the Mesh tool or by applying the Create Gradient Mesh command.

Generally, you'll be happiest using the Create Gradient Mesh command, which creates a mesh object with regularly spaced mesh lines and mesh points. The Create Gradient Mesh dialog box is shown in Figure 10. The Mesh tool adds a mesh point and its intersecting mesh lines where you click. The tool is most effective when you want to add a particular mesh point (say, for a highlight) to an existing mesh.

The Create Gradient Mesh command is always the best choice when converting complex objects.

Once a mesh object has been created, it cannot be converted back into a simple path. Complex mesh objects are a memory drain and may affect your computer's performance. When creating mesh objects, keep in mind that it's better to create a few simple mesh objects than a single complex one.

FIGURE 9
Elements of a mesh object

Mesh line

Mesh point (with red applied)

Mesh patch (with yellow applied)

Direction lines

FIGURE 10
Create Gradient Mesh dialog box

Create Gradient Mesh

Rows: 4   OK

Columns: 4   Cancel

Appearance: Flat ▼   ☐ Preview

Highlight: 100 %

FIGURE 11
Mesh points can be moved, just like anchor points

1. Open AI 7-4.ai, then save it as **Circle Mesh**.
2. Select the circle, click **Object** on the Application bar, then click **Create Gradient Mesh**.
3. Type **2** in the Rows text box and **2** in the Columns text box, then click **OK**.
4. Deselect, then click the **edge of the circle** with the Direct Selection tool ![tool icon].
5. Select the center mesh point, then click a **yellow swatch** on the Swatches panel.
6. Move the center mesh point to the green X, as shown in Figure 11.
7. Move the direction lines at the top, bottom, left, and right of the circle's edge, as shown in Figure 12.

(continued)

FIGURE 12
The shape of the mesh is manipulated by direction lines

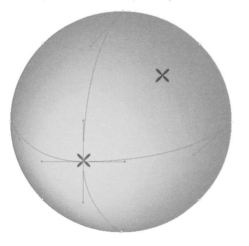

8. Click the **Mesh tool** 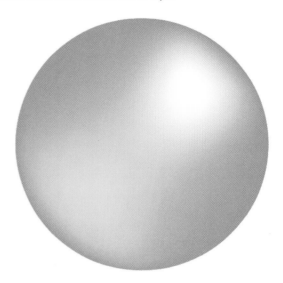, then click the **blue X**.

   TIP Press [Shift] while you click the Mesh tool to add a mesh point without changing to the current fill color.

9. Click the **white swatch** on the Swatches panel to change the color of the mesh point to white.

10. Click the **Selection tool**, deselect, then hide Layer 2.

   Your work should resemble Figure 13.

11. Save your work, then close the Circle Mesh document.

You applied a gradient mesh to a circle with the Create Gradient Mesh command, changed the color of a mesh point, then moved the mesh point. You then used the Mesh tool to expand the mesh. You changed the color of the new mesh point to white to add a highlight to the sphere.

FIGURE 13
Gradient meshes add dimension to an object

FIGURE 14
Selecting a mesh point

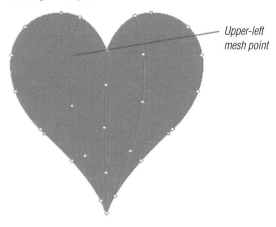

Upper-left
mesh point

Manipulate a gradient mesh

1. Open AI 7-5.ai, then save it as **Heart Mesh**.

2. Select the heart, click **Object** on the Application bar, then click **Create Gradient Mesh**.

3. Type **4** in the Rows text box and **4** in the Columns text box, then click **OK**.

4. Deselect, then click the **edge of the heart** with the Direct Selection tool ▶.

5. Click the **upper-left mesh point**, as shown in Figure 14, then change the mesh point color to 10% black, using the Color panel.

   The new color gradates out from the mesh point.

6. Click the **Mesh tool** ▦ .

7. Press and hold **[Shift]**, then drag the **mesh point** along the mesh path to the left, as shown in Figure 15.

(continued)

FIGURE 15
Mesh points can be moved without changing the shape of the mesh

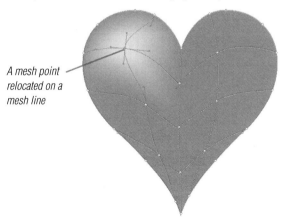

A mesh point
relocated on a
mesh line

8. Repeat Steps 5-7 for the upper-right mesh point, then deselect so that your work resembles Figure 16.

9. Click the **Direct Selection tool** ▶, press and hold **[Shift]**, then select the 20 mesh points and anchor points along the edge of the heart.

> TIP Mesh points appear as diamonds and have the same properties as anchor points, with the added capability of accepting color.

10. Apply a black fill to the selected mesh points.

    The selected anchor points are unaffected. Your work should resemble Figure 17.

11. Deselect, then select the three mesh points at the lower third of the heart, then apply a 60% black fill so that your work resembles Figure 18.

12. Select the mesh point at the center of the heart (between the two 10% black highlights).

13. Apply a 60% black fill, deselect, then compare your work to Figure 19.

14. Save your work, then close the Heart Mesh document.

You applied a gradient mesh to a heart shape, then created highlights by changing the color of two mesh points. Next, you relocated the highlight mesh points without changing the shape of the mesh lines. You then darkened the color of other mesh points to add contrast and dimension to the artwork.

FIGURE 16
The mesh, reconfigured on both sides of the object

FIGURE 17
Selecting mesh points

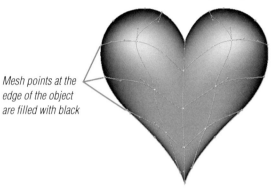

Mesh points at the edge of the object are filled with black

FIGURE 18
Mesh points are like anchor points, with the added functionality of accepting color assignments

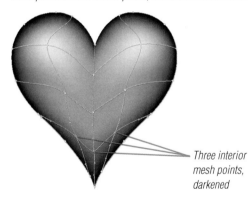

Three interior mesh points, darkened

FIGURE 19
Meshes offer the ability to manipulate gradients precisely

Working with Distortions, Gradient Meshes, Envelopes, and Blends

WORK WITH ENVELOPES

What You'll Do

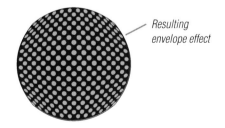

In this lesson, you will create envelope distortions in three ways: using a top object, using a mesh, and using a warp.

Defining Envelopes

Envelopes are objects that are used to distort other selected objects; the distorted objects take on the shape of the envelope object.

Imagine that you have purchased a basketball as a gift, and you want to wrap it with paper that has a polka-dot pattern. If these were objects in Illustrator, the basketball would be the envelope object, and the sheet of wrapping paper would be the object to be distorted. Figure 20 is a good example of what an envelope distortion looks like.

You can make envelopes with objects that you create, or you can use a preset warp shape or a mesh object as an envelope. You can use envelopes with compound paths, text objects, meshes, and blends. Using envelopes, you can add a lot of life to otherwise dull text. For example, you can create wavy text by applying the Wave or the Flag style in the Warp Options dialog box. Powerful effects can be achieved by applying envelopes to linear gradient fills or pattern fills.

FIGURE 20

An envelope created using a top object

Objects to be distorted

Object to be used as an envelope

Resulting envelope effect

Creating Envelopes with Top Objects, Meshes, and Warps

You create an envelope by using the Envelope Distort command on the Object menu. The Envelope Distort command offers you three options for creating an envelope: Make with Warp, Make with Mesh, and Make with Top Object. The top object is the topmost selected object. Warps are simply 15 premade shapes to choose from, to use as your top object. Warps are especially useful when you don't want to draw your own top object. The envelope in Figure 21 was created using the Flag warp. Meshes are the same as gradient meshes made with the Mesh tool. Creating an envelope with a mesh allows you to apply a mesh to multiple objects, which is not the case when you create a mesh using the Create Gradient Mesh command or the Mesh tool. The envelope in Figure 22 was created using a mesh.

Applying Envelopes to Gradient and Pattern Fills

Envelopes can be used to distort objects that have linear gradient fills or pattern fills, but you must first activate the option to do so. In the Envelope Options dialog box, you can check the Distort Linear Gradients or Distort Pattern Fills check box to apply an envelope to either of the fills. Figure 23 shows the options in the Envelope Options dialog box.

FIGURE 21
An envelope created using a warp

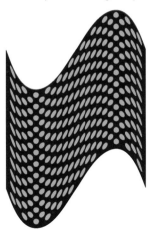

FIGURE 22
An envelope created using a mesh

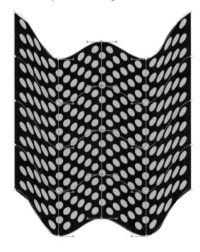

FIGURE 23
Envelope Options dialog box

Select to distort linear gradients

Select to distort pattern fills

Working with Distortions, Gradient Meshes, Envelopes, and Blends

FIGURE 24

A round envelope distorting a flat star pattern

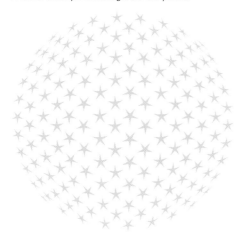

Create an envelope distortion with a top object

1. Open AI 7-6.ai, then save it as **Envelope Top Object**.

2. Copy the yellow circle, paste in front, then hide the copy.

3. Select all, click **Object** on the Application bar, point to **Envelope Distort**, then click **Make with Top Object**.

   Your work should resemble Figure 24.

4. Show all, then fill the yellow circle with the Purple Berry gradient on the Swatches panel.

5. Send the circle to the back, so that your work resembles Figure 25.

6. Save your work, then close the Envelope Top Object document.

You used a circle as the top object in an envelope distortion. Because you cannot apply a fill to the circle after it's been used to make the envelope, you filled a copy of the circle with a gradient, then positioned it behind the distorted objects to achieve the effect.

FIGURE 25

A radial blend enhancing the effect of an envelope distortion

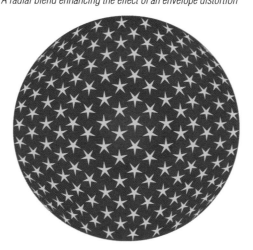

Create an envelope distortion with a mesh

1. Open AI 7-7.ai, then save it as **Envelope Mesh**.

2. Select all, click **Object** on the Application bar, point to **Envelope Distort**, then click **Make with Mesh**.

3. Type **4** in the Rows text box and **4** in the Columns text box, then click **OK**.

   There are five mesh points on each horizontal line.

4. Deselect, then select the second and fourth column of mesh points, using the Direct Selection tool ⬉, as shown in Figure 26.

5. Press and hold **[Shift]**, press ↑ two times, then release [Shift].

   Pressing an arrow key in conjunction with [Shift] moves a selected item ten keyboard increments.

   | TIP   The keyboard increment value can be adjusted in the General Preferences dialog box.

6. Select the middle column of mesh points.

7. Press and hold **[Shift]**, press ↓ two times, deselect, then compare your screen to Figure 27.

8. Save your work, then close the Envelope Mesh document.

You applied an envelope distortion with a mesh to a series of rectangles, then moved the mesh points to create a wave effect.

FIGURE 26
Two columns of mesh points, selected

Select all of the mesh points in the second and fourth columns

FIGURE 27
An envelope distortion created using a mesh

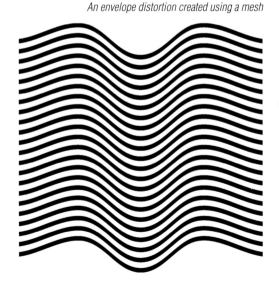

FIGURE 28

An envelope distortion created using a warp

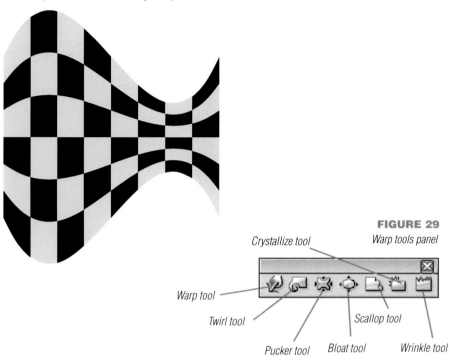

FIGURE 29

Warp tools panel

Crystallize tool

Warp tool

Twirl tool

Scallop tool

Pucker tool   *Bloat tool*   *Wrinkle tool*

Create an envelope distortion with a warp effect

1. Open AI 7-8.ai, then save it as **Envelope Warp**.
2. Select all, click **Object** on the Application bar, point to **Envelope Distort**, then click **Make with Warp**.
3. Click the **Style list arrow**, click **Fish**, then click **OK**.

   Your screen should resemble Figure 28.
4. Undo the distort, then make Layer 2 visible.
5. Select all.

(continued)

Using the Warp tools

The Warp tool, found on the Tools panel, applies a "warp effect" to objects on the artboard. Simply drag the Warp tool over an object and watch it change before your eyes. Objects do not have to be selected before you apply the tool. To adjust the Warp tool settings before you use it, double-click the Warp tool to open the Warp Tool Options dialog box. Hiding behind the Warp tool are six more tools offering you interesting ways to distort your text and graphics. As shown in Figure 29, these tools include Twirl, Pucker, Bloat, Scallop, Crystallize, and Wrinkle. Like the Warp tool, each has its own Options dialog box.

6. Click **Object** on the Application bar, point to **Envelope Distort**, then click **Make with Top Object**.

As shown in Figure 30, you get the same result as you did using the fish-style warp. The reason for this is that using the Envelope Distort feature with a warp is the same as using the feature with a top object—the difference is that warps are pre-made shapes that you can choose, instead of making your own.

7. Save your work, then close the Envelope Warp document.

You applied an envelope distortion with a warp effect—in this case, the Fish warp. You then used an object in the shape of the Fish warp as the top object in a new envelope, with the same result as in the first distortion. Through this comparison, you got a better sense of how Illustrator creates warp effects with envelopes.

FIGURE 30

An envelope distortion using a premade shape

Printing color blends and gradient meshes

Print and prepress professionals have long known that some output devices have trouble printing color blends. The most common problem is banding, an effect in which the transitions of the gradient are visibly harsh rather than smooth. This problem was especially common on early PostScript devices. In addition, gradient meshes (which are a newer feature in Illustrator) may print incorrectly, even on PostScript Level 3 printers. If you are having trouble outputting either color blends or meshes, you can print them as bitmaps instead of vectors. To do so, display the Flattener Preview panel, choose settings on the panel, then save the preset with a descriptive name by clicking the Flattener Preview panel list arrow, then clicking the Save Transparency Flattener Preset. When you are ready to print your document, click File on the Application bar, click Print, click the Advanced category on the left side of the Print dialog box, select the Print as Bitmap check box, choose your named preset from the Preset list arrow, then click Print. Anyone who has experience with printing bitmaps knows that the quality can vary greatly. Use this option only if you are having problems, then decide if the output is acceptable. If not, you may need to go to a professional prepress department to output the file.

CREATE BLENDS

What You'll Do

 In this lesson, you will use blends to manipulate shapes and colors for various effects.

Defining a Blend

A **blend** is a series of intermediate objects and colors between two or more selected objects. If the selected objects differ in color—if they have different fills, for example—the intermediate objects will be filled with intermediate colors. Therefore, in a blend, both shapes and colors are "blended." Figure 31 is an example of a blend using shapes and colors.

Blends are created with either the Blend tool or the Make Blend command. You can make blends between two open paths, such as two different lines. You can make blends between two closed paths, such as a square and a star. You can blend between objects filled with gradients. You can even blend between blends, as shown in Figure 32.

FIGURE 31
In a blend, both shapes and colors are blended

Specifying the Number of Steps in a Blend

The fewer the number of steps in a blend, the more distinct each intermediary object will be. At a greater number of steps, the intermediate objects become indistinguishable from one another, and the blend creates the illusion of being continuous or "smooth."

In the Blend Options dialog box, select from the following options for specifying the number of steps within a blend.

- Specified Steps. Enter a value that determines the number of steps between the start and the end of the blend.
- Specified Distance. Enter a value to determine the distance between the steps in the blend. The distance is measured from the edge of one object to the corresponding edge on the next object.

- Smooth Color. Illustrator determines the number of steps for the blend, calculated to provide the minimum number of steps for a smooth color transition. This is the default option, which poses a bit of a problem in that the minimum number of steps will not always give you the effect you desire, as shown in Figure 33.

FIGURE 32
A blend between blends

Blend #3

Blend #1   Blend #2

FIGURE 33
Sometimes, the Smooth Color option doesn't produce the blend effect you desire

A blend between two similar colors, made with the Smooth Color blend option

A blend between the same two colors, made with 256 specified steps

Manipulating Blends

Once a blend is created, you can change its appearance by making changes to one or more of the original objects. For example, using the Direct Selection tool, you can select one of the original objects, then change its fill color, stroke color, or stroke weight. Illustrator will automatically update the appearance of the steps to reflect newly added attributes, thus changing the appearance of the entire

blend. You can also change a blend by transforming one or more of the original objects, for example by scaling, rotating, or moving them.

You can affect the appearance of a blend by manipulating its spine. When a blend is created, a path is drawn between the starting and ending objects. Illustrator refers to this path as the spine, but it can be manipulated like a path. For example, you can add anchor points to the spine with the

Pen tool, then move them with the Direct Selection tool. The blend is updated when you alter the spine. Figure 34 shows how a blend's spine can be manipulated.

One of the most stunning manipulations of a blend happens when you replace its spine. Draw any path with the Pen tool, then select it along with any blend. Apply the Replace Spine command, and the blend replaces its spine with the new path!

FIGURE 34
Manipulating the blend's spine changes the blend

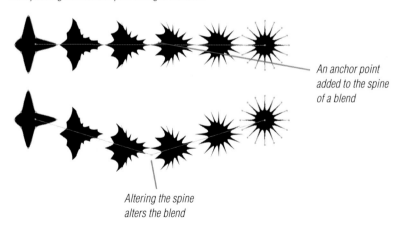

*An anchor point
added to the spine
of a blend*

*Altering the spine
alters the blend*

Create blends between shapes

1. Open AI 7-9.ai, then save it as **Blended Shapes**.

2. Click the **Blend tool** ⬚, click anywhere on the orange square, then click anywhere on the green square.

   | TIP You can click the Blend tool on two or more unselected objects to blend them.

3. Click the **Selection tool** ▶, select the red and blue squares, then double-click the **Blend tool** ⬚.

4. Click the **Spacing list arrow**, click **Specified Steps**, type **5** in the Spacing text box, then click **OK**.

5. Click **Object** on the Application bar, point to **Blend**, then click **Make**.

   Five intermediary squares are created, as shown in Figure 35.

   (continued)

(continued)

FIGURE 35
The red and blue objects blended with five steps

Recording steps as a reusable action

An action is a series of steps and commands that you record and are stored in the Actions panel. Once recorded, those steps are available to you to use over and over again on other objects or files. For example, let's say your work often calls for you to flatten a file, convert it to CMYK then save it as an Illustrator EPS. You can record those steps as an action. Then, in the future, rather than step through every time, simply execute the action in the Actions panel and the process happens automatically. You can even "batch process" an action on multiple files all at once. The Actions panel functions like a tape recorder. Simply click New Action in the Actions panel menu then click the Record button at the bottom of the panel. The Actions panel records the steps you are making. Once you are done, click the Stop Playing/Recording button. All the steps will be listed in the panel under the name you give to the action. Even after you close the file or quit Illustrator, the action remains and will be available when you start the program again.

Working with Distortions, Gradient Meshes, Envelopes, and Blends

FIGURE 36

Blends are very effective for adding dimension to objects

6. Switch to the Selection tool ▶, then deselect the blend.

7. Click the **Blend tool** , then click the **three purple shapes**.

8. Keeping the purple blend selected, click **Object** on the Application bar, point to **Blend**, then click **Blend Options**.

   > TIP You can also access the Blend Options dialog box by double-clicking the Blend tool.

9. Click the **Spacing list arrow**, click **Specified Steps**, type **2** in the Steps text box, then click **OK**.

   The intermediary steps are reduced to two.

10. Deselect the purple blend.

11. Select the Heart view on the View menu.

12. Double-click the **Blend tool** , change the Specified Steps to 256, then click **OK**.

13. Click the **heart**, click the **small pink circle** in the center of the heart, then deselect.

   The 256 intermediary steps blend the heart to the circle in both color and shape. Your screen should resemble Figure 36.

14. Save your work, then close the Blended Shapes document.

You used the Blend tool to create a smooth blend and evenly distributed shapes between two sets of squares. You created a blend between differing shapes, then used the Blend Options dialog box to change the number of steps in the blend. You also used a smooth blend to add dimension to the heart.

Create a clockwise color blend

1. Open AI 7-10.ai, then save it as **Clockwise Blend**.

2. Double-click the **Blend tool** 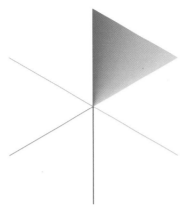, click the **Spacing list arrow**, click **Specified Steps**, type **256** in the Spacing text box, then click **OK**.

3. Click the top of the green line, then click the top of the yellow line to create a blend, as shown in Figure 37.

   TIP   The Blend tool pointer turns black when it is successfully positioned over an anchor point.

4. Click the remaining five lines, ending with the green line, to make five more blends, so that your work resembles Figure 38.

5. Draw a circle over the blend that does not exceed the perimeter of the blend.

6. Select all, click **Object** on the Application bar, point to **Clipping Mask**, then click **Make**.

7. Click the **Selection tool** , deselect, then compare your image to Figure 39.

8. Save your work, then close the Clockwise Blend document.

You created blends among six lines. You specified the number of steps between each pair of paths to be 256, which resulted in a visually uninterrupted blend. You then masked the blend with a circle.

FIGURE 37
A blend between two open paths

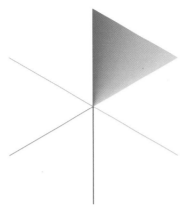

FIGURE 38
This color effect could not be reproduced with a gradient

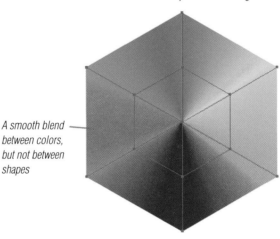

A smooth blend between colors, but not between shapes

FIGURE 39
The blended paths are masked by a circle

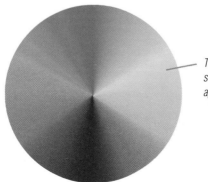

The use of 256 specified steps improves the appearance of the blend

FIGURE 40

Blends can be applied to paths

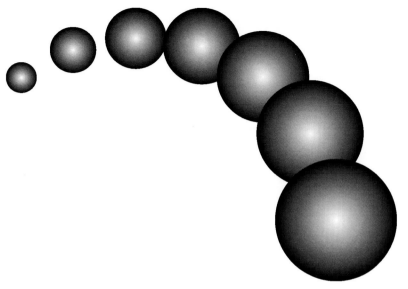

Working with multiple documents

In addition to multiple artboards, you can work with multiple documents open at the same time. When you have multiple documents open, you can have them open as tabbed documents or as individual floating windows. To choose how you would like to view multiple documents, click Edit (Win) or Illustrator (Mac) on the Application bar, point to Preferences, then click User Interface. Add or remove the check mark in the Open Documents As Tabs check box. You can also use the new Arrange Documents menu on the Application bar to manage and view multiple document windows. The Arrange Documents menu includes many options for viewing multiple documents in a single window, such as 2-Up, 3-Up, 4-Up, and 5-Up. You can choose to tile the windows vertically or horizontally, or in a grid. This allows you to move objects across documents. Click Consolidate All button to return all open documents to tabbed documents.

1. Open AI 7-11.ai, then save it as **Blends on a Path**.

2. Click the **blended objects** with the Selection tool ▶.

3. Click **Object** on the Application bar, point to **Blend**, then click **Reverse Front to Back**.

   The stacking order of the blended objects is reversed.

4. Click **Object** on the Application bar, point to **Blend**, then click **Reverse Spine**.

   The order of the objects on the path is reversed.

5. Select all.

6. Click **Object** on the Application bar, point to **Blend**, click **Replace Spine**, then deselect.

   The curved path becomes the new spine for the blend, as shown in Figure 40.

7. Save your work, then close the Blends on a Path document.

You reversed the stacking order of a blend, then reversed its spine. You then replaced the spine with a curved path to create a 3-D effect.

Create color effects with blends

1. Open AI 7-12.ai, then save it as **Chrome**.

2. Double-click the **Blend tool** , then change the number of specified steps to **256**, if necessary.

3. Switch to Outline mode, click the **Selection tool** , then select the five paths at the bottom of the artboard.

   Two of the paths are stroked with white and cannot be seen in Preview mode.

4. Switch to Preview mode, click the **Blend tool** , then, starting from the bottom of the artboard, create a blend between each pair of paths, so that your work resembles Figure 41.

5. Position the text over the blend.

6. Keeping the text selected, click **Object** on the Application bar, point to **Compound Path**, then click **Make**.

7. Select all, click **Object** on the Application bar, point to **Clipping Mask**, then click **Make**.

8. Deselect all, click **Select** on the Application bar, point to **Object**, then click **Clipping Mask**.

9. Apply a 2-point black stroke to the mask.

10. Deselect, save your work, compare your screen to Figure 42, then close the Chrome document.

You created blends between five paths, then masked the blend with text.

FIGURE 41
A simple blend between open paths

CHROME

FIGURE 42
Chrome letters created with a blend and a mask

Edit colors and distort objects.

1. Create a new 6" × 6" CMYK Color document, then save it as **Distort Skills**.
2. Create a 4" circle with a yellow fill and no stroke.
3. Apply the Add Anchor Points command.
4. Apply the Bloat effect at 35%.
5. Apply the Twist effect at 50°.
6. Use the Scale Tool Options dialog box to make a 50% copy of the object.

7. Apply the Transform Again command twice.
8. With the top object still selected, fill it with a dark shade of blue.
9. Select all, then use the Edit Colors command to blend the objects from front to back.
10. Save your work, deselect, compare your illustration with Figure 43, then close the document.

Work with gradient meshes.

1. Open AI 7-13.ai, then save it as **Mesh Skills**.
2. Select the yellow hexagon.
3. Apply the Create Gradient Mesh command with 4 rows and 4 columns.

FIGURE 43
Completed Skills Review

4. Click the Direct Selection tool, deselect the hexagon, then click the edge of it.

5. Select the top row of mesh points, then click orange on the Swatches panel. (*Hint*: Click and drag the Direct Selection tool on the artboard to create a selection box that includes the top row of mesh points.)

6. Select the middle row of mesh points, then click red on the Swatches panel.

7. Select the four mesh patches at the bottom of the hexagon, then click a shade of orange on the Swatches panel. (*Hint*: Select each mesh patch one at a time.)

8. Select the five mesh points at the bottom of the hexagon, then click a shade of red on the Swatches panel.

9. Save your work, deselect, then compare your mesh object with Figure 44.

10. Close the Mesh Skills document.

Work with envelopes.

1. Open AI 7-14.ai, then save it as **Envelope Skills**.

2. Click Object on the Application bar, point to Envelope Distort, then click Envelope Options.

FIGURE 44
Completed Skills Review

3. Verify that there is a check mark in the Distort Pattern Fills check box and in the Distort Appearance check box, then click OK.

4. Position a triangle above the square with the pattern fill. (*Hint*: Click the Polygon tool, click the artboard, type 3 in the Sides text box, then click OK.)

5. Scale the triangle so that it covers most of the square below it, if necessary.

6. Select all, click Object on the Application bar, point to Envelope Distort, then click Make with Top Object.

7. Enlarge the size of the illustration, if you wish to.

8. Save your work, deselect, compare your illustration to Figure 45, then close the Envelope Skills document.

Create blends.

1. Open AI 7-15.ai, then save it as **Star**.

2. Create a 15% copy of the star.

3. Fill the copy with White.

4. Double-click the Blend tool, then change the Specified Steps value to 256 if necessary.

5. Blend the two stars.

6. Save your work, deselect, then compare your illustration to Figure 46.

7. Close the Star document.

FIGURE 45
Completed Skills Review

FIGURE 46
Completed Skills Review

The owner of Tidal Wave Publishing hires your design firm to redesign their logo. She shows you her original logo—a meticulous line drawing of a wave. She explains that the line drawing has been their logo for more than 25 years, and she feels that it's time for something "more contemporary." She cautions you that she doesn't want anything that feels "too artificial" or looks like "cookie-cutter computer graphics."

1. Create a new 6" × 6" document, then save it as **Tidal Wave**.
2. Create an ellipse that is 2.5" wide and 2.25" tall, then fill it with any color and no stroke.
3. Apply the Add Anchor Points command three times.
4. Apply the Pucker & Bloat effect at −80%.
5. Apply the Twist effect at 200°.
6. Deselect, save your work, compare your illustration to Figure 47, then close the Tidal Wave document.

FIGURE 47
Completed Project Builder 1

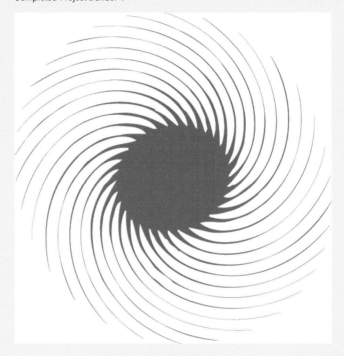

Miltie Berger, a famous journalist from Los Angeles, commissions your design firm to create a logo for her new column, which will be titled "Poison Pen." She explains that it will be a gossip column that will "skewer" all the big names in Hollywood. Refer to Figure 48 as you perform the steps.

1. Open AI 7-16.ai, then save it as **Poison Pen**.
2. Double-click the Blend tool, set the number of specified steps to 40, click OK, then click anywhere on the two white objects on the right side of the artboard to blend them. (*Hint*: They do not need to be selected first.)
3. Deselect, then click the Direct Selection tool.
4. Select only the bottom object of the blend, then change its fill color to Black and its stroke color to White. (*Hint*: Refer to this new object as the "feather" blend.)
5. Click the Selection tool, select the very narrow white curved stroke at the center of the artboard, copy it, paste in front, then hide the copy.
6. Select the white stroke again, click Object on the Application bar, point to Path, then click Outline Stroke.
7. Deselect all, double-click the Blend tool, change the number of steps to 256, then blend the white outlined stroke with the pointy black quill shape that is behind it.

8. Lock the new blend, then show all. The hidden white stroke appears and is selected.
9. Click the Selection tool, press and hold [Shift], then click the "feather" blend to add it to the selection.

10. Click Object on the Application bar, point to Blend, then click Replace Spine.
11. Save your work, compare your illustration with Figure 48, then close the Poison Pen document.

FIGURE 48
Completed Design Project

You create graphics for a video game company. Your assignment for the morning is to create an illustration for a steel cup that will be used to store magical objects in a game.

1. Open AI 7-17.ai, then save it as **Steel Cup**.
2. Select the gray object, then apply the Create Gradient Mesh command using 7 rows and 3 columns.
3. Deselect, then click the edge of the mesh object with the Direct Selection tool.
4. Press and hold [Shift], then click the four vertical mesh points, fourth in the third row from the left edge of the cup.
5. Click the Color panel list arrow, then click Grayscale, if necessary.
6. Make sure the Fill button is active on the Tools panel, then drag the K slider on the Color panel to 20% to lighten the selected mesh points.
7. Select the top right mesh patch and darken it, using the Color panel.
8. Select the mesh points along the left edge and the bottom edge of the "steel cup," then click Black.
9. Continue selecting vertical rows of mesh points and lighten or darken them to create a stainless steel effect. (*Hint*: The mesh points at the bottom edge of the cup should remain black.)
10. Hide the gradient mesh object.

11. Click the edge of the black object with the Direct Selection tool, then select the five horizontal mesh points in the second row from the top.
12. Fill the row of mesh points with White.

FIGURE 49
Completed Design Project

13. Deselect, then show all.
14. Save your work, compare your steel cup with Figure 49, then close the Steel Cup document.

Working with Distortions, Gradient Meshes, Envelopes, and Blends

You own a small design firm in the Caribbean, and you have just been contracted to do a major project for the island of Bellucia, a new nation in the West Indies. Having recently gained independence, Bellucia wants you to consult with their new government on the design of their flag. After the first meeting, you begin working on a composite illustration. Your only direction from the government group is that the flag must be composed of abstract shapes—no words, stars, symbols, etc.

1. Create a new 6" × 6" CMYK Color document, then save it as **Bellucia Flag**.
2. Search the Internet and collect pictures of as many flags from Caribbean nations as you can find.
3. Experiment with different width-to-height ratios in determining the shape of the banner.
4. Garner fabric samples from local merchants and textile designers.
5. Sketch a design, then recreate the design in Illustrator with an envelope distort so that the flag appears to be waving.
6. Save your work, compare your illustration to Figure 50, then close the document.

FIGURE 50
Completed Portfolio Project

ADOBE ILLUSTRATOR CS4

WORKING WITH
TRANSPARENCY, RECOLORING ARTWORK, EFFECTS, AND GRAPHIC STYLES

1. Use the Transparency panel and the Color Picker

2. Recolor Artwork

3. Apply effects to objects

4. Use the Appearance panel

5. Work with graphic styles

WORKING WITH
TRANSPARENCY, RECOLORING ARTWORK, EFFECTS, AND GRAPHIC STYLES

Adobe Illustrator was always—from the get-go—a sophisticated software package. However, if you could compare the first version of Illustrator to the current CS4 version, you would be amazed at how much Illustrator has evolved over the years and the many added upgrades added into this powerhouse application, especially in the areas of color and special effects.

In this chapter, we'll explore four advanced features that you can use to produce effects that would have been unimaginable in the early days of Illustrator: transparency, recoloring artwork, effects, and graphic styles.

The Transparency panel allows you to control the **opacity** of an object—the degree to which it is "see through." The Transparency panel also includes a list of **blending modes** to choose from. Blending modes are fun, preset filters that control how colors blend when two objects overlap.

Recolor Artwork is the umbrella name given to a powerful set of features that allow you to manipulate color dynamically. Recolor Artwork includes the Color Guide panel,

which contains color groups—sets of swatches based on various established color models. You can use the color groups to help you choose colors that work well together, and you can also use them for inspiration when you're choosing colors to work with.

The Recolor Artwork dialog box allows you to take selected artwork and manipulate its color dynamically by dragging various sliders and controls. It is a gigantic step forward and truly takes Illustrator to a whole new level in terms of color control.

Appearance attributes are properties that you apply to an object that affect only the look of the object; its underlying structure is not affected. After you apply an appearance attribute to an object, you can later remove it, leaving the original object—and any other attributes—unaltered. **Effects** are a type of appearance attribute and are listed on the Effect menu. **Graphic styles** are named sets of appearance attributes that are stored on the Graphic Styles panel. Graphic styles can be easily—and consistently—applied to other objects.

Tools You'll Use

USE THE TRANSPARENCY
PANEL AND THE
COLOR PICKER

What You'll Do

▶ *In this lesson, you will use the Transparency panel to change the opacity and blending modes of objects, and you will use the Color Picker to specify a new fill color.*

Understanding Opacity

The term **opacity** derives from the word "opaque," which describes an object that is neither transparent nor translucent, that is not "see through." By default, objects in Illustrator are created with 100% opacity—that is, they are opaque. Whenever one object overlaps another on the artboard, the top object hides all or part of the object behind it. If you were drawing a face behind a veil, clouds in a blue sky, or fish in a tinted goldfish bowl, the ability to affect the opacity of objects would be critical to creating the illustration. Figure 1 shows an example of opacity.

Working with the Transparency Panel

The Transparency panel allows you to control the degree to which an object is transparent. You can change the opacity amount by dragging the Opacity slider in the panel. The Opacity slider works with percentages, with 100% being completely opaque and 0% being completely transparent, or invisible.

Working with Blending Modes

Blending modes are preset filters in the Transparency panel that vary the way that the colors of objects blend with the colors of underlying objects when they overlap them. You cannot determine the amount or intensity of a blending mode; you can simply choose whether or not to apply one. Thus, you will find yourself working with blending modes by trial and error. Blending modes are fun to experiment with. Apply a blending mode—if you like it, keep it. If not, try another.

Of all the blending modes, the most essential is Multiply. The Multiply blending mode makes the top object transparent and blends the colors of the overlapped and overlapping objects in an effect that is similar to overlapping magic markers. Objects that overlap black become black, objects that overlap white retain their original color, and as with magic markers, objects with color darken when they overlap other colors.

Imagine you were drawing a puddle of pink lemonade spilled on a black, white, and yellow tiled floor. You would use the Multiply blending mode on the object you draw to represent the lemonade, as shown in Figure 2. The color of the lemonade would not change where it overlapped the white tiles, because multiplying a color with white produces no change in the color. The lemonade would appear black where it overlapped the black tiles, because any color multiplied with black produces a black result. Where the pink lemonade overlapped the yellow tiles, the area would appear as a dark orange.

Because the Multiply blending mode reproduces real-world color situations, it is important for you to identify it as an essential component of your skills set. Don't forget that it's there!

FIGURE 1

Reducing opacity causes objects to appear translucent

FIGURE 2

Multiply blending mode mimics the effect of overlapping transparent ink, like a magic marker

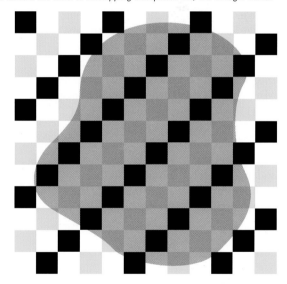

Working with the Color Picker

You use the Color Picker to specify new colors to be used as fills, strokes, or part of effects, such as drop shadows. The easiest way to access the Color Picker is to double-click the Fill or Stroke button on the Tools panel.

In addition to allowing you to choose a new color, the Color Picker offers a valuable opportunity for studying the most fundamental color model, HSB, or Hue, Saturation, and Brightness.

The **hue** is the color itself. Blue, red, orange, and green are all hues. The Color Picker identifies hues based on the concept of a color wheel. Because there are 360 degrees to a circle, the hues on the color wheel are numbered 0–360. This is why you see a small degree symbol beside the H (hue) text box in the Color Picker dialog box. The color wheel is represented in the Color Picker by the vertical color slider. Move the triangles along the color slider and watch the number in the H (hue) text box change to identify the corresponding hue on the color slider.

Does this mean that only 360 colors can be specified in the Color Picker? No, because each hue is modified by its saturation and brightness value.

Saturation refers to the intensity of the hue. A comparison of the colors of a tomato and a cranberry would be a fine illustration of different saturation values. Both have hues that fall within a "red" range. However, the tomato's red is far more intense, or saturated. In the Color Picker, 100% is the highest degree of saturation. A saturation value of 0% means that there is no hue, only a shade of gray. A black-and-white photo, for example, has no saturation value.

The reds of the tomato and cranberry also differ in brightness. The tricky thing about understanding the brightness component of a color is that the term "brightness" is so common that it's difficult to know how it applies specifically to colors. A good example is a room with no windows filled with furniture and artwork. If you flood the room with light, all of the colors of the objects in the room will appear at their most vivid. If you have only a single, dim light source (like a flickering candle), the colors will appear less vivid, and many hues will be indistinguishable from others. If there were no light source whatsoever, no colors would appear, because in the absence of light there is no color.

In the Color Picker, 100% is the highest degree of brightness. A brightness of 0% is always black, regardless of the hue or saturation value specified. Thus, 100% saturation and 100% brightness produce a "pure" hue. Any lesser amount of saturation or brightness is a degradation of the hue.

QUICKTIP

Many effects listed on the Effect menu are available only for documents in the RGB Color mode. If you are working in CMYK Color mode, these effects will be unavailable. If you apply one of these effects, and then convert the document to CMYK Color mode, you will lose the effect. For these reasons, be aware that some effects that you apply in RGB Color mode may be difficult—if not impossible—to print. If you plan to print the illustration, download the file to your printer in RGB Color mode as a test.

The Color Picker, shown in Figure 3, is made up of a large color field. The color field represents the current hue and all of its variations of saturation and brightness. By dragging the circle around in the color field, you can sample different saturation and brightness values of the selected hue. Saturation values lie on the horizontal axis; as you move the circle left to right, the saturation of the color increases from 0% to 100%. Note that the colors along the left edge of the color field are only shades of gray. This is because the colors along the left edge have 0% saturation.

Brightness values lie on the vertical axis. All the colors at the bottom of the field are black (0% brightness). The color's brightness increases as you move up. Thus, the pure hue (100% saturation and 100% brightness) is at the top-right corner of the field.

For a hands-on example of these essential color concepts, you can drag the circle cursor around the color field. As the sampled color changes, you'll see that the H (hue) number remains constant while the S (saturation) and B (brightness) numbers change. You can change the hue by dragging the triangles along the color slider.

FIGURE 3
Color Picker dialog box

Color field

Selected hue

Saturation values range from 0% to 100%

Brightness values range from 0% to 100%

Selected hue

Current color

Drag triangles along color slider to change hue

Color slider

Hexadecimal number

Color Picker

Select Color:

OK

Cancel

Color Swatches

H: 193 °
S: 54 %
B: 56 %

R: 66   C: 76 %
G: 128   M: 37 %
B: 142   Y: 37 %
#: 42808E K: 5 %

Only Web Colors

Change the opacity and blending mode of objects

1. Open AI 8-1.ai, then save it as **Transparency**.

2. Click **Window** on the Application bar, then click **Transparency**.

3. Select both the yellow circle and the letter T.

   The selection appears on the Transparency panel.

4. Click the **Opacity list arrow**, then drag the **Opacity slider** to 50.

5. Select the cyan and magenta circles, click the **Opacity list arrow**, then drag the **Opacity slider** to 20 so that your screen resembles Figure 4.

6. Select the T and the three circles, then change the opacity to 100%.

7. Click the **Blending Mode list arrow**, click **Multiply**, then deselect all so that your screen resembles Figure 5.

8. Save your work, then close the Transparency document.

You explored the results of changing the opacity of objects and the color effects achieved when you applied the Multiply blending mode to overlapping objects.

FIGURE 4
The three circles and the T at reduced opacity

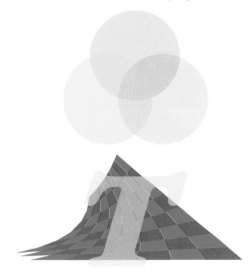

FIGURE 5
Effect of the Multiply blending mode on overlapping objects

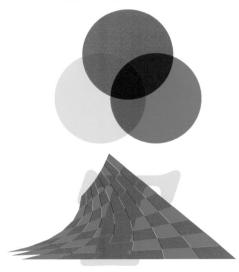

FIGURE 6

Small circle indicates the saturation and brightness values of the selected hue

50% saturation and 50% brightness

The color in this box is the same color as the selected hue inside the circle

---

Applying transparency options to objects

An opacity mask functions like any other masking objects except that you use the opacity mask along with a masking object to alter the transparency of masked artwork. The opacity mask functions as the mask: it's the window through which other objects show. The masking object defines which areas are of the masked object are transparent and the degree of that transparency. You can use any colored object or raster image as the masking object. The masking object appears in the Transparency panel and functions with the same concept as masks do in Photoshop: Where the opacity mask is white, the artwork is fully visible. Where the opacity mask is black, the artwork is hidden. Shades of gray in the mask result in varying degrees of transparency in the artwork.

1. Open AI 8-2.ai, then save it as **Limeade**.
2. Click **File** on the Application bar, point to **Document Color Mode**, then verify that RGB Color is checked.
3. Double-click the **Fill button** on the Tools panel to open the Color Picker.
4. Type **180** in the H (hue) text box.
5. Type **50** in the S text box, then press [**Tab**].

   The circle in the color field moves to 50% of the width of the color field, and the values in the CMYK and RGB text boxes are updated to reflect the change.
6. Type **50** in the B text box, then press [**Tab**].

   The color circle moves down to 50% of the height of the color field, as shown in Figure 6.
7. Type **40** in the R text box, type **255** in the G text box, type **0** in the B text box, then click **OK**.
8. Add the new color to the Swatches panel, name it **Lime Green**, then close the Limeade document.

You used the Color Picker to select a new fill color. You entered specific values for hue, saturation, and brightness, and entered specific values for red, green, and blue. You then added the new color to the Swatches panel.

RECOLOR ARTWORK

What You'll Do

In this lesson, you will manipulate color with color groups and with the Recolor Artwork dialog box.

Recoloring Artwork

To put it simply, the Recolor Artwork dialog box is a giant step for color management in Adobe Illustrator. Why is it so revolutionary? Because it puts to rest the select objects/fill objects paradigm that has been the sole color management procedure since Illustrator 88.

The Recolor Artwork feature uses the Color Guide panel and the Recolor Artwork dialog box as an interface for unprecedented ability to affect color in an entire illustration dynamically—rather than fill objects with various colors, you can now drag sliders and watch the colors in your illustration change *as you drag*.

Recoloring artwork starts with the Color Guide panel, shown in Figure 7. The Color Guide uses Harmony Rules, which are based on color models with complementary colors, to help you select colors for your illustration that work well together.

In Figure 7, note the base color. Whenever you click a swatch on the Swatches panel or a color on the Color panel, that color automatically becomes the base color for the current Harmony Rules in the Color Guide. Figure 8 shows some of the harmony rules available for the red base color.

When you select an object on the artboard then choose a harmony rule in the Color Guide, the selected object does not change color. Instead, the Color Guide loads a group of swatches, called **variations**, based on the harmony rule. These are swatches that you can choose from to colorize your illustration, swatches that all work well together.

FIGURE 7
Color Guide panel

Base color

Figure 9 shows the Color Guide panel with a harmony rule named Analogous 2. Note the variations available. In addition, you can modify any set of variations on the Color Guide panel menu, as shown in Figure 10. Figure 11 shows the same harmony rule and the same base color, but the variations are based on the Show Warm/Cool option.

Assigning Color in the Recolor Artwork Dialog Box

You can access the Recolor Artwork dialog box by clicking the Edit or Apply Colors button on the Color Guide panel. If you do so with art selected, any changes you make in the Recolor Artwork dialog box will affect the selected art.

The Recolor Artwork dialog box functions based on two modes—Assign and Edit. Both have essentially the same effect—they just use different methods to manipulate color. Figure 12 shows the dialog box in Assign mode. When working in Assign mode, you choose a harmony rule, and that harmony rule alters the colors of the selected artwork.

In the figure, a harmony rule named Compound 2 has been loaded. The Current Colors column shows that the selected artwork contains 8 colors—six chromatic colors plus black and white. The New column shows each of the six colors from the Compound 2 harmony rule. It's important to understand that each of the six new colors has been randomly assigned to one of the six current colors. By default, black and white are not affected.

You can at any time reassign the new colors from the harmony rule to different current

FIGURE 8
Harmony Rules available for the red base color

FIGURE 9
Analogous 2 harmony rule and the variations available

FIGURE 10
Color Guide panel menu

colors simply by dragging and dropping them. Figure 13 shows the same set of original colors and the harmony rule. Compare this to Figure 12 to see how the new colors have been reassigned. For example, red is now assigned to the light tan original current color; any object in the illustration filled with the light tan color will now be red.

Your options for manipulating color in the Recolor Artwork dialog box are literally unlimited, and that means that you are not limited to using only the colors in the harmony rule that you selected. Click any of the new colors in the new column, and you can manipulate the sliders at the bottom of the dialog box to change that color to any

color you choose. As you drag the sliders, you will see the color in the illustration change dynamically. Figure 14 shows that the red color in the New column has been changed to lime green.

Editing Color in the Recolor Artwork Dialog Box

As we said in the previous section, Edit and Assign modes in the Recolor Artwork

dialog box essentially provide the same options for manipulating color—they just use different methods. However, whenever you see the Recolor Artwork dialog box demonstrated, it's Edit mode that gets all the attention because it's so visually interesting and easier to understand what's going on.

Figure 15 shows the Recolor Artwork dialog box in Edit Mode. The top illustration of the cat is the original, and the bottom is the selected art being manipulated. (When the Recolor Artwork dialog box is open, selection marks are automatically hidden for selected artwork on the artboard.)

FIGURE 11

Variations modified by the Show Warm/Cool option

FIGURE 12

Recolor Artwork dialog box in Assign mode

Current Colors column

New column

The six circles in the dialog box represent the six colors for the loaded harmony rule, and each corresponds to one of the six chromatic colors in the original artwork. The circles are called **color tools**, and the color tool with the heavy border is the base color for the loaded harmony rule.

The big difference between Edit mode and Assign mode is that Edit mode does not show you a list of your current colors. Instead, when in Edit mode, the illustration on the artboard is your only reference to your current colors and how they're being affected.

In Edit mode, you adjust color by moving the color tools to different positions on the color wheel, and the corresponding colors in the artwork are thus affected. In Figure 16, the base color circle has been repositioned. By default, when you move the base color tool, the other tools move with it. Note the effect on the illustration.

If you click the Unlink harmony colors button, you can move the color tools independently of one another. In addition, you can select any of the color tools, then modify that color with the color sliders at the bottom of the dialog box. In Figure 17, the color tools have been unlinked and repositioned independently. The brightness of each color tool has been increased with the Adjusts brightness slider immediately below the color wheel.

FIGURE 13

Reassigning colors from the chosen harmony rule

New column

Current Colors column

FIGURE 14

Modifying a new color

FIGURE 15

Recolor Artwork dialog box in Edit mode

Edit mode

Reducing an Illustration's Colors in the Recolor Artwork Dialog Box

In most cases, when you select artwork, and then choose a harmony rule in the Recolor Artwork dialog box, the harmony rule will not have the same number of colors as the number of colors in the selected artwork. When the harmony rule contains fewer colors than what is selected in the artwork, the color in the artwork must be reduced to whatever is available in the harmony rule. This is achieved with tints.

For example, if you have six objects with six different colors selected, and you choose a harmony rule that contains only three colors, each of the three colors in the harmony rule creates a second tint version of itself to assign to the three additional colors.

In Figure 18, the six current colors have been reduced to a harmony rule that contains only three colors. Where two colors can use only one color from the harmony rule, a tint is created. Thus, the illustration at the bottom is painted with only three colors—red, yellow, and blue—but the light red, light yellow, and light blue tints effectively maintain the illustration's six-color appearance.

Reducing Artwork to a Two-Color Job

The Recolor Artwork dialog box's ability to reduce color results in the most practical feature that the utility has to offer: the ability to take multi-colored artwork and quickly create a two-color spot color job.

FIGURE 16

Repositioning the base color tool

Color tools

Base color

Unlink harmony colors button

FIGURE 17

Repositioning the color tools independently of one another

Adjust brightness slider

It is very common for a designer to design a piece as a "two-color job" which in most cases is black and a spot color, such as a Pantone color. If you are working with artwork that has already been filled with multiple colors, the Recolor Artwork dialog box can quickly convert those colors to various shades of a spot color that you choose.

Figure 19 shows five current colors all reduced to a single color in the Assign mode. In addition, the red new color has been specified as PANTONE 185, and the black colors in the original are, by default, unaffected. Thus, if this illustration were to be color separated, it would separate into black and six tints of PANTONE 185.

Using Isolation Mode

In addition to locking and unlocking or hiding and showing objects and layers, isolation mode is a feature that helps you to select groups of objects with ease. When you use isolation mode, the selected group appears in full color, while all the remaining objects on the art board are dimmed and unable to be selected. This allows you to access the isolated group without any of the other objects getting in the way.

To work in Isolation mode, select any grouped objects on the artboard and the Isolate selected group button appears on the Control panel. You can click the button to enter Isolation mode, or you can simply double-click the grouped objects. When in Isolation mode, the button changes to Exit isolation mode. Click it to return to the normal view of the art board.

When you are in Isolation mode, the Layers panel displays only the artwork in the isolated sublayer or group. You cannot access any other layers. When you exit isolation mode, the other layers and groups reappear on the Layers panel.

FIGURE 18

Reducing six colors to a three-color harmony rule

FIGURE 19

Reducing six colors to six tints of one spot color

Explore the Color Guide panel

1. Open AI 8-3.indd, then save it as **El Gato**.

2. Click the **Magenta swatch** on the Swatches panel.

3. Click the **Color Guide button** to open the Color Guide panel.

4. Click the **Harmony Rules list arrow**.

   As shown in Figure 20, the Color Guide panel contains a long list of harmony rules, all of them sets of color swatches grouped together based on various established color models.

5. Note that the first color—the leftmost swatch—in all of the Harmony Rules is the magenta swatch that you clicked on the Swatches panel.

   Whenever you click a swatch on the Swatches panel, that swatch automatically becomes the base color on the Color Guide panel. All of the Harmony Rules in the current list use the magenta swatch as the basis for their individual color groupings.

6. Click **Analogous** from the Harmony Rules list so that your Color Guide panel resembles Figure 21.

   The rows of swatches below the Analogous harmony rule are referred to as the **variation grid**. The center column in the variation grid, as shown in Figure 21, contains the same colors from the Analogous harmony rule. The swatches to the left and right of this column are darker and lighter shades, all based on the same Analogous harmony rule.

   (continued)

FIGURE 20
A list of harmony rules in the Color Guide panel

Harmony rules

FIGURE 21
Color Guide panel showing the Analogous harmony rule for the magenta swatch

Analogous harmony rule

Working with Transparency, Recoloring Artwork, Effects, and Graphic Styles

FIGURE 22
Lion illustration painted with swatches from the Analogous harmony rule

FIGURE 23
Base color indicated on the Color Guide panel

Set base color to the
current color button

TIP If the colors on your Color Guide panel differ from the figure, click the Color Guide list arrow then verify that Show Tints/Shades is checked.

7. Apply various swatches from this variation grid to the illustration of the lion.

   Figure 22 shows one example.

8. Click **File** on the Application bar, then click **Revert** to remove the colors that you applied to the illustration.

You explored the Color Guide panel, viewing various harmony rules. You then chose the Analogous harmony rule and applied swatches from that collection to the illustration. You then reverted the file to its original state.

Set a base color and save a color group

1. Verify that the Color Guide panel is showing, verify in the Tools panel that the foreground color is active and in front of the stroke color, then click the **Pure Cyan swatch** on the Swatches panel.

   The Pure Cyan swatch becomes the base color, as indicated by the Set base color to the current color button shown in Figure 23. All the harmony rules are updated to reflect that change.

   TIP Whenever you click a swatch on the Swatches panel or click a color on the Color panel, that color automatically becomes the base color in the Color Guide.

2. Click the **Selection tool** , then click the **orange square** above the illustration.

   (continued)

The harmony rules on the Color Guide panel do not change. However, the orange from the selected item now appears in the Set base color to the current color button on the Color Guide panel.

3. On the Color Guide panel, click the **Set base color to the current color button**, then click the **Harmony Rules list arrow**.

   As shown in Figure 24, the Color Guide panel and all the harmony rules update, with the orange from the selected item now the new base color.

4. Click the **Harmony Rules list arrow** again (if necessary), then click **Analogous 2**.

5. Click the **Save color group to Swatch panel button** ⊡⁺ on the Color Guide panel, then go to the Swatches panel to see the color group.

   Figure 25 shows the color group on the Swatches panel.

6. Use the color group on the Swatches panel to paint the illustration as shown in Figure 26.

7. Save your work, then close El Gato.

You clicked a swatch on the Swatches panel, noting that it automatically became the base color on the Color Guide panel. You then selected an object on the artboard and set it as the base color. You chose a harmony rule and then applied those colors to the illustration.

Use isolation mode to examine groups in an illustration

1. Open AI 8-4.indd, then save it as **Mayan Warrior**.

(continued)

FIGURE 24
Color Guide panel with the new base color

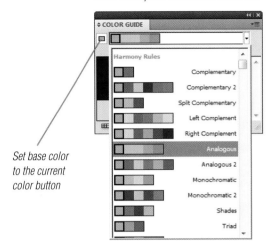

Set base color
to the current
color button

FIGURE 25
Color group on the Swatches panel

New color group

FIGURE 26
Illustration painted with swatches from the new color group

Working with Transparency, Recoloring Artwork, Effects, and Graphic Styles

FIGURE 27

Illustration in isolation mode

2. Verify that the Control panel is visible.

   The illustration features five colors plus black and white.

3. Click the **Selection tool** , then click one of the turquoise blue "jewels."

   All of the jewels are selected because they are grouped.

4. Click the **Isolate Selected Object button** on the Control panel.

   As shown in Figure 27, the selected group remains visible, but the selection marks disappear. All of the other non-selected objects in the illustration are dimmed. Note that the jewels are the only objects in the illustration painted blue.

5. Click any of the dimmed objects in the illustration.

   In isolation mode, dimmed objects cannot be selected.

6. Click any one of the blue jewels.

   Only one jewel is selected. In isolation mode, grouped objects are selected individually—even with the Selection tool.

7. Click the **Exit Isolation Mode button** on the Control panel.

8. Click **Edit** (Win) or **Illustrator** (Mac) on the Application bar, point to **Preferences**, then click **General**.

9. Verify that the Double Click To Isolate check box is checked, then click **OK**.

10. Double-click the **headdress**.

    Double-clicking isolates the group in isolation mode. The headdress and the eyelid are painted dark brown.

(continued)

11. Click the **Exit Isolation Mode button** ⬚ on the Control panel, then double-click the **gold wristband**.

    Gold is the third color you have viewed in isolation mode.

12. Click the **Exit Isolation Mode button** ⬚ on the Control panel, then double-click the **gray belt**.

    Gray is the fourth color you have viewed in isolation mode.

13. Click the **Exit Isolation Mode button** ⬚ on the Control panel, then double-click the **face**.

    The group is shown in isolation mode. Tan is the fifth color you have viewed in isolation mode.

14. Click the **Exit Isolation Mode button** ⬚ on the Control panel.

You used the isolation mode feature to view five groups in an illustration and to get a clear sense of the colors in the illustration and which objects are painted with which colors.

Assign colors with the Recolor Artwork dialog box

1. Click the **tan face object**, then click the **Set base color to the current color button** ▣ on the Color Guide panel.

2. Select all, click the **Edit or Apply Colors button** ⬯ on the Color Guide panel, click the **Edit button** at the top of the Recolor Artwork dialog box, then compare your screen to Figure 28.

    Note that the selection marks on the art are automatically hidden. Note too that, because

    (continued)

FIGURE 28
Recolor Artwork dialog box

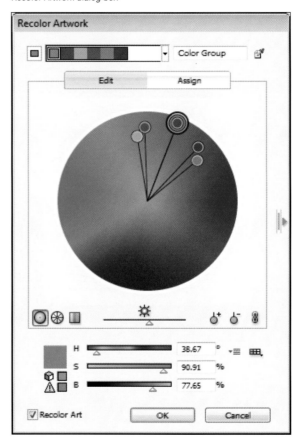

you had selected art when you clicked the Edit or Apply Colors button, the Recolor Art check box is automatically checked.

> TIP Depending on the last settings you chose, the dialog box may show different colors from what you see in the figure.

3. Click the **Assign button** so that the Recolor Artwork dialog box is in Assign mode.

4. Click the **Harmony Rules list arrow**, then experiment with different harmony rules, noting how each affects the art.

5. Click the **Pentagram harmony rule** from the list, then compare your art and your Recolor Artwork dialog box to Figure 29.

Like the illustration itself, the Pentagram harmony rule has five colors. In the Recolor Artwork dialog box, the list of colors on the left —five colors plus black and white— represent the original colors used in the illustration. The smaller color squares to the right represent the new colors assigned with the Pentagram harmony rule. Because we chose a five color harmony rule, the relationship between the original and the new colors is 1 to 1. For example, the turquoise used to paint the jewelry has now been changed to navy blue, and the original gray on the belt and the paddle have now changed to red.

6. Click and drag the **red color box** in the New column up and release it on top of the purple color box.

The swap is reflected in the art—the jewels are now red, and the belt and paddle are now purple.

(continued)

FIGURE 29

Pentagram harmony rule applied to the artwork

7. Double-click the **green color box** in the New column.

The Color Picker opens.

8. Type **237**, **184**, and **107** in the R, G, and B text boxes, respectively, then click **OK**.

The dialog box and the artwork are updated with the change.

9. Click the **purple color box** one time to select it, drag the **hue slider** at the bottom of the dialog box to 29° then compare your artwork and your Recolor Artwork dialog box to Figure 30.

10. Click the **New Color Group button** ◻⁺ at the top of the dialog box.

The new color group is saved. You may need to expand the dialog box to see the New Color Group button. Note that this saved group is not the Pentagram harmony rule that you first selected. The saved group is the Pentagram harmony rule with all of the edits that you made to it.

11. Click **OK**, deselect, then save your work.

You used the Assign mode of the Recolor Artwork dialog box to assign a harmony rule to an illustration, then you modified the new colors in the Recolor Artwork document to control how they affected the artwork.

Edit colors with the Recolor Artwork dialog box

1. Select all, then click the **Edit or Apply Colors button** 🎨 on the Color Guide panel.

(continued)

FIGURE 30

Illustration with new colors assigned in the Recolor Artwork dialog box

FIGURE 31

Recolor Artwork dialog box in Edit mode

FIGURE 32

Positioning the base color tool

Base color tool

FIGURE 33

The result of moving the base color

2. Verify that the Assign button is active, click the **Harmony Rules list arrow**, then click **Pentagram**.

   This is the same harmony rule that you applied in the previous lesson; the color in the artwork is updated.

3. Click the **Edit button**, then look at Figure 31.

   In Edit mode, the Recolor Artwork dialog box shows you harmony rules in relation to a color wheel. In Figure 31, note how the Pentagram harmony rule has five points on the color wheel, all of them equidistant from one another—just like a pentagram. Each of the five points corresponds to a color in the illustration; the color tool with the heavy circle is the base color of the active harmony rule.

4. Click and drag the **base color tool** to the position shown in Figure 32.

   All of the colors in the illustration change dynamically with the movements in the dialog box. When you move the base color tool, the other color tools move with it, thus maintaining the original relationship established by the Pentagram harmony rule. The illustration in Figure 33 shows the result of the move; by definition, the new colors are all in mathematical harmony with one another, despite the change.

5. Click and drag the **base color tool** halfway to the center of the color wheel.

   All the color tools move with the base color tool. The color in the illustration is desaturated, because in a color wheel, colors with the highest saturation are at the outside of the wheel.

   (continued)

Lesson 2   Recolor Artwork

6. Click and drag the **Brightness slider** to 50, then compare your dialog box and illustration to Figure 34.

7. Click and drag the **Brightness slider** to 100.

8. Drag the **base color tool** back to the outside of the color wheel.

9. With the base color tool still selected, type **0**, **100**, and **100** in the H, S, and B dialog boxes, respectively.

10. Experiment with various hues by dragging the **H slider** to various locations.

    Dragging the Hue slider with the base color tool selected is the same as dragging the base color tool by hand—all of the color tools move with the base color tool and the relationships are maintained.

11. Drag the **H slider** back to 0, then click the **Unlink harmony colors button** 🗗.

    The solid lines connecting the color tools become dotted, representing that the colors are no longer linked.

12. Click the **top (gold) color tool**, drag it to the location shown in Figure 35, then note the effect on the illustration.

    Only the "skin" group is affected, because the color tool you moved represents that group in the illustration.

13. Drag the **B slider** to 80%.

    Only the "skin" group is affected.

14. Click the **Display segmented color wheel button** ⊕, then drag the **green "headdress" color tool** to the location shown in Figure 36.

(continued)

FIGURE 34
Adjusting the brightness

Brightness slider

FIGURE 35
New location of the gold color tool

FIGURE 36
New location of the green color tool

Working with Transparency, Recoloring Artwork, Effects, and Graphic Styles

FIGURE 37

New location of the red and navy blue color tools

FIGURE 38

Result of adjusting the hue of the green color tool

FIGURE 39

Viewing the Test harmony rule

FIGURE 40

New location of dark green

15. Drag the **red base color tool** to the same location on the opposite side of the color wheel, then drag the **navy blue color tool** to the bright yellow segment, as shown in Figure 37.

16. Click the **Link harmony colors button** ✵, click the **green color tool** to select it, type **72** in the Hue slider text box, press **[Tab]**, then compare your illustration to Figure 38.

17. Click the **Show color group storage button** to expose the right side of the dialog box, then click the **New Color Group button** ⊡⁺.

18. Click **OK**, save your work, then close the file.

You edited the colors in the illustration using the Recolor Artwork dialog box.

Reduce colors in the Recolor Artwork dialog box

1. Open AI 8-5.ai, then save it as **2-Color Job**.

2. Select all, click the **Edit or Apply Colors button** 🔘 on the Color Guide panel, then click the **Assign button**.

3. Click **Test** in the Color Groups section, then compare your dialog box to Figure 39.

   The five original colors in the illustration correspond to each of the five colors in the Test harmony rule.

   TIP This step is not necessary for reducing colors—you did this only so that your illustration and dialog box are working with the same colors shown in Figure 39.

4. Click the **Hide color group storage button** ◁.

5. Click and drag the **fifth color** in the list— dark green—on top of the first color in the list so that your dialog box resembles Figure 40.

(continued)

6. Click and drag the remaining three colors up to the top of the list so that your dialog box resembles Figure 41.

7. Compare your illustration to Figure 42.

All five original colors in the illustration have been replaced by tints of the base color of the Test harmony group. The black border lines and white eye remain untouched.

8. Click the **Limits the color group to colors in a swatch library button** ▦ , point to **Color Books**, then click **PANTONE solid coated**.

Colors in the color group can now be only those found in the PANTONE solid coated swatch library.

9. Double-click the **tan color box** in the New column to the right of the five combined colors, click **PANTONE Blue 072 C**, then click **OK**.

10. Click **OK** to close the Recolor Artwork dialog box, save changes when prompted, then compare your illustration to Figure 43.

The five colors in the illustration are now all tints of PANTONE Blue 072 C. However, the tints are all very similar, making it difficult to distinguish various objects in the illustration.

(continued)

FIGURE 41
Result of dragging the remaining three colors

FIGURE 42
Illustration with tints of the base color

FIGURE 43
Illustration with tints of PANTONE Blue 072 C

Working with Transparency, Recoloring Artwork, Effects, and Graphic Styles

FIGURE 44
Final illustration

11. Click the **Color button** to display the Color panel.

12. Deselect all, click the **Selection tool**, click the **face** (skin group), then note that the group is filled with an 80% tint of PANTONE Blue 072 C.

13. Drag the **slider** to 10%.

14. Using this method, use the Color panel to distinguish the various objects in the illustration with tints of PANTONE Blue 072 C.

    Figure 44 shows one outcome.

    | TIP Feel free to use the Direct Selection tool and colorize objects in groups with different tips.

15. Save your work, then close 2-Color Job.

    This illustration will color separate into Black and PANTONE Blue 072 C.

You reduced the number of colors used in the illustration using the Recolor Artwork dialog box.

Using the Keyboard Shortcuts dialog box

Shortcuts are keyboard commands and combinations you use rather than clicking menu items to allow you to work faster. Illustrator lets you view a list of all shortcuts, and edit or create shortcuts. The Keyboard Shortcuts dialog box works like a shortcut editor; it includes all commands that can be accessed with a keyboard shortcut.

You can define your own sets of shortcuts, change individual shortcuts within a set, and switch between sets of shortcuts. To do so, follow the following steps: Click Edit on the Application bar, then click Keyboard Shortcuts. Choose a set of shortcuts from the Set menu at the top of the Keyboard Shortcuts dialog box.

Choose to modify either Menu Commands or Tools from the menu at the top of the dialog box. To activate the set of shortcuts, click OK.

To change a shortcut, click in the Shortcut column of the scroll list and type a new shortcut.

APPLY EFFECTS
TO OBJECTS

What You'll Do

▶ *In this lesson, you will work with a series of useful effects, using the Effect menu.*

Working with Effects

The commands listed on the Effect menu can be applied to objects to alter their appearance without altering the object itself. You can apply effects that distort, transform, outline, and offset a path—among other effects—without changing the original size, anchor points, and shape of the object. The object in Figure 45 is a simple square with a number of effects applied to it, creating the appearance of a complex illustration.

So what is the point of working with effects? The best answer is that working with effects offers you the ability to change your mind and change your work at any point, because each effect can be easily removed from an object without disturbing other effects that may be applied to it.

Many effect dialog boxes include a color box that, when clicked, opens up the Color Picker dialog box, or simply the Color

Picker. Of all the ways to choose colors in Illustrator, using the Color Picker is the most sophisticated. In this dialog box, you can specify colors numerically as CMYK, RGB, HSB, or hexadecimal (a numbering system based on 16). You can also access the

Color Picker by double-clicking the Fill or Stroke buttons on the Tools panel.

When you work with effects, all of your actions are recorded and listed on the Appearance panel. You can, at any time,

select an effect on the panel and modify its settings or delete it.

The Appearance panel also provides a useful record of what you've done to create an illustration.

FIGURE 45
One square with multiple effects applied

Apply a Bloat effect

1. Open the Limeade document that you started working on in Lesson 1.

2. Click **Window** on the Application bar, then click **Appearance**.

3. Click the **Selection tool** , then click each letter object in LIMEADE so that they are all selected.

   The Appearance panel displays a new entry called Mixed Objects, meaning that mixed objects are selected. The A and the D are compound paths, while the remaining letters are regular closed paths.

4. Click **Effect** on the Application bar, point to **Distort & Transform** in the Illustrator Effects section, then click **Pucker & Bloat**.

5. Type **11** in the text box, then click **OK**.

   The Pucker & Bloat item is listed on the Appearance panel.

6. Compare your image to Figure 46.

   The selection marks represent those of the letters *before* the Bloat effect was applied, reflecting the fact that the original objects have not been actually changed by the effect.

You applied a Bloat effect to letter objects. You noted that the effect was listed on the Appearance panel and that the selection marks of the object did not change as a result of the applied effect.

FIGURE 46
Pucker & Bloat effect applied to letter objects

Selection marks show that the original objects have not been changed by the Bloat effect

FIGURE 47

Inner Glow effect affects the black stroke

FIGURE 48

Inflate Warp effect

Apply an Inner Glow and a Warp effect

1. Fill the LIMEADE letter objects with Lime Green.

2. Click **Effect** on the Application bar, point to **Stylize** in the Illustrator Effects section, then click **Inner Glow**.

3. Verify that Mode is set to Screen, that Opacity is set to 75%, that the Edge option button is selected, then type **.15** in the Blur text box.

   TIP If your dialog box does not show inches, type **.15 in** in the Blur text box.

4. Click the **color box** next to the Mode list arrow to open the Color Picker.

5. Type **10** in the C text box, **0** in the M text box, **100** in the Y text box, and **0** in the K text box, then click **OK**.

6. Click **OK** again to close the Inner Glow dialog box.

7. Click the **Stroke button** on the Tools panel, click **Black** on the Swatches panel, then on the Stroke panel, click the **Weight list arrow**, then click **3 pt** so that your work resembles Figure 47.

   The stroke does not appear black because the Inner Glow effect is altering its appearance.

8. Click **Effect** on the Application bar, point to **Warp** in the Illustrator Effects section, then click **Inflate**.

9. Type **30** in the Bend text box.

10. Type **-30** in the Horizontal text box, click **OK**, then hide the selection marks.

    Your work should resemble Figure 48.

You applied the Inner Glow effect to the letter objects, increased the Blur value, then specified the color of the glow, using the Color Picker. You applied a 3-pt Black stroke, creating an interesting effect in conjunction with the Inner Glow effect. You then applied the Inflate Warp effect.

Apply a Drop Shadow effect

1. Show the selection marks of the LIMEADE letter objects.

2. Click **Effect** on the Application bar, point to **Stylize** in the Illustrator Effects section, then click **Drop Shadow**.

3. Click the **Mode list arrow**, then click **Normal**.

4. Click the **Opacity list arrow**, then drag the **Opacity slider** to 100.

5. Verify that the X and Y Offset text boxes are both set to 0.1 in and that Blur is set to 0.07 in.

6. Click the **Color option button**, then click the **color box** to open the Color Picker.

7. Type **240** in the H text box, type **100** in the S and B text boxes, then click **OK**.

   The new color appears in the color box in the Drop Shadow dialog box.

8. Click **OK** to close the Drop Shadow dialog box.

   The Drop Shadow effect is listed on the Appearance panel.

9. Compare your screen to Figure 49.

You applied the Drop Shadow effect, using the Normal blending mode. You also accessed the Color Picker from within the Drop Shadow dialog box to determine the color of the shadow.

FIGURE 49
Drop Shadow effect with a Normal blending mode

Normal blending mode produces an opaque drop shadow

FIGURE 50
Grain effect, isolated on its own layer

FIGURE 51
Grain effect, multiplied at 25% opacity

Apply a Grain effect

1. Verify that the LIMEADE letter objects are still selected, copy them, then paste in front.

2. Verify that the Layers panel is displayed, create a new layer, then move the selected art to the new layer.

   TIP Move the selected art by dragging the Indicates Selected Art button on Layer 1 to the new layer.

3. Click **Effect** on the Application bar, point to **Texture** in the Photoshop Effects section, then click **Grain**.

4. Verify that the Grain Type is set to Regular, type **71** in the Intensity text box, type **61** in the Contrast text box, then click **OK**.

5. Click the **Toggles Visibility button** 👁 on Layer 1 to hide Layer 1 so that you can see the results of the effect on Layer 2, as shown in Figure 50, then click the **Toggles Visibility button** ☐ again to show the layer.

   Note that the drop shadow areas were included when the Grain effect was applied.

6. Click the **Opacity list arrow** on the Transparency panel, then drag the **Opacity slider** to 25.

   TIP When you change the opacity of a layer, all objects on the layer are affected.

7. Click the **Blending Mode list arrow**, then click **Multiply**.

8. Deselect, save your work, then compare your screen to Figure 51.

You viewed LIMEADE on a new layer to view the Grain effect independently. You changed the opacity of the copied letters, then changed the blending mode to Multiply, allowing the original letters to be seen through the effect.

USE THE
APPEARANCE PANEL

What You'll Do

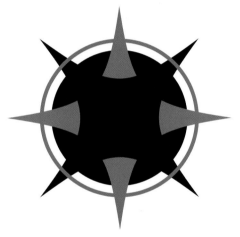

In this lesson, you will explore the role of the Appearance panel in controlling the appearance attributes of objects.

Working with the Appearance Panel

The Appearance panel does far more than simply list appearance attributes. It is the gateway for controlling and manipulating all of the appearance attributes of your artwork. The Appearance panel, as shown in Figure 52, shows you the fills, strokes, and effects that have been applied to your artwork and offers you the ability to manipulate those attributes.

When you select an object on the artboard, the Appearance panel lists the associated attributes. Fills and strokes are listed according to their stacking order (front to back), and effects are listed in the order in which they are applied. You can double-click an effect on the Appearance panel to open the effect's dialog box, which will show the settings you used to apply the effect. This is an extremely valuable function of the panel. Imagine opening an illustration after six months and trying to remember how you built it! The Appearance panel provides a trail.

When you have applied a set of effects to an object, and you then draw a new object, you can use the Appearance panel to decide whether or not the new object is created with the effects you've been working with. Click the Appearance panel list arrow, and note the New Art Has Basic Appearance menu item. By default it will be checked and active. When it's active, any new object you create will have a "basic appearance," which means it will be a normal Illustrator object, with a simple fill and stroke but with no effects pre-applied.

To remove all appearances from an object—including the fill and stroke—click the Clear Appearance button on the Appearance panel.

If you remove the check mark next to the New Art Has Basic Appearance menu item, any new objects you create will "inherit" the effects you've applied to previous objects.

If you want to remove all effects from a selected object, simply click the Appearance panel list arrow, then click Reduce to

Basic Appearance. The object will only retain the current fill and stroke on the Tools panel.

Duplicating Items on the Appearance Panel

A strange operation that you can execute with the Appearance panel is the application of multiple fills (and strokes) to a single object. Simply select the Fill attribute on the Appearance panel, then click the Duplicate Selected Item button on the panel. You can also duplicate an attribute by clicking the Appearance panel list arrow, then clicking Duplicate Item.

The Appearance panel is the only place where you can duplicate a fill. One would likely ask oneself, "Why would I need two fills anyway?" The answer is that you don't need two fills. The Appearance panel uses the second fill as a means to create a new object as part of the illustration. The second fill can be distorted and transformed and made to appear as an additional object, as shown in Figure 53. In this figure, the black circle is the original fill, and the yellow and pink objects are duplicate fills. Note that the distortion (Pucker) and transformation (Rotate) of the duplicate fills

are *effects*. Thus, this is a single object despite its appearance.

Changing the Order of Appearance Attributes

You can change the order of attributes on the Appearance panel simply by dragging them up or down. The hierarchy of attributes directly affects the appearance of the object. For example, if you dragged the yellow fill attribute on the Appearance panel above the pink fill attribute, the illustration would appear as shown in Figure 54.

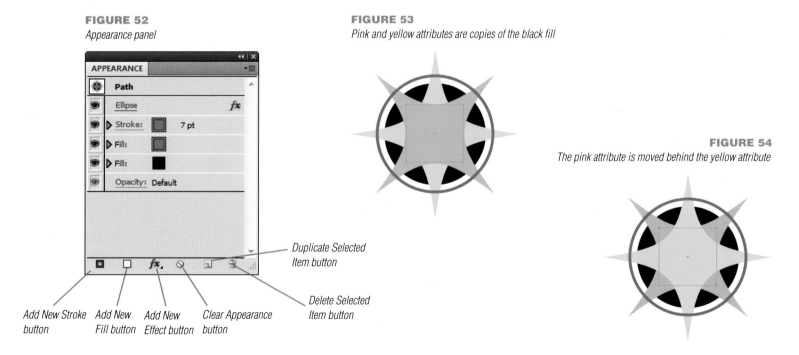

FIGURE 52
Appearance panel

Add New Stroke button *Add New Fill button* *Add New Effect button* *Clear Appearance button*

Duplicate Selected Item button

Delete Selected Item button

FIGURE 53
Pink and yellow attributes are copies of the black fill

FIGURE 54
The pink attribute is moved behind the yellow attribute

Modify effects

1. Hide Layer 2.

2. Select the LIMEADE letter objects on Layer 1, then click **Drop Shadow** on the Appearance panel.

3. Click the **Mode list arrow**, then click **Multiply**.

4. Type **.15** in the X Offset text box, then click **OK**.

   Your work should resemble Figure 55.

5. Click the **Inner Glow layer** (not the underlined name) on the Appearance panel, click the **Appearance panel list arrow**, then click **Duplicate Item**.

   The Inner Glow effect is intensified.

6. Deselect, then compare your work to Figure 56.

You double-clicked the Drop Shadow item on the Appearance panel to access the effect's dialog box, which listed the parameters of the effect as you previously applied it. You changed the blending mode of the effect to Multiply, which allowed you to see the lime wallpaper through the blue shadow. You also changed the horizontal offset of the drop shadow. On the Appearance panel, you duplicated the Inner Glow effect.

FIGURE 55
Drop Shadow effect with a Multiply blending mode

Multiply blending mode produces transparent drop shadow

FIGURE 56
Inner Glow effect is intensified when duplicated on the Appearance panel

Working with Transparency, Recoloring Artwork, Effects, and Graphic Styles

FIGURE 57
Line inherits the current attributes on the Appearance panel

FIGURE 58
Add Arrowheads dialog box

Start window

End window

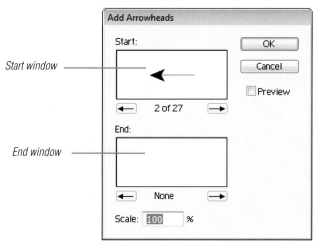

Remove effects from new art

1. Click the **Appearance panel list arrow**, then select the New Art Has Basic Appearance menu item in order to remove the check mark.

   | TIP If the check mark is already removed, do not select the menu item.

   | TIP New Art Has Basic Appearance is a setting that is checked and active by default. When it is active, any new art you create has a basic appearance, with no effects applied.

2. Change the fill to [None] and the stroke to Black on the Tools panel.

3. Click the **Pen tool** , click to the left of the number 5, press [**Shift**], then click directly below the L so that your work resembles Figure 57.

   Because New Art Has Basic Appearance is *not* checked on the Appearance panel, the line automatically inherits the effects on the Appearance panel.

4. Click the **Appearance panel list arrow**, then click **Reduce to Basic Appearance**.

   The effects are removed from the new line.

5. Using the Stroke panel, click the **Round Cap button** , click the **Dashed Line check box**, type **6** in the first dash text box, then press [**Enter**] (Win) or [**return**] (Mac).

6. Click **Effect** on the Application bar, point to the **first Stylize command**, then click **Add Arrowheads**.

7. Click the **right arrow** below the Start window until you see arrowhead 2 of 27.

8. Click the **left arrow** below the End window until you see None, as shown in Figure 58, then click **OK**.

(continued)

The Add Arrowheads effect is listed on the Appearance panel.

TIP If the arrowhead is overlapping the "5," move the right anchor point on the path to the left.

9. Click the **Appearance panel list arrow**, then click **New Art Has Basic Appearance** to add a check mark (if necessary).

When the New Art Has Basic Appearance option is active, newly created art will not inherit the current attributes.

10. Click the **Rectangle tool** , draw a rectangle around the lime wallpaper background, then remove the dashes so that the stroke is solid.

The rectangle does not inherit the Add Arrowheads effect.

11. Show Layer 2, then deselect so that your screen resembles Figure 59.

12. Save your work, then close the Limeade document.

You created a simple line, noting that it automatically inherited the effects on the Appearance panel, then you removed the effects. You added the Add Arrowheads effect. You then chose the New Art Has Basic Appearance button on the Appearance panel, and, when you drew a rectangle, noted that it did not inherit any effects.

FIGURE 59
Black rectangle has a basic appearance

FIGURE 60
Appearance panel

Stroke color

Stroke weight

Stroke effect

Fill effect

1. Create a new 6" × 6" CMYK Color document, then save it as **Triple Fill**.

2. Create a 2" square with a black fill and no stroke.

3. Click **Effect** on the Application bar, point to **Convert to Shape**, then click **Ellipse**.

4. Verify that the Relative option button is selected, type **.25** in the Extra Width text box, type **.25** in the Extra Height text box, then click **OK**.

   The square appears as a larger circle.

5. Click the **Stroke item** on the Appearance panel, then use the options that appear beside the item to set the color to **CMYK Green** and the weight to **7 pt**.

   TIP You will need to expand the Stroke item on the panel to see the Outline Object listed.

6. Compare your Appearance panel with Figure 60.

(continued)

7. Click **Effect** on the Application bar, point to **Path** in the Illustrator Effects section, click **Offset Path**, type **.25** in the Offset text box, then click **OK**.

   Your screen should resemble Figure 61.

8. Click the **Fill item** on the Appearance panel, then click the **Duplicate Selected Item button** 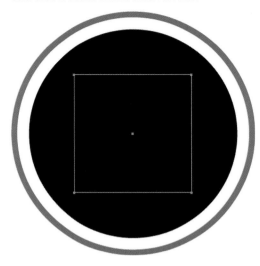 on the Appearance panel.

9. Click the **color swatch list arrow** beside the new Fill item, then click **CMYK Green**.

10. Click **Effect** on the Application bar, point to **Distort & Transform** in the Illustrator Effects section, click **Pucker & Bloat**, type **-65** in the text box, then click **OK**.

    The green fill is distorted above the original black fill, as shown in Figure 62.

    (continued)

FIGURE 61
Outer circle is created with the Offset Path effect

FIGURE 62
Duplicated fill effect is distorted

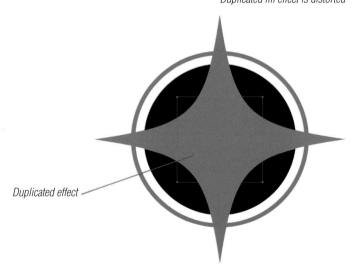

Duplicated effect

Working with Transparency, Recoloring Artwork, Effects, and Graphic Styles

FIGURE 63

Rotation on the third fill is an effect

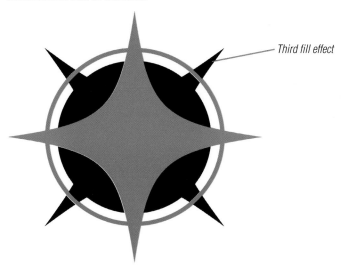

— Third fill effect

FIGURE 64

Changing the order of effects changes appearance

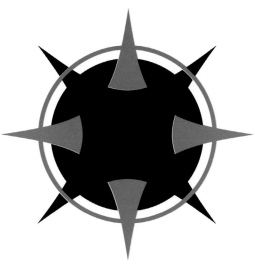

11. Click the **Green Fill layer** on the Appearance panel so that it's highlighted, then click the **Duplicate Selected Item button** on the Appearance panel.

12. Click the **middle Fill item**, click **Effect** on the Application bar, point to **Distort & Transform**, click **Transform**, type **45** in the Angle text box, then click **OK**.

13. Click the **color swatch list arrow** beside the middle Fill item, then change it to black so that your work resembles Figure 63.

14. Drag the **middle Fill item** above the top Fill item, deselect so that your work resembles Figure 64, then save and close the Triple Fill document.

    Note that the illustration is a single object—as such, it can be used as a style.

You applied a number of effects to a simple square, creating the appearance of multiple objects. You also changed the appearance of the illustration by changing the order of the items on the Appearance panel.

WORK WITH
GRAPHIC STYLES

What You'll Do

In this lesson, you will create and apply graphic styles.

Creating and Applying Graphic Styles

Graphic styles are named sets of appearance attributes that are accessed on the Graphic Styles panel. To create a new style, select the artwork whose attributes you want to save as a style, then do one of the following:

- Click the New Graphic Style button on the Graphic Styles panel.
- Drag a selected object from the artboard into the Graphic Styles panel.
- Drag a thumbnail from the Appearance panel into the Graphic Styles panel.

A graphic style can include fills, strokes, effects, patterns, opacity settings, blending modes, gradients, and effects. However, a graphic style can be created from a *single* set of attributes only. Only one object needs to be selected in order to create a new graphic style. The Graphic Styles panel is shown in Figure 65.

Merging graphic styles

You can create new graphic styles by merging two or more graphic styles on the Graphic Styles panel. [Ctrl] click (Win) or ⌘ click (Mac) to select all the graphic styles that you want to merge, click the Graphic Styles panel list arrow, then click Merge Graphic Styles. The new graphic style will contain all of the attributes of the selected graphic styles and will be added to the Graphic Styles panel as a new graphic style.

When you apply a graphic style to an object, the new graphic style overrides any graphic style that was previously applied to the object. When you apply a graphic style to a group or a layer, all objects in the group or on the layer take on the graphic style's attributes. Graphic styles are associated with the layers they are applied to. If you remove an object from a layer that has a graphic style applied to it, the object will lose the graphic style attributes.

FIGURE 65
Graphic Styles panel

Default graphic styles

Break Link to Graphic Style button

New Graphic Style button

Delete Graphic Style button

Create a new graphic style

1. Open AI 8-6.ai, then save it as **Dolphin Blue**.

2. Create a rectangle that is 1" wide and 2" tall.

3. Fill the rectangle with the Blue Radial swatch and remove any stroke.

4. Click the **Gradient tool** , then drag the **Gradient tool pointer** from just below the top-left corner to the bottom-right corner of the rectangle.

   Try to make your fill resemble Figure 66.

5. Click **Effect** on the Application bar, point to **Stylize** in the Illustrator Effects section, click **Round Corners**, type **.15** in the Radius text box, then click **OK**.

6. Click **Effect** on the Application bar, point to **Stylize** in the Illustrator Effects section, then click **Outer Glow**.

7. Verify that the Mode is set to Multiply and that the Opacity is set to 75%, change the color to black in the Color Picker (if necessary), click **OK**, type **.1** in the Blur text box, then click **OK**, so that your work resembles Figure 67.

8. Click **Window** on the Application bar, then click **Graphic Styles**.

9. Select all, then drag the **thumbnail** next to Path to the Graphic Styles panel, as shown in Figure 68.

10. Double-click the **new swatch** on the Graphic Styles panel, then name it **Dolphin Blue**.

You created an illustration with the Round Corners and Outer Glow effects, then saved the appearance attributes as a new graphic style on the Graphic Styles panel.

FIGURE 66
Applying the gradient to the rectangle

FIGURE 67
An Outer Glow effect added to the rectangle

FIGURE 68
Creating a new graphic style

Drag the appearance thumbnail to the Graphic Styles panel to create a new graphic style

Working with Transparency, Recoloring Artwork, Effects, and Graphic Styles

FIGURE 69
Dolphin Blue graphic style applied to an object

Dolphin blue

1. Cut the rectangle from the artboard.
2. Click **Object** on the Application bar, then click **Show All**.

   A dolphin object and the words Dolphin blue appear.
3. Deselect all, select the dolphin artwork, click **Dolphin Blue** on the Graphic Styles panel, then deselect.

   Your work should resemble Figure 69.

You applied a graphic style to a simple object.

Apply a graphic style to text

1. Click the **Graphic Styles panel list arrow**; if there is a check mark to the left of Override Character Color, click **Override Character Color** to remove the check mark.

2. Select the text, then click **Dolphin Blue** on the Graphic Styles panel.

   The text takes on all the attributes of the graphic style except the fill color, which remains black.

3. Undo your last step.

4. Click the **Graphic Styles panel list arrow**, click **Override Character Color**, then apply the Dolphin Blue graphic style to the Dolphin blue text.

   Your work should resemble Figure 70.

5. Undo your last step, click **Type** on the Application bar, then click **Create Outlines** to convert the text to outlines.

6. Ungroup the outlines, then apply the Dolphin Blue graphic style to the objects so that your work resembles Figure 71.

7. Compare the text fills in Figure 71 to those in Figure 70.

You explored three ways of applying a graphic style to text and text outlines for different effects.

FIGURE 70
Dolphin Blue graphic style applied to text

FIGURE 71
Dolphin Blue graphic style applied to each object

FIGURE 72

Artwork modified with a stroke and a second Outer Glow effect

Duplicate outer glow
added to dolphin

1. Select all, then apply a 1.5-pt. green stroke to the dolphin and the letters.

2. Deselect, select only the dolphin, click the **Outer Glow item** on the Appearance panel, then click the **Duplicate Selected Item** button ▣ .

3. Double-click the **duplicate Outer Glow item** on the Appearance panel, then change the opacity to 17% in the Outer Glow dialog box.

4. Click the **color box** in the Outer Glow dialog box to open the Color Picker.

5. Type **32** in the H (hue) text box, **100** in the S (saturation) text box, and **100** in the B (brightness) text box, then click **OK**.

6. Click **OK** again to close the Outer Glow dialog box, then deselect all.

   Your work should resemble Figure 72.

7. Press and hold [**Alt**] (Win) or [**option**] (Mac), then drag the **thumbnail** from the Appearance panel directly on top of the Dolphin Blue graphic style on the Graphic Styles panel.

   The Dolphin Blue graphic style is updated to include the green stroke and the orange outer glow.

8. Save your work, then close Dolphin Blue.

You modified the Dolphin Blue graphic style by changing the settings on the Appearance panel, then replacing the old graphic style with the new appearance attributes.

Use the Transparency panel and the Color Picker.

1. Open AI 8-7.ai, then save it as **Channel Z**.
2. Double-click the Fill button on the Tools panel to open the Color Picker, create a color using the following values: hue = 59, saturation = 34, and brightness = 74, then drag the new color to the Swatches panel.
3. Select the square on the artboard, show the Gradient panel (if necessary), click the black color stop on the gradient slider, press [Alt] (Win) or [option] (Mac), then click the new color swatch on the Swatches panel.
4. Change the opacity of the square to 60%.
5. Save your work.

Apply effects to objects.

1. On the Appearance panel, duplicate the Fill item.
2. Click the new Fill item again to activate it, click Effect on the Application bar, point to Texture, click Grain, click the Grain Type list arrow, then click Regular.
3. Type **70** for the Intensity and **60** for the Contrast, then click OK.

4. Click the Stroke item on the Appearance panel, then change its weight to 1 pt and its color to orange. (*Hint*: Use any orange swatch.)
5. Click Effect on the Application bar, point to Path, click Offset Path, type **.1** in the Offset text box, then click OK.
6. Save your work.

Use the Appearance panel.

1. Click the top Fill item on the Appearance panel.
2. Click Effect on the Application bar, point to the first Stylize command, click Round Corners, type **.5** in the Radius text box, then click OK.
3. On the Transparency panel, change the blending mode to Multiply.
4. Select the bottom Fill item, then apply the Grain effect using the same settings that you previously used.
5. Expand the top Fill item (if necessary), click the word Grain to open the Grain dialog box, then change the Intensity to 100.

6. Duplicate the top Fill item, then change the Color attribute of the middle Fill item to the original Orange Black gradient on the Swatches panel.
7. On the top Fill item, drag the *fx* icon next to the Round Corners item to the Delete Selected Item button on the Appearance panel to remove the effect from the top item.
8. Collapse the three Fill items on the Appearance panel.
9. Save your work.

Work with graphic styles.

1. Show the Graphic Styles panel (if necessary).
2. Drag the thumbnail from the Appearance panel to the Graphic Styles panel.
3. Name the new graphic style **Noise**.
4. Cut the artwork from the artboard.
5. Click Object on the Application bar, click Show All, then change the fill on the text to None.
6. Verify that Override Character Color is checked on the Graphic Styles panel menu.
7. Apply the Noise style to the text.

8. Expand the Stroke item on the Appearance panel, then change its color to Black and its weight to 1.5 pt.

9. Double-click the Offset Path item, then change the offset to .15.

10. Delete the Round Corners effect from the middle Fill item.

11. Update the Noise graphic style with the new attributes by pressing [Alt] (Win) or [option] (Mac) as you drag the thumbnail on the Appearance panel on top of the Noise style on the Graphic Styles panel.

12. Save your work, compare your screen to Figure 73, then close Channel Z.

Recolor Artwork.

1. Open AI 8-8.ai, then save it as **Jaguar**.

2. Double-click the orange nose to see the orange group in isolation mode.

3. Click the Exit Isolated Group button on the Control panel.

4. Click the Eyedropper tool, sample the orange color from the nose, then click the Set base color to the current color button on the Color Guide panel.

5. Select all, then click the Edit or Apply Colors button on the Color Guide panel.

6. Click the Assign button (if necessary), so that the Recolor Artwork dialog box is in Assign mode.

7. Click the Harmony Rules list arrow, then choose the Pentagram harmony rule from the list.

8. Click and drag the red color box in the New column up and release it on top of the color box at the top.

9. Double-click the green color box in the New column, type **237**, **184**, **107** in the R, G & B text boxes, respectively, then click OK.

10. Click the navy blue color box in the New column one time to select it, drag the hue slider at the bottom of the dialog box to 133°.

11. Click OK, deselect, save your work, then compare your illustration to Figure 74.

FIGURE 73
Completed Skills Review, Part 1

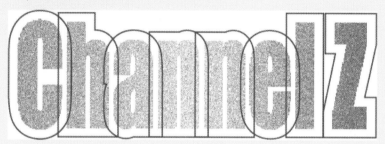

FIGURE 74
Completed Skills Review, Part 2

Working with Transparency, Recoloring Artwork, Effects, and Graphic Styles

The local VFW has contracted you to design their monthly newsletter. You are happy, because it means a regular monthly payment. However, since their budget is modest, you want to streamline your work as much as possible. One design element of the newsletter that is used every month is a red and blue frame positioned around pictures. You decide to create this as a graphic style in Illustrator.

1. Open AI 8-9.ai, then save it as **Frame**.
2. Show the Brushes panel, then apply the 10 pt Round brush to the square.
3. Click Effect on the Application bar, point to Stylize, then click Feather.
4. Accept the default settings in the Feather Radius text box, then click OK.
5. On the Appearance panel, duplicate the stroke, then change the duplicate stroke color to blue.
6. Click the Offset Path command on the Effect menu. (*Hint*: Point to Path.)

7. Type **.18** in the Offset text box, then click OK.
8. Save the appearance attributes as a new graphic style on the Graphic Styles panel.

9. Name the new graphic style **Picture Frame**.
10. Save your work, compare your screen to Figure 75, then close the Frame document.

FIGURE 75
Completed Project Builder 1

Working with Transparency, Recoloring Artwork, Effects, and Graphic Styles

You are a designer and you have just finished a color illustration when your client calls to tell you that the project is being changed. Because of budgetary constraints, it's going to be reduced from a 4-color to a 2-color job. The client tells you to use black ink plus any red PANTONE color that you think will work best.

1. Open AI 8-10.ai, then save it as **2 Color Jaguar**.

2. Select all, click the Edit or Apply Colors button on the Color Guide panel, then click the Assign button.

3. Click the Harmony Rules list arrow, then choose the Pentagram harmony rule from the list.

4. Click and drag the fifth color in the Current Colors list—red—on top of the first color in the list.

5. Click and drag the remaining three colors up to the top of the list (don't move the black and white colors).

6. Click the Limits the color group to colors in a swatch library button, point to Color Books, then click PANTONE solid coated.

7. Double-click the color box in the New column to the right of the five combined colors, click PANTONE 200 C, then click OK.

8. Click OK to close the Recolor Artwork dialog box, save changes when prompted, then compare your illustration to Figure 76.

Save your work, then close 2 Color Jaguar.

FIGURE 76
Completed Project Builder 2

Starlight.com, a local Web site that lists the schedules of the city's nightlife, has hired you to redesign their site. Part of that redesign will require a new masthead. They give you no specific direction on how they want their name displayed, but they do tell you that whatever design you create will be applied to other headlines throughout the site.

1. Open AI 8-11.ai, then save it as **Starlight**.
2. Select the black square, then duplicate its fill on the Appearance panel.
3. Click the Free Distort command on the Effect menu. (*Hint*: Point to Distort & Transform.)
4. Move the top two selection handles down and outward, as shown in Figure 77, then click OK.
5. Select the top Fill item on the Appearance panel, click Effect on the Application bar, point to Stylize, click Feather, type **.05** in the Feather Radius text box, then click OK.
6. Change the color of the top Fill item to 40% Black.
7. Select the bottom Fill item on the Appearance panel, then click Inner Glow on the Effect menu. (*Hint*: Point to Stylize.)
8. Specify the color for the glow as hue = 56, saturation = 100, and brightness = 84, change the blending mode to Normal and the Blur to .1, then click OK.
9. Save the attributes as a new graphic style named Starlight Glow on the Graphic Styles panel.

10. Cut the artwork from the artboard.
11. Type the word **STARLIGHT** in 72-point Impact.

12. Apply the Starlight Glow graphic style to the text.
13. Save your work, compare your screen to Figure 78, the close Starlight.

FIGURE 77
Free Distort dialog box

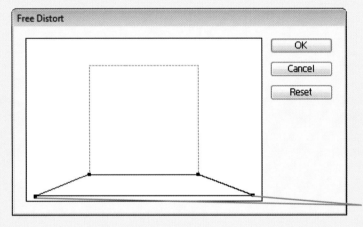

Drag top two selection handles down and outward to these positions

FIGURE 78
Completed Design Project

In this exercise, you will use the Recolor Artwork dialog box to convert a color Illustrator graphic to a 2-Color graphic with one black and one PANTONE ink. Your group is free to choose which PANTONE color to use and how to apply it to the graphic.

1. Open AI 8-12.ai, then save it as **2 Color Mask**.

2. Select all, then open the Recolor Artwork dialog box.

3. Reduce all the colors (except black and white) to a single color.

4. Change the single color to any PANTONE color of your choice.

5. Modify the color areas of the image to your liking.
   Figure 79 shows one outcome.

6. Save your work, then close 2 Color Mask.

FIGURE 79
Completed Portfolio Project

chapter

9

CREATING GRAPHS
IN ILLUSTRATOR

1. Create a graph

2. Edit a graph using the Graph Data window

3. Use the Group Selection tool

4. Use the Graph Type dialog box

5. Create a combination graph

6. Create a custom graph design

7. Apply a custom design to a graph

8. Create and apply a sliding-scale design

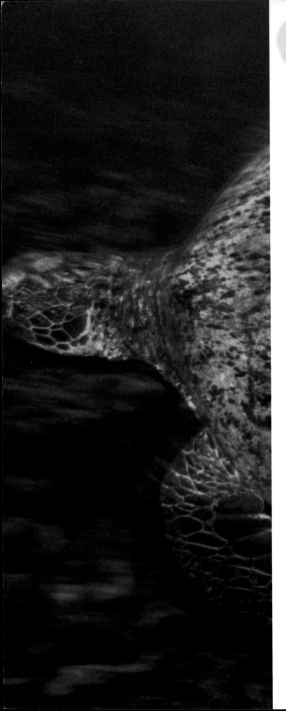

CREATING GRAPHS
IN ILLUSTRATOR

chapter 9

When you think of graphs, you probably think of those premade, click-a-button graphs that you can make with any presentation or financial software package. As a designer, you'll be really excited by the graphs that you can create with Illustrator's graph tools. When your project calls for a graph, you can enter the data directly into Illustrator, then have all of Illustrator's design and drawing power behind you when it comes to designing the graph.

For the right project, visually interesting and smartly designed graphs are a very powerful tool for conveying information. Think of using graphs as an opportunity for expressing data artistically. Since people naturally pay more attention to a well-designed graph than to blocks of text, using graphs in a presentation will help you to make your points more persuasively.

Tools You'll Use

Group
Selection
tool

Graph tools

CREATE A GRAPH

What You'll Do

In this lesson, you will enter data and create a column graph.

Defining a Graph

A **graph** is a diagram of data that shows relationships among a set of numbers. A set of data can be represented by a graphic element, such as a bar, line, or point. Different types of graphs are used to emphasize different aspects of a display.

Illustrator offers nine types of graphs:
- Column
- Stacked column
- Bar
- Stacked bar
- Line
- Area
- Scatter
- Pie
- Radar

The right type of graph can help you to simplify complex data and communicate a message more effectively. In Illustrator, you can convert one type of graph into another type and create custom designs that you can then apply to the graph.

Creating a Graph

Before you create a graph, it is important to understand how data is plotted in Illustrator's Graph Data window. The first column (vertical axis) of the Graph Data window is reserved for category labels, while the first row (horizontal axis) is reserved for legend labels. See Figure 1.

Category labels describe non-numeric data, such as the months of the year, the days of the week, or a group of salespersons' names.

Legend labels describe numeric data that may change, such as weekly sales totals, payroll amounts, or daily temperatures; they appear in a box next to the graph, called the legend.

The legend, like a map legend, contains the legend labels and small boxes filled with colors that represent the columns on the graph.

FIGURE 1

Entering category labels and legend labels

Category labels

Legend labels

Create a column graph

1. Open AI 9-1.ai, then save it as **Graph**.

2. Verify that you are using inches as your General unit of measure by checking your Units & Display Performance Preferences.

3. Click the **Column Graph tool** , then click the center of the artboard.

4. Type **6** in the Width text box and **4** in the Height text box, as shown in Figure 2, then click **OK**.

   The Graph Data window appears in front of the graph. The Graph Data window consists of rows and columns. The intersection of a row and a column is called a **cell**. The first cell, which is selected, contains the number 1.00 as sample data to create a temporary structure for the graph. The appearance of the graph will change after you enter your own data.

5. Press [**Delete**] (Win) or [**delete**] (Mac), then press [**Tab**] to eliminate the 1.00 from the first cell and select the next cell in the first row.

   You must always remove the number 1.00 from the first cell before entering new data.

6. Type **Low**, press [**Tab**], type **High**, press [**Tab**], then type **Average**.

   You have entered three legend labels.

   (continued)

FIGURE 2
Graph dialog box

Height text box   Width text box

Changing the number of decimal points in graph data

Numbers in the Graph Data window are initially displayed with two decimals. For example, if you type the number 86, it appears as 86.00. To modify the number of decimals in any or all cells in the Graph Data window, click the cell(s) that you want to change, then click the Cell style button in the Graph Data window. The Cell Style dialog box opens. Increase or decrease the number in the Number of decimals text box to change the decimal place (set it to 0 if you do not want any decimal place), then click OK. You can also increase or decrease the column width in the Cell Style dialog box by changing the value in the Column width text box.

FIGURE 3

Graph Data window

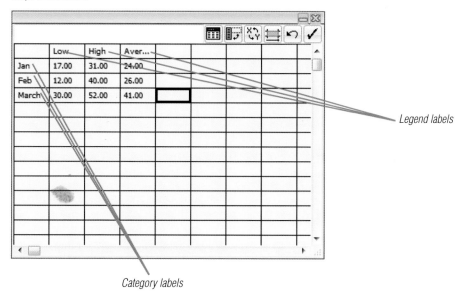

Legend labels

Category labels

FIGURE 4

Column graph

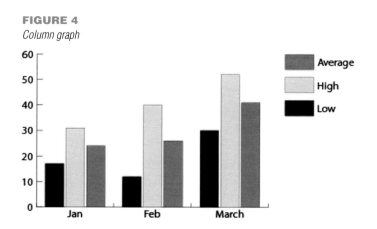

7. Click the **second cell** in the first column, type **Jan**, press [**Enter**] (Win) or [**return**] (Mac), type **Feb**, press [**Enter**] (Win) or [**return**] (Mac), type **March**, then press [**Enter**] (Win) or [**return**] (Mac).

   You have entered three category labels. Compare the positions of your labels with those shown in Figure 3.

   TIP   Category labels are listed vertically and legend labels are listed horizontally in the Graph Data window. If you enter your labels incorrectly, you can click the Transpose row/column button in the Graph Data window to switch them.

8. Enter the remaining data shown on the artboard, using [Tab] and [Enter] (Win) or [Tab] and [return] (Mac), and the four arrow keys on your keyboard to move between cells.

   TIP   Often you will want to create labels that consist of numbers, such as a ZIP code or the year 2010. Since these labels are meant to describe categories, they must be set in quotes ("2010") so that Illustrator will not mistake them for data that should be plotted.

9. Close the Graph Data window, saving the changes you made, then reposition the graph on the artboard (if necessary).

10. Deselect, save your work, then compare your graph to Figure 4.

You defined the size of the graph, then entered three legend labels, three category labels, and numbers in the Graph Data window.

EDIT A GRAPH USING THE
GRAPH DATA WINDOW

What You'll Do

	Low	High	Aver...			
Jan	17.00	31.00	24.00			
Feb	12.00	40.00	26.00			
March	34.00	52.00	43.00			

 In this lesson, you will change the data that is the basis of the column graph, then update the graph to reflect the new data.

Editing Data and Graphs

A project that calls for a graph often calls for edits to the graph. Fortunately, it is easy to make changes to the data that defines the graph . . . and just as easy to update the graph. For every graph in Illustrator, the data that was used to plot it is stored in the Graph Data window. The data is editable; when you make changes to the data, simply click the Apply button in the Graph Data window to preview the changes to the graph.

When you create text and data in another program that you want to use in an Illustrator graph, the document must be saved as a text-only file with commas separating each number from the next. If you are importing an Excel worksheet, it must be saved as a text (tab-delimited) file for Illustrator to support it.

Importing data from other software programs

You can import graph data from a text file or a Microsoft Excel worksheet into the Graph Data window in Illustrator. To import data, you must have the Graph Data window open and selected. Click the Import data button. You will then be prompted to open the file you wish to import.

FIGURE 5

Changing data in the Graph Data window

Entry text box

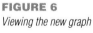

FIGURE 6

Viewing the new graph

Edit data in a graph

1. Click **View** on the Application bar, then click **Hide Print Tiling**, (if necessary).

2. Click the **Selection tool** ▶, then select and delete the text at the top of the artboard.

3. Click the **graph**, click **Object** on the Application bar, point to **Graph**, then click **Data**.

    TIP The separate objects that make up the graph are automatically grouped when the graph is created.

4. Click the cell that contains the number 30.00, type **80**, press [**Enter**] (Win) or [**return**] (Mac), then compare your screen to Figure 5.

    When you click a cell, the number in the cell becomes highlighted in the Entry text box of the Graph Data window, allowing you to change it to a new number.

5. Click the **Apply button** ✓ in the Graph Data window, then compare your graph to Figure 6.

6. Change the number 80.00 to **34**, click the cell that contains the number 41.00, type **43**, then press [**Enter**](Win) or [**return**](Mac).

7. Close the Graph Data window, then save changes when prompted.

    TIP To remove data from cells in the Graph Data window select the cells from which you want to delete the data, click Edit on the Application bar, then click Clear.

You edited the graph's data in the Graph Data window, then clicked the Apply button to view the changes to the graph.

USE THE GROUP
SELECTION TOOL

What You'll Do

In this lesson, you will use the Group Selection tool to easily select different areas of the graph for modification.

Using the Group Selection Tool

Graphs are grouped objects, consisting of many individual groups grouped together. Each set of colored columns represents an individual group within the larger group. For example, all of the black columns in Figure 7 represent the low temperatures for each month. The gray columns are the average-temperature group, and the light gray columns are the high-temperature group.

The Group Selection tool allows you to select entire groups within the larger group for the purpose of editing them with the Illustrator tools and menu commands.

FIGURE 7
Individual groups within a graph

FIGURE 8

Changing the color of the low-temperature group to red

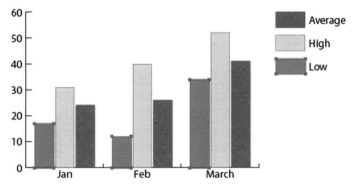

FIGURE 9

Column graph with new colors applied

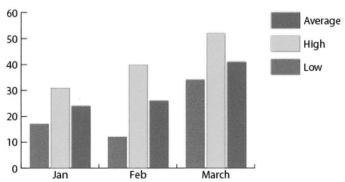

1. Click the artboard to deselect the graph.

2. Click the **Group Selection tool** ▸⁺ .

   The Group Selection tool is hidden beneath the Direct Selection tool.

3. Click the **first black column** above the Jan label, then click it again.

   The first click selects the first black column, and the second click selects the two remaining black columns.

4. Click the **first black column** a third time to select the low-temperature legend box.

   If you click too many times, you will eventually select the entire graph instead of an individual group. In that case, deselect and try again.

5. Change the fill color of the selected columns to red, as shown in Figure 8.

6. Click the **first light gray column** above the Jan label, click it again, click it a third time, then change the fill color of the high-temperature columns and legend box to yellow.

7. Select the gray columns and legend box, change the fill color to green, then deselect all.

   Your graph should resemble Figure 9.

8. Save your work.

   TIP The text labels, value axis labels, and legend labels are also individual groups within the larger graph group. Click twice to select them, then change their font, size, or color as desired.

You used the Group Selection tool to select groups within the graph quickly and easily, then changed the colors of the columns and the legend boxes.

USE THE GRAPH
TYPE DIALOG BOX

What You'll Do

In this lesson, you will modify the graph using the Graph Type dialog box.

Using the Graph Type Dialog Box

The Graph Type dialog box provides a variety of ways to change the look of your graph. For example, you can add a drop shadow behind the columns in a graph or change the appearance of the tick marks.

Tick marks are short lines that extend out from the value axis, which is the vertical line to the left of the graph. Tick marks help viewers interpret the meaning of column height by indicating incremental values on the value axis. You can also move the value axis from the left side of the graph to the right side, or display it on both sides.

Values on the value axis can be changed, and symbols such as $, %, and ° can be added to the numbers for clarification.

Choosing a chart type

Keep in mind the following guidelines when choosing a chart type:
- Pie or column charts are typically used to show quantitative data as a percentage of the whole.
- Line or bar charts are used to compare trends or changes over time.
- Area charts emphasize volume and are used to show a total quantity rather than to emphasize a portion of the data.
- Scatter or radial charts show a correlation among variables.

FIGURE 10
Graph Type dialog box

Graph Options
list arrow

Graph types

Add Drop Shadow
check box

FIGURE 11
Choosing options for the value axis

Length list arrow

FIGURE 12
Graph with full-width tick marks and a drop shadow

Use the Graph Type dialog box

1. Click the **Selection tool** , then click the **graph**.

    The entire graph must be selected to make changes in the Graph Type dialog box.

2. Click **Object** on the Application bar, point to **Graph**, then click **Type**.

3. Click the **Add Drop Shadow check box**, as shown in Figure 10.

4. Click the **Graph Options list arrow**, then click **Value Axis**.

    All of the options in this window now refer to the value axis, which is the vertical line located to the left of the columns on the graph.

5. Click the **Length list arrow** in the Tick Marks section of the window, click **Full Width**, compare your Graph Type dialog box to Figure 11, then click **OK**.

6. Deselect the graph, save your work, then compare your graph to Figure 12.

    TIP   The Graph Type dialog box does not provide an option for displaying the number or value that each column in the graph represents. For example, it will not display the number 32 on top of a column that represents 32°. If you want to display the actual values of the data on the chart, you must add those labels manually, using the Type tool.

You used the Graph Type dialog box to add a drop shadow to the graph and to extend the tick marks to run the full width of the graph.

CREATE A
COMBINATION GRAPH

What You'll Do

In this lesson, you will create a combination graph to show one set of data as compared to other data.

Defining a Combination Graph

A **combination graph** is a graph that uses two graph styles to plot numeric data. This type of graph is useful if you want to emphasize one set of numbers in comparison to others. For example, if you needed to create a column graph showing how much more paper than glass, plastic, or aluminum is recycled in a major city over a one-year period, you could plot the paper recycling data as a line graph, leaving the other recycling categories as columns. Your audience would be able to compare how much more paper is recycled than the other three products by looking at the line in relationship to the columns on the graph.

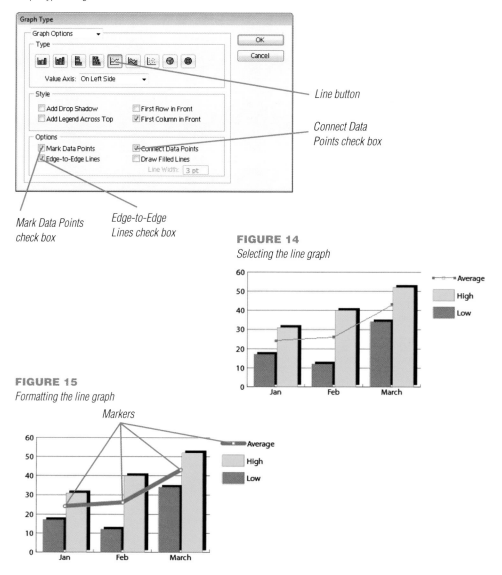

FIGURE 13
Graph Type dialog box

Line button

Connect Data
Points check box

Mark Data Points
check box

Edge-to-Edge
Lines check box

FIGURE 14
Selecting the line graph

FIGURE 15
Formatting the line graph

Markers

Create a combination graph

1. Click the **Group Selection tool** , then select all four items of the Average (green) group.

2. Click **Object** on the Application bar, point to **Graph**, then click **Type**.

3. Click the **Line button** , then click the **Add Drop Shadow check box** to remove the check mark.

4. Click the **Edge-to-Edge Lines check box**, make sure that there are check marks in the Mark Data Points and Connect Data Points check boxes, as shown in Figure 13, then click **OK**.

   The four green columns are replaced by four small square markers.

5. Click the **artboard** to deselect the graph.

6. Click the **Group Selection tool** , then click the first line segment connecting the markers three times to select the entire line and the corresponding information in the legend, as shown in Figure 14.

7. Click **Object** on the Application bar, point to **Arrange**, then click **Bring to Front**.

8. Change the stroke weight to 10 pt, the fill color of the line to [None], the stroke color of the line to green, and the cap to a round cap.

9. Deselect, select the four gray markers using the Group Selection tool , change their fill color to White, then deselect again.

10. Save your work, compare your graph to Figure 15, then close the Graph document.

You created a combination graph.

CREATE A CUSTOM
GRAPH DESIGN

What You'll Do

In this lesson, you will define artwork that will be used for a custom graph.

Creating a Custom Graph Design

This is where Illustrator really shines as a design tool for graphs. A **custom graph design** is a picture of something used to replace traditional columns, bars, or markers in Illustrator graphs. For example, when reporting on financial news, newspapers such as *USA Today* often print graphs made with custom designs of coins or dollars instead of columns and bars.

Only vector-based objects can be used for custom graph designs. You cannot use bitmaps, objects created with the Paintbrush tool, or objects filled with gradients.

Illustrator contains predefined column and marker designs as well as graph designs. These files are located in Adobe Illustrator CS4/Cool Extras/Sample Files. To use these designs, first open one of the sample files, create a new document and then create a new graph. Select the graph, click Object on the Application bar, point to Graph, then click Column. All of the column designs will appear in the Graph Column dialog box.

Using supplied custom graph designs

Illustrator comes with two documents full of custom designs that you can apply to graphs. These designs include flags, cats, hammers, diamonds, dollar signs, stars, and men and women. In addition, three-dimensional objects such as cylinders, hexagons, cubes, arrows, and pyramids are available.

FIGURE 16
Creating a custom graph design

Part A

Part B

Part C

Two guides

Rectangle is the same
height as the pencil

Rectangle is behind
the pencil and both
are selected

FIGURE 17
Graph Design dialog box

Pencil design

Create a custom graph design

1. Open AI 9-2.ai, then save it as **Pencil**.

2. Click **View** on the Application bar, then click **Pencil**.

3. Click the **Selection tool** ▶, drag a selection marquee around the entire pencil to select all of it, then group it.

4. Show the rulers (if necessary), then align two guides with the top and bottom of the pencil, as shown in Part A of Figure 16.

5. Deselect the pencil, if necessary, then change the fill and stroke colors to [None] on the Tools panel.

6. Click the **Rectangle tool** ▭, then create a rectangle around the pencil that snaps to the top and bottom guides, as shown in Part B of Figure 16.

   The height of the rectangle should exactly match the height of the custom design, to ensure that data values are represented correctly on the graph.

7. While the rectangle is still selected, click **Object** on the Application bar, point to **Arrange**, then click **Send to Back**.

   The rectangle must be behind the illustration.

8. Select both the rectangle and the pencil, as shown in Part C of Figure 16, click **Object** on the Application bar, point to **Graph**, then click **Design**.

9. Click **New Design**, click **Rename**, name the design **Pencil**, then click **OK**.

   The pencil design appears in the Graph Design dialog box, as shown in Figure 17.

10. Click **OK** to close the Graph Design dialog box, then save your work.

You created a custom design for graphs, using the Graph Design dialog box.

APPLY A CUSTOM
DESIGN TO A GRAPH

What You'll Do

In this lesson, you will apply the pencil custom design to a graph.

Applying a Custom Design to a Graph

Custom designs are typically applied to column graphs and line graphs. Illustrator provides four options for displaying custom designs on a graph: uniformly scaled, vertically scaled, repeating, and sliding.

Uniformly scaled designs are resized vertically and horizontally, whereas vertically scaled designs are resized only vertically. Figure 18 shows an example of a uniformly scaled design, and Figure 19 shows an example of a vertically scaled design. Repeating designs assign a value to the custom design and repeat the design as many times as necessary. For example, if the pencil is assigned a value of 1 school, 3 pencils would represent 3 schools. Sliding-scale designs allow you to define a point on the custom design from which the design will stretch, thereby leaving everything below that point uniform.

FIGURE 18
A uniformly scaled custom design

Hours of homework per week

FIGURE 19
A vertically scaled custom design

Hours of homework per week

Apply a custom graph design

1. Click **View** on the Application bar, then click **Fit Artboard in Window**.

2. Click the **graph** with the **Selection tool** .

3. Click **Object** on the Application bar, point to **Graph**, then click **Column**.

   The Graph Column dialog box shows a list of custom designs you can apply to your graph.

4. Click **Pencil**, then verify that Vertically Scaled is selected for the Column Type, and that the Rotate Legend Design check box is not checked, as shown in Figure 20.

   (continued)

FIGURE 20
Graph Column dialog box

Pencil design

Rotate Legend Design check box

Column Type list arrow

Using the Glyph and OpenType panels to obtain special characters

OpenType is a type of font formatting. OpenType fonts often come with alternative characters. For example, when the letter f is followed by the letter i, an OpenType font might offer you a ligature character that is one character of the f and i combined. Click Window on the Application bar, point to Type, then click OpenType to specify your preferences for applying alternate characters in OpenType fonts. For example, you can specify that you want to use standard ligatures for a given font, or you could choose to use dingbat characters to make checkboxes or radio buttons. Note that the OpenType panel works hand-in-hand with the Glyphs panel. You can view all the characters in any given font using the Glyphs panel.

FIGURE 21

Pencil custom design applied to the graph

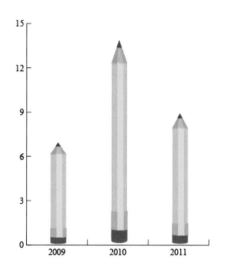

students with full scholarships

5. Click **OK**.

   The three columns on the graph are replaced with pencils, each a different length, indicating how many scholarships were given out.

6. Click the **artboard** to deselect the graph, so that your work resembles Figure 21.

7. Save your work.

   | TIP   To remove a custom design from a graph, select the graph, then click None in the Graph Column dialog box.

You selected a custom design in the Graph Design dialog box, you selected Vertically Scaled for the column type, and then you applied the custom design to a graph. The artwork is scaled vertically—taller or shorter—to represent the graph data.

CREATE AND APPLY A
SLIDING-SCALE DESIGN

What You'll Do

 In this lesson, you will define the area on the pencil design that will be affected by a sliding-scale design. Then you will apply a sliding-scale design to the existing graph.

Creating a Sliding-Scale Design and Applying It to a Graph

When you apply a vertically scaled design style to a column graph, the entire design stretches to accommodate the value assigned to it. This expansion may present a problem if the custom design needs to maintain an aspect ratio. For example, a custom logo design might become unreadable if it is stretched too far. For this reason, a vertically scaled design can sometimes be unsatisfactory.

The answer to the problem is the sliding-scale design, which allows you to define a point on the custom design from which the graph will stretch. Thus a portion of the design can be specified to remain at its original size and not stretch. Figure 22 shows an example of a sliding-scale design. Note how only the handles lengthen in the graph, while the "shovels" at the bottom are not scaled.

FIGURE 22

A sliding-scale design

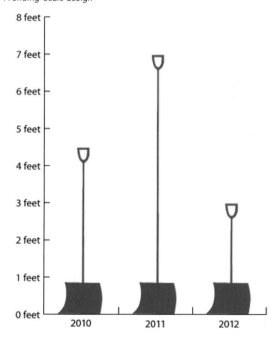

Create and apply a sliding-scale design

1. Return to the Pencil view, click **View** on the Application bar, point to **Guides**, click **Clear Guides**, then set the stroke color to Black on the Tools panel.

2. Using the **Pen tool** 🖉, draw a black line across the pencil, as shown in Figure 23, Part A.

3. Click the **Selection tool** 🔦, select the entire line, click **View** on the Application bar, point to **Guides**, then click **Make Guides**.

   The black line turns into a guide, as shown in Figure 23, Part B.

4. Click **View** on the Application bar, point to **Guides**, then verify that there is not a check mark to the left of Lock Guides.

5. Select the pencil, the rectangle, and the guide, so that all three objects are selected, as shown in Figure 23, Part C.

   TIP Drag a selection marquee around the pencil to make sure you select the rectangle too, or switch to Outline view to see the outline of the rectangle. Because the rectangle has no fill or stroke, it is "invisible" in Preview.

   (continued)

(continued)

FIGURE 23
Creating a sliding-scale design

Short, straight, black line

Part A

Line converted to a guide

Part B

Part C

Rectangle, pencil, and guide selected

Viewing and modifying document metadata information

Metadata contains basic information about a file, such as the author's name, the file's resolution, copyright information, the color space, and keywords that have been "tagged" to the file. You can use metadata to streamline your workflow and organize your files. The File Info dialog box in Illustrator is command central for viewing and modifying metadata: The File Info dialog box displays camera data, file properties, an edit history, copyright, and author information, and it also displays custom metadata panels. You can add new metadata information for a file directly in the File Info dialog box. To access the dialog box, click File Info on the File menu.

FIGURE 24
Graph Column dialog box

Sliding Pencil design

Column Type
list arrow

6. Click **Object** on the Application bar, point to **Graph**, then click **Design**.

7. Click **New Design**, click **Rename**, name the design **Sliding Pencil**, click **OK**, then click **OK** again to close the Graph Design dialog box.

8. Hide the guides, fit the document in the window, then select the graph.

9. Click **Object** on the Application bar, point to **Graph**, click **Column**, click **Sliding Pencil**, click **Sliding** from the Column Type list, as shown in Figure 24, then click **OK**.

10. Deselect, then save your work.

Notice that the metal and the eraser tip of the three pencils remain unscaled and identical despite the varying lengths, as shown in Figure 25.

11. Close the Pencil document.

You created a guide on top of the pencil design to identify the area of the artwork that will not be scaled in the graph. You then saved the new artwork as a new sliding-scale design.

FIGURE 25
Completed graph

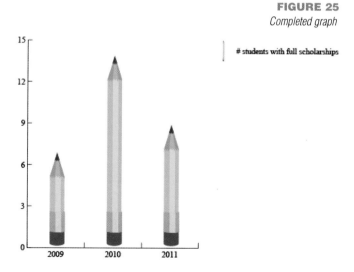

students with full scholarships

Create a graph.

1. Open AI 9-3.ai, then save it as **Nice Weather**.
2. Click the Column Graph tool, then click the artboard.
3. Type **6** in the Width text box, type **4** in the Height text box, then click OK.
4. Delete the number 1.00 from the first cell in the Graph Data window.
5. Press [Tab] to select the next cell in the first row.
6. Type **Rain**, press [Tab], type **Sun**, press [Tab], type **Clouds**, then press [Tab].
7. Click the second cell in the first column, type **June**, press [Enter] (Win) or [return] (Mac), type **July**, press [Enter] (Win) or [return] (Mac), type **August**, then press [Enter] (Win) or [return] (Mac).
8. Enter the rest of the data that is supplied in the upper-left corner of the artboard to fill in the cells underneath Rain, Sun, and Clouds.
9. Close the Graph Data window, saving your changes to it.
10. Move the graph onto the artboard, if necessary.

Edit a graph using the Graph Data window.

1. Hide the print tiling, (if necessary).
2. Delete the text at the top of the artboard.
3. Click the graph to select it.
4. Click Object on the Application bar, point to Graph, then click Data.
5. Click the cell that contains the number 7, and change it to 8.
6. Click the cell that contains the number 20, and change it to 19.
7. Drag the Graph Data window down slightly to view the artboard, then click the Apply button in the Graph Data window.
8. Close the Graph Data window.
9. Save your work.

Use the Group Selection tool.

1. Deselect the graph, then click the Group Selection tool.
2. Click the first black column above the June label, click a second time, then click a third time to select the Rain group.
3. Change the fill color of the selected columns to green.

4. Change the fill color of the Sun group to yellow.
5. Change the fill color of the Clouds group to a shade of blue.
6. Save your work.

Use the Graph Type dialog box.

1. Click the Selection tool, then click the graph.
2. Click Object on the Application bar, point to Graph, then click Type.
3. Click the Add Drop Shadow check box, if necessary, to add a drop shadow.
4. Click the Graph Options list arrow, then click Value Axis.
5. Click the Length list arrow in the Tick Marks section of the window, then click Full Width, if necessary.
6. Click OK.
7. Save your work.

Create a combination graph.

1. Deselect the graph, then, using the Group Selection tool, select the entire Sun group.
2. Click Object on the Application bar, point to Graph, then click Type.
3. Click the Line button.
4. Click the Add Drop Shadow check box to deselect the option.
5. Click the Edge-to-Edge Lines check box.
6. Verify that both the Mark Data Points and Connect Data Points check boxes are checked, then click OK.
7. Click the artboard to deselect the graph.
8. Using the Group Selection tool, select the line that connects the markers and the small corresponding line in the legend.
9. Change the stroke weight of the line to 10 pt.
10. Remove the fill color from the line, then change the stroke color of the line to yellow.
11. Save your work, compare your graph to Figure 26, then close the Nice Weather document.

Create a custom graph design.

1. Open AI 9-4.ai, then save it as **Flower Graph**.
2. Click View on the Application bar, then click Flower.
3. Click View on the Application bar, then click Show Rulers, if necessary.
4. Drag two guides from the horizontal ruler; position one at the very top of the flower, and the other at the bottom of the stem.

5. Lock the guides, then set the fill and stroke colors to [None] on the Tools panel.
6. Create a rectangle that is slightly wider than the width of the flower, and that snaps to the top and bottom of the guides.
7. Send the rectangle to the back. (*Hint*: If you deselect the rectangle and cannot see it, switch to Outline view, repeat Step 7, then switch back to Preview view.)
8. Select the flower and the rectangle.
9. Click Object on the Application bar, point to Graph, then click Design.
10. Click New Design, click Rename, name the design **Flower**, click OK, then click OK again.

FIGURE 26
Completed Skills Review, Part 1

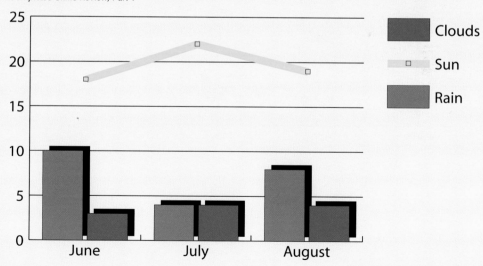

11. Delete the flower artwork at the top of the document window, then hide the guides.

Apply a custom design to a graph.

1. Click View on the Application bar, then click Graph.
2. Select the graph with the Selection tool.
3. Click Object on the Application bar, point to Graph, then click Column.
4. Click Flower, then make sure that Vertically Scaled is chosen for the Column Type.
5. Click the Rotate Legend Design check box to remove the check mark, then click OK.
6. Click the artboard to deselect the graph.
7. Save your work, then compare your graph to Figure 27.

Create and apply a sliding-scale design.

1. Click the graph with the Selection tool.
2. Click Object on the Application bar, point to Graph, then click Column.
3. Click the Column Type list arrow, then click Repeating.
4. Type **10** in the units text box next to "Each Design Represents."
5. Verify that there is not a check mark in the Rotate Legend Design check box.
6. Click the For Fractions list arrow, then click Chop Design.
7. Click OK, then save your work.
8. Deselect the graph, compare your graph to Figure 28, then close the Flower Graph document.

FIGURE 27
Completed Skills Review, Part 2

 Flower Sales (Thousands)

FIGURE 28
Completed Skills Review, Part 3

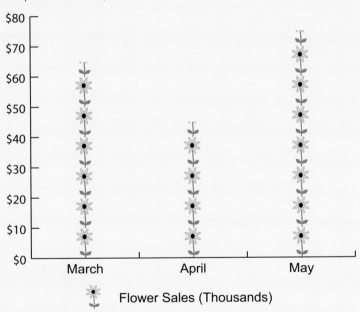

Flower Sales (Thousands)

Your apartment is heated and cooled electrically, and your monthly bills vary month to month. You decide to create a graph to get an idea of which months are most costly.

1. Open AI 9-5.ai, then save it as **Electrical Expenses**.

2. Create a 6" wide by 4" tall column graph.

3. Delete 1.00 from the first cell, then press [Tab].

4. Type **Monthly Electrical Expenses**. (*Hint*: Don't worry if the title is not in full view.)

5. Enter the data as shown in Figure 29.

6. Close the Graph Data window, saving your changes to the data.

7. Change the fill color of the graph columns and legend box to the Jade swatch.

8. Place a drop shadow behind the columns.

9. Click Object on the Application bar, point to Graph, click Type, click the Graph Options list arrow, click Value Axis, type **$** in the Prefix text box, then click OK.

10. Click Object on the Application bar, point to Graph, click Type, click the Graph Options list arrow, click Value Axis, click the Length list arrow under Tick Marks, click Full Width, then click OK.

11. Compare your graph to Figure 30, save your work, then close the Electrical Expenses document.

FIGURE 29
Project Builder 1 data

FIGURE 30
Completed Project Builder 1

You own an independent market research consulting business that specializes in the television industry. You have recently conducted a survey of 1000 people who describe their television-watching habits as "regularly watch television." The question they were asked was "What is your favorite TV program?" Your research assistants have tabulated the data and supplied the breakdown to you as a column graph in an Illustrator file. You note that the words under the columns are running into each other, and you decide the graph would work better as a pie chart.

1. Open AI 9-6.ai, then save it as **Television**.
2. Create a 6" wide by 4" tall column graph.
3. Delete 1.00 from the first cell, then press [Tab].
4. Type **What is your favorite TV program?**
5. Using the information at the top of the art-board, enter the rest of the data.
6. Close the Graph Data window, saving your changes to the data.
7. Verify that the graph is selected, click Object on the Application bar, point to Graph, then click Type.
8. Click the Pie button, remove the check mark in the Add Drop Shadow check box, if necessary, then click OK.

9. Click Object on the Application bar, point to Graph, then click Data.
10. Click the Transpose row/column button in the Graph Data window. (*Hint*: The Transpose row/column button is the second button in the Graph Data window.)
11. Close the Graph Data window, save changes, then delete the information at the top of the artboard.
12. Choose colors that you like for each section of the pie graph and the corresponding legend box.
13. Save your work, compare your graph to Figure 31, then close the Television document.

FIGURE 31
Completed Project Builder 2

What is your favorite TV program?

You are a freelance designer, and you are hired by a small market research company that specializes in television. They are submitting an annual report to one of their network clients. The report contains a number of pie charts. They want you to design a look that is more "eye catching."

1. Open AI 9-7.ai, then save it as **Designer Pie**.
2. Click the Group Selection tool, then click the largest wedge two times. (*Hint*: The largest wedge and the Drama legend box are selected.)
3. Change the fill of the two objects to any red.
4. Moving clockwise, fill the remaining wedges and legend boxes with any of the orange, yellow, green, blue, and violet swatches, respectively.
5. Deselect all, click the Direct Selection tool, drag a marquee to select the pie chart only, then scale the chart 150%.
6. Deselect, click the Type tool, type **34%** on top of the red wedge, change the font size to 27 pt, then set the fill color to White.
7. Moving clockwise, type the following percentage values on the remaining wedges: **25**, **9**, **18**, **5**, and **9**. (*Hint*: Change the fill color of the values on top of the yellow and orange wedges to Black.)
8. Using the Direct Selection tool, move each word from the legend over its corresponding wedge. (*Hint*: The words "Game Show"

and "Soap Opera" must be positioned outside of their corresponding wedge because they are too long.)
9. Change the fill color of Sports and Drama to White.
10. Hide the legend boxes, then reposition the What is your favorite TV program? text, and any other objects if necessary.
11. Select only the wedges of the graph, using the Direct Selection tool.

12. Click Effect on the Application bar, point to Stylize, click Round Corners, type **.139**, then click OK.
13. Apply a 2-point Black stroke to the pie wedges.
14. Save your work, compare your graph to Figure 32, then close Designer Pie.

FIGURE 32
Completed Design Project

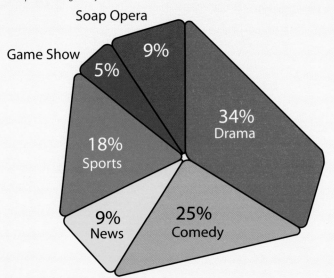

What is your favorite TV program?

PORTFOLIO PROJECT

You are the chief designer of an in-house design group in a large department store. The head of the Digital Department has asked you to help with a presentation that shows how computers, scanners, and printers have been selling in comparison to one another over the last four weeks. Specifically, she wants you to create a graph that emphasizes how many more scanners she sells each week than computers or printers.

1. Gather the weekly sales data from each of the three departments, which is as follows:

	Computers	Printers	Scanners
Week One	11	13	55
Week Two	12	15	40
Week Three	14	6	61
Week Four	9	11	35

2. Draw a simple bar graph on scrap paper, showing the sales relationships among the three products.
3. Think about what would be the best type of graph to convey the data.
4. Decide the colors and fonts that will be used in the graph.
5. Create a new CMYK Color document, then save it as **Sales**.
6. Create a column graph that is 4" wide by 4" high.

7. Enter the data (from Step 1) in the Graph Data window.
8. Close the Graph Data window, saving changes to it.
9. Select the Scanners group, using the Group Selection tool, then apply the line graph type to it.

FIGURE 33
Completed Portfolio Project

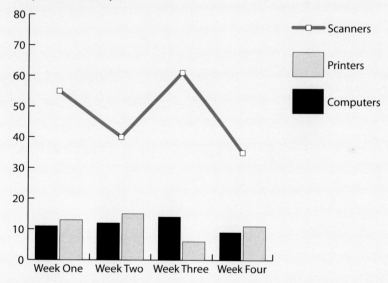

10. Change the color and thickness of the line graph so that it is easy to see.
11. Format the rest of the graph (labels, Printers group, and Computers group) if desired.
12. Save your work, compare your graph to Figure 33, then close the Sales document.

Creating Graphs in Illustrator

ILLUSTRATOR 9-33

chapter

10

DRAWING
WITH SYMBOLS

1. Create symbols

2. Place symbol instances

3. Modify symbols and symbol instances

4. Create symbol instance sets

5. Modify symbol instance sets

In Illustrator, the file size of a document is largely determined by the number and complexity of objects in the document. The greater the number of objects in the document, the greater the file size. A large number of objects with gradients, blends, and effects *greatly* increases the file size. When you are creating graphics for the World Wide Web, file size becomes a serious concern.

Symbols are one solution for creating complex files while maintaining a relatively low file size. Symbols are graphic objects that you create and store on the Symbols panel.

Imagine that you were drawing a field of flowers, and you have drawn a pink, a blue, and a yellow flower. Each flower has a radial gradient in its center and color blends to add dimension to the petals and green leaves. Now imagine that you must drag and drop 200 copies of each to create

your field of flowers! Along with a cramp in your hand, you would have an unusually large Illustrator file.

With the three flowers defined as symbols, you can create 200 symbol instances of each flower symbol quickly and easily. The key is: You haven't actually added the complex artwork multiple times, because the instances don't really exist as artwork. They are merely a reference to the original artwork that is the symbol; the instances function only to show the positioning of the symbol artwork on the artboard. Think of it this way: Symbol instances are merely virtual representations of a symbol.

Symbolism tools allow you to edit large numbers of symbol instances quickly and effectively. Whenever you are using the same artwork multiple times in a document, consider using symbols to save time and disk space.

Tools You'll Use

Symbols panel

Symbolism tools

CREATE
SYMBOLS

What You'll Do

 In this lesson, you will create symbols from Illustrator artwork and save them on the Symbols panel.

Creating Symbols

A **symbol** is artwork that you store on the Symbols panel and reuse in the document. You can create symbols from any Illustrator artwork, including text, compound paths, and grouped paths. Symbols may also include blends, effects, brush strokes, gradients, and even other symbols. The Symbols panel, as shown in Figure 1, is a great place to store artwork that you plan to use again. When you use symbol artwork, you can modify it on the artboard, while retaining its original appearance on the panel. In this way, you can think of the Symbols panel as a database of your original art.

FIGURE 1
Symbols panel

Symbol Libraries Menu

Place Symbol Instance button

Break Link to Symbol button

Symbol Options button

New Symbol button

Delete Symbol button

FIGURE 2

Symbol Options dialog box

Symbol Options

Name: Ski Lodge

OK

Type: ● Graphic   ○ Movie Clip

Cancel

Flash Registration:

☐ Enable Guides for 9-slice scaling

Create symbols

1. Open AI 10-1.ai, then save it as **Trail Map**.
2. Click the **Symbols button** ♣ to open the Symbols panel.
3. Select the brown house picture in the scratch area.
4. Click the **Symbols panel list arrow**, then click **New Symbol**.
5. Type **Ski Lodge** in the Name text box of the Symbol Options dialog box, click the **Graphic option button**, then compare your Symbol Options dialog box to Figure 10-2.
6. Click **OK**.
   The Ski Lodge symbol becomes a new symbol on the Symbols panel.
7. Select the green circle icon in the scratch area, then drag it into the Symbols panel. The Symbol Options dialog box opens automatically.
8. Type **Novice** in the Name text box, click the **Graphic option button**, then click **OK**. Throughout this chapter, all symbols that you create should be Graphic types.
9. Add the blue square icon to the Symbols panel, then name it **Intermediate**.
10. Add the black diamond icon to the Symbols panel, then name it **Expert**.
11. Add the red square icon to the Symbols panel, then name it **First Aid**.
12. Add the yellow oval icon to the Symbols panel, then name it **Chairlift**.
    Your Symbols panel should resemble Figure 3.
13. Delete the Ski Lodge, Novice, Intermediate, Expert, First Aid, and Chairlift icons in the scratch area, then save your work.

You created new symbols by using the Symbols panel menu and by dragging and dropping.

FIGURE 3

Symbols panel with new symbols added

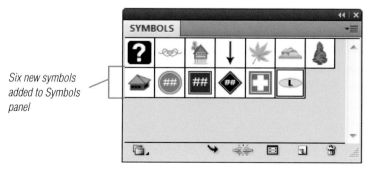

Six new symbols added to Symbols panel

PLACE SYMBOL INSTANCES

What You'll Do

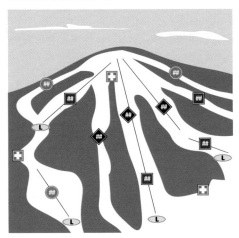

In this lesson, you will place symbol instances on the artboard.

Placing Instances of Symbols

If a symbol is artwork that is stored on the Symbols panel, then the artwork—when put to use in the document—is called a **symbol instance**. You can place a symbol instance on the artboard by first selecting the symbol on the Symbols panel, then dragging it to the artboard, or by selecting it, then clicking the Place Symbol Instance button on the Symbols panel, as shown in Figure 4. You can also use the Place Symbol Instance command on the Symbols panel menu.

Symbol instances are "linked" to their corresponding symbols on the panel. This relationship introduces powerful functionality when you work with symbol instances. For example, you can select all the instances of a symbol by selecting the symbol on the panel and then clicking the Select All Instances command on the panel menu.

FIGURE 4
Placing a symbol instance

Symbol instance placed on artboard

Selected symbol

Place Symbol Instance button

FIGURE 5

Positioning symbol instances

FIGURE 6

Positioning copies of the Chairlift symbol instance

FIGURE 7

Positioning the Novice, Intermediate, Expert, and First Aid symbol instances

Place instances of a symbol

1. Click the **Novice symbol** on the Symbols panel.

2. Click the **Symbols panel list arrow**, then click **Place Symbol Instance**.

    A single Novice symbol instance appears on the artboard.

3. Drag the **Novice symbol instance** to the location shown in Figure 5.

4. Click the **Intermediate symbol** on the Symbols panel, then drag it to the artboard above the Novice symbol instance.

5. Drag a **symbol instance** of the Expert, First Aid, and Chairlift symbols onto the artboard, then position them as shown in Figure 5.

6. Click the **Chairlift symbol instance** on the artboard, press and hold **[Alt]** (Win) or **[option]** (Mac), drag and drop three copies, then position the copies as shown in Figure 6.

7. Copy and reposition the Novice, Intermediate, Expert, and First Aid symbol instances so that your screen resembles Figure 7.

    Dragging and dropping copies is the easiest way to duplicate the symbol instances.

8. Save your work.

You placed symbol instances of five symbols on the artboard. You then duplicated the symbol instances and positioned them on the artboard.

MODIFY SYMBOLS AND
SYMBOL INSTANCES

What You'll Do

In this lesson, you will modify both symbol instances and the symbols themselves.

Modifying Symbol Instances

When working with symbol instances, approach them as you would any other Illustrator artwork. You can transform symbol instances by using commands on the Object menu or by using any of the transform tools. You can cut, copy, and drag and drop copies of symbol instances. You can perform any operation from the Transparency, Appearance, and Graphic Styles panels. For example, you can reduce the opacity of a symbol instance and you can apply effects, such as a drop shadow or a distortion.

Symbols are most often composed of multiple objects, such as you would expect to find in a drawing of a butterfly or a flower, for example. When you select a symbol instance on the artboard, its selection marks show only a simple bounding box, as shown in Figure 8; the individual elements of the artwork are not selected.

You can, however, select the individual components of a symbol instance by using the Expand command on the Object menu. The bounding box disappears, and the individual elements of the artwork are available to be selected (and modified), as shown in Figure 9.

Modifying Symbols

Once you have modified a symbol instance, you can use the modified artwork to redefine the associated symbol on the panel by replacing the original symbol. When you do so, all existing symbol instances are updated and reflect the changes to the symbol. If you don't want a particular symbol instance to be updated, you can select the instance and break the link to the symbol. The symbol instance will no longer be associated with the symbol.

You can also modify a symbol instance on the artboard and use it to create a new symbol without affecting the original symbol that it is based on. Thus, the Symbols panel is very useful for storing subtle or dramatic variations of artwork. For example, if you are drawing a landscape that features a wind farm, you can draw a single windmill, save it as a symbol, rotate the blades on the original artwork, then save a new symbol, and so on.

QUICKTIP

Symbols, ideal for web graphics, can be output as Scalable Vector Graphics (SVG) or Flash files (SWF). To output your symbol artwork as SVG, click File on the Application bar, click Save As, then click SVG from the Save as type list arrow. To output your symbol artwork as Flash, click File on the Application bar, click Export, then click Flash (SWF) from the Save as type list arrow. Both formats offer an Options dialog box for you to make further specifications about your final product.

FIGURE 8

When you select a symbol instance, the individual elements of the artwork are not selected

FIGURE 9

The Expand command allows you to select the individual elements of the artwork

Edit symbol instances

1. Select the green Novice symbol instance in the lower-left corner of the artboard.

   A bounding box identifies the selection. The elements of the artwork cannot be selected individually.

2. Click **Object** on the Application bar, then click **Expand**.

3. In the Expand dialog box, verify that the Object check box is checked and the Fill check box is not checked, then click **OK**.

   The elements of the symbol instance are selected individually.

4. Deselect the symbol instance, click the **Type tool** T, highlight the two # signs in the symbol instance, then type **1**.

   Your screen should resemble Figure 10.

   TIP   If you receive a message stating that the text was created in a previous version of Illustrator, click OK.

5. Using the same method, expand the Novice, Intermediate, and Expert symbol instances, then change their numbers to those shown in Figure 11.

6. Select all of the symbol instances and each of the blue lines, then hide them.

   TIP   Do not use the Select All command to select the symbol instances and the blue lines.

   Your screen should resemble Figure 12.

You used the Expand command to allow you to select individual elements of a symbol instance and edit those elements.

FIGURE 10
Editing a symbol instance

Replace ## with 1

FIGURE 12
The artboard with the symbol instances hidden

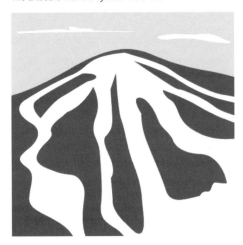

FIGURE 11
Adding numbers to symbol instances

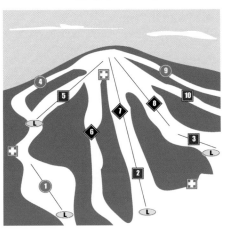

FIGURE 13

Positioning four symbol instances of the Ski Lodge symbol

FIGURE 14

Updated instances of the Ski Lodge symbol

This ski lodge graphic is not updated because it is no longer linked to the Ski Lodge symbol

Edit a symbol

1. Position four symbol instances of the Ski Lodge symbol, as shown in Figure 13.

2. Select the bottom-right Ski Lodge symbol instance, then click the **Break Link to Symbol button** on the Symbols panel.

3. Select the top Ski Lodge symbol instance, then click the **Break Link to Symbol button** .

4. Scale the top ski lodge artwork 50%.

5. Press and hold **[Alt]** (Win) or **[option]** (Mac), then drag the **scaled artwork** on top of the Ski Lodge symbol on the Symbols panel.

   The three symbol instances of the Ski Lodge symbol are updated, as shown in Figure 14. The bottom ski lodge artwork does not change.

6. Click the **Sequoia symbol**, then place one instance of the symbol in the scratch area.

7. Click the **Break Link to Symbol button** .

8. Deselect, click the **Direct Selection tool** , remove the brown "tree trunk" areas from the symbol instance, then reduce the artwork 50%.

9. Press and hold **[Alt]** (Win) or **[option]** (Mac), then drag the **edited tree artwork** on top of the Sequoia symbol on the Symbols panel.

10. Delete the Sequoia symbol instance in the scratch area.

You edited symbols by modifying instances, then replacing the original symbols with the edited artwork. You protected a symbol instance from modification by breaking its link.

Transform symbol instances

1. Select the six green objects within the snow area of the artboard, then change their fill color to a light blue swatch so that your screen resembles Figure 15.

   TIP   Use the Color panel to mix a new light blue color (if necessary).

2. Click the **Sequoia symbol** on the Symbols panel.

3. Click the **Place Symbol Instance button** ↘ on the Symbols panel, then position the instance on the artboard, as shown in Figure 16.

4. Drag and drop nine copies of the Sequoia symbol instance on the artboard, so that your screen resembles Figure 17.

(continued)

FIGURE 15
Six objects filled with a new color

FIGURE 16
Positioning the Sequoia symbol instance

FIGURE 17
Positioning nine copies of the Sequoia symbol instance

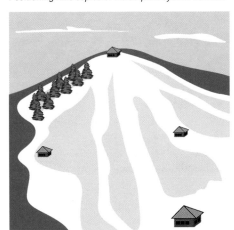

Drawing with Symbols

FIGURE 18

Positioning 14 copies of the Sequoia symbol instance

5. Verify that the Sequoia symbol is still selected on the Symbols panel, click the **Symbols panel list arrow**, then click **Select All Instances**.

   All instances of the Sequoia symbol are selected on the artboard.

6. Scale the symbol instances 75%.

7. Drag and drop 14 copies of the newly scaled Sequoia symbol instance to the opposite side of the artboard, as shown in Figure 18.

   TIP   Press [Alt](Win) or [option](Mac) while dragging to create copies.

8. Save your work.

You positioned one instance of a symbol on the artboard, then copied it nine times. You used the Select All Instances command to quickly select the ten instances of the symbol, scaled them 75%, then positioned 14 copies of the scaled symbol instance.

Customizing and using SWF presets

The Adobe Flash (SWF) file format is a vector-based graphics file format. Because it is vector based, it is effective for the creation of fully scalable and low-file-size graphics for the web. And also because it is vector based, it's ideal for exporting Illustrator graphics to Flash. Because the file format is vector-based, the artwork maintains its image quality at any resolution. In Illustrator, you can create individual animation frames on layers and then export the image layers into individual frames for use on a website. You can also define symbols in an Illustrator file to reduce the size of an animation. When exported, each symbol is defined only once in the SWF file. You can save artwork as an SWF file by using the Export command or the Save For Web & Devices command. Benefits of each include: The Export (SWF) command provides the most control over animation and bitmap compression. The Save For Web & Devices command provides more control over the mix of SWF and bitmap formats in a sliced layout.

CREATE SYMBOL
INSTANCE SETS

What You'll Do

▶ *In this lesson, you will use the Symbol Sprayer tool to create sets of symbol instances and mixed symbol instance sets.*

Creating a Symbol Instance Set

Instead of creating symbol instances one at a time using the Symbols panel, you can use the Symbol Sprayer tool to create multiple symbol instances quickly. Imagine that you have a symbol of a star and you want to draw a night sky filled with stars. The Symbol Sprayer tool would be a good choice for applying the star symbol multiple times.

Symbol instances created with the Symbol Sprayer tool are called **symbol instance sets**. Incorporate the term "set" into your work with symbols to differentiate the multiple symbol instances created with the Symbol Sprayer tool from individual instances of a symbol that you create using the Symbols panel.

To create a symbol instance set, click the symbol that you want to use on the Symbols panel, then drag the Symbol Sprayer tool where you want the symbols to appear on the artboard.

Working with Symbol Instance Sets

When you create a symbol instance set with the Symbol Sprayer tool, the entire set of symbols is identified within a bounding box, as shown in Figure 19. If the set is selected and you begin dragging the Symbol Sprayer tool again, the new symbol instances will be added to the selected set—even if the new symbol instances are outside of the existing set's bounding box. (The bounding box will expand to encompass the new symbol instances.)

You can also create mixed symbol instance sets. Mixed symbol instance sets include symbol instances based on more than one symbol. To create a mixed symbol instance set, create your first set of symbol instances, click a different symbol on the Symbols panel, then drag the Symbol Sprayer tool where you want the new symbols to appear on the artboard. The new symbol instances will be added to the existing set, as shown in Figure 20.

Even though a symbol instance set, by definition, appears as multiple objects, it is best to think of it as a single object. A symbol instance set can be modified and transformed (as a whole). Figure 21 shows a symbol instance set that has been reflected using the Reflect tool.

FIGURE 19

A symbol instance set created with the Symbol Sprayer tool

FIGURE 20

A mixed symbol instance set

FIGURE 21

A symbol instance set transformed with the Reflect tool

Setting Options for the Symbol Sprayer Tool

The Symbol Sprayer tool has many options to help you control the dispersion of symbol instances. You can access these options in the Symbolism Tools Options dialog box by double-clicking the Symbol Sprayer tool on the Tools panel.

The Diameter setting determines the brush size of the tool. Use a larger brush size to disperse symbol instances over a greater area of the artboard. Note that the brush size does not determine the size of the symbol instances themselves.

The Intensity setting determines the number of instances of the symbol that will be sprayed. The higher the intensity setting, the greater the number of symbol instances that will be dispersed in a given amount of time.

The Symbol Set Density setting determines how closely the symbol instances will be positioned to each other. The higher the density setting, the more closely packed the instances will appear. Figure 22 shows a symbol instance set with a high symbol set density, and Figure 23 shows a symbol instance set with a low symbol set density.

FIGURE 22

A symbol instance set with a high symbol set density

FIGURE 23

A symbol instance set with a low symbol set density

Expanding a Symbol Set

Despite the many options available with the Symbol Sprayer tool, it is often difficult to position multiple symbols exactly where you want them. For this reason alone, it is best to think of the Symbol Sprayer tool as a means to quickly disperse symbol instances but not as a tool to position symbols precisely.

Once you have created a symbol instance set that contains roughly the number of symbol instances you want to work with and have positioned them roughly where you want them to be on the artboard, you can then apply the Expand command to release the set into individual symbol instances. Figure 24 shows a symbol instance set expanded into individual symbol instances.

The power of this operation cannot be overstated. Once expanded, all the symbol instances of the set are available to you to be transformed, repositioned, duplicated, or deleted. Expand the individual symbol instances to be able to select their component parts.

FIGURE 24
A symbol instance set expanded into individual symbol instances

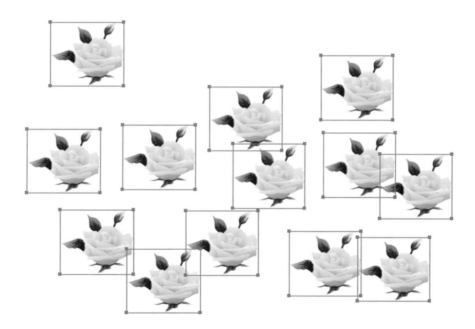

Use the Symbol Sprayer tool

1. Click the **Sequoia symbol** on the Symbols panel (if necessary).

2. Double-click the **Symbol Sprayer tool** 📷.

3. Type **.5** in the Diameter text box, type **3** in the Intensity text box, type **5** in the Symbol Set Density text box, then click **OK**.

4. Click and drag the **Symbol Sprayer tool** to spray instances of the Sequoia symbol over the gray areas so that your artboard resembles Figure 25.

   > TIP Don't try to create all the instances in one move. Click and drag the Symbol Sprayer tool multiple times in short bursts. Your results will vary from the figure.

5. Press and hold [**Alt**] (Win) or [**option**] (Mac), then click the **Symbol Sprayer tool** over symbol instances that you do not want to include to remove them (if necessary).

6. Select the symbol set, click **Object** on the Application bar, click **Expand**, verify that only the Object check box is checked, then click **OK**.

7. Deselect, then using the Direct Selection tool ▶, move the individual Sequoia symbol instances so that your work resembles Figure 26.

   You may also copy and/or delete instances (if necessary).

8. Click **Object** on the Application bar, click **Show All**, then while the hidden objects are still selected, bring them to the front, then deselect.

   Your screen should resemble Figure 27.

9. Save your work, then close Trail Map.

You defined the diameter, the intensity, and the symbol set density for the Symbol Sprayer tool. You then used the Symbol Sprayer tool to create a set of Sequoia symbols.

FIGURE 25
Instances of the Sequoia symbol created with the Symbol Sprayer tool

FIGURE 26
Moving and deleting symbol instances from the set

FIGURE 27
The majority of the trail map artwork is created with symbol instances

FIGURE 28
Spraying instances of the Red Stone symbol

FIGURE 29
Spraying instances of the Purple Stone symbol

FIGURE 30
Spraying instances of the Green Stone, Orange Stone, and Tan Stone symbols

FIGURE 31
Masking the mixed symbol instance set

Create a mixed symbol instance set

1. Open AI 10-2.ai, then save it as **Fish Tank**.

2. Click the **Red Stone symbol** on the Symbols panel.

3. Double-click the **Symbol Sprayer tool** 🅱.

4. Type **1** in the Diameter text box, type **8** in the Intensity text box, type **5** in the Symbol Set Density text box, then click **OK**.

5. Click and drag the **Symbol Sprayer tool** over the "sand," as shown in Figure 28.

6. Click the **Purple Stone symbol**, then drag the **Symbol Sprayer tool** over the "sand," as shown in Figure 29.

   The Purple Stone symbols are added to the set, creating a mixed symbol instance set.

7. Add the Green Stone, Orange Stone, and Tan Stone symbols to the set, so that your screen resembles Figure 30.

8. Select the sand object, copy it, paste in front, then bring the copy to the front.

9. Press and hold [**Shift**], then click the **mixed symbol instance set** so that the sand and the set of rocks are selected.

10. Click **Object** on the Application bar, point to **Clipping Mask**, click **Make**, deselect, then save your work.

    The sand acts as a mask to hide the rocks that extend beyond the sand object, as shown in Figure 31.

You used five different symbols and the Symbol Sprayer tool to create a mixed set of symbol instances.

MODIFY SYMBOL
INSTANCE SETS

What You'll Do

▶ *In this lesson, you will use various symbolism tools to modify symbol instance sets.*

Using Symbolism Tools

Illustrator offers seven symbolism tools that you can use to modify symbol instances or sets of symbol instances. You will most often use the symbolism tools to affect symbol instances within a set, since individual symbol instances are easy to select and modify directly with transform tools and menu commands. Table 10-1 lists each symbolism tool and its function. Figure 32 shows an illustration of a symbol instance set with each tool applied to the set.

TABLE 10-1: Symbolism Tools

symbolism tool	function
Symbol Sprayer tool	Places symbol instances on the artboard.
Symbol Shifter tool	Moves symbol instances and/or changes their stacking order in the set
Symbol Scruncher tool	Pulls symbol instances together or apart
Symbol Sizer tool	Increases or decreases the size of symbol instances
Symbol Spinner tool	Rotates symbol instances
Symbol Stainer tool	Changes the color of symbol instances gradually to the current fill color on the Tools panel
Symbol Screener tool	Increases or decreases the transparency of symbol instances
Symbol Styler tool	Applies the selected style on the Styles panel to symbol instances

When you apply symbolism tools to mixed symbol instance sets, each corresponding symbol must be selected on the Symbols panel in order for each type of symbol instance to be modified by the tool. For example, imagine you have created a mixed symbol instance set of four types of flowers (daisy, tulip, rose, and lily) and only the daisy symbol is selected on the Symbols panel. If you apply a symbolism tool to the mixed symbol instance set, only the instances of the daisy symbol will be modified.

When working with symbolism tools, it is also important that you set realistic goals. The symbolism tools are particularly useful if you have created a symbol set that is intended to appear random. For example, if you use symbol instances to render multiple stars in the night sky, the symbolism tools will be an excellent choice for modifying their orientation on the artboard. However, if your goal is to position symbol instances precisely in your artwork, you should expand the symbol set and use the selection tools and transform tools to modify each instance directly.

FIGURE 32
Applying the symbolism tools

*Applying the Symbol
Shifter tool*

*Applying the Symbol
Sizer tool*

*Applying the Symbol
Spinner tool*

*Applying the Symbol
Stainer tool*

*Applying the Symbol
Screener tool*

*Applying the Symbol
Scruncher tool*

*Applying the Soft Cast
Shadow style with the
Symbol Styler tool*

Lesson 5   Modify Symbol Instance Sets

Use the Symbol Stainer tool

1. Click **Object** on the Application bar, then click **Unlock All**.

2. Deselect, then select the set of fish symbol instances.

3. Change the fill color on the Tools panel to green.

4. Click the **Symbol Stainer tool** 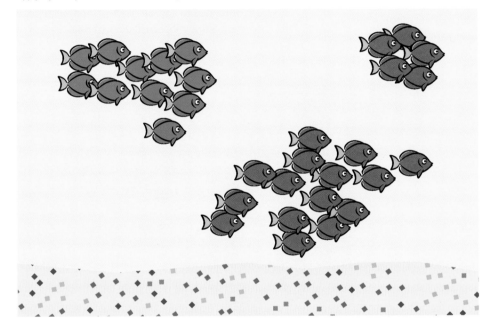.

   The Symbol Stainer tool is hidden beneath the Symbol Sprayer tool.

   > TIP Press and hold the current Symbol tool until you see all of the Symbol tools, then click the Tearoff tab at the end of the row of tools to create a floating panel of all of the symbolism tools.

5. Click and drag the **Symbol Stainer tool** over the 11 fish symbol instances in the upper-left region of the artboard so that your work resembles Figure 33.

   > TIP Using the Symbol Stainer tool results in increased file size and may tax your computer's performance.

6. Position the Symbol Stainer tool over the bottommost fish symbol instance in the same group.

   (continued)

FIGURE 33
Applying the Symbol Stainer tool with a green fill

FIGURE 34
Applying the Symbol Stainer tool with a yellow fill

7. Press and hold [**Alt**] (Win) or [**option**] (Mac), then press and hold the mouse button for approximately two seconds.

   Pressing [Alt] (Win) or [option] (Mac) while using the Symbol Stainer tool gradually removes color applied by the Symbol Stainer tool. The symbol instance that you clicked returns to its original blue color. The surrounding symbol instances are not affected as directly; their color changes toward the original blue color, but remains somewhat green. Your results may vary.

8. Change the fill color on the Tools panel to yellow.

9. Drag the **Symbol Stainer tool** over the five fish symbol instances in the upper-right region of the artboard, so that your work resembles Figure 34.

You used the Symbol Stainer tool to modify the color of symbol instances within a set.

Use the Symbol Shifter tool

1. Double-click the **Symbol Shifter tool** to open the Symbolism Tools Options dialog box.

   The Symbol Shifter tool is hidden beneath the current symbolism tool.

2. Type **.25** in the Diameter text box, then click **OK**.

3. Position the Symbol Shifter tool over any of the green fish, press and hold [**Shift**], then click the **fish instance**.

   The symbol instance is brought to the front of the set.

   TIP It's usually a good idea to enter a small diameter setting when you want to affect the stacking order of instances in a set. A larger brush will affect the stacking order of surrounding instances.

4. Press and hold [**Shift**][**Alt**] (Win) or [**Shift**][**option**] (Mac), then click a **green fish**.

   The symbol instance is sent to the back. Figure 35 shows an example of the green fish instances after the stacking order has been affected by the Symbol Shifter tool. Compare your choices and results.

5. Change the diameter setting of the Symbol Shifter tool to 2.5.

6. Click and drag the **Symbol Shifter tool** over the yellow fish until they no longer touch each other, as shown in Figure 36.

   Your results may vary.

You used the Symbol Shifter tool to change the stacking order of instances within the symbol set and to move symbol instances within the set.

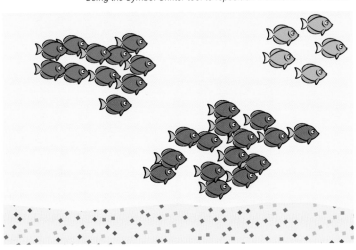

Drawing with Symbols

FIGURE 37
Using the Symbol Spinner tool on the green fish

Use the Symbol Spinner tool

1. Double-click the **Symbol Spinner tool** .

2. Type **2.6** in the Diameter text box, type **10** in the Intensity text box, then click **OK**.

3. Position the Symbol Spinner tool over the center of the green fish group.

4. Click and drag slightly to the right, so that the fish rotate, as shown in Figure 37.

   Your results may vary.

   > TIP   The blue arrows that appear when you click and drag the Symbol Spinner tool are not always reliable predictors of the final rotation of the symbol instances. The diameter and intensity settings and the location of the tool in regard to the instances all affect the impact of the rotation.

5. Position the Symbol Spinner tool over the center of the yellow fish group.

6. Click and drag slightly to the upper-left so that the yellow fish rotate, as shown in Figure 38.

   Your results may vary.

You used the Symbol Spinner tool to rotate symbol instances within the set.

FIGURE 38
Using the Symbol Spinner tool on the yellow fish

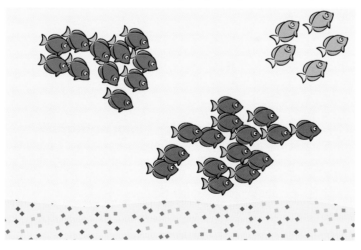

Use the Symbol Sizer tool

1. Double-click the **Symbol Sizer tool** .

2. Type **2** in the Diameter text box, type **8** in the Intensity text box, then click **OK**.

3. Position the Symbol Sizer tool over the center of the green fish group.

4. Press and hold the mouse button for approximately two seconds so that your work resembles Figure 39.

   Your results may vary.

5. Position the Symbol Sizer tool over the center of the blue fish group.

(continued)

FIGURE 39
Using the Symbol Sizer tool to enlarge symbol instances

Preparing a document for Flash authoring

When you import Illustrator text into Flash you have a number of options: You can import the text as "live" editable test, as outlines, or as a flattened bitmap image. If your text has more complex effects applied to it, like blend modes, Illustrator effects, or reduced opacity, import the text into Flash as a movie clip, because that preserves the editability of compatible visual effects. By default, Illustrator text imports as editable Flash text.

Drawing with Symbols

FIGURE 40

Using the Symbol Sizer tool to reduce symbol instances

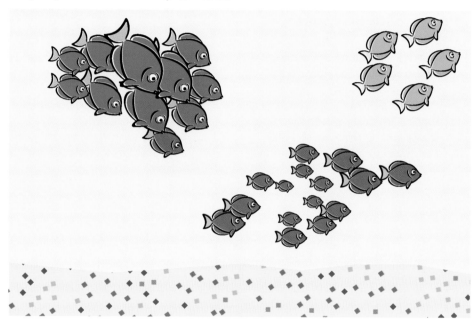

6. Press and hold **[Alt]** (Win) or **[option]** (Mac), then press and hold the mouse button for approximately three seconds.

7. Deselect all, then save your work.

   Your screen should resemble Figure 40. Your results may vary.

8. Close the Fish Tank document.

You used the Symbol Sizer tool to change the size of symbol instances within the set.

Create symbols.

1. Open AI 10-3.ai, then save it as **Winter Ball Fun**.
2. Show the Brushes panel, then drag the Radiant Star brush onto the artboard.
3. Verify that the Symbols panel is displayed, then drag the Radiant Star artwork into the Symbols panel.
4. Name the new symbol **Snowflake**.
5. Delete the Radiant Star artwork from the artboard.

Place symbol instances.

1. Click the Snowflake symbol on the Symbols panel.
2. Click the Place Symbol Instance button on the Symbols panel.
3. Position the symbol instance between the words ball and December.

Modify symbols and symbol instances.

1. Scale the Snowflake symbol instance 35%, then reposition the Snowflake symbol instance (if necessary).
2. Click Effect on the Application bar, point to Distort & Transform, click Pucker & Bloat, type **50** in the text box, then click OK.
3. Change the opacity of the symbol instance to 75%.

4. Click the Break Link to Symbol button on the Symbols panel.
5. Press [Alt] (Win) or [option] (Mac), then drag the modified snowflake artwork directly on top of the Snowflake symbol on the Symbols panel.

Create symbol instance sets.

1. Double-click the Symbol Sprayer tool.
2. Type **1** for the Diameter, **2** for the Intensity, and **1** for the Symbol Set Density in the Symbolism Tools Options dialog box.
3. Spray approximately 25 symbol instances of the Snowflake symbol evenly over the artboard.

Modify symbol instance sets.

1. Use the Symbol Sizer tool to enlarge and reduce symbol instances.
2. Expand the symbol set.
3. Move or delete symbols to your liking.
4. Save your work, then compare your illustration to Figure 41. (*Hint*: Your results will vary from the figure.)
5. Close Winter Ball Fun.

FIGURE 41
Completed Skills Review

You work in the design department of a major Internet portal site. As part of the promotion of this year's Hooray for Hollywood Awards, your site will link to the Awards' site. You are asked to create a banner that says "click here to meet the stars" against a starry sky.

1. Open AI 10-4.ai, then save it as **Hollywood Stars**.
2. Double-click the Symbol Sprayer tool.
3. Type **2** for the Diameter, **1** for the Intensity, and **10** for the Symbol Set Density.

4. Click the 5 Point Star symbol on the Symbols panel, then drag the Symbol Sprayer tool across the gradient-filled rectangle.
5. Repeat Step 4, using the 8 Point Star symbol on the Symbols panel.
6. Expand the symbol set.
7. Use the Symbol Shifter tool to move or delete symbol instances that overlap each other.
8. Use the Symbol Sizer tool to enlarge and reduce symbol instances to add depth and variety.

9. Show all to reveal the semitransparent text.
10. Save your work, compare your illustration to Figure 42, then close the Hollywood Stars document.

FIGURE 42
Completed Project Builder 1

You work at a busy design firm. Your boss e-mails you an Illustrator file. He tells you that the file contains a symbol of the American flag that he saved some months ago. He wants you to update the existing symbol on the Symbols panel so that the flag is scaled 25% and the opacity of the flag is 50%. He also wants the new symbol to show the flag waving.

1. Open AI 10-5.ai, then save it as **American Flag Symbol**.
2. Show the Symbols panel (if necessary), then place an instance of the American Flag symbol on the artboard.
3. Break the link between the symbol instance and the symbol.
4. Click Object on the Application bar, point to Envelope Distort, then click Make with Warp.
5. Click the Style list arrow, then click Flag.
6. Type **-35** for the Bend value, then click OK.
7. Scale the artwork 25%.
8. Show the Transparency panel (if necessary), then change the opacity of the artwork to 50%.
9. Replace the original American Flag symbol with the modified artwork, then remove the flag artwork from the artboard.
10. Save your work, then compare your Symbols panel with Figure 43.
11. Close the American Flag Symbol document.

FIGURE 43
Completed Project Builder 2

The nice lady who works at your town's Chamber of Commerce has created a poster for this year's Memorial Day parade and asks you if you could jazz it up. Since your firm is very busy, your improvements must be quick and simple. You e-mail a file containing a symbol of the American flag to an employee with instructions for updating the symbol. He e-mails the file back to you with the updated symbol, and you paste the parade text into the file.

1. Open AI 10-6.ai, then save it as **Memorial Day Parade**.
2. Fill the black rectangle with orange, then hide it.
3. Select all the elements on the artboard, then hide them.
4. Place an instance of the American Flag symbol in the lower-left corner of the artboard.
5. Create a pattern out of the American Flag symbol instances that covers the entire artboard. (*Hint*: Refer to Figure 44 for ideas.)
6. Select all the symbol instances, group them, then send them to the back.
7. Show all, then deselect all.
8. Select the orange rectangle and the symbol instances, then make a clipping mask.
9. Apply a 10% cyan fill and a 3-point Black stroke to the clipping mask.
10. Save your work, compare your screen to Figure 44, then close Memorial Day Parade.

FIGURE 44
Completed Design Project

Town of Springfield

Memorial Day Parade

Memorial Day at 11 am

Starts at the Page Street Armory

Ends at the Common Park

Bring the family!

You own a design firm in Silicon Valley that specializes in solutions for Web sites. You are approached by a representative of Black Swan Technologies, a global company noted for engineering breakthrough devices in the medical field. The representative tells you that he wants you to redesign the splash page of their Web site to convey the fact that they work with all sectors of the medical industry. The company's motto is "We Are Everywhere."

1. Open AI 10-7.ai, then save it as **Black Swan**.
2. Think about ways to design the Black Swan Technologies logo.
3. Do you think that parts of the logo suggest a bat more than a bird?
4. How do you think that the concept "We Are Everywhere" can be incorporated visually into the splash page?
5. Discuss how reproducing the logo as a symbol presents possibilities for a splash page design based on the phrase "We Are Everywhere."
6. Create a new symbol using the swan artwork. (*Hint*: Modify the artwork using any Illustrator tools or features that you want before adding the new symbol to the Symbols panel.)

7. Use the swan symbol and the symbolism tools to create a new splash page for Black Swan Technologies.

FIGURE 45
Completed Portfolio Project

8. Save your work, then compare your results with Figure 45.
9. Close the Black Swan document.

Drawing with Symbols

chapter

11

CREATING
3D OBJECTS

1. Extrude objects

2. Revolve objects

3. Manipulate surface shading and lighting

4. Map artwork to 3D objects

11 CREATING
3D OBJECTS

Creating 3D objects is one of the more exciting features in Illustrator CS4. With unprecedented ease, you can transform a simple two-dimensional (2D) object into an eye-popping three-dimensional (3D) graphic. You can extrude 2D objects to give them depth, and you can add interesting details by applying a bevel edge. You can revolve 2D objects around an axis to create stunning 3D graphics, complete with surface shading and highlights. You

have a number of options for manipulating that surface shading. Apply diffuse shading for subtle highlights, or apply plastic shading to make the object reflect light as though its surface were shiny. You can even add and delete light sources to dramatically change the way a 3D graphic is lit. If that's not enough, once you've designed the 3D object, you can "map" 2D graphics, making them appear to "wrap around" the 3D object. Very cool!

Tools You'll Use

EXTRUDE OBJECTS

What You'll Do

In this lesson, you will use the 3D Extrude & Bevel effect to extrude objects.

Extruding Objects

Illustrator's **Extrude & Bevel** effect applies a three-dimensional effect to two-dimensional objects. A two-dimensional object has two axes: an X axis representing the width and a Y axis representing the height. When you **extrude** an object you add depth to an object by extending it on its Z axis, as shown in Figure 1. An object's Z axis is always perpendicular to the object's front surface.

Figure 2 shows four 2D objects before and after being extruded. Note the changes to each object's fill color on the front surface and the light and dark shadings on the other surfaces. These shadings create the 3D effect and are applied automatically when the Extrude & Bevel effect is applied.

QUICKTIP

3D effects may produce fills with flaws. These are usually screen aberrations—an issue with your monitor—and don't show when you print the document.

FIGURE 1
Identifying the Z-axis on an extruded object

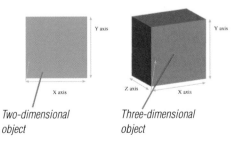

Two-dimensional object

Three-dimensional object

FIGURE 2
Four objects before and after being extruded

Before being extruded

After being extruded

You determine the degree of extrusion by changing the Extrude Depth value in the 3D Extrude & Bevel Options dialog box, shown in Figure 3. Extrusion depth is measured in points. The greater the value, the more the object is extended on its Z axis, as shown in Figure 4.

Use the Cap buttons in the 3D Extrude & Bevel Options dialog box to make extruded objects appear solid or hollow. The Turn cap on for solid appearance button is the default setting. It produces an object in which the front and back faces (surfaces) are solid, as shown in Figure 5. The Turn cap off for

FIGURE 3

3D Extrude & Bevel Options dialog box

*Click to expose
Extrude Depth slider*

FIGURE 4

Two objects extruded to different depths

Less extrusion   *More extrusion*

FIGURE 5

Activating the "solid cap" button

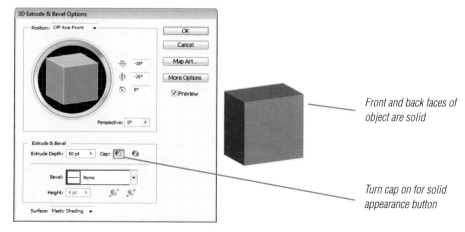

Front and back faces of object are solid

Turn cap on for solid appearance button

hollow appearance button makes the front and back faces invisible, producing an object that appears hollow, as shown in Figure 6.

Rotating 3D Objects

The 3D Extrude & Bevel Options dialog box offers controls for rotating extruded objects.

You can rotate the object manually by dragging the rotation cube, shown in Figure 7. The three text boxes to the right of the cube represent the selected object's X, Y, and Z axes. When you rotate the cube, the values in these text boxes update to reflect the changes you make. You may also enter values in these text boxes to rotate the selected object at specific angles.

Once an object has been extruded, you can use the rotation cube to view any surface of the object—front, back, left, right, etc. The surface shading will update whenever you rotate an object.

FIGURE 6
Activating the "hollow cap" button

Turn cap off for
hollow appearance
button

Front and back
faces of object
are hollow

FIGURE 7
Options for rotating 3D objects

Specify rotation around
the X axis text box

Specify rotation around
the Y axis text box

Specify rotation around
the Z axis text box

Object is rotated

Rotation cube

Extruding Compound Paths

Applying the Extrude & Bevel effect to a compound path can yield results that are visually very interesting. Figure 8 shows a simple compound path—a circle with a square "knocked out" from its center—positioned in front of a light blue square. Figure 9 shows the same object after being extruded.

Generally speaking, the more surfaces that an object has, the more interesting the 3D effect will be. Figure 10 shows a complex compound path, and Figure 11 shows the results when the Extrude & Bevel effect is applied.

FIGURE 8
Simple compound path

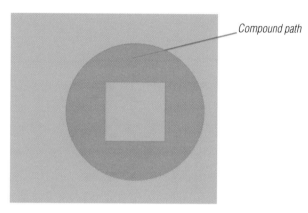

Compound path

FIGURE 10
Complex compound path

FIGURE 9
Simple compound path, extruded

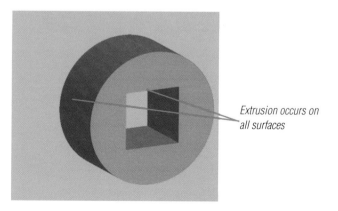

Extrusion occurs on all surfaces

FIGURE 11
Complex compound path, extruded

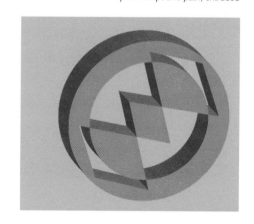

Applying a Bevel Edge to an Extruded Object

The dictionary defines the term **bevel** as the angle that one surface makes with another when they are not at right angles.

Figure 12 shows an example of a graphic with a bevel edge.

The Bevel menu, shown in Figure 13, offers ten pre-defined bevel shapes that you can apply to the edges of extruded objects.

The width of the bevel edge is controlled by the Height slider. Figure 14 shows six objects, each with a different bevel shape applied to its edge. Each bevel has a width of 4 points.

FIGURE 12

Identifying a bevel edge

FIGURE 13

Viewing the Bevel menu

Choose from 1 of 10 bevel shapes

FIGURE 14

Six objects with bevel shapes applied to edges

Classic

Complex 2

Cove

Jaggy

Rolling

Rounded

As shown in Figure 15, text can be extruded without first having to convert it to outlines. Once extruded, you can add a bevel edge to text. Figure 16 shows the same text with the Rounded bevel shape.

Because many letters are complex shapes, applying a bevel to extruded text often causes problems. Simply put, the shapes are too intricate to be rendered with a bevel edge. In Figure 16, the two Ts and the E handle the

bevel edge quite well, but you can see that the X is becoming disfigured. In Figure 17, the Classic bevel shape has been applied. The X isn't rendered properly with the Classic bevel shape applied to its edge.

The "X" is becoming disfigured

The "X" isn't rendered properly

Whenever Illustrator is having difficulty rendering an object with a bevel edge, a warning appears in the 3D Extrude & Bevel Options dialog box, shown in Figure 18. When problems do occur, sometimes there is no solution. Your best bet, however, is to reduce the width of the bevel. Figure 19 shows the same text with the same Classic bevel shape shown in Figure 17, but in this figure, the bevel width has been reduced from four points to three points. The dialog box continues to warn that there may be problems with the bevel edge. Though that may be the case, the problems are less obvious.

Warning regarding a bevel edge

Warning

FIGURE 19
Reducing the width of a bevel edge

The "X" is rendered fairly well

Creating 3D Objects

When you apply a bevel shape to an object's edge, you can decide how the bevel will be applied to the object using the Bevel Extent In and Bevel Extent Out buttons in the 3D Extrude & Bevel Options dialog box. The

Bevel Extent In button produces a bevel edge that carves away from the edge of the existing object. The Bevel Extent Out button adds the bevel edge to the object. Figure 20 shows the Bevel Extent Out and

Bevel Extent In buttons. Generally speaking, the Bevel Extent In option is the better choice, because it stays within the already-established boundaries of the object.

FIGURE 20
Bevel Extent Out and Bevel Extent In buttons

Extrude an object

1. Open AI 11-1.ai, then save it as **Extrude Objects**.

2. Click **View** on the Application bar, then click **Blue Square**.

3. Click the **Selection tool**, select the **blue square**, click **View** on the Application bar, then click **Hide Edges**.

4. Click **Effect** on the Application bar, point to **3D**, then click **Extrude & Bevel**.

5. Position the 3D Extrude & Bevel Options dialog box so that you can see the blue square, then click the **Preview check box**.

   As shown in Figure 21, the blue square is extruded 50 points on the Z axis.

6. Click the **Extrude Depth list arrow**, drag the **slider** to 96 pt, then click **OK**.

(continued)

FIGURE 21

Applying the 3D Extrude & Bevel effect

50-pt extrusion

Creating 3D Objects

FIGURE 22
Viewing the effect on the Appearance panel

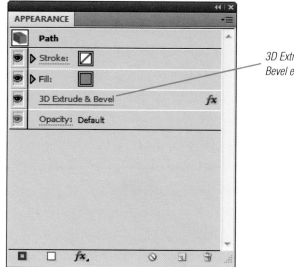

3D Extrude &
Bevel effect

7. Click the **Appearance button** ⊙ to display the Appearance panel.

   As shown in Figure 22, the Appearance panel lists the 3D Extrude & Bevel effect applied to the object.

8. Click **3D Extrude & Bevel** on the Appearance panel to open the dialog box, then click the **Preview check box**.

9. Click the **Turn cap off for hollow appearance button** ⊙ .

   The object's front and back "capping faces" become transparent, making the object appear hollow.

10. Click **OK**, then compare your work to Figure 23.

You applied the 3D Extrude & Bevel effect to a selected object, increased the depth of the extrusion, then changed the cap so that the 3D object would appear hollow.

FIGURE 23
Viewing the extrusion with hollow caps

Extrude and rotate an object

1. Click **View** on the Application bar, then click **Orange Star**.

2. Click the **star**, click **Effect** on the Application bar, point to **3D**, then click **Extrude & Bevel**.

   Hide the Selection Edges for all the remaining lessons in this chapter.

3. Click the **Preview check box**, then change the Extrude Depth value to 60 pt.

4. Position your cursor over the top-front edge of the rotation cube so that a rotate cursor appears, as shown in Figure 24.

5. Click and drag to rotate the cube, noting that the value in the Specify rotation around the X axis text box is the only value that changes as you drag.

(continued)

FIGURE 24
Manipulating the rotation cube manually

Top front edge of
rotation cube

Creating 3D Objects

FIGURE 25
Entering rotation values

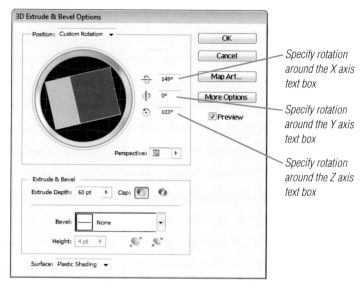

Specify rotation
around the X axis
text box

Specify rotation
around the Y axis
text box

Specify rotation
around the Z axis
text box

6. Experiment with different rotations by dragging the rotation cube from all sides, and note the changes to the orange star object on the page.

7. Double-click the **Specify rotation around the X axis text box** to select its contents, type **149**, then press **[Tab]**.

   TIP Include the negative sign when you select the contents in the Specify rotation around the X axis text box.

8. Type **0** in the Specify rotation around the Y axis text box, press **[Tab]**, type **103** in the Specify rotation around the Z axis text box, press **[Tab]**, then compare your dialog box to Figure 25.

9. Click **OK**, then compare your work to Figure 26.

You applied the 3D Extrude & Bevel effect to a star-shaped object, then manipulated the rotation cube to rotate the object.

FIGURE 26
Viewing the rotated star

Extrude a compound path

1. Click **View** on the Application bar, then click **Target**.

2. Select all three circles, click **Object** on the Application bar, point to **Compound Path**, then click **Make**.

3. Click **Effect** on the Application bar, point to **3D**, then click **Extrude & Bevel**.

4. Click the **Preview check box**, then change the Extrude Depth value to 100 pt.

5. Experiment with different rotations by dragging the rotation cube from all sides.

6. Double-click the **Specify rotation around the X axis text box**, type **28**, then press **[Tab]**.

   TIP   If the negative sign is not selected when you double-click the value in the Specify rotation around the X axis text box, make sure you select it before you type 28.

7. Type **-26** in the Specify rotation around the Y axis text box, press **[Tab]**, type **8** in the Specify rotation around the Z axis text box, then press **[Tab]**.

8. Click **OK**, then compare your work to Figure 27.

You created a compound path, applied the 3D Extrude & Bevel effect, then rotated the graphic, all the time noting the visual effect created by applying the effect to a compound path.

FIGURE 27
Viewing the 3D Extrude & Bevel effect applied to a compound path

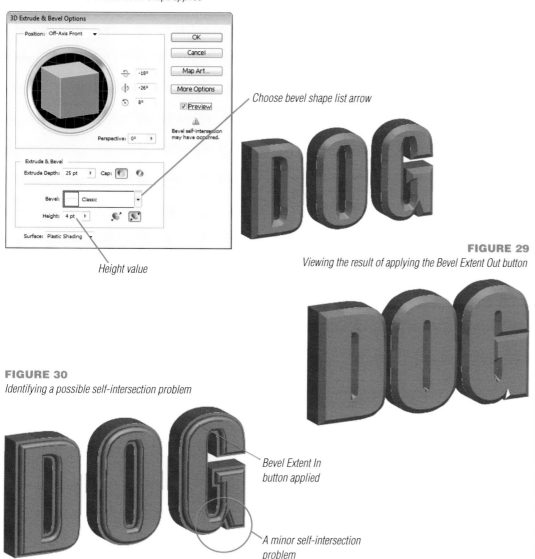

FIGURE 28

Text outlines with the Classic bevel shape applied

Choose bevel shape list arrow

Height value

FIGURE 29

Viewing the result of applying the Bevel Extent Out button

FIGURE 30

Identifying a possible self-intersection problem

*Bevel Extent In
button applied*

*A minor self-intersection
problem*

Apply a bevel shape to an object's edge

1. Click **View** on the Application bar, then click **DOG**.

   The text has been converted to outlines and made into a compound path.

2. Click the **Selection tool** ▶, click any letter of the text, click **Effect** on the Application bar, point to **3D**, then click **Extrude & Bevel**.

3. Click the **Preview check box**, then change the Extrude Depth value to 25 pt.

4. Click the **Choose bevel shape list arrow**, click **Classic**, verify that the Height value is set to 4 pt, then compare your screen to Figure 28.

5. Note that the Bevel Extent In button is pressed, click the **Bevel Extent Out button** , then note the change to the graphic, as shown in Figure 29.

6. Click the **Bevel Extent In button** , click the **Choose bevel shape list arrow**, then click **Complex 2**.

7. Note the warning in the dialog box that says Bevel self-intersection may have occurred, then compare your graphic to Figure 30.

8. Click **OK**, save your work, then close Extrude Objects.

You applied two bevel shapes to extruded text outlines. You also experimented with the Bevel Extent In and Bevel Extent Out buttons.

REVOLVE
OBJECTS

What You'll Do

In this lesson, you will use the 3D effect to revolve objects.

Revolving Objects

In addition to extruding, **revolving** is another method that Illustrator provides for applying a 3D effect to a 2D object. Imagine taking a large, hard cover book and opening it so much that its front and back covers touch. The pages would fan out from one cover to the other, all of them with their inside edges adhering to the spine of the book. This example is similar to what happens when the Revolve effect is applied to an object.

Revolving an object "sweeps" a path in a circular direction around the Y axis. Figure 31 shows a familiar shape—the letter E—before and after the Revolve effect is applied. The blue selection

FIGURE 31
The letter E before and after being revolved

Original path

marks show the original path, and the left edge of that path is the Y axis around which the path was revolved. The surface shading is applied automatically with the effect.

By default, an object is revolved around a vertical axis that represents its leftmost point. An example of this is shown in Figure 32. The 3D Revolve Options dialog box, shown in Figure 33, also offers the

option to revolve the object from its right edge. Revolving the object from its right edge yields an entirely different result, shown in Figure 34.

FIGURE 32

Revolving an object around its left edge

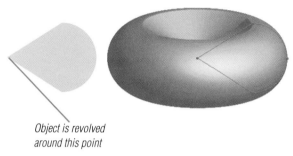

Object is revolved around this point

FIGURE 33

Choosing the edge for the revolution

Options for revolving objects

FIGURE 34

Revolving an object around its right edge

Object is revolved around this point

Because a revolution occurs around a vertical axis, in most cases, the starting path will depict half of the object you want to revolve. This is more easily explained with examples. Figure 35 shows the original path and the result of applying the Revolve effect to that path. Note how the original path is a two-dimensional half of the revolved three-dimensional object.

Once revolved, an object can be rotated by manipulating the rotation cube in the 3D Revolve Options dialog box. This feature is extremely powerful with a revolved graphic. You can use the rotation cube to present all surfaces of the graphic. Figure 36 shows four sides of the bottle graphic, all of them created by manipulating the rotation cube.

Revolving Multiple Objects

You can apply the Revolve effect to multiple paths simultaneously. Paths to be revolved

FIGURE 35

Identifying the path used to produce the revolved 3D graphic

FIGURE 36

A revolved graphic rotated four ways

can be open or closed paths. As shown in Figure 37, when multiple paths are selected and the Revolve effect is applied, each path is revolved around its own axis. For this reason, it is often best to align the left edges of multiple paths on the same Y axis, as shown in Figure 38.

As the figure shows, aligning separate paths on the same Y axis can be useful when revolving. However, unwanted results can occur when rotating those paths, even when they are aligned on the same Y axis. Figure 39 shows the same two paths being rotated. Note that because they are separate paths, they rotate separately—each on its own axis. This problem can be resolved by grouping the paths.

FIGURE 37
Multiple paths revolved on their own axis

Two separate objects   *Two separate objects—each revolved around its own axis*

FIGURE 39
Multiple paths rotated on their own axis

Separate, ungrouped paths rotate separately

FIGURE 38
Multiple paths aligned on the same axis then revolved

Two separate objects aligned on their left edges   *Two separate objects—each revolved around their own axis*

Revolving Grouped Objects

When grouped, multiple paths are revolved around a single axis. This can yield unexpected results. In Figure 40, the two paths (left) are grouped, but they don't share the same Y axis. When revolved, both paths revolve around the leftmost axis.

When multiple paths are grouped and revolved, they will also rotate together. Figure 41 shows four versions of two grouped and revolved paths after they have been rotated in the 3D Revolve Options dialog box. In every case, the two paths rotate together because they are grouped. Compare this to Figure 39, in which the two ungrouped paths rotated separately, each on their own axes.

Applying an Offset to a Revolved Object

By default, an object is revolved around a vertical axis that represents its leftmost point. Figure 42 illustrates this point.

FIGURE 40
Two grouped paths revolved around a single Y-axis

Two paths, grouped

Grouped paths revolved around the leftmost axis

Leftmost axis

FIGURE 41
Four grouped paths after being revolved and rotated

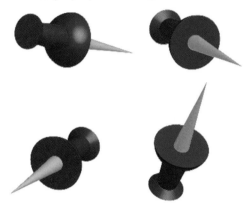

FIGURE 42
Object revolved around its leftmost point

Leftmost point

Leftmost point

Increasing the Offset value in the 3D Revolve Options dialog box, shown in Figure 43, increases how far from the Y axis the object is revolved. Figure 44 shows the same revolved object shown in Figure 42 with a 90-point offset value. The path revolves around the same Y axis, but it does so at a distance of 90 points. Figure 45, in which the object has been rotated, shows the offset more clearly. Try to visualize that the object is a series of half circles rotated around a single vertical axis—90 points from that vertical axis.

FIGURE 43
Offset slider in the 3D Revolve Options dialog box

Offset value

FIGURE 44
Object revolved with a 90-point offset from its Y-axis

FIGURE 45
Rotated object shows 90-point offset more clearly

Revolve an object

1. Open AI 11-2.ai, then save it as **Green Bottle**.

2. Click the **Selection tool** ▶, click the **green object**, click **View** on the Application bar, then click **Hide Edges** (if necessary).

3. Click **Effect** on the Application bar, point to **3D**, click **Revolve**, then click the **Preview check box**.

   As shown in Figure 46, the object is revolved on its axis and appears as a bottle. Highlights and shadows are applied automatically.

4. Click **OK**, save your work, then close Green Bottle.

You revolved a simple object to produce a three-dimensional graphic.

Revolve multiple objects

1. Open AI 11-3.ai, then save it as **Revolve Objects**.

2. Select the second row of blue objects, click **Effect** on the Application bar, point to **3D**, then click **Revolve**.

3. Click the **Preview check box**.

   Each object is revolved on its own axis.

4. Click **OK**, then compare your work to Figure 47.

   The graphic on the left has a hard edge because the original object was a rectangle. The round edge of the original object on the right produced a 3D graphic that also has a round edge.

(continued)

FIGURE 46
Revolving an object

Highlights and shadows applied automatically

FIGURE 47
Revolving multiple objects

FIGURE 48
Revolving three objects

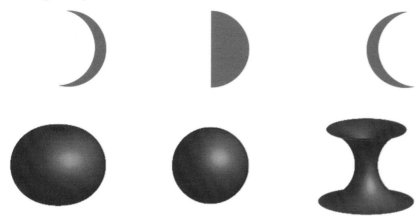

FIGURE 49
Rotating a revolved object

5. Select the second row of red objects, click **Effect** on the Application bar, point to **3D**, then click **Revolve**.

6. Click **OK**, deselect all, then compare your work to Figure 48.

   The first two graphics produced spheres when revolved, but only the middle graphic is a perfect sphere. The two crescent shapes, because they face in opposite directions, produce two drastically different results when revolved.

7. Deselect all, select the rightmost red object, double-click **3D Revolve** on the Appearance panel, manipulate the rotation cube to rotate the graphic any way that you like, then click **OK**.

   Figure 49 shows one possible result.

8. Save your work, then close Revolve Objects.

You selected multiple objects, applied the 3D Revolve effect, then noted that each object was revolved on its own axis. You compared the results with the original objects, then rotated one of the revolved objects.

Revolve grouped objects

1. Open AI 11-4.ai, then save it as **Push Pins**.

2. Click **View** on the Application bar, click **Green Pin**, then select the two objects in the Green Pin view.

   | TIP The two objects in Green Pin view are not grouped.

3. Click **Effect** on the Application bar, point to **3D**, then click **Revolve**.

4. Click the **Preview check box**, then note the effect on the objects on the page.

5. Manipulate the rotation cube in any direction.

   As shown in Figure 50, the two objects are each rotated on their own axis and the illustration is no longer realistic.

   | TIP Because your rotation will differ, your results will differ from the figure.

6. Click **OK**, click **View** on the Application bar, click **Red Pin**, click one of the objects in the Red Pin view.

   | TIP The two objects are grouped.

7. Click **Effect** on the Application bar, point to **3D**, click **Revolve**, then click the **Preview check box**.

   As shown in Figure 51, because the two objects are grouped, they are both revolved around the same axis.

   (continued)

FIGURE 50
Rotating revolved objects that are not grouped

FIGURE 51
Two grouped objects revolved around the same axis

Creating 3D Objects

FIGURE 52

Two grouped objects revolved around the same axis

FIGURE 53

Rotating revolved objects that are grouped

8. Click **OK**, click **View** on the Application bar, click **Blue Pin**, select the two objects, click **Object** on the Application bar, then click **Group**.

9. Click **Effect** on the Application bar, point to **3D**, click **Revolve**, then click the **Preview check box**.

   As shown in Figure 52, the two grouped objects are revolved around the same axis. Because they both share the same axis (their left edge) the illustration is realistic.

   > TIP   The selection edges are showing in the figure so that you can see the left edge that both graphics share.

10. Manipulate the rotation cube in any direction that you like.

    Figure 53 shows one possible result.

11. Click **OK**, save your work, then close Push Pins.

You explored the results of revolving grouped and ungrouped objects. With the green pin, you noted that ungrouped objects cannot be rotated together. With the red pin, you noted that grouped objects are revolved around the same axis. With the blue pin, you noted that grouped objects can be rotated together.

Offset a revolved object

1. Open AI 11-5.ai, then save it as **Desk Lamp**.

2. Select the silver object, click **Effect** on the Application bar, point to **3D**, click **Revolve**, then click **OK**.

3. Select the gold diagonal line, click **Effect** on the Application bar, point to **3D**, click **Revolve**, then click the **Preview check box**.

   As shown in Figure 54, the object's leftmost point is the axis around which it is revolved.

   (continued)

FIGURE 54
Revolving an object around its leftmost point

Leftmost point of
original object

Creating 3D Objects

FIGURE 55

Revolving an object with a 50-pt offset from its axis

50-pt offset from
leftmost point

4. Double-click the **Offset text box**, type **50**, press **[Tab]**, then compare your work to Figure 55.

   The object is revolved at a radius that is 50 points from its axis.

5. Click **OK**, save your work, then close Desk Lamp.

You used an increased offset value to manipulate how an object is revolved in relation to its axis.

MANIPULATE SURFACE
SHADING AND LIGHTING

What You'll Do

▶ *In this lesson, you will familiarize yourself with the controls that allow you to manipulate the highlight effects of a 3D object.*

Applying Surface Shading

When the Extrude & Bevel effect or the Revolve effect is applied to an object, surface shading and lighting are applied automatically. However, you can manipulate these effects.

Surface shading controls how the object's surface appears. When an object is revolved, four surface shadings are available: Wireframe, No Shading, Diffuse Shading, and Plastic Shading. Examples of all four are shown in Figure 56.

Plastic shading is the default surface shade. With plastic shading, the object reflects light as though it were made of a shiny plastic material. Distinct highlight areas appear on the surface of an object.

Diffuse shading offers a surface that reflects light in a soft, diffuse pattern. With Diffuse Shading, no distinct highlights appear on the surface of the object.

The Wireframe option makes all surfaces transparent and shows the object's geometry. The No Shading option, as its name suggests, applies no new shading to the object. Its surface is identical to that of the 2D object.

Manipulating Lighting Controls

When you choose Diffuse Shading or Plastic Shading, a number of lighting controls are available for you to manipulate the lighting effects that are applied to the object automatically.

- Lighting Intensity controls the strength of the light on the object. The range for lighting intensity is 0-100, with 100 being the default.
- Ambient Light is a very useful control. It determines how the object is lit globally. The range for Ambient Light is 0-100. Any changes that you make with the Ambient Light slider affect the brightness of the object uniformly, though the effect is much more pronounced in the shadow areas than in the highlights. Decreasing the ambient light noticeably makes the shadow areas darker, which increases the overall contrast of the object, from shadow to

FIGURE 56
Four surface shading choices

Wireframe   No shading   Diffuse shading   Plastic shading highlight. Figure 57 shows two objects, one with 60% ambient light and one with 20% ambient light.

- As its name implies, Highlight Intensity controls how intense a highlight appears. The more intense the highlight, the more white it appears. Figure 58 shows two objects, one with 100% highlight intensity and one with 60% highlight intensity.

Note that at 100%, the highlight is too white and "glaring." At 60%, the highlight is a good mixture of white and the object's color.

- Highlight Size controls how large the highlights appear on the object.
- Blend Steps controls how smoothly the shading appears on the object's surface and is most visible in the transition

from the highlight areas to the diffusely lit areas. The range for blend steps is 1-256, with higher numbers producing more paths and therefore smoother transitions. If your computer can handle it, use 256 blend steps, but be aware that the higher the number, the more computer memory will be required to render the object.

FIGURE 57
Comparing ambient lighting

FIGURE 58
Comparing highlight intensity

60% ambient lighting

20% ambient lighting

100% highlight intensity

60% highlight intensity

Creating 3D Objects

Manipulating Light Sources

In addition to manipulating lighting controls, you can manipulate the light itself. When Diffuse Shading or Plastic Shading is chosen as the surface shading, a default light source, shown in Figure 59, is applied.

You can drag the light source to a new location to light the object from a different angle, as shown in Figure 60. This can be very effective for manipulating the overall lighting of the object.

In addition to relocating the default light source, you can add additional light sources by clicking the New Light button. By default, the new light source appears at the center of the lighting key, but it too can

FIGURE 59

Viewing default light source settings

Default light source

Default light
source settings

FIGURE 60

Relocating a light source

Drag to relocate

be relocated, as shown in Figure 61. You can apply different light intensity values to individual light sources. It is often a good idea for one light source to be more dominant than the other(s).

You delete a light source by selecting it and then clicking the Delete Light button. The Move selected light to back of object button moves the light source to the back of the object. This is often most effective when there's a background object that allows the back light to be more apparent. In Figure 62, the second light has been moved behind the object; the highlights on the right side of the object are from the back light.

FIGURE 61
Relocating a second light source

Second light source

FIGURE 62
Using a light source as a back light

Back light source

Move selected light to back of object button

Highlight from back light source

FIGURE 63
Viewing the object with the Plastic Shading surface applied

1. Open AI 11-6.ai, then save it as **Surface Lighting**.

2. Click the **object** to select it, then double-click **3D Revolve** on the Appearance panel.

3. Click the **Preview check box**, then note the subtle lighting effects on the object.

   The Diffuse Shading surface type is applied to the object.

4. Click the **Surface list arrow**, then click **No Shading**.

5. Click the **Surface list arrow**, then click **Wireframe**.

6. Click the **Surface list arrow**, click **Plastic Shading**, then compare your artwork to Figure 63.

You examined four types of surface shadings as applied to a revolved object.

Manipulate lighting controls

1. Click **More Options** in the dialog box.

2. Click the **Ambient Light list arrow**, then drag the **slider** to 20.

3. Click the **Highlight Intensity list arrow**, then drag the **slider** to 75.

4. Click the **Highlight Size list arrow**, then drag the **slider** to 75.

5. Click the **Light Intensity list arrow**, drag the **slider** to 50, note the change in the object, then drag the **slider** to 100.

6. Click the **Blend Steps list arrow**, then drag the **slider** to 128.

7. Click **OK**, then compare your artwork to Figure 64.

You manipulated five surface shading controls, noting their effect on a 3D object.

Manipulate light sources

1. Verify that the green object is selected, double-click **3D Revolve** on the Appearance panel, then click the **Preview check box**.

2. Drag the **light** to the top center of the sphere, as shown in Figure 65.

(continued)

FIGURE 64
Manipulating surface shading on a 3D object

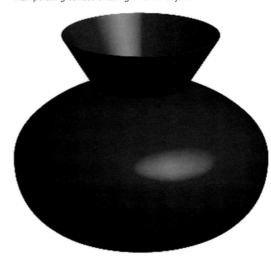

FIGURE 65
Relocating a light

Relocated light source

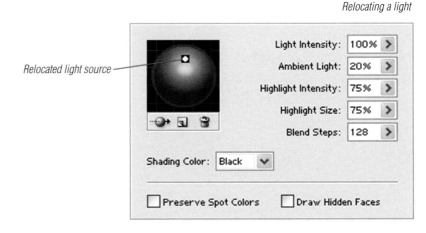

Creating 3D Objects

FIGURE 66
Relocating the new light

New light source

3. Click the **New Light button** ▣ to add a second light.

   TIP By default, a new light is positioned at the center of the sphere.

4. Drag the **new light** to the top-right corner of the sphere, as shown in Figure 66.

5. Click the **New Light button** ▣ to add a third light, then move it to the location shown in Figure 67.

6. Click **OK**, compare your work to Figure 68, then compare Figure 68 to Figure 64 to see the results of adding the two lights.

7. Save your work, then close Surface Lighting.

You added and positioned lights to modify the lighting effects applied to the 3D object.

FIGURE 67
Relocating the third light

Third light source

FIGURE 68
The object with different lighting

MAP ARTWORK TO
3D OBJECTS

What You'll Do

In this lesson, you will map 2D artwork to a 3D object .

Mapping Artwork

Once you have created a three-dimensional object, you can "map" two-dimensional artwork to the three-dimensional object. A good example of this concept is a soup can and a soup label. The two dimensional soup label is designed and printed. It is then wrapped around the three-dimensional soup can.

FIGURE 69
Viewing 3D object and 2D artwork to be mapped

The process of mapping a 2D object to a 3D object first includes converting the 2D object to a symbol. Figure 69 shows a revolved 3D object and 2D artwork that will be mapped to it.

To map the artwork, you first select the 3D object, then click Map Art in the 3D Revolve Options dialog box. In the Map

2D Illustrator artwork ——

3D object ——

Art dialog box, shown in Figure 70, you must first choose which surface you intend to map the art to. When you click the surface buttons, the active surface is shown in red wireframe on the 3D object. In this example, we are mapping the wrapping paper to surface 1 of 4, which is shown in Figure 71.

The grid pattern represents the *complete* surface of surface 1 of 4. Understand that this means not only the surface that you see—the front surface—but the entire surface, all the way around. For this exercise, we're interested in mapping the wrapping paper to the surface that we can see—the front surface. That area is defined by the curved lines, identified in Figure 71.

FIGURE 70
Map Art dialog box

FIGURE 71
Identifying the surface to be mapped

First Surface button

Previous Surface button

Next Surface button

Interior of curved lines represents visible surface (1 of 4)

Last Surface button

Once you have chosen the surface, you then choose the symbol to be mapped by clicking the Symbol list arrow and selecting the appropriate symbol. When you do so, the symbol artwork is centered on the grid. In this example, the symbol is named Wrapping Paper. For this exercise, we drag the artwork so that it completely covers the curved lines that represent the front face, as shown in Figure 72.

Once the artwork is mapped, it reshapes itself to the three-dimensional object, as shown Figure 73.

FIGURE 72
Positioning the symbol artwork

Wrapping Paper
symbol selected

FIGURE 73
Viewing the mapped art

FIGURE 74

Creating the "tea can" and "lid"

1. Open AI 11-7.ai, then save it as **Tea Can**.

2. Select all, click **Effect** on the Application bar, point to **3D**, click **Revolve**, then click **OK**.

   Your artwork should resemble Figure 74.

3. Open AI 11-8.ai, select all, click **Edit** on the Application bar, click **Copy**, close the document, then return to Tea Can.ai.

4. Click the **Symbols button** ♣ to display the Symbols panel, click **Edit** on the Application bar, click **Paste**, then drag the pasted artwork into the Symbols panel.

   The Symbol Options dialog box opens.

5. Name the new symbol **Elephant Rectangle**, click the **Graphic option button**, then click **OK**.

6. Delete the pasted artwork from the artboard.

7. Open AI 11-9.ai, select all, copy the artwork, close the document, return to Tea Can.ai, then paste the artwork.

8. Drag the pasted artwork into the Symbols panel, name it **Elephant Circle**, click the **Graphic option button**, then click **OK**.

9. Delete the pasted artwork from the artboard.

You used the 3D Revolve effect to create the artwork to which the 2D artwork will be mapped. You then created two symbols, one for each part of the 2D artwork.

Map rectangular artwork

1. Click the **Selection tool** ▸, click the **silver-object**, then press ↑ eight times so that the silver artwork is fully "under" the purple lid.

2. Double-click **3D Revolve** on the Appearance panel to open the 3D Revolve Options dialog box, click the **Preview check box**, then click **Map Art**.

3. Note that the Surface text box reads 1 of 3 and that a red line indicates that surface on the object, as shown in Figure 75.

4. Click the **Next Surface button** ▶ two times, so that the Surface text box reads 3 of 3.

   The light gray areas of the layout grid represent the visible area of the silver object at this viewing angle.

5. Click the **Symbol list arrow**, then click **Elephant Rectangle**.

6. Drag the **top-left and bottom-right resizing handles** on the symbol's bounding box so that the artwork fits into the light gray areas of the layout grid, as shown in Figure 76.

   (continued)

FIGURE 75
Viewing surface 1 of 3 in the Map Art dialog box

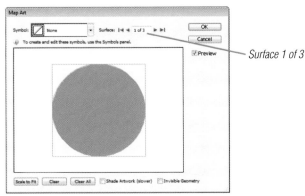

Surface 1 of 3

Red line identifies surface

FIGURE 76
Resizing the artwork to the visible area

Resizing handles

Creating 3D Objects

FIGURE 77

Adjusting surface shading and lighting

—Light source

FIGURE 78

Viewing the mapped art

7. Drag the **bottom-middle resizing handle** up slightly so that the silver "can" will show beneath the "elephant label."

8. Click the **Shade Artwork (slower) check box**.

9. Click **OK**, click **More Options** (if necessary), change the Ambient Light setting to 65%, change the Highlight Intensity setting to 80%. change the number of blend steps to 128, then move the light to the location shown in Figure 77.

10. Click **OK**, deselect all, then compare your work to Figure 78.

In the Map Art dialog box, you selected the symbol that you wanted to map and the surface that you wanted to map it to. You resized the symbol artwork so that it fit onto the surface properly, then you activated the shading option to make the artwork appear more realistic as a label. You modified surface shading settings and lighting to improve the appearance of the artwork.

Map round artwork

1. Click the **purple "cover" object**, double-click **3D Revolve** on the Appearance panel, click the **Preview check box**, then click **Map Art**.

2. Click the **Next Surface button** ▶ once, so that the Surface text box reads 2 of 5.

3. Click the **Symbol list arrow**, then click **Elephant Circle**.

4. Point to the **upper-right resizing handle** until a rotate cursor appears, then drag to rotate the graphic to the position shown in Figure 79.

5. Click **OK** to close the Map Art dialog box, click **OK** again, deselect all, then compare your artwork to Figure 80.

You mapped a circular piece of 2D artwork to an oval 3D object.

FIGURE 79
Rotating the mapped art

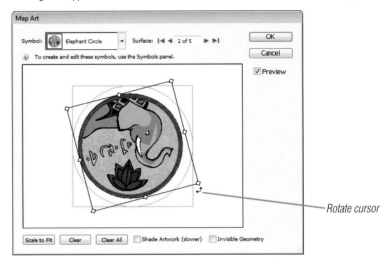

Rotate cursor

FIGURE 80
Viewing the mapped art

Creating 3D Objects

FIGURE 81
Positioning the artwork

FIGURE 83
Viewing the finished artwork

FIGURE 82
Relocating the light

Map texture artwork

1. Open AI 11-10.ai, select all, copy the artwork, close the document, then return to Tea Can.ai.

2. Verify that the Symbols panel is visible, click **Edit** on the Application bar, click **Paste**, then drag the pasted artwork into the Symbols panel.

3. Name the new symbol **Cover Texture**, click the **Graphic option button**, then click **OK**.

4. Delete the pasted artwork from the artboard.

5. Click the **purple "cover" object**, double-click **3D Revolve (Mapped)** on the Appearance panel, click the **Preview check box**, then click **Map Art**.

6. Click the **Next Surface button** ▶ until the Surface text box reads 5 of 5.

7. Click the **Symbol list arrow**, then click **Cover Texture**.

8. Position the symbol artwork so that it covers the entire light gray area, as shown in Figure 81.

9. Click **OK** to close the Map Art window, then drag the light to the location shown in Figure 82.

10. Click **OK**, deselect all, then compare your work to Figure 83.

11. Save your work, then close Tea Can.

You mapped artwork to the front face of a 3D object to add texture.

Extrude objects.

1. Open AI 11-11.ai, then save it as **Extrude & Bevel Skills**.
2. Click the Selection tool, select the blue octagon, click View on the Application bar, then click Hide Edges.
3. Click Effect on the Application bar, point to 3D, click Extrude & Bevel, then click the Preview check box.
4. Click the Extrude Depth list arrow, then increase the depth to 75 pt.
5. Click the Turn cap off for hollow appearance button, then click OK.
6. Select the orange letter H, click Effect on the Application bar, point to 3D, then click Extrude & Bevel.
7. Click the Preview check box, then change the Extrude Depth value to 60 pt.
8. Double-click the Specify rotation around the X axis text box to select its contents, type **17**, then press **[Tab]**.
9. Type **-17** in the Specify rotation around the Y axis text box, press [Tab], type **-31** in the Specify rotation around the Z axis text box, then click OK.
10. Select the green octagon and the two objects inside it, click Object on the Application bar, point to Compound Path, then click Make.
11. Click Effect on the Application bar, point to 3D, then click Extrude & Bevel.
12. Click the Preview check box, then experiment with different rotations by clicking and dragging the rotation cube from all sides.

13. Double-click the Specify rotation around the X axis text box, type **26**, then press [Tab].
14. Type **-9** in the Specify rotation around the Y axis text box, press [Tab], then type **5** in the Specify rotation around the Z axis text box.
15. Click OK.
16. Select the hollow blue octagon at the top of the artboard, then double-click 3D Extrude & Bevel on the Appearance panel.

FIGURE 84
Completed Skills Review, Part 1

17. Click the Preview check box, then click the Turn cap on for solid appearance button.
18. Click the Bevel list arrow, click Complex 3, then drag the Height slider to 6.
19. Click the Bevel Extent Out button, click Ok, then compare your work to Figure 84.
20. Save your work, then close Extrude & Bevel Skills.

Revolve objects.

1. Open AI 11-12.ai, then save it as **Gold Urn**.
2. Click the Selection tool, select all, click View on the Application bar, then click Hide Edges (if necessary).
3. Click the Horizontal Align Left button on the Align panel.
4. Click Effect on the Application bar, point to 3D, click Revolve, then click the Preview check box.
5. Manipulate the rotation cube in any direction, note that the three objects all rotate on their own axes, then click Cancel.
6. Click Object on the Application bar, then click Group.
7. Click Effect on the Application bar, point to 3D, click Revolve, then click the Preview check box.
8. Manipulate the rotation cube in any direction.
9. Click Cancel.
10. Click Effect on the Application bar, point to 3D, click Revolve, then click the Preview check box.
11. Click the Offset list arrow, change the offset value to 48, then click OK.

Manipulate surface shading and lighting.

1. Double-click 3D Revolve on the Appearance panel.
2. Click the Preview check box, click the Surface list arrow, then click No Shading.
3. Click the Surface list arrow, then click Diffuse Shading.
4. Click the Surface list arrow, then click Plastic Shading.
5. Click More Options (if necessary), click the Ambient Light list arrow, then drag the slider to 45.
6. Drag the light to the top center of the sphere.
7. Click the New Light button to add a second light.
8. Drag the Light Intensity slider to 30.

Map artwork to 3D objects.

1. Drag the Offset slider to 0, then click Map Art.
2. Click the Next Surface button until the Surface text box reads 5 of 13.

3. Click the Symbol list arrow, then click Wrapping Paper.
4. Click OK.
5. Click OK, then compare your work to Figure 85.
6. Save your work, then close Gold Urn.

FIGURE 85
Completed Skills Review, Part 2

You are a freelance illustrator, and you have been hired to draw an old-fashioned lava lamp to be part of a montage. To begin work on the illustration, you decide to draw three paths, then use the 3D Revolve effect.

1. Open AI 11-13.ai, then save it as **Lava**.
2. Click the Selection tool, then drag the three path segments so that they are aligned with the blue guide.
3. Hide the guides.
4. Select all, click Effect on the Application bar, point to 3D, then click Revolve.
5. Click the Preview check box, note the results, then click Cancel.
6. Group the three paths, apply the Revolve effect again, then click the Preview check box.
7. Click More Options (if necessary), apply Plastic Shading as the surface shading, then drag the Ambient Light slider to 45.
8. Click OK, deselect all, then compare your work to Figure 86.
9. Save your work, then close Lava.

FIGURE 86
Completed Project Builder 1

You are a designer for a game company, and you are designing the packaging for a chess game. You decide to use basic shapes and the 3D Revolve effect to create a graphic for the cover art.

1. Open AI 11-14.ai, then save it as **Chess**.
2. Click the Selection tool, then align each shape with the black rules.
3. Hide the Assembled layer, then verify that the Pawn Parts layer is targeted.
4. Select all on the Pawn Parts layer, then hide edges.

5. Click Effect on the Application bar, point to 3D, then click Revolve.
6. Click the Preview check box, note the results, then click Cancel.
7. Click the Horizontal Align Left button on the Align panel.
8. Press and hold [Alt] (Win) or [option] (Mac), then click the Unite button on the Pathfinder panel.
9. Click Effect on the Application bar, point to 3D, click Revolve, then click the Preview check box.

10. Select the contents of the Specify rotation around the X axis text box, type **-57**, then click OK.
11. Click the White Pawn swatch on the Swatches panel, then compare your work to Figure 87.
12. Save your work, then close the Chess document.

FIGURE 87
Completed Project Builder 2

Creating 3D Objects

You are a designer for a T-shirt company. Presently, your assignment is to develop shirts that feature peoples' names in 3D. To come up with a design, you experiment using your own name.

1. Create a new 8" × 8" document, then save it as **T-Shirt**.
2. Type your first name in a bold font at a large point size. (*Hint*: The typeface used in Figure 88 is Franklin Gothic Heavy, 134 point. Try to use the same or a similar typeface at the same point size in your work.)
3. Change the fill color to something other than black.
4. Click Effect on the Application bar, point to 3D, then click Extrude & Bevel.
5. Click the Preview check box, then change the Extrude Depth value to 115 pt.
6. Double-click the Specify rotation around the X axis text box to select its contents, type **–8**, then press [Tab].
7. Type **0** in the Specify rotation around the Y axis text box, press [Tab], type **0** in the Specify rotation around the Z axis text box, press [Tab], then press [Tab].

8. Slowly drag the Perspective slider to 95°.
9. Click the More Options button (if necessary) to expand the dialog box, then position the light source to your liking.
10. Click OK, then compare your result to Figure 88. (*Hint*: Illustrator sometimes has trouble displaying 3D effects correctly. If you do not get good results, try again.)
11. Save your work, then close the file.

FIGURE 88
Sample Completed Design Project

This portfolio project is designed to challenge your ability to visualize simple paths and how they will appear when the 3D Revolve effect is applied. You will look at nine graphics, all of which are simple paths to which the 3D Revolve effect has been applied. Use a piece of paper and a pencil and try to draw the simple path that is the basis for each graphic. Note that for each 3D graphic, no rotation or offset has been applied—each is the result of simply applying the 3D Revolve effect to a simple path. Note also that two of the simple paths are open paths, and the other seven are all closed paths.

1. Refer to Figure 89.
2. Look at Graphic #1, and try to visualize what it would look like if the 3D Revolve effect were removed.
3. Using a pencil and paper, draw the original path that was used to create the graphic.
4. Do the same for the remaining eight graphics.
5. Open AI 11-15.ai, then save it as **Mystery Shapes**.
6. Select each graphic, then delete the 3D Revolve effect from the Appearance panel.
7. Compare your pencil drawings to the graphics in the file.
8. Save Mystery Graphics, then close the file.

FIGURE 89
Reference for Portfolio Project

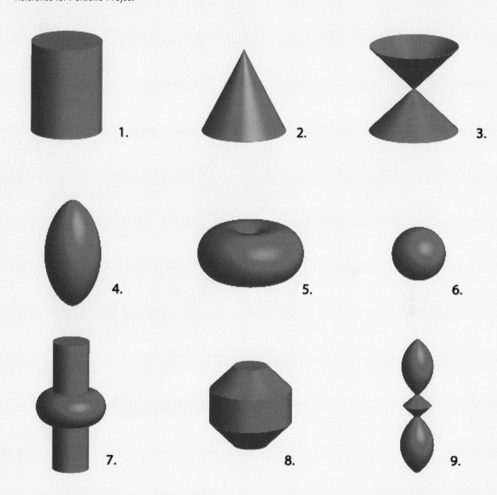

1.

2.

3.

4.

5.

6.

7.

8.

9.

chapter

12

PREPARING A DOCUMENT
FOR PREPRESS
AND PRINTING

ADOBE ILLUSTRATOR CS4

12 PREPARING A DOCUMENT
FOR PREPRESS
AND PRINTING

Illustrator is so widely praised for its excellence as a drawing tool, it's easy to forget that the application is also a top-notch page layout solution. Illustrator CS4 is a powerhouse print production utility, a state-of-the-art interface with the world of professional prepress and printing. Everything that you need to produce an output-ready document is there—crop marks, trim marks, reliable process tints, the full PANTONE library of non-process inks—all backed by a sophisticated color separations utility. If you are new to the world of prepress and printing, Illustrator CS4 makes for an excellent training ground, with straightforward, easy-to-use panels and dialog boxes. If you are experienced, you will admire how Illustrator seamlessly transitions from design and drawing to layout and output, thoughtfully and thoroughly encompassing the gamut of a printer's needs, demands, and wishes.

Tools You'll Use

EXPLORE BASIC
COLOR THEORY

What You'll Do

 In this lesson, you will learn basic color theory to gain an understanding of the role of CMYK ink in offset printing.

Exploring Basic Color Theory

All of the natural light in our world comes from the sun. The sun delivers light to us in waves. The entirety of the sun's light, the electromagnetic spectrum, contains an infinite number of light waves—some at high frequencies, some at low frequencies—many of which will sound familiar to you. X-rays, gamma rays, and ultraviolet rays are all components of the electromagnetic spectrum.

The light waves that we see in our world are only a subset of the electromagnetic spectrum. Scientists refer to this subset—this range of wavelengths—as visible light. Because this light appears to us as colorless (as opposed to, say, the red world of the planet Mars), we refer to visible light as "white light."

From your school days, you may remember using a prism to bend light waves to reveal what you probably referred to as a rainbow. It is through this bending, or "breaking down" of white light, that we see color. The rainbow that we are all so familiar with is called the visible spectrum, and it is composed of seven distinct colors: red, orange, yellow, green, blue, indigo, and violet. Though the colors are distinct, the color range of the visible spectrum is infinite; for example, there's no definable place in the spectrum where orange light ends and yellow light begins.

Colors in the visible spectrum can themselves be broken down. For example, because red light and green light, when combined, produce yellow light, yellow light can, conversely, be broken down, or reduced, to those component colors.

Red, green, and blue light (RGB) are the additive primary colors of light, as shown in Figure 1. The term **primary** refers to the fact that red, green, and blue light cannot themselves be broken down or reduced. The term **additive** refers to the fact that these same colors combine to produce other colors. For example, red and blue light, when combined, produce violet hues. As primary colors, red, green, and blue light are the irreducible component colors

of white light. Therefore, it logically follows that when red, green, and blue light are combined equally, they produce white light.

Finally, you'll note that nowhere in this paradigm is the color black. That is because, in the natural world, there is no such color as black. True black is the absence of all light.

FIGURE 1

Red, green, and blue are the additive primary colors of light

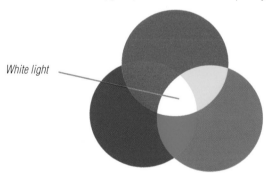

White light

Understanding Subtractive Primary Colors

Three things can happen when light strikes an object: the light can be reflected, absorbed, or transmitted, as shown in Figure 2.

Reflection occurs when light strikes an object and "bounces" off the object. Any object that reflects all of the light that strikes it appears as pure white.

Absorption occurs when light strikes an object and is not reflected, but instead is absorbed by the object. Any object that absorbs all of the light that strikes it appears as pure black.

Transmission occurs when light strikes an object and passes through the object. Any object that transmits all of the light that strikes it becomes invisible.

There are no truly invisible objects in our world (only some gasses are invisible). Nor are there any purely white or purely black objects. Instead, depending on the physical properties of the object, varying amounts of light are reflected, absorbed, and transmitted.

If an object absorbs some light, it logically follows that not all the white light that strikes the object will be reflected. Put another way, red, green, and blue light will not be reflected in full and equal amounts. What we perceive as the object's color is based on the percentages of the red, green, and blue light that are reflected and the color that that combination of light produces.

An object appears as cyan if it absorbs all of the red light that strikes it and also reflects or transmits all of the green and all of the blue light. An object that absorbs all of the green light that strikes it and also reflects or transmits all of the red and all of the blue light appears as magenta. An object that absorbs all of the blue light that strikes it and also reflects or transmits all of the red and all of the green light appears as yellow, as shown in Figure 3.

Cyan, magenta, and yellow are called **subtractive primary colors**. The term subtractive refers to the fact that each is produced by removing or subtracting one of the additive primary colors, and overlapping all three pigments would absorb all colors.

QUICKTIP

You may be thinking back to your school days and remembering that red, blue, and yellow are primary colors. They are. Red, blue, and yellow are the primary colors for mixing opaque (nontransmissive) paint, but that is entirely extraneous to the concepts covered in this chapter.

FIGURE 2

Visual representations of reflection, absorption, and transmission

reflection   absorption   transmission

FIGURE 3

Printers often refer to cyan as "minus red," magenta as "minus green," and yellow as "minus blue"

cyan   magenta   yellow

Understanding the Theory of Four-Color Process Printing

Color printing uses the three subtractive primary colors (plus black) to produce a color image or tint. To understand this, read the two points below carefully:

- The standard color for paper is white. The paper appears as white because it is manufactured to reflect RGB light in equal amounts.
- Cyan, magenta, and yellow inks are transparent—they are manufactured so that light passes through them. For example, cyan ink is manufactured to absorb red light and transmit green and blue light.

Here is the key to the whole theory: The color that you see when you look at a printed page is *not* reflected off the inks; it is light reflected off the paper. The light that is reflected off the paper is that which has not been absorbed (or *subtracted*) by the inks. Figure 4 demonsrates this concept.

FIGURE 4

The color of the printed image is reflected off the paper, not the inks

paper

Creating a rich black

For many designers, black is the most powerful "color" on the panel. No other color can provide such contrast. Black can be used to trigger emotions. Black is neutral, but it's never silent. Use black ink (K) for text and lines and small areas of your artwork. When you have designed artwork with large black areas that you want to be dramatically black, keep in mind that black ink alone may not be enough to produce the effect. To produce deep blacks, printers create a process tint that is 100% K plus 50% C. The cyan ink overlapped with the black produces a dark, rich black . . . which is why printers refer to this tint as a "rich black." Keep the idea in mind when you are working with black, but remember also that rich blacks are never used for text or lines.

Understanding CMYK Inks

CMYK inks are called process inks. Process inks are manufactured by people, so by definition, they're not perfect. For example, no cyan ink can be manufactured so that it absorbs 100% of the red light that strikes it. Some is reflected, and some is transmitted, as shown in Figure 5. Perfect magenta and yellow inks cannot be manufactured either. In addition, an ink's ability to transmit light is not perfect. That same cyan ink should, if it were a true cyan, transmit both blue and green light. Manufactured cyan inks actually absorb a small percentage of blue and green light.

These imperfections become crucial when you try to use cyan, magenta, and yellow (CMY) to print dark areas of an image. In theory, if you overlapped all three inks, the area would appear black because each would absorb an additive primary, and no light would be reflected off the paper, as shown in Figure 6.

FIGURE 5

Cyan ink in theory vs. reality

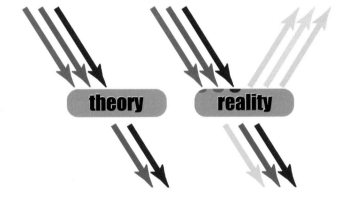

FIGURE 6

If "perfect" inks were overlapped, no light would be reflected; the area of the overlap would appear black

Preparing a Document for Prepress and Printing

Because, in reality, the inks are unable to achieve 100% absorption and some light gets through and is reflected off the paper, CMY inks are unable to produce satisfactory shadows and dark areas of an image, as shown in Figure 7.

To compensate, black ink is used to produce deep shadows and fine detail. Printers refer to black ink as "K." They do not refer to it as "B" because "B" could be confused with blue, and blue could be confused with cyan. Also, printers have long referred to black as the "key" for aligning (registering) the four colors. Thus, the K in CMYK, though not a subtractive primary, is nevertheless essential to the subtractive printing process, as shown in Figure 8.

FIGURE 7
In reality, CMY inks are insufficient to produce black areas

FIGURE 8
The image on the left was printed with only CMY inks; black ink adds contrast and depth to the image on the right

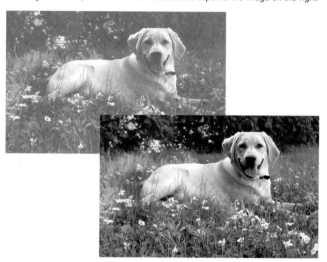

Coping with color confusion
If all of this color theory talk is making your head spin, don't worry about it. Working in Illustrator and producing a printed project *does not require* that you have these theories in your head. As you become more experienced with the printing process (and if you generally like this kind of stuff), these concepts will make more sense. Until then, remember the two essential points of this discussion: The offset printing process uses transparent CMYK inks; the color you see on a printed page is reflected off the paper, not the inks.

WORK IN
CMYK MODE

What You'll Do

In this lesson, you will use Illustrator's Color Picker, Color panel, and print options in CMYK Color mode.

Understanding Color Gamut

RGB, CMYK, and HSB are all known as **color models**. The **color mode** determines the color model used to display and print Illustrator documents. Illustrator offers two color modes for documents: RGB and CMYK.

As we've discussed, offset color printing is based on the CMYK color model. All light-emitting devices, such as your television or your monitor, produce color based on the RGB color model. If you flick a drop of water at your television screen, you will be able to see that the image is composed of very small red, green, and blue pixels. The full range of color that you perceive when you watch TV is the result of the additive properties of light; the red, green, and blue light are combining to produce the image.

Color gamut refers to the range of colors that can be printed or displayed by a given color model. A good monitor, based on the RGB color model, can produce a color gamut of more than 16 million colors. However, the spectrum of colors that can be viewed by the human eye is wider than any man-made method for reproducing color.

Setting up color management

For the print and prepress professional, Illustrator's Color Settings dialog box simplifies the goal of setting up a color-managed workflow by bringing most of the standard color management controls to a single place. Click Edit on the Application bar, then click Color Settings to open the Color Settings dialog box. You can choose RGB or CMYK working spaces and color management policies. The predefined configurations offer a set of color management options that are designed to achieve color consistency in a production workflow. In most cases, the predefined color settings will provide enough color management controls to meet the demands of a prepress environment.

The CMYK color model is substantially smaller than the RGB color model. Therefore, when you are creating computer graphics, remember that some colors that you can see on your monitor cannot be reproduced by the CMYK printing process.

Illustrator addresses this reality in different ways. For example, if you are working in RGB mode and choosing colors in the Color Picker or the Color panel, Illustrator will warn you if you have chosen a color

that is "out-of-gamut"—that is, a color that cannot be printed. Also, if you have created an image in RGB mode and you convert to CMYK mode, Illustrator will automatically replace the out-of-gamut colors applied to images with their closest CMYK counterparts.

As shown in Figure 9, the colors in RGB that are out-of-gamut for the CMYK color model are the brightest, most saturated, and most vibrant hues.

Don't despair. As you have certainly noted from looking at art books, posters, and even some high-quality magazines, the CMYK color model can be used to reproduce stunning color images. (Note: Because this book is a printed product and therefore based on the CMYK color model, we are unable to show you examples of out-of-gamut colors.)

FIGURE 9
CMYK color model is unable to reproduce the brightest and most saturated hues that you can see on your screen

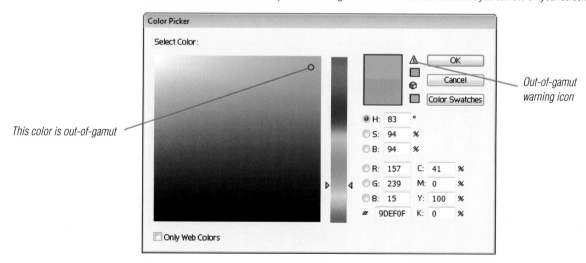

This color is out-of-gamut

Out-of-gamut warning icon

Specifying CMYK Tints

Tints are, quite simply, colors that you print by mixing varying percentages of CMYK inks. The lightest colors are produced with small percentages of ink, and darker colors with higher percentages. You can purchase process tint books that show you—with a high degree of fidelity—a large number of the color combinations available in the CMYK gamut.

In Illustrator, you specify CMYK tints by entering percentages in the Color Picker and the Color panel, as shown in Figure 10. If this idea is setting off alarms in your head . . . good for you! All the color produced by your monitor is based on the RGB color model. By definition, you cannot "see" the CMYK color model (or real CMYK tints, for that matter) on your monitor.

In the early days of desktop publishing, this contradiction generated enormous fear in the hearts of print professionals and created an entire cottage industry of color calibration hardware and software. Despite

FIGURE 10

Specifying a process tint on the Color panel

Dragging sliders on the Color panel is referred to as "specifying" or "mixing" a color

---

Using Creative Suite color settings

If you use other programs in the Adobe Creative Suite, such as InDesign and Photoshop, you'll be glad to know that there is a way to ensure that color settings can be synchronized across each CS4 program. Before you start your work on a new document or even an old one, you should synchronize your color settings. Adobe Bridge is the tool for this job. Simply open Bridge from your current application by clicking File on the Application bar, then clicking Browse in Bridge. In Bridge, click Edit on the Application bar, then click Creative Suite Color Settings.

To see all of the color settings, click the Show Expanded List Of Color Setting Files check box. Once you choose a color setting, click Apply. You can also install a custom settings file, such as a file you received from a printer or service bureau. To choose a custom settings file, click the Show Saved Color Settings Files button, then navigate to its location on your hard drive.

the dire warnings, however, color calibration problems turned out to be a phantom menace; simply put, the majority of print work produced is not so color-critical that variation in color is a problem (if the variation is even noticed).

Practically speaking, you must accept that the colors in your illustration on-screen will *never* be an exact match to the printed version. However, the numbers that you enter when specifying percentages of CMYK are *exactly* the percentages that will be output when the illustration goes to the printer. Therefore, if you *must* have a specific tint, find the color in a process tint book, and enter the percentages as specified.

Then, don't worry about how the tint looks on your screen. If it looks close, that's great. If not, it doesn't matter. The printer is contractually responsible to be able to reproduce the tint that you specified.

Printing transparent artwork

Whenever you have a document with transparent objects (objects whose opacity is set to less than 100%), you should be sure to check the transparency preferences before printing the file. When you print or save artwork that contains transparency, Illustrator performs a process called flattening. When flattening, Illustrator identifies transparent artwork, then isolates the areas that are overlapped by the transparent object by dividing the areas into components. Illustrator then analyzes those components to determine if they can be output with vector data or if they must be rasterized (converted to pixels). The flattening process works very well in most cases. However, if you are unsatisfied with the appearance of the high-resolution output, you may want to step in and rasterize the artwork yourself. Before outputting the file, you can use Illustrator's Overprint Preview mode (found on the View menu), which approximates how transparency and blending will appear in color-separated output.

When working in Illustrator, you have the option to specify a fill or a stroke to overprint. However, in most cases, only separation devices support overprinting. When you print to a composite, or when your artwork contains overprinted objects that interact with transparent objects, you need to choose what to do with the objects you have set to overprint. You can choose to simulate the overprint or to discard the overprint altogether. Choose File on the Application bar, then click Print. Select Advanced on the left side of the Print dialog box. Select Simulate or Discard from the Overprints list arrow.

Specify process tints in the Color Picker

1. Open AI 12-1.ai, then save it as **Oahu**.

2. Select the placed image, then hide it.

3. Double-click the **Fill or Stroke button** on the Tools panel to open the Color Picker, then type **189** for the hue, **100** for the saturation, and **100** for the brightness.

   The out-of-gamut warning icon appears, as shown in Figure 11.

4. Click the **blue square** under the out-of-gamut warning icon.

   The closest process color is specified as the new fill color.

5. Click **OK** to close the Color Picker dialog box.

6. Add the new color to the Swatches panel, then name it **Maverick**.

You chose a color in the Color Picker that was out-of-gamut for CMYK. You chose the process match that the out-of-gamut warning offered as a new fill color, then added it to the Swatches panel.

FIGURE 11
Out-of-gamut warning in the Color Picker

Out-of-gamut warning icon

Blue square

Creating templates

Templates are used for documents that share common settings like size and design elements. For example, if you design all the business cards for new employees at the company you work for, you can create a template at the specific size, view settings (such as guides), and print options. The template can also contain the company logo and specific color swatches, like your company's logo color. You could then use this template for every card you create. To create a template, open a new or existing document. Set up the document the way you want it to appear in terms of size, or with specific guides, etc. Create any artwork you want to appear in new documents you create from the template. Delete any existing swatches, styles, brushes, or symbols, you don't want to retain. Click File on the Application bar, then click Save as Template.

FIGURE 12

Applying process tints to the artwork

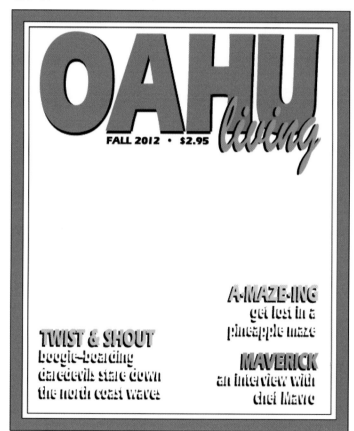

1. Click **Window** on the Application bar, then click **Color** to show the Color panel (if necessary).

2. Click the **Color panel list arrow**, then click **CMYK** (if necessary).

3. Using the sliders on the panel, mix a process tint that is 5C/70M/100Y, then press [**Enter**] (Win) or [**return**] (Mac).

   In standard notation for process tints, zero is not specified. As there is no black in this tint, the K percentage is not noted.

   TIP   You will not see the new color on the Color panel if the cursor is still flashing in the last text box that you entered a new value in. Pressing [Tab] advances your cursor to the next text box.

4. Add the new color to the Swatches panel, then name it **Living**.

5. Mix a new process tint that is 5C/40M/5Y.

6. Add the new color to the Swatches panel, then name it **Amazing**.

7. Mix a new process tint that is 30M/100Y.

8. Add the new color to the Swatches panel, then name it **Twist**.

9. Apply the four new tints that you have added to the Swatches panel to the artwork, as shown in Figure 12.

10. Save your work.

You mixed three different process tints on the Color panel, saved them on the Swatches panel, then applied the four tints you have created so far in this chapter to the artwork.

SPECIFY SPOT COLORS

What You'll Do

In this lesson, you will create and apply spot colors.

Understanding Spot Colors

Though printing is based on the four process colors CMYK, it is not limited to them.

Imagine that you are an art director designing the masthead for the cover of a new magazine. You have decided that the masthead will be an electric blue, vivid and eye-catching. If you were working with process tints only, you would have a problem. First, you would find that the almost-neon blue that you want to achieve is not within the CMYK gamut; it can't be printed. Even if it could, you would have an even bigger problem with consistency issues. You want that blue to be the same blue on every issue of the magazine, month after month. But process tints will vary on press; as the cover is printed, the blue color in the masthead will shift in tone, sometimes sharply.

Designers and printers use non-process inks to solve this problem. Non-process inks are special premixed inks that are printed separately from process inks. The color gamut of non-process inks available far exceeds that of CMYK. Non-process inks also offer consistent color throughout a print run.

Tabbing through the Color panel

The easiest way to mix process tints on the Color panel is to start out by double-clicking the C text box to select the current value, then enter the percentage of cyan that you want for the new tint. Press [Tab] to advance to the next text box, enter the new percentage, and so on. After you have entered the percentage in the B (black) text box, be sure to press [Tab] again. If you want to reverse direction, press and hold [Shift] while tabbing.

Preparing a Document for Prepress and Printing

The print world refers to non-process inks by a number of names:

- Spot colors: Refers to the fact that non-process inks print on the "spots" of the paper where the process inks do not print.
- Fifth color: Refers to the fact that the non-process ink is often printed in addition to the four process inks. Note, however, that non-process inks are not necessarily the "fifth" color. For example, many "two-color" projects call for black plus one non-process ink.
- PANTONE color: Pantone is a manufacturer of non-process inks.
- PMS color: An acronym for PANTONE Matching System.

Loading Spot Colors

In Illustrator, you use the Swatch Libraries menu item to select from a range of color systems (or libraries), including PANTONE, the standard library for non-process inks. When you import the PANTONE library, it appears as a separate panel, as shown in Figure 13.

QUICKTIP

To access the Pantone color library in Illustrator, click Window on the Application bar, point to Swatch Libraries, then point to Color Books.

FIGURE 13

PANTONE solid coated library appears as a separate panel

Rasterizing artwork

Illustrator is a vector-based drawing program; the graphics you create are called vector graphics. However, Illustrator is not exclusively vector-oriented, nor are Illustrator graphics limited to vectors. For a number of reasons, you may wish to convert a vector graphic into a bitmap graphic, a process called rasterization. If your Illustrator file is very complex, rasterizing it will convert it to a simple bitmap image. Output devices sometimes have trouble with complex objects and effects, such as gradient meshes and transparent objects. If you rasterize the graphic, you will see immediately if the effects translated properly. If so, the artwork is ready to print, as a simple, standard bitmap image. When rasterizing a vector graphic for output, whether for high-resolution printing or to appear on the Internet, you must determine the resolution (the number of pixels per inch) that the resulting bitmap will contain. You can input the desired resolution for the resulting bitmap file using the Document Raster Effects Settings dialog box. Click Document Raster Effects Settings on the Effect menu.

Outputting Documents with Spot Colors

All spot colors in the PANTONE library have a process match, which is of course a misnomer: if the process tint *matched* the spot color, there would be no need for the spot color in the first place. Some process tints—especially in the yellow hues—can come close to matching a spot color. Others—especially deep greens and blues—don't even come close.

When a four-color document is printed on a printing press, each of the four colors is printed separately: first yellow, then magenta, then cyan, then black. When an Illustrator document is output for printing, the document must be output as separations. Separations isolate each of the four process colors on its own "plate."

Clarifying resolution issues

The reckless misuse of the terms "resolution" and "DPI" by designers, printers, and even software programmers has resulted in widespread confusion over this concept and countless dollars and hours lost in struggling with files whose resolution settings are incorrect. And despite all of the confusion, the concepts are surprisingly simple and easy to understand. In general, when the term "resolution" is used, it is in reference to the number of pixels per inch in a bitmap image, or PPI. Unfortunately, seemingly everybody uses the term DPI instead of PPI; PPI is the only correct term for the resolution of a bitmap image. DPI stands for "dots per inch," which is the resolution of an output device. Dots are dots, and pixels are pixels; they are mutually exclusive. The resolution of your laser printer is probably 600 DPI or 1200 DPI, which is a satisfactory number of printing device dots to print text and lines that appear to be smooth. For bitmap images and blends, a minimum resolution of 2400 DPI is required for the output device to produce the smooth transitions of tone. Add to this confusion a third type of resolution, the resolution of a printed document. Lines per inch, LPI, or "line screen" is the number of lines of halftone dots (ink dots) in a printed image (professionally printed, not output from a desktop printer). Many printers refer to this resolution as, you guessed it, DPI, which is wholly incorrect. Lines are lines, and dots are dots. LPI is the only correct term for the resolution of a printed image. Standard line screens for color printing are 133 LPI and 150 LPI. A fluency with resolution terminology will help you in Illustrator when you want to rasterize a vector graphic (convert it to a bitmap image). When doing so, you must determine the resolution of the resulting bitmap image, the PPI. The PPI for a bitmap graphic that is to be used on the Internet is 72 PPI. The PPI for a bitmap graphic that is to be printed is twice the LPI.

When a color document is printed with four colors and a spot color, the spot color requires its own plate on the printing press so that the non-process ink can be laid down separately from the process inks.

In Illustrator, all spot colors that you use in a document will automatically be converted to their process match when separated, unless you *deselect* the Convert to Process option in the Separation Setup dialog box, which you access through the Print dialog box. See Figure 14.

See Figure 14.

FIGURE 14

Spot colors are converted to their process match when seperated

Understanding the output resolution of a vector graphic

Curved lines that you draw in Illustrator are, in terms of output, defined by small straight lines. "Curves" are made up of lines so small that your eye blends them together to create the appearance of a smooth curve. Therefore, the smaller the line segments, the smoother the curve. Of course, if the line segments are smaller, more of them are needed to draw the curve. Therefore, vector graphics have an output resolution, the number of line segments that will be used to draw the curve. Yet another term comes into play, and that is "flatness." The output resolution determines the flatness of the curve. A lower output resolution results in longer and fewer line segments to draw a curve. A higher output resolution increases the number of line segments and the file size. Sometimes, you will get a printer error if a document contains many long curved paths, simply because the file information is too much for the printer's processor to handle. In that case, you may want to reduce the default output resolution. Illustrator's default output resolution setting is 800 dots per inch (DPI). You can modify the flatness setting in the Graphics windows of the Print dialog box. In the Paths section of the window, drag the slider toward Quality for a lower flatness setting and a higher quality.

Import and apply spot colors

1. Click **Window** on the Application bar, point to **Swatch Libraries**, point to **Color Books**, then click **PANTONE solid coated**.

   A new panel appears with small sample colors of each color in the library, as shown in Figure 15.

   TIP You can purchase PANTONE swatch books from the Pantone web site at *www.pantone.com*.

2. Click in the Find text box in the PANTONE solid coated panel.

   TIP If the Find text box is not available, click the PANTONE solid coated panel list arrow, then click Show Find Field.

3. Type **663** in the Find text box.

   Color number 663 C is selected on the PANTONE solid coated panel.

   TIP To display the number for each PANTONE color, click the PANTONE solid coated panel list arrow, then click List View.

   (continued)

FIGURE 15
PANTONE solid coated panel library appears as a separate panel

Working with legacy text

Text that was created in Illustrator 10 or earlier must be updated if you plan on editing it in Illustrator CS4. If you don't need to update the text, it can remain as "legacy text." Legacy text can be moved and printed but it cannot be updated. There are two ways to update legacy text. You can update it upon opening the document when you are prompted to, or, open the document, click Type on the Application bar, point to Legacy Text, then click Update All Legacy Text.

If you only wish to update some legacy text but not all of it, simply select the text object you wish to update, click Type on the Application bar, point to Legacy Text, then click Update Selected Legacy Text.

Updated text is treated just like CS4 text and can take advantage of all of the text and paragraph formatting features in Illustrator CS4. If you save an Illustrator CS4 document as a Legacy Format (Version 10 or earlier), you may lose text editing features applied in CS4.

FIGURE 16

Spot color applied to the artwork

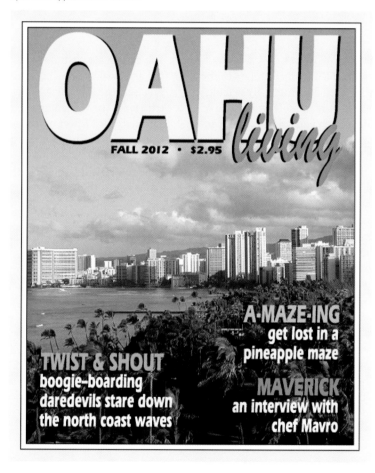

4. Click the **OAHU letters**, then click the **PANTONE 663 C color swatch**.

   The PANTONE 663 C color swatch is added to the standard Swatches panel.

5. Double-click the **PANTONE 663 C swatch** on the standard Swatches panel.

6. Click the **Color Mode list arrow**, then click **CMYK**.

7. Note that Spot Color is listed as the Color Type in the Swatch Options dialog box.

8. Note the CMYK values.

   The CMYK values represent the values you would use to create the closest possible match of PANTONE 663 C with process inks.

9. Click **Cancel** to close the Swatch Options dialog box.

10. Change the fill of the red frame to PANTONE 663 C.

11. Show all, then send the placed image to the back.

   Your work should resemble Figure 16.

12. Save your work, then close the Oahu document.

You displayed the PANTONE solid coated library of swatches. You then applied a spot color to artwork.

CREATE CROP MARKS

What You'll Do

 In this lesson, you will set up documents to print with crop marks.

Creating Crop Marks

The **trim size** of a document refers to the size of the finished document. By default, Illustrator crops the artwork at the size of the artboard, which you specify when you create the document. The document size is the trim size. **Crop marks** are short, thin lines that you can use to define areas of the page that you want be trimmed after the document is printed. Figure 17 shows crop marks around a graphic. When the trim size and the document size (the size of the artboard) are the same, you don't need to create your own crop marks.

You can create custom-sized crop marks on the artboard by drawing a rectangle that is precisely the same size as the document's trim size. Then, keeping the rectangle selected, click Effect on the Application bar, then click Crop Marks in the Illustrator Effects section of the menu. Crop marks will be added, representing the same size as the selected rectangle.

Illustrator CS4 adds crop marks as effects. Like all effects, crop marks are listed on the Appearance panel.

Editing Crop Marks

Once you've created crop marks, you cannot directly select them to edit them. Because they are added as effects, you must first expand the appearance to select and edit the crop marks. Click Object on the Application bar, then click Expand Appearance.

Creating Multiple Crop Marks for Multiple Objects

You can select multiple objects of different sizes on a page and create crop marks for each of those objects. The method is the same as for a single object: select the objects, click Effect on the Application bar, then click Crop Marks.

This situation often occurs when you "gang up" artwork on a page. For example, when printing business cards, printers use a standard sized 8.5" x 11" sheet of paper. Printing a single business card on that size paper would be a waste, so printers position multiple copies of the card on one sheet. Each of those copies must be trimmed, as shown in Figure 18.

When you apply the Crop Marks effect to multiple objects, you will often find that the effect creates redundant and/or overlapping crop marks. Simply expand the appearance and remove the crop marks you don't need.

FIGURE 17

Crop marks define the trim size of the artwork

FIGURE 18

Multiple crop marks define marks for multiple cuts

Create crop marks

1. Open AI 12-2.ai, then save it as **Crop Marks**.
2. Click **View** on the Application bar, then click **Business Card**.

   The view of the artwork is enlarged.
3. Select the 2" × 3.5" rectangle.

   2" × 3.5" is the standard size for business cards.

   | TIP   Switch to Outline mode if you have trouble selecting the rectangle.
4. Click **Effect** on the Application bar, then click **Crop Marks**.

   The rectangle remains; crop marks appear that define the trim size as that of the rectangle. Your screen should resemble Figure 19.
5. Save your work, then close the Crop Marks document.

You selected a rectangle, then you applied the Crop Marks effect.

FIGURE 19
Applying crop marks

Creating print presets

When you print a file, you often have to choose between a number of options that will affect the output of the file. Once you have specified the options you want to use, you can save those options as a print preset. Once saved, you will no longer need to specify these options again. You can simply choose the print preset containing the options. Using print presets is a fast, reliable way to print jobs that require consistently accurate settings for many options in the Print dialog box. To save a print preset, do one of the following:

1. Choose File on the Application bar, then click Print, adjust print settings, then click the Save Preset button next to the Print Preset list arrow. Type a name or use the default, and then click OK. With this method, the preset is saved in the preferences file.
2. Choose Edit on the Application bar, click Print Presets, and then click New. In the Print Presets dialog box, type a new name or use the default, adjust print settings, and then click OK to return to the Print Presets dialog box.

FIGURE 20

Applying crop marks

Use the Create Crop Marks effect

1. Open AI 12-3.ai, then save it as **Multiple Crop Marks**.

2. Select all.

   The artwork is locked. Only the eight rectangles that represent each business card are selected.

3. Click **Effect** on the Application bar, click **Crop Marks**, then deselect.

   As shown in Figure 20, crop marks appear for each rectangle.

4. Note that Crop Marks is listed on the Appearance panel.

5. Select all, click **Object** on the Application bar, then click **Expand Appearance**.

   The rectangles are deleted. All of the crop marks become selectable.

6. Select the crop marks shown in Figure 21.

   All of these crop marks are redundant; they all define the same cuts that are defined by the crops outside of the artwork.

7. Delete the selected crops.

8. Save your work, then close the file.

You applied crop marks to eight objects, expanded the appearance of the effect, then deleted the redundant crop marks.

FIGURE 21

Delete crop marks that lie on trim lines

CREATE
BLEEDS

What You'll Do

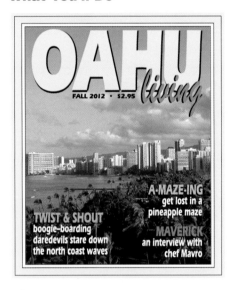

In this lesson, you will modify artwork to accommodate bleeds.

Creating Bleeds and Safety Guides

Artwork that extends to the trim is referred to as a "bleed" element, or simply a **bleed**, based on printer lingo meaning that to print correctly, the ink must bleed off the page.

Imagine that you have designed a business card that shows white lettering against a black background. You have used the Crop Marks effect so that the marks define the "live area" as 2" × 3.5". When the cards are trimmed, if the cutter is off by the slightest amount, $\frac{1}{10}$ of an inch, for example, your black business card will have a white line on one edge.

To accommodate variations in trimming, a printer will ask you to "build a bleed." What he or she is asking you to do is to extend bleed artwork so that it exceeds the cropped area by a minimum of .125". Artwork can bleed off any one or all four sides of the trim. Two of the most straightforward ways of doing this are to create a bleed object with the Offset Path command, or to extend the existing artwork off the artboard using the Move command for precision. Figure 22 shows an example of using bleeds.

In addition to bleeds, as a designer you should be conscious of your safety margin. All elements that aren't designed to bleed should be kept a minimum of .125" from the trim edge. This practice is known as maintaining safety or type safety. As with bleeds, safety guides anticipate variations in the trim cut and are designed to keep artwork from being accidentally trimmed off the page.

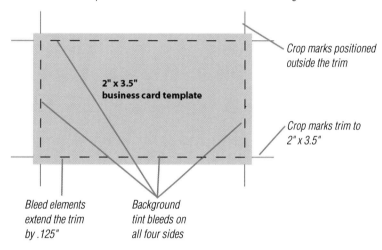

FIGURE 22
Bleeds extend the crop marks to accommodate variations when trimming

2" x 3.5"
business card template

Crop marks positioned outside the trim

Crop marks trim to 2" x 3.5"

Bleed elements extend the trim by .125"

Background tint bleeds on all four sides

Creating a PDF preset

A PDF preset is a collection of specified settings that affect the process of creating a PDF. When specifying PDF options, the choice often involves balancing file size with quality. With Illustrator files, file size is seldom an issue, unless the file contains large size placed bitmap graphics. In that case, you need to specify a compression setting to reduce the size of the placed bitmap artwork and thus reduce the size of the PDF itself. PDF settings are not only used for conserving file size. The PDF format offers a number of useful options. You can choose whether or not the resulting PDF shows crop marks and printer marks, for example, or you can choose whether the filename and the date and time of the creation of the PDF is listed at the top. You also specify whether the resulting file will be in the CMYK or RGB color space. Most users rely on pre-defined presets in the PDF dialog box. Most predefined presets are shared across Adobe Creative Suite components, including InDesign, Illustrator, Photoshop, and Acrobat. However, you can always create and save your own unique settings as new presets.

Create a bleed using the Offset Path command

1. Open AI 12-4.ai, then save it as **Oahu Bleed**.

2. Select the frame of the artwork that is filled with PANTONE 663 C.

3. Click **Object** on the Application bar, point to **Path**, then click **Offset Path**.

4. Type **.125** in the Offset text box, then click **OK**.

   The Offset Path command creates a new object, in this case, a bleed object that extends the artboard .125" on all sides. Your artwork should resemble Figure 23.

5. Verify that the new bleed object is still selected, then send it to the back.

6. Save your work, then close the Oahu Bleed document.

You used the Offset Path command to extend the edges of a bleed object .125".

FIGURE 23
A bleed object created with the Offset Path command

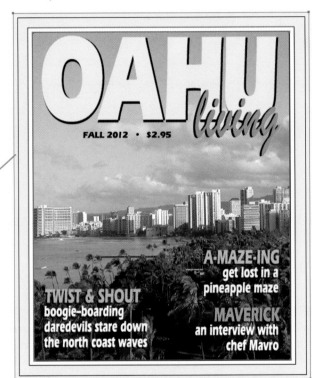

.125" bleed

FIGURE 24
Three sides of the blue rectangle must bleed

.125" bleed

FIGURE 25
The rule, too, must bleed

.125" bleed

Create a bleed using the Move command

1. Open AI 12-5.ai, then save it as **Three Sided Bleed**.

2. Click **View** on the Application bar, then click **Business Card**.

3. Select the black-stroked rectangle, click **Effect** on the Application bar, then click **Crop Marks**.

4. Click **Object** on the Application bar, click **Expand Appearance**, then use the Direct Selection tool ▸. to delete the black rectangle.

5. Click the bottom edge of the blue rectangle.

6. Click **Object** on the Application bar, point to **Transform**, click **Move**, type **0** in the Horizontal text box, type **-.125** in the Vertical text box, then click **OK**.

7. Select the left edge of the blue rectangle, then move it -.125" to the left.

8. Select the right edge of the blue rectangle, then move it .125" to the right.

   The blue rectangle bleeds on all three sides, as shown in Figure 24.

9. Select *only* the left anchor point of the black line, then move the point -.125" horizontally.

10. Select *only* the right anchor point of the black line, then move the point .125" horizontally, so that your work resembles Figure 25.

11. Save your work, then close the Three Sided Bleed document.

You extended individual lines and anchor points outside the crop marks as bleeds.

Explore basic color theory.

1. List the seven distinct colors of the visible spectrum.
2. What are the three additive primary colors?
3. What are the three subtractive primary colors?
4. When red, green, and blue light are combined equally, what color light do they produce?
5. Explain the term "subtractive" in terms of the subtractive primary colors.
6. Explain the term "transmission" in terms of light striking an object.
7. Which additive primary color would be 100% absorbed by a perfect cyan ink?
8. Which additive primary color would be 100% absorbed by a perfect magenta ink?
9. Which additive primary color would be 100% absorbed by a perfect yellow ink?
10. What is the fourth color in the four-color printing process, and why is it necessary?

Work in CMYK mode.

1. Open AI 12-6.ai, then save it as **Sleep Center**.
2. Using the Color panel, create a new process tint that is 55M/75Y.
3. Save the process tint on the Swatches panel as **text color**.
4. Fill the words THE SLEEP CENTER with the text color swatch.
5. Deselect the text, then save your work.

Specify spot colors.

1. Click Window on the Application bar, point to Swatch Libraries, point to Color Books, then click PANTONE solid coated.
2. Select the object with the gradient on the artboard.
3. Select the black color stop on the gradient slider on the Gradient panel.
4. Press [Alt] (Win) or [option] (Mac), then click a purple swatch in the PANTONE solid coated panel.
5. Save your work.

Create crop marks.

1. Click Effect on the Application bar, then click Crop Marks.
2. Click Object on the Application bar, then click Expand Appearance.
3. Save your work.

Create bleeds.

1. Deselect, then click the left edge of the rectangle with the Direct Selection tool.
2. Click Object on the Application bar, point to Transform, then click Move.
3. Type **-.125** in the Horizontal text box, type **0** in the Vertical text box, then click OK.
4. Select the top edge of the rectangle.
5. Open the Move dialog box, type **0** in the Horizontal text box, type **.125** in the Vertical text box, then click OK.
6. Select the right edge of the rectangle.
7. Open the Move dialog box, type **.125** in the Horizontal text box, type **0** in the Vertical text box, then click OK.
8. Save your work, compare your illustration to Figure 26, then close the document.

FIGURE 26
Completed Skills Review

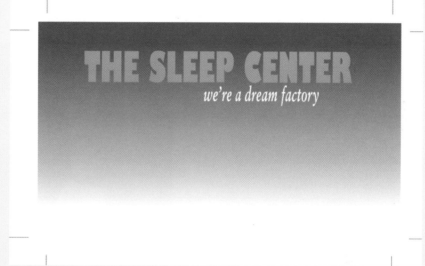

You work in the computer department at a small print shop. Your boss brings you an Illustrator file for a business card for USAchefs, an Internet company that works with the top chefs and restaurants in the city. Your boss asks you to create a print proof, which she will show to the customer. She asks you to create a rich black, add crops, and build a bleed, then says, with a wink, "But not necessarily in that order." You realize that she's challenging you to figure out the right order in which to get all three processes accomplished.

1. Open AI 12-7.ai, then save it as **USAchefs**.
2. Select the black rectangle, click Effect on the Application bar, then click Crop Marks.
3. Click Object on the Application bar, then click Expand Appearance.
4. Use the Offset Path command to offset the black rectangle path .125" on all four sides.
5. Keeping the rectangle selected, increase the cyan portion of its fill color 50% to create a rich black.
6. Save your work, then compare your illustration to Figure 27.
7. Close the document.

FIGURE 27
Completed Project Builder 1

You own a design firm in a small town. A new client delivers his logo to you on disk, telling you that it has two colors: PANTONE 255 and 70% PANTONE 5767. He tells you, "It's all set to go." You know that this client knows only enough to be dangerous. You open his file and, sure enough, you note immediately that all of the tints are process tints. You must change the fills and strokes to the proper PANTONE colors. Because this is a complex logo, and because you know that your client's knowledge of Illustrator is limited, you are aware that you must be very careful not to miss any elements.

1. Open AI 12-8.ai, then save it as **City Square**.
2. Apply the Show All command, just to avoid any potential surprises.
3. Delete the green letters.
4. Display the PANTONE solid coated panel.
5. Select the letter C in the center.
6. Click Select on the Application bar, point to Same, then click Fill Color.
7. Apply PANTONE 255 C to the fill, then hide the selection (*Hint*: If the Find Field text box does not work, you'll have to scroll around to find the correct swatch.)
8. Select the top white rectangle.
9. Click Select on the Application bar, point to Same, then click Stroke Color.
10. Apply PANTONE 255 C to the stroke, then hide the selection.

11. Click the green square in the center, then change the black stroke to PANTONE 255 C.
12. Click Select on the Application bar, point to Same, then click Fill Color.
13. Apply PANTONE 5767 C to the fill.
14. Display the Color panel (if necessary), then drag the slider to 80%.

FIGURE 28
Completed Project Builder 2

15. Hide the selection.
16. Select all and note that all the remaining items have a white fill.
17. Show all, save your work, then compare your illustration with Figure 28.
18. Close the City Square document.

You are the assistant art director for OAHU magazine. The art director tells you that, at the last minute, the editor in chief has changed the cover photo. You place the new photo in the Illustrator file and realize immediately that the colors that worked so well with the previous photo no longer work with this new photo.

1. Open AI 12-9.ai, then save it as **Oahu 2**.
2. Choose a new PANTONE color for the title and the frame.
3. Mix a new process tint, then apply it to the word "living."
4. Mix three new process tints, then apply them to the three subheads.
5. Save your work, compare your illustration with Figure 29, then close Oahu 2.

FIGURE 29
Completed Design Project

You are the head of the film output department for a small printer. You receive an Illustrator file for the business card for USAchefs. The file is complete with a rich black, crop marks, and bleeds. With so many years' experience, you know how best to lay out and print standard-sized business cards for maximum cost-effectiveness. However, you have a group of six new workers whom you hired for the third shift, and you realize that the issues involved with preparing this job would make for a great lesson.

1. Open AI 12-10.ai, then save it as **Chef Output**. (*Hint*: The single card is 2" wide by 3.5" tall. The document is 8.5" by 11.")

2. What would be the most cost-efficient layout for the card on an 8.5" × 11" sheet? How many cards can be positioned on the sheet while still keeping a minimum .25" margin from the edge of the sheet?

3. Once you have calculated the number of cards that can fit on the page, calculate the size of the total area (without bleeds) covered by the artwork.

4. Use the Move dialog box to position 12 cards (4 across, 3 down) centered on the 8.5" × 11" page.

5. Select just the black rectangles, copy them, paste in front, then bring them to the front.

6. Open the Pathfinder panel, then click the Unite button. (*Hint*: The 12 rectangles are united as one rectangle.)

7. Hide the new rectangle.

8. Select just the black rectangles again, click Effect on the Application bar, then click Crop Marks.

9. Click Object on the Application bar, then click Expand Appearance.

10. Deselect, then use the Direct Selection tool to move the outside crop marks onto the 8.5" × 11" document. (*Hint*: Move the crops close to the black rectangles, but don't let them touch.)

11. Select the black rectangles, then hide them.

12. Delete all the redundant interior crop marks so that your document resembles Figure 30.

13. Reveal the hidden objects, then deselect.

14. Select the large black rectangle, click Object on the Application bar, point to path, then click Offset path.

15. Type .125 in the Offset text box, then click OK.

16. Click Object on the Application bar, points Arrange, then click Send to Back.

17. Deselect all, click the center of the large black triangle to select it, then delete it.

18. Compare your results to Figure 31, save your work, then close the file.

FIGURE 30
Interior crop marks deleted

FIGURE 31
Completed Portfolio Project

13

PREPARING GRAPHICS
FOR THE WEB

1. Create slices

2. Specify slice type and slice options

3. Use the Save for Web & Devices

   dialog box

4. Create an image map

It's funny to think that, when Illustrator debuted in the late 80s, there was only one type of output for an Illustrator file—print. No Internet, no cell phones, no iPods—it was either on the screen, or it was on paper.

So much has, of course, changed since then, and the World Wide Web has had an impact on all design and layout programs—Illustrator included. It's had its impact on Adobe as well—who could have foreseen that Dreamweaver would become an Adobe product?

Fortunately for Illustrator lovers who don't necessarily want to design in

Dreamweaver or Flash, Adobe has blessed Illustrator with the ability to convert a layout into slices and the ability to optimize those slices for download.

With the success of Dreamweaver and Flash as industry standards for web page and web graphic creation, it's unlikely that you'll see Illustrator used exclusively to create a website. Nevertheless, it's good to know that you can still use Illustrator to create web pages and that Illustrator is fully conversant with Dreamweaver and Flash.

Tools You'll Use

CREATE
SLICES

What You'll Do

In this lesson, you will create slices using guides. You will also combine slices.

Understanding Web Graphics

When you create graphics for the web, you will need to pay attention to different considerations than you would when designing graphics for print. The web is an entirely different medium, and you will be required to become familiar with, if not fluent in, many issues.

Color is an essential consideration when producing web graphics. Since a computer's monitor functions as a light source, it produces color based on the additive model; color is created by combining light. Thus, graphics that you create must be saved in RGB mode.

For the designer, this is good news: The RGB color gamut is much larger than the CMYK color gamut. When designing for the web, you can use the brightest, most saturated colors. However, the colors you see on your artboard aren't necessarily the colors that will appear in your web browser. Color choices, file formats, and the degree of compression all affect the appearance of color.

Resolution is another essential consideration when using bitmap graphics on the web. If you place a bitmap graphic in your Illustrator file, remember that 72 pixels per inch (PPI) is the standard resolution for bitmap graphics on the web.

Two other considerations when choosing the correct file format for your web graphics are file size and display characteristics. Two standard compression file formats for bitmap graphics—JPEG and GIF—both reduce file size significantly, but through dramatically different processes. Knowing which to choose, and then choosing the degree to which each compresses the file, require understanding and experience.

Understanding Sliced Artwork

When you create graphics for the web, file size is a fundamental consideration. Smaller file sizes enable web servers to store and transmit images more efficiently, and allow viewers to download images more quickly.

When creating graphics for the web, you often find that the file size of the entire document is too large to be acceptable. For this reason, Illustrator allows you to divide your work into slices: You literally divide the artwork into areas to be output as individual—and therefore smaller—files.

Imagine a 100-piece puzzle whose pieces are all rectangular. Imagine that the entire puzzle, when put together, weighs exactly one pound. It would stand to reason that each of the 100 pieces weighs far less than one pound. This is a good analogy for understanding sliced artwork. Each slice is like a piece of the puzzle, smaller in area and—more importantly—smaller in size.

The analogy is not apt in one area: When a puzzle is completed, you can see the lines between the pieces. With sliced artwork, the slices in the work are invisible when it is viewed in a web browser.

Slices provide another important function. Web pages can contain many different kinds of elements, such as HTML text and bitmap images. In Illustrator, if you use slices to divide the different elements, you can then output them differently. For example, if you create a slice that contains a bitmap image and another that contains HTML text, you can output the bitmap slice as a JPEG file and the text slice as an HTML file.

Creating artwork by using variables

Variable libraries enable designers and developers to coordinate their work through an XML file. The developer can then use the XML file to link variables and data sets to a database and write a script to render the final artwork. To import variables into Illustrator from an XML file, choose Load Variable Library from the Variables panel menu. To export variables from Illustrator to an XML file, choose Save Variable Library from the Variables panel menu.

Creating Slices with the Make Slice Command and the Slice Tool

The Make Slice command creates a slice whose dimensions match those of the bounding box of the object. This command also creates a slice that captures text with its basic formatting characteristics. With the Make Slice command, the object is the slice, and vice versa. If you move or modify the object, the slice automatically adjusts to encompass the new artwork.

The Slice tool allows you to draw a rectangular slice anywhere on the artboard. Slices that you create with the Slice tool are independent of the underlying artwork. In other words, if you move the artwork, the slice does not move with the artwork.

Whether you use the Make Slice command or the Slice tool to create slices, Illustrator generates automatic slices that cover the remainder of the artboard. Illustrator does this to create a complete HTML table, in case the document is saved as a web page.

In Figure 1, slice 3 was drawn with the Slice tool. Slices 1, 2, and 4 were generated automatically.

Put quite simply, automatic slices are cumbersome, tricky, and hard to work with. Every time you add or edit slices, Illustrator must regenerate automatic slices; thus, the slice pattern on the artboard continues to change.

FIGURE 1

Slice 3 was created with the Slice tool; slices 1, 2, and 4 were generated automatically

Creating Slices from Guides

You can use standard ruler guides to define how you want artwork to be divided into slices. Figure 2 shows three guides that were positioned so as to isolate the graphic of the dog.

By definition, guides extend across and beyond the artboard. Therefore, when you use guides to define areas to be sliced, the length of the guide can get in the way. For example, the two vertical guides in Figure 2 extend up beyond the dog area into the headline. Thus, the headline is unnecessarily divided into three sections.

This problem can sometimes seem extreme. Figure 3 shows two additional horizontal guides positioned on the artwork to isolate each of the three photos and their corresponding text on the right. Each will be used as a link that will take the viewer to a different page. Therefore, it is necessary to create a slice for each link. Note, however, that the horizontal guides extend across the dog area, dividing that artwork into three parts.

FIGURE 2

Guides isolate the dog graphic into its own area

FIGURE 3

Two additional horizontal guides divide the dog graphic into three sections

Horizontal guide   Two vertical guides

When you apply the Create from Guides command, Illustrator generates slices for each area defined by a guide, as shown in Figure 4. Twelve slices are unnecessary to save this artwork for the web. For exam-

ple, slices 04, 07, and 10, if combined, could be saved as a very small file. Also, one might want to try to save the dog graphic as one file. Breaking the dog artwork into three slices runs the risk that

each slice might vary slightly in color because of the file format and the compression that is applied.

FIGURE 4

The Create from Guides command generates only slices—no automatic slices

Note, however, that each slice . . . is a slice! The Create from Guides command generates only slices—no automatic slices. Each slice can be selected with the Slice Selection tool. Therefore, slices can be easily combined, as shown in Figure 5.

Of the three main ways that Illustrator offers for making slices, using guides and then combining excess slices is the simplest, most straightforward, and hassle-free method.

FIGURE 5
Slices can be combined easily

Make slices

1. Open AI 13-1.ai, then save it as **SDS**.

2. Close all panels except for the Tools panel.

3. Change the style of the guides to Dots and the color of the guides to Yellow.

   TIP If you are using Macintosh OS 10, your preference settings are on the Illustrator menu.

4. Show the rulers, then position a guide on all four sides of the photo, as shown in Figure 6.

5. Position a vertical guide to the left of the three text buttons, then position another guide to the right of the three text buttons.

6. Position a horizontal guide above the large purple text at the bottom, as shown in Figure 7.

7. Position a horizontal guide above and below the "purchase show tickets" button, as shown in Figure 8.

8. Verify that your guides are unlocked.

9. Click **Object** on the Application bar, point to **Slice**, then click **Create from Guides**.

   Thirty slices are generated, as shown in Figure 9.

   TIP The View menu has commands to hide and show slices.

You positioned guides, then used them to create slices.

FIGURE 6
Positioning guides on all four sides of the photo

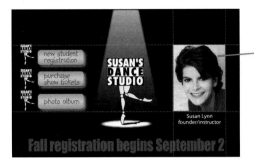

Position guides on all four sides of this photo

FIGURE 7
Positioning a guide above the text

Horizontal guide above text

FIGURE 8
Positioning guides above and below the "purchase show tickets" button

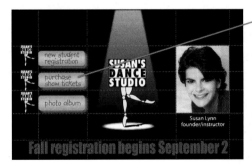

Purchase show tickets button

FIGURE 9
Thirty slices generated from guides

Preparing Graphics for the Web

FIGURE 10
Slices 06, 11, and 16 selected

Slices 06, 11, and 16

FIGURE 11
Three slices combined into one

Newly combined slice

FIGURE 12
After combining slices, 14 slices remain

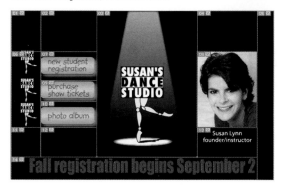

Combine slices

1. Click the **Selection tool** 🔺, then click any-where in the scratch area to deselect the slices.

2. Click the **Slice Selection tool** 📋.

   TIP The Slice Selection tool is hidden beneath the Slice tool.

3. Using [Shift], select slices 06, 11, and 16 as shown in Figure 10.

   TIP The easiest way to select a slice is to click the slice number.

4. Click **Object** on the Application bar, point to **Slice**, then click **Combine Slices**.

   The three slices are combined into one slice; all of the slices are renumbered, as shown in Figure 11.

5. Hide the guides.

6. Using the same method, combine the four slices that contain all of the purple "Fall registration text."

7. Combine the six black slices on the right-hand margin.

8. Combine the three slices that contain the photo.

9. Combine the five slices that contain the logo in the spotlight, so that your slices corre-spond to Figure 12.

10. Save your work.

You combined slices to create single slices for specific areas of the artwork.

SPECIFY SLICE TYPE
AND SLICE OPTIONS

What You'll Do

 In this lesson, you will specify slices as Image or No Image, and you will add URL links to image slices.

Specifying Slice Types

A slice's type and the options assigned to it determine how the artwork contained in the slice will function on a web page. A slice must be selected in order for you to assign a type and apply options to it. The Slice Options dialog box allows you to specify one of three categories for a slice's type. Basically, a slice's type defines its content.

The Image type is used when you want the content of a slice to become a linked image file on a web page.

The No Image type is used when you want the area to contain text or a solid color. You enter the text or the color information directly into the Slice Options dialog box. You cannot view No Image slice content in Illustrator; you must use a web browser to preview it.

Choosing between Image and No Image is not always as straightforward as it would at first seem. Consider slice 2 in Figure 13, for example. It contains no artwork, and

certainly would not function as a link. However, it does contain a background color—the same background color that is shared by all of the slices.

If you were to define the slice type of slice 2 as No Image, it would by default have no background color. If you saved the file for the web, the content of slice 2 would appear white on the web page. You could apply a background color in the Slice Options dialog box, and specify the color to have the same RGB values as the background color in the Image slices. This solution may work well. However, you also have the option of specifying slice 2's type as Image—a single color image with no links. In this case, slice 2 would be output using the same file format as the other slices, logically a safer bet for color consistency.

The third type of slice is HTML Text, which you use if you want to capture Illustrator text and its basic formatting. You can only create this type of slice using the Make Slice command.

Generally, you will use Illustrator to create display text—text that is intended to be used as a design element, such as a headline. Rather than saving display text as text for the web, it is a smart decision to simply save a version of your artwork with display text converted to outlines and defined as an image. With this method, you know for certain that your text will appear exactly as you designed it, with no risk of its being modified by or being in conflict with a browser's preset preferences.

Setting Options for Image Content Slices

When you specify a slice as an Image slice, you have the following options in the Slice Options dialog box:

- **Name**: By default, the slice name is used as the file name when you save the web page. By default, the slice is named with the slice number. It is a good idea to rename an important slice with a name that is more descriptive of its content.
- **URL**: Specify a URL to make the slice a hotspot on the web page.
- **Target**: If you've specified a URL, the target specifies the frame that you want the link to target. You can enter the name of a target frame, or you can use one of the standard targets in the pop-up menu. If you are unfamiliar with frames, note that _parent and _blank are the most common. _blank means that a new browser window will be opened, or "spawned," to show the linked page. _parent, the more standard of the two, means that the current window will change to show the linked page.
- **Message**: The information you type in the Message text box is what will appear in the status bar of a browser window when you position your cursor over the corresponding image slice. Messages usually convey information about the current image, or information about what the image links to.
- **Alt**: Think of Alt as an "alternative" to an image. Alternative text is for sight impaired web surfers. They will hear the alt text rather than see the image.
- **Background**: If you are saving a bitmap image with a transparent background, you can specify a color for the background behind the transparent areas.

FIGURE 13

Slice 2 could be specified as an Image or a No Image type

Setting Options for No Image Content Slices

In the Slice Options dialog box, you can set the following options:

- **Text**: In the Text Displayed in Cell text box, you can enter text that will appear in the slice. You can format the text using standard HTML tags. Be careful not to enter more text than can fit in the slice. If you do, the overflow will extend into neighboring slices. Because you cannot view the text in Illustrator, you will need to save the file for the web and open it in a browser to view your work.

- **Alignment**: Use the Horiz and Vert list arrows to specify the horizontal and vertical alignment of the text.

- **Background**: Choose a background color for the slice.

QUICKTIP

Using Illustrator CS4, you can build interactivity into your graphics that will be used on the web. Using the SVG Interactivity panel, select the object that you plan on exporting as an SVG file, choose an event, such as `onmouseover`, from the Event list arrow, then enter your JavaScript in the JavaScript text box. When the graphic is placed in a browser, the event assigned to it will trigger the JavaScript command and cause another event such as a rollover or a pull-down menu to appear.

Using Device Central

With the omnipresence of iPods and cell phones, it seems only natural that Illustrator CS4 would incorporate utilities for exporting graphics to various handheld and other devices. But if you think back to even just five years ago—who would have ever thought of exporting an Illustrator graphic to a phone?!?

Device Central is a mini application that interfaces all the applications in the Creative Suite. Design Central is equipped with presets for output to a large number of handheld devices, and that output can include basic graphics, video files, and even HTML. With Device Central, creative professionals and developers can preview how different types of files—Photoshop files, Illustrator files, Flash files—will appear on a handheld device.

But Device Central goes beyond just previewing. With Device Central, you can scale and position graphics in a visual rendering of various cell phone designs. And you can rely on Design Central's size presets to be sure that your graphic is sized correctly and will appear exactly as it's previewed.

Device Central supports a long list of file formats: SWF, JPG, JPEG, PNG, GIF, WBM, MOV, 3GP, M4V, MPG, MPEG, AVI, HTM, HTML, XHTML, CHTML, URL, and WEBLOC. You can access Device Central through the Save for Web & Devices dialog box.

FIGURE 14
Slice Options dialog box for slice 03

Message text box

Alt text box

Slice Type list arrow

1. Click the **Slice Selection tool** , then click **slice 03** (if necessary).

2. Click **Object** on the Application bar, point to **Slice**, then click **Slice Options**.

3. Click the **Slice Type list arrow**, then click **Image**.

4. Type **Susan's Dance Studio** in both the Message and Alt text boxes, as shown in Figure 14.

5. Click **OK** to close the Slice Options dialog box.

6. Click **File** on the Application bar, then click **Save** to update your slice numbers.

7. Click **slice 14**, click **Object** on the Application bar, point to **Slice**, click **Slice Options**, specify it as an Image slice, type **Fall registration** in the Message and Alt text boxes, click **OK**, then save.

8. Click **slice 01**, define it as No Image, click the **Background list arrow**, click **Black**, click **OK**, then save.

   The black background will be coded in HTML. If you wanted to use the underlying black object as the black background, you would specify the slice type as an image, just as you did the logo.

9. Repeat Step 8 to specify slices 02, 04, 05, 11, and 12 as No Image slices with a black background, one at a time.

   TIP You cannot apply Slice Options to multiple slices simultaneously.

10. Save your work.

You used the Slice Options dialog box to specify slices as Image slices and No Image slices.

Formatting a story

Along with being a great drawing program, Illustrator remains a great layout program. You can use any of the shapes you create as text boxes, and Illustrator provides you the standard layout options that you'd find in a layout program like InDesign. You can "thread" text between objects, meaning you can flow text from one object to another. When you add text to an object, it becomes a text object with an "in port" and an "out port." To thread text, click the out port of an object that contains text, then click the in port of the object you want to thread to. If the object you are threading to isn't already defined as a text object, click on the path of the object. Another method for threading text between objects is to select an area type object, select the object (or objects) you want to thread to, and then choose Type on the Application bar, point to Threaded Text, and then click Create. You will see visual icons representing threads. To view threads, choose View on the Application bar, point to Show Text Threads and then select a linked object.

Set options for image content slices

1. Click the **Slice Selection tool** (if necessary), click **slice 13**, click **Object** on the Application bar, point to **Slice**, then click **Slice Options**.

2. Click the **Slice Type list arrow**, then click **Image**.

3. Type **http://www.sds.com/bio/index.html** in the URL text box.

   In a web browser, clicking slice 13 will link to an HTML biography page.

4. Click the **Target list arrow**, then click **_parent**.

   In a web browser, clicking slice 13 will change the current window to the HTML biography page.

5. Type **Susan Lynn bio** in the Message and Alt text boxes, as shown in Figure 15, click **OK**, then save.

   TIP   Each time you make changes to a slice or combine slices, the slice numbering is thrown off. Saving your work reapplies the correct slice numbers to the slices.

   (continued)

FIGURE 15
Slice Options dialog box for slice 13

URL text box

Locating and replacing fonts inside a document

You can replace a given font in a document with another font using the Find Font utility. Click Type on the Application bar, then click Find Font. All the fonts used in the document are listed. Select the name of the font you want to find; the first occurrence of the font is highlighted in the document window. Select a replacement font from the Replace with Font From list arrow. You can click Change to change just one occurrence of the selected font, or click Change All to change all occurrences of the selected font. Note that when you replace a font using the Find Font command, all other type attributes applied to the original remain applied to the replacement font.

FIGURE 16

Slice Options dialog box for slice 07

FIGURE 17

Slice Options dialog box for slice 09

FIGURE 18

Slice Options dialog box for slice 10

6. Click **slice 08**, open the Slice Options dialog box, repeat Steps 2–5 so that slice 08 contains the same slice information as slice 13, then save.

7. Click **slice 06**, open the Slice Options dialog box, verify that the Slice Type is set to Image, click **OK**, then save.

8. Click **slice 07**, open the Slice Options dialog box, type the information shown in Figure 16, click **OK**, then save.

9. Specify the slice options for slice 09 as shown in Figure 17, then save.

10. Specify the slice options for slice 10 as shown in Figure 18, then save.

Because the target for slice 10 is _blank, slice 10, when clicked, will open a new browser window for the photo album page.

11. Save your work.

You used the Slice Options dialog box to specify URLs to which the image slices will link when clicked in a browser application.

USE THE SAVE FOR
WEB & DEVICES DIALOG BOX

What You'll Do

In this lesson, you will optimize slices for the web, using the Save for Web & Devices dialog box.

Optimizing Artwork for the Web and Other Devices

Most artwork, even when sliced, requires optimization. **Optimization** is a process by which the file size is reduced through standard color compression algorithms.

Illustrator CS4 offers a number of optimization features to save artwork in different web graphics file formats. Your choice of a file format will have the greatest effect on the optimization method that is performed on the artwork.

The Save for Web & Devices dialog box presents many options for previewing images. The tabs at the top of the image area define the display options. The Original display presents the artwork with no optimization. The Optimized display presents the artwork with the current optimization setting applied. The 2-Up

display presents two versions of the artwork—the original and the optimized version—side by side, and the 4-Up display presents the original beside three optimized versions.

Optimizing with the GIF File Format

GIF is a standard file format for compressing images with flat color, which makes it an excellent choice for many types of artwork generated in Illustrator. GIFs provide effective compression; for the right type of artwork, GIFs maintain excellent quality with crisp detail. In many cases, the compression has no noticeable effect on the image.

GIF compression works by lowering the number of colors in the file. The trick with GIFs is to lower the number of available colors as much as possible without adversely affecting the appearance of the image. Generally, if the number of colors is too low, problems with the image are obvious, as shown in Figure 19.

Optimizing with the JPEG File Format

JPEG is a standard file format for compressing continuous-tone images, gradients, and blends. JPEG compression relies on "lossy" algorithms—lossy referring to a loss of data. In the JPEG format, data is selectively discarded.

You choose the level of compression in the JPEG format by specifying the JPEG's quality setting. The higher the quality setting, the more detail is preserved. Of course, the more detail preserved, the less the file size is reduced.

When JPEG compression is too severe for an image, the problems with the image are obvious and very unappealing, as shown in Figure 20.

JPEG has emerged as one of the most used, if not the most used, file formats on the Internet. As a result, many designers ignore GIFs in favor of JPEGs, though many times GIFs would be the better choice.

FIGURE 19

A GIF file with too few colors available to render the image adequately

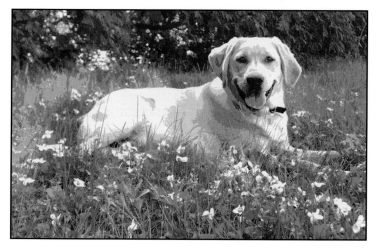

FIGURE 20

Problems with JPEGs are obvious and very unappealing

Optimize a slice as a JPEG

1. Click **File** on the Application bar, then click **Save for Web & Devices**.

2. Click the **Optimized tab** (if necessary).

   The Optimized view shows you the artwork with the current optimization settings applied.

3. Click the **Slice Select tool** ✂ in the Save for Web & Devices dialog box, click **slice 03**, click the **Preset list arrow**, then click **JPEG High**.

   The selected slice is updated.

4. Click the **4-Up tab**.

   The image area is divided into four views of the artwork. The upper-right window is selected.

5. Click the **Hand tool** ✋ in the Save for Web & Devices dialog box, then drag the upper-right window until all of slice 03 is visible, as shown in Figure 21.

   > TIP Use the Zoom tool to zoom in or out (if necessary).

6. Compare the file size of the original to the other three.

7. Compare the download times and quality settings, as listed in the upper-right and bottom windows.

8. Examine the three images.

   The quality of the lower-right image is unsatisfactory. Distracting pixels are visible at the edges of the logo and on the legs.

9. Click the **lower-left window**, click the **Quality list arrow**, then drag the **slider** to 40.

10. Keep the Save for Web & Devices dialog box open.

You used the 4-Up view of the Save for Web & Devices dialog box to compare three optimized JPEG files, each with different settings.

FIGURE 21
Save for Web & Devices dialog box

File size

Download time

Quality setting

FIGURE 22

Slice 14, optimized as a GIF using 8 colors

Change in
file size

Color
Table

1. Click the **Optimized tab**.

2. Click the **Slice Select tool**, click **slice 06**, press and hold [**Shift**], then click **slice 13** to add it to the selection.

3. Click the **Preset list arrow**, then click **GIF 32 Dithered**.

4. Remove the check mark from the Transparency check box.

5. Deselect, click **slice 06** only, then click the **Color Table tab** to the right of the image window.

    The Color Table shows the 32 total colors that are used to represent the artwork.

6. Click **slice 14**, click the **Preset list arrow**, then click **GIF 32 No Dither**.

    Note the change to the swatches in the Color Table. Though the setting is for 32 colors, only 17 colors are required to reproduce the artwork.

7. Note the file size in the lower-left corner.

8. Click the **Colors list arrow**, then click **8**.

    Note the change in the Color Table and the change in file size, as shown in Figure 22. Note also the high quality of the artwork with only eight colors.

9. Remove the check mark from the Transparency check box.

10. Keep the Save for Web & Devices dialog box open.

You optimized a slice as a GIF. You lowered the number of colors available to draw the image, noting the changes in image quality and file size.

Compare and contrast JPEG vs. GIF formats

1. Click the **Slice Select tool** (if necessary), click **slice 07**, press and hold [**Shift**], then click slices **09** and **10** to add them to the selection.

2. Click the **Preset list arrow**, click **JPEG High**, then click the **4-Up tab**.

3. Compare the quality of the three JPEGs to the original.

   The High quality JPEG in the upper-right window is the only version with acceptable quality. Note that the file size is over 9K, as shown in Figure 23.

   TIP Your file size may slightly differ.

4. Click the **Optimized tab**.

5. Click the **Preset list arrow**, click **GIF 128 No Dither**, then remove the check mark from the Transparency check box.

6. Click the **4-Up tab**, then use the Hand tool (if necessary), to see as much of the three buttons as possible.

   (continued)

FIGURE 23

Slices 07, 09, and 10 optimized as a high-quality JPEG

File size is large

FIGURE 24

Slices 07, 09, and 10 optimized as a GIF

7. Click the **lower-left window**, then note that its Selective palette is 64 colors, one-half that of the image in the upper-right window.

8. Click the **Colors list arrow**, then click **32**.

   The Selective palette of the image in the lower-left corner is reduced by half, yet the quality remains acceptable.

9. Click the **Colors list arrow**, then click **16**.

   The reduced palette does not contain enough colors to represent the buttons' drop shadows smoothly.

10. Click the **Colors list arrow**, then click **32**.

    The file size is around 6 kilobytes—⅔ that of the acceptable JPEG—and the quality is almost indistinguishable from the original, as shown in Figure 24.

11. Keep the Save for Web & Devices dialog box open.

You experimented with optimizing a slice as both a JPEG and GIF, comparing file size and image quality. You found that the GIF format was able to optimize the slice with higher quality at a lower file size than the JPEG format.

Create photo effects with a GIF

1. Click the **Optimized tab**.

2. Click the **Slice Select tool** 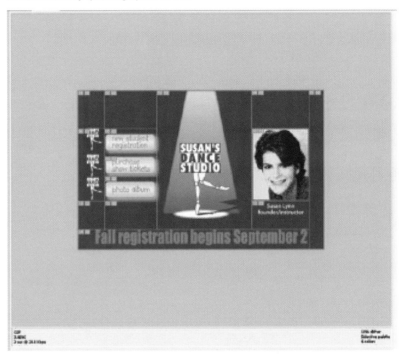 (if necessary), then click **slice 08**.

3. Click the **Preset list arrow**, then click **GIF 32 Dithered**.

4. Click the **Color Table tab** (if necessary).

   The Color Table shows the 32 total colors that are used to present the photo in slice 08.

5. Click the **Colors list arrow**, then click **16**.

   The number of colors in the Color Table is reduced.

6. Click the **Colors list arrow**, click **8**, then note the effect on the photo and the file size shown in the lower-left corner of the dialog box.

7. Click the **Colors list arrow**, click **4**, click the **Dither list arrow**, then drag the **slider** to 10%.

8. Click the **Specify the dither algorithm list arrow**, then click **Noise** so that the photo resembles Figure 25.

9. Keep the Save for Web & Devices dialog box open.

You specified an Image slice as a GIF, then lowered the number of colors available to reproduce the image, noting the effect on the image. You then added noise as the type of dither algorithm to create a special effect.

FIGURE 25

An effect created by optimizing a photo as a GIF

FIGURE 26
Web page shown in a browser window

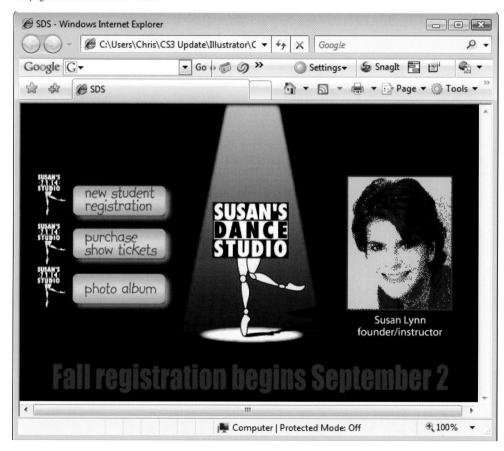

1. Click **Save**, name the file **SDS.html**, then click **Save**.

2. Launch your web browser, such as Safari or Internet Explorer.

   TIP If you do not have access to a web browser, proceed to the next lesson.

3. Open SDS.html in your web browser application.

4. Point to different images and note the messages that you entered in the Slice Options dialog box, in the status bar of the browser window.

   TIP If you do not see messages in the status bar, your browser may be set to block specific content.

   Your screen should resemble Figure 26.

5. Close (Win) or Quit (Mac) your browser, then save and close the SDS document.

You saved the file with the optimization settings that you specified in the Save for Web & Devices dialog box. You then viewed the HTML file in a web browser application.

CREATE AN IMAGE
MAP

What You'll Do

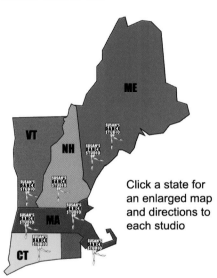

Click a state for
an enlarged map
and directions to
each studio

*In this lesson, you will change the colors
in an illustration to web safe colors and
create polygonal image maps with URLs
attached to them for use on web page.*

Working with Web Safe Colors

Given all of the variables that might affect
color display on the Internet—different
monitors with different settings, different
web browsers with different settings,
among many other conditions—you can
never be certain that the colors that you
specify in your document will appear the
same way when viewed as a web page. You
can't even be certain that they'll be consistent from computer to computer. To allevi-
ate this problem to some degree, Illustrator
offers a Web Safe RGB mode on the Color
panel and a Web swatch library. The Web
swatch library contains predefined colors
that are coded so as to be recognized by
most computer displays, and by the common web browser applications. When color
is critical, it is best to think of the web safe
gamut as a safe bet for achieving reasonable
consistency, understanding that a guaran-
tee is a bit too much to expect.

Creating vector-based web graphics

Though bitmap images are the most common graphics on the web, vector-based
graphics make for excellent web graphics. Unlike bitmap graphics, which tend
toward higher file sizes and lose quality when enlarged, vector graphics are scalable,
compact, and able to maintain their image quality at different resolutions. The Flash
SWF file format supports vector graphics for the web. SWF also recognizes symbols
in your artwork. When the artwork is saved or exported as an SWF, each symbol is
defined only once, which can substantially lower the file size. The SWF format also
provides excellent support of complex Illustrator artwork, such as gradients, mesh
objects, and patterns.

Understanding Image Maps

Image maps allow you to define an area of an illustration as a link. In a web browser, when a user clicks the area of the image defined as a link, the web browser loads the linked file.

Unlike using slices to create links, using image maps stores the artwork and the links in a single file; using slices causes artwork to be exported in different files. Another main difference is that slices are always rectangular, while image maps enable you to create links from polygons and odd-shaped objects, as shown in Figure 27.

Image maps are quite simple to make in Illustrator. The Attributes panel contains an Image list arrow, which allows you to choose a shape for your image map. You can then enter the URL for the link. The resulting image map is not visible—not in Illustrator and not in the browser. The area that the user clicks on the image map is also known as a **hotspot**.

FIGURE 27

Image maps enable you to define odd-shaped areas of an image as links to a URL

Choose web safe colors

1. Open AI 13-2.ai, then save it as **New England Map**.

2. Show the Color panel.

3. Click the **Color panel list arrow**, then click **Web Safe RGB**.

4. Verify that the Fill button is in front of the Stroke button on the Tools panel, click the **Selection tool** , then click the **state of Maine**.

   The Color panel, as shown in Figure 28, shows the current fill color, the Out of Web Color Warning button, and the In Web Color button. The In Web Color button shows the closest possible web safe color to the green fill.

5. Click the **In Web Color button** on the Color panel.

   The object's fill color changes to a web safe color.

6. Click the **state of New Hampshire**, then click the **In Web Color button** on the Color panel.

7. Using the same method, change the fill color of the state of Vermont to a web safe color.

You used the In Web Color button on the Color panel to change objects' fills to web safe colors.

FIGURE 28
Color panel in Web Safe RGB mode

Current fill color button

Out of Web Color Warning button

In Web Color button

Customizing language dictionaries

Illustrator comes complete with Proximity language dictionaries, which are used for spelling and hyphenation. Each dictionary contains information for standard syllable breaks for literally hundreds of thousands of words. You can assign a language to an entire document or apply a language to selected text. To apply a language to all text Choose Edit (Win) or Illustrator (Mac) on the Application bar, point to Preferences, then click Hyphenation. Select a dictionary from the Default Language list arrow, then click OK. To assign a language to selected text, first select the text. In the Character panel, choose the appropriate dictionary from the Language menu. You may need to expand the Character panel to see the Language menu.

FIGURE 29
The image map artwork, optimized as a GIF

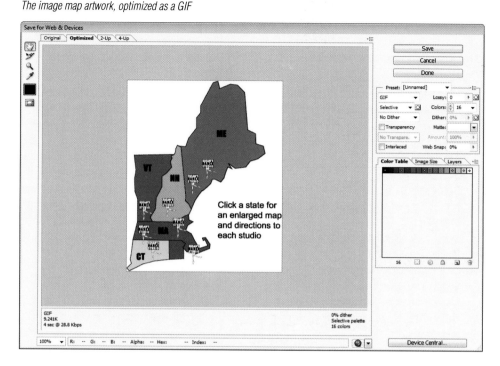

1. Select the state of Maine, click **Window** on the Application bar, then click **Attributes**.

2. Click the **Image Map list arrow** on the Attributes panel, then click **Polygon**.

   An invisible hotspot that closely follows the outline of the selected object is created.

3. Type **http://www.sds.com/map/me** in the URL text box.

4. Select the state of New Hampshire, click the **Image Map list arrow**, then click **Polygon**.

5. Type **http://www.sds.com/map/nh** in the URL text box.

6. Add polygon hotspots using the following URLs to Vermont, Massachusetts, and Connecticut. **http://www.sds.com/map/vt**, **http://www.sds.com/map/ma**, and **http://www.sds.com/map/ct**.

7. Click **File** on the Application bar, click **Save for Web & Devices**, then click the **Optimized tab** (if necessary).

8. Click the **Preset list arrow**, then click **GIF 32 No Dither**.

9. Click the **Colors list arrow**, then click **16**.

10. Remove the check mark from the Transparency check box. Your screen should resemble Figure 29.

11. Click **Save**, accept the current file name, then click **Save**.

12. Save and close New England Map.

You created five polygonal image maps with corresponding URLs. You then used the Save for Web & Devices dialog box to specify the artwork as a GIF file.

Adjusting and applying hyphenation

Illustrator has a preferences panel dedicated to hyphenation. Click Edit (Win) or Illustrator (Mac) on the Application bar, point to Preferences, then click Hyphenation. Hyphenation in Illustrator is applied automatically based on the language dictionary that is in use. You can turn automatic hyphenation on and off or change the hyphenation default settings in the Hyphenation dialog box. To access the Hyphenation dialog box, click the Paragraph panel list arrow, then click Hyphenation. To turn hyphenation off, remove the check mark in the Hyphenation check box.

Create slices.

1. Open AI 13-3.ai, then save it as **Hana**.
2. Show rulers, then place a horizontal guide just above the five photos. (*Hint*: Change your guides to a darker color.)
3. Place a horizontal guide just below the five photos (above the blue text).
4. Place a vertical guide between each photo and the next, for a total of four vertical guides.
5. Verify that your guides are unlocked.
6. Click Object on the Application bar, point to Slice, then click Create from Guides.
7. Deselect all.
8. Click the Slice Selection tool.
9. Select slices 01 and 02, click Object on the Application bar, point to Slice, click Combine Slices, then save.
10. Combine slices 02, 03, and 04, then save.
11. Combine slices 08 and 09, then save.
12. Combine slices 10 and 11, then save.
13. Save your work. (*Hint*: It's important that you save after Steps 9, 10, 11, and 12.)

Specify slice type and slice options.

1. Select slice 01, click Object on the Application bar, point to Slice, then click Slice Options.
2. Define slice 01 as an Image slice, click OK, then save.
3. Select slice 02, click Object on the Application bar, point to Slice, then click Slice Options.
4. Define slice 02 as a No Image slice, click the Background list arrow, click White, click OK, then save.
5. Select slice 08, define slice 08 as a No Image slice, click the Background list arrow, click White, click OK, then save.
6. Select slice 09, click Object on the Application bar, point to Slice, then click Slice Options.
7. Define slice 09 as an Image slice, click OK, then save.
8. Select slice 03, define it as an Image slice, then type **http://www.hana.com/photo1** in the URL text box.
9. Click the Target list arrow, then click _blank.
10. Type **Explore by car** in the Message and Alt text boxes, then click OK.
11. Save your work.

Use the Save for Web & Devices dialog box.

1. Click File on the Application bar, then click Save for Web & Devices.
2. Click the Slice Select tool (if necessary), click slice 01, click the Preset list arrow, click GIF 32 Dithered, then remove the check mark from the Transparency check box.
3. Click slice 09, click the Preset list arrow, click GIF 32 Dithered, remove the check mark from the Transparency check box, click the Colors list arrow, then click 8.
4. Click slice 03, click the Preset list arrow, then click JPEG High.
5. Click the 4-Up tab, click the Hand tool, then drag the Hand tool over the selected window until slice 03 is visible in all four windows.
6. Compare the quality and file sizes of the three optimized images.
7. Click Done.

Create an image map.

1. Click Window on the Application bar, then click Attributes (if necessary).
2. Click the Selection tool, then click the purple diamond in slice 01.
3. Click the Image list arrow on the Attributes panel, then click Polygon.
4. Type **http://www.hana.com/car** in the URL text box on the Attributes panel.
5. Click the gold diamond.
6. Click the Image list arrow on the Attributes panel, then click Polygon.
7. Type **http://www.hana.com/horse** in the URL text box.
8. Click the green diamond.
9. Click the Image list arrow on the Attributes panel, then click Polygon.
10. Type **http://www.hana.com/foot** in the URL text box.
11. Click the blue diamond.
12. Click the Image list arrow on the Attributes panel, then click Polygon.
13. Type **http://www.hana.com/bike** in the URL text box.
14. Save your work, then compare your window to Figure 30.
15. Close the Hana document.

FIGURE 30
Completed Skills Review

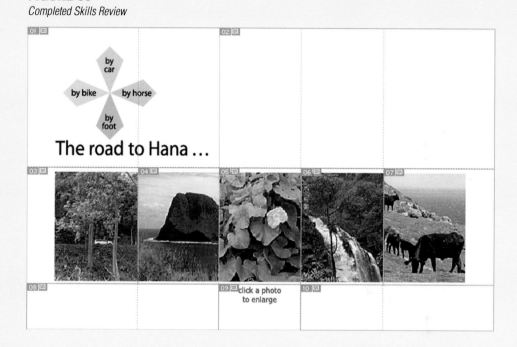

You work in the online department of *OAHU* magazine as an art manager. Every month, when the magazine hits the newsstands, you update the magazine's website with the new online issue. The top page always features this month's cover of the magazine (reduced 50% to fit on the page). The print department sends you an Illustrator file. Your job is to prepare the file to be used on the web. You dislike this month's cover choice—a dark, busy, and out-of-focus image—and note that the subheads must remain bright when they are converted to web safe colors.

1. Open AI 13-4.ai, then save it as **Oahu Online**.
2. Click File on the Application bar, point to Document Color Mode, then click RGB Color.
3. Click Window on the Application bar, then click Color (if necessary).
4. Click the Color panel list arrow, then click Web Safe RGB.
5. Select the word OAHU. (*Hint*: The magazine cover frame is grouped to the Oahu text.)
6. Click the In Web Color button on the Color panel.
7. Select the word "living."

8. Click the In Web Color button on the Color panel.
9. Change the colors for the three subheads (TWIST & SHOUT, A-MAZE-ING, and MAVERICK) to web safe colors.

10. Save your work, then compare your document to Figure 31.
11. Close the Oahu Online document.

FIGURE 31
Completed Project Builder 1

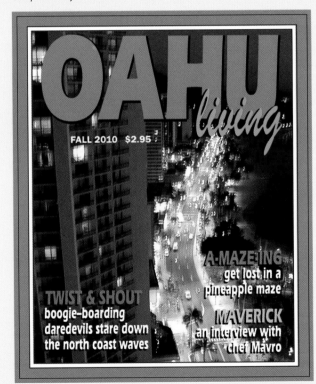

You work in the online department of *OAHU* magazine as a webmaster. Every month, you receive the color-corrected version of this month's cover, which you position on the top page of the website. The cover is one of your favorite features of the *OAHU* magazine website: Users can click the three featured cover stories and go immediately to the online article. You create the slices and specify the slice options.

1. Open AI 13-5.ai, then save it as **Oahu Magazine**.
2. Show the rulers (if necessary), then place a vertical guide between the A and H in OAHU.
3. Place a horizontal guide beneath the word "*living.*"
4. Place a horizontal guide above the word A-MAZE-ING.
5. Place a horizontal guide above the word MAVERICK.
6. Use the guides to make slices.
7. Combine slices 5 and 7, then save.
8. Define the options for slice 5 as follows:
   Slice Type: Image
   URL: http://www.oahu.com/twist
   Target: _blank
9. Save your work.
10. Define the options for slice 6 as follows:
    Slice Type: Image
    URL: http://www.oahu.com/amazeing
    Target: _blank

11. Save your work.
12. Define the options for slice 7 as follows:
    Slice Type: Image
    URL: http://www.oahu.com/maverick
    Target: _top

FIGURE 32
Completed Project Builder 2

13. Save your work.
14. Define slices 1, 2, 3, and 4 as Image slices.
15. Save your work, then compare your document to Figure 32.

You work in the online department of *OAHU* magazine as an art director. Every month, you personally optimize the cover image for the website. You feel strongly that the process of compressing a cover image demands a critical eye to maintain image quality. You note that you'll be able to optimize the image substantially: the photo is so busy and out-of-focus that it will be hard to see any flaws created by compression. Your goal is to compress each slice to approximately 8K or less, while maintaining acceptable quality.

1. Open AI 13-6.ai, then save it as **Oahu Cover**.
2. Click File on the Application bar, then click Save for Web & Devices.
3. Click the Optimized tab (if necessary).
4. Select all seven slices.
5. Click the Preset list arrow, then click JPEG High.
6. Click the 4-Up tab.
7. Note that the quality of the JPEG with the quality setting of 30 is unacceptable, then click the Optimized tab.
8. Note the file size and download time of the total image.
9. Deselect by clicking outside the magazine cover, then select each slice, noting the file size of each one in the lower-left corner of the window.
10. Select all of the slices.

11. Click the Preset list arrow, then click GIF 64 Dithered; note the file size.
12. Click the Preset list arrow, then click GIF 32 Dithered, as shown in Figure 33.
13. Note any changes in quality.

14. Deselect all, then select each slice, noting the file size of each one.
15. Click Done, then close the Oahu Cover document.

FIGURE 33
Completed Design Project

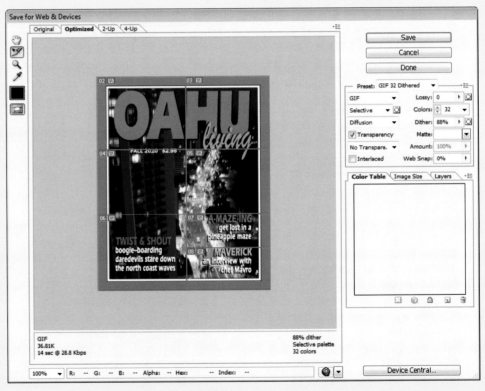

You work for a design consulting group. Lately, your company has enjoyed much new business from Internet companies who want your team to assess the design quality of their websites. Your newest client is Boston Chefs, a national website for chefs and the restaurant industry that features high-quality food photography.

1. Connect to the Internet, go to www.bostonchefs.com, click the search by restaurant list arrow, then click Casablanca. (Your screen may differ from Figure 34.)
2. Print the web page.
3. Draw lines on your copy that represent guides to be used as slices.
4. Assess the quality of the graphics on the page—all the graphics, not just the picture of the food.
5. Do you think the food slices are JPEGs or GIFs?

FIGURE 34
Completed Portfolio Project

Adobe Illustrator CS4 Ace Grid

Topic	Objective	Chapter Number	Page Number(s)
1.0 Working with Illustrator documents	1.1 Given a scenario, choose the correct document options or create a custom document profile.	1	4-5
	1.2 Given a scenario, create a document template.	12	14
	1.3 Given a scenario, save a document with the appropriate format and options. (Options include: various "Save..." commands, export, file formats)	6	7
	1.4 Given a scenario, select the proper settings in the Preferences dialog box.	1 2 3 4 6 7	5 4 11 14 6 18
	1.5 Given a scenario, create Guides, Grids, and use Smart Guides.	1 2 2 1	36 11 11 27
	1.6 Manage Illustrator workspace and panels. (Options include opening/closing/docking panels and saving workspaces)	1	8-11
	1.7 Build a document structure based on layers. (Options include moving and copying objects to layers)	5	Entire chapter
	1.8 Given a scenario, choose a preview mode to visualize the document.	1 5 12	14 6 13
	1.9 Customize keyboard shortcuts by using the Keyboard Shortcuts dialog box.	8	27
	1.10 Control object size and other options by using the control bar.	1 4 8	8-9 8 15
	1.11 Given a scenario, create and use multiple artboards. (Options include create, move, duplicate, and adjust artboard dimensions)	1 1	6 10

Topic	Objective	Chapter Number	Page Number(s)
	1.12 Given a scenario, work with multiple documents. (Option include views, tabbed documents, n-up arrangement)	3 7	6 27
	1.13 View and modify document metadata information.	9	24
2.0 Drawing and transforming objects	2.1 Create and modify a vector object using the Pen tool and bezier controls.	3	2-23
	2.2 Given a scenario, customize the Stroke panel settings to achieve the proper visual appearance.	3	24-36
	2.3 Given a scenario, cut, erase or delete portions of an object by using the appropriate tool.	3 4 6	5 24 23
	2.4 Use Isolation Mode to edit objects, groups, symbols, or layers.	8	15
	2.5 Given a scenario, create either a clipping mask or layer clipping to hide parts of objects.	4	30-31
	2.6 Given a scenario, use a mix of open/closed path, compound path, and compound shapes. (Options include Pathfinder operations)	4	12-23
	2.7 Align or distribute objects precisely on an artboard.	4	26
	2.8 Select one or more objects and arrange their stacking order.	2 3	28-29 29
	2.9 Modify an object with one or more transformation tools.	1	30-31
	2.10 Create and apply a pattern swatch.	6	8-10
	2.11 Record steps as a reusable action.	7	24
3.0 Managing color and transparency	3.1 Given a scenario, set up Color Management settings and proof color on screen.	12	10
	3.2 Given a scenario, create or load swatches, organize them, and apply them to objects.	1	22-23
	3.3 Apply transparency options to objects. (Options include Opacity, Color Mode, and Opacity mask)	8 12	4-7 13
	3.4 Recolor and fine-tune artwork color by using Live Color.	8	10-15
	3.5 Explore color combinations using Color Guide.	8	10-12
	3.6 Given a scenario, use the appropriate tools to create, modify, save, and apply color gradients to objects.	2	20-33

Topic	Objective	Chapter Number	Page Number(s)
4.0 Using type	4.1 Given a scenario, create the appropriate text object. (Options include point type, area text, and text on path)	2	2-19
	4.2 Format type by using character and paragraph attributes.	2	2-19
	4.3 Create and apply character and paragraph styles to text.	2	2-13
	4.4 Use the Glyph and OpenType panels to obtain special characters.	2 9	2-9 20
	4.5 Format a story. (Options include threading text frames and text wrap)	13	15
	4.6 Locate or replace fonts inside a document.	13	16
	4.7 Given a scenario, customize language dictionaries.	13	28
	4.8 Given a scenario, adjust and apply hyphenation.	13	29
5.0 Controlling effects, appearances, and graphic styles	5.1 Given a scenario, adjust the appearance of objects by using the Appearance panel. (Options include fill, stroke, effect, and transparency)	8	34-35
	5.2 Given a scenario, save and apply Graphic Styles.	8	42-43
	5.3 Given a scenario, apply the appropriate Live Effect to an object.	3 8	36-44 10-15
	5.4 Use the Eyedropper to copy attributes between elements.	3	24
6.0 Building graphic objects	6.1 Create and format a graph. (Options include entering data, controlling type options, and design)	9	Entire chapter
	6.2 Produce a smooth color mix by using and controlling a gradient mesh.	7	9-14
	6.3 Given a scenario, adjust the settings for the Blend tool.	7	21-23
	6.4 Given a scenario, choose or create the appropriate brush.	6	20-22
	6.5 Create and use a symbol. (Options include placing it onto the artboard, editing it, and manipulating it with Symbolism tools)	10	Entire chapter
	6.6 Create and edit a Live Paint Group.	3	40-43
	6.7 Apply and edit an object distortion envelope.	7	15-20
	6.8 Given a scenario, use the Eraser tool or Blob Brush. (Including editing the tool options)	6 6	35-37 23
	6.9 Given a scenario, prepare and create artwork by using variables.	13	5

Topic	Objective	Chapter Number	Page Number(s)
7.0 Working with images	7.1 Import images into your document.	3	18-20
	7.2 Manage assets with the Links panel.	7	6
	7.3 Turn an image into a vector object with Live Trace.	3	36-38
8.0 Preparing for Web and Flash	8.1 Given a scenario, choose the proper settings to save Illustrator artwork for Web or mobile devices.	13 13	14 18-20
	8.2 Prepare a document for Flash authoring. (Options include Symbols, Flash Text, and Release to Layers)	10 10	9 26
	8.3 Given a scenario, export to SWF. (Options include customizing and using SWF presets)	10 10	9 13
9.0 Preparing for print	9.1 Analyze the content of a document by using the Document Info panel.	6	5
	9.2 Use the Flattener Preview to preview and create custom settings to control the transparency flattening process.	7	20
	9.3 Given a scenario, choose the correct overprinting options. (Options include Preserve, Discard, or Simulate)	12	13
	9.4 Preview and analyze on screen color separations.	12	18
	9.5 Given a scenario, choose the correct print options and create custom print presets.	12	24
	9.6 Given a scenario, choose the correct PDF presets or customize options.	12	27

Files used in this book

Chapter	Data File Supplied*	Student Creates File	Used in
1		The Lay of the Land	L1
	AI 1-1.ai		L2
		Basic Shapes	L3–L6
	AI 1-2.ai		L7
		Flag	Skills Review
	AI 1-3.ai		Project Builder 1
		Iris Vision Design	Project Builder 2
	AI 1-4.ai		Design Project
	AI 1-5.ai		Portfolio Project
2	AI 2-1.ai		L1–L6
	AI 2-2.ai		L2
	AI 2-3.ai		Skills Review
		Desert Oasis	Project Builder 1
	AI 2-4.ai		Project Builder 2
		Vanish	Design Project
		Firehouse Chili	Portfolio Project
3	AI 3-1.ai		L1
	AI 3-2.ai AI 3-3.ai		L2
	AI 3-4.ai		L3–L4
		Snowball Assembled	L5–L6
	AI 3-5.ai AI 3-6.ai AI 3-7.ai AI 3-8.ai		L7
	AI 3-9.ai AI 3-10.ai AI 3-11.ai		Skills Review
		Peppermill	Project Builder 1
		Boston chefs	Project Builder 2
		Sleek Design	Design Project
		Shape	Portfolio Project

*See Support Files List at end of table for a list of files students do not open, but need in order to work with the Data Files.

Chapter	Data File Supplied*	Student Creates File	Used in
4	AI 4-1.ai AI 4-2.ai AI 4-3.ai		L1
	AI 4-4.ai AI 4-5.ai		L2
	AI 4-6.ai AI 4-7.ai		L3
	AI 4-8.ai AI 4-9.ai AI 4-10.ai AI 4-11.ai		L4
	AI 4-12.ai AI 4-13.ai AI 4-14.ai		L5
	AI 4-15.ai AI 4-16.ai AI 4-17.ai		Skills Review
	AI 4-18.ai		Project Builder 1
	AI 4-19.ai		Project Builder 2
		New Tie	Design Project
		Dartboard	Portfolio Project
5	AI 5-1.ai AI 5-2.ai		L1–L4
	AI 5-3.ai		Skills Review
	AI 5-4.ai		Project Builder 1
	AI 5-5.ai		Project Builder 2
	AI 5-6.ai		Design Project
	AI 5-7.ai		Portfolio Project

*See Support Files List at end of table for a list of files students do not open, but need in order to work with the Data Files.

Chapter	Data File Supplied*	Student Creates File	Used in
6		Checkerboard	L1
	AI 6-1.ai AI 6-2.ai		L2
	AI 6-3.ai		L3
	AI 6-4.ai		L4
	AI 6-5.ai		L5
	AI 6-6.ai		L6
		Polka Dot Pattern	Skills Review
	AI 6-7.ai AI 6-8.ai		
		New Curtain	Project Builder 1
	AI 6-9.ai		Project Builder 2
	AI 6-10.ai		Design Project
		Wedding Plaid	Portfolio Project
7	AI 7-1.ai AI 7-2.ai AI 7-3.ai		L1
	AI 7-4.ai AI 7-5.ai		L2
	AI 7-6.ai AI 7-7.ai AI 7-8.ai		L3
	AI 7-9.ai AI 7-10.ai AI 7-11.ai AI 7-12.ai		L4
		Distort Skills	Skills Review
	AI 7-13.ai AI 7-14.ai AI 7-15.ai		
		Tidal Wave	Project Builder 1
	AI 7-16.ai		Project Builder 2
	AI 7-17.ai		Design Project
		Bellucia Flag	Portfolio Project

*See Support Files List at end of table for a list of files students do not open, but need in order to work with the Data Files.

Chapter	Data File Supplied*	Student Creates File	Used in
8	AI 8-1.ai AI 8-2.ai		L1
	AI 8-3.ai AI 8-4.ai AI 8-5.ai		L2
	Limeade.ai**		L3-L4
		Triple Fill	L4
	AI 8-6.ai		L5
	AI 8-7.ai AI 8-8.ai		Skills Review
	AI 8-9.ai		Project Builder 1
	AI 8-10.ai		Project Builder 2
	AI 8-11.ai		Design Project
	AI 8-12.ai		Portfolio Project
9	AI 9-1.ai		L1–L5
	AI 9-2.ai		L6–L8
	AI 9-3.ai AI 9-4.ai		Skills Review
	AI 9-5.ai		Project Builder 1
	AI 9-6.ai		Project Builder 2
	AI 9-7.ai		Design Project
		Sales	Portfolio Project
10	AI 10-1.ai		L1–L4
	AI 10-2.ai		L4–L5
	AI 10-3.ai		Skills Review
	AI 10-4.ai		Project Builder 1
	AI 10-5.ai		Project Builder 2
	AI 10-6.ai		Design Project
	AI 10-7.ai		Portfolio Project

**Students open Limeade.ai which they created in Lesson 1 and continue to work on it in Lesson 3 and Lesson 4.

*See Support Files List at end of table for a list of files students do not open, but need in order to work with the Data Files.

Chapter	Data File Supplied*	Student Creates File	Used in
11	AI 11-1		L1
	AI 11-2		L2
	AI 11-3		
	AI 11-4		
	AI 11-5		
	AI 11-6		L3
	AI 11-7		L4
	AI 11-8**		
	AI 11-9**		
	AI 11-10**		
	AI 11-11		Skills Review
	AI 11-12		
	AI 11-13		Project Builder 1
	AI 11-14		Project Builder 2
		T-Shirt	Design Project
	AI 11-15		Portfolio Project
12	AI 12-1.ai		L2–L4
	AI 12-2.ai		L4
	AI 12-3.ai		
	AI 12-4.ai		L5
	AI 12-5.ai		
	AI 12-6.ai		Skills Review
	AI 12-7.ai		Project Builder 1
	AI 12-8.ai		Project Builder 2
	AI 12-9.ai		Design Project
	AI 12-10.ai		Portfolio Project
13	AI 13-1.ai		L1–L3
	AI 13-2.ai		L4
	AI 13-3.ai		Skills Review
	AI 13-4.ai		Project Builder 1
	AI 13-5.ai		Project Builder 2
	AI 13-6.ai		Design Project
		No solution file, class discussion	Portfolio Project

**Artwork is copied from Files 11-8, 11-9, and 11-10 and pasted into Tea Can file. Students do not save these files.

*See Support Files List at end of table for a list of files students do not open, but need in order to work with the Data Files.

Chapter	Support Files
1	No files
2	No files
3	Dog Sketch.psd, Peppermill.tif, Snowball Sketch.tif, BW photo.tif, Montag Sketch.tif, Skills Photo Trace.psd
4	Mona Lisa.psd
5	Living Room Original.tif
6	Brushes.tif

Absorption

Occurs when light strikes an object and is absorbed by the object.

Additive primary colors

Refers to the fact that Red, Green, and Blue light cannot themselves be broken down but can be combined to produce other colors.

Adobe Bridge

A sophisticated, stand-alone file browser, tightly integrated with the four CS4 applications. The main role of Bridge is to help you locate, browse and organize files—also called "assets"—more easily.

Ambient light

Determines how an object is lit globally.

Art brushes

A brush style that stretches an object along the length of a path.

Attributes

Formatting which has been applied to an object that affects its appearance.

Bevel

The angle that one surface makes with another when they are not at right angles.

Bevel join

Produces stroked lines with squared corners.

Bitmap images

Graphics created using a grid of colored squares called pixels.

Bleed

Artwork that extends to the trim and must extend the trim size by .125" to allow for variations when trimmed.

Blend

A series of intermediate objects and colors between two or more selected objects.

Blend Steps

Controls how smoothly shading appears on an object's surface and is most visible in the transition from the highlight areas to the diffusely lit areas.

Blending modes

Preset filters that control how colors blend when two objects overlap.

Bridge

See Adobe Bridge.

Brightness

The degree of lightness of a color.

Butt caps

Squared ends of a stroked path.

Calligraphic brushes

Brush style that applies strokes that resemble those drawn with a calligraphic pen.

Caps

The ends of stroked paths.

Clipping mask

An object whose area crops objects behind it in the stacking order.

Clipping set

Term used to distinguish clipping paths used in layers from clipping paths used to mask non-layered artwork.

CMYK

Cyan, Magenta, Yellow, and Black; four inks essential to professional printing.

Color gamut

Refers to the range of colors that can be printed or displayed within a given color model.

Color mode

Illustrator setting determining the color model of a document: RGB or CMYK.

Color model

A system used to represent or reproduce color.

Color Picker

A sophisticated dialog box for specifying colors in Illustrator.

Color tools

Circle icons in the Live Color dialog box which represent the colors for the loaded harmony rule.

Combination graph

A graph that uses two graph styles to plot numeric data; useful for emphasizing one set of data in comparison to others.

Compound path

Two or more paths that define a single object. When overlapped, the overlapped area becomes a negative space.

Compound shape
A term used to distinguish a complex compound path from a simple one. Compound shapes generally assume an artistic rather than a practical role.

Corner point
An anchor point joining two straight segments, one straight segment, and one curved segment, or two curved segments.

Crop marks
Short, thin lines that define where artwork is trimmed after it is printed.

Custom graph design
Artwork used to replace traditional columns, bars, or markers in Illustrator graphs.

Direction lines
Emanating from an anchor point, they determine the arc of a curved segment.

'Drag & drop' a copy
Pressing [Alt](Win) or [option](Mac) when moving an object; creates a copy of the object.

Edge
Similar to a stroke, an edge is a new shape or area created by the overlap of Illustrator objects, when the Live Paint Bucket Tool is applied. Edges appear as strokes but can be filled with color using the Live Paint Bucket Tool.

Effect
A type of appearance attribute which alters an object's appearance without altering the object itself.

Envelopes
Objects that are used to distort other objects into the shape of the envelope object.

Extrude
To add depth to an object by extending it on its Z axis. An object's Z axis is always perpendicular to the object's front surface.

Extrude & Bevel effect
A 3D effect that applies a three-dimensional effect to two-dimensional objects.

Flatten Artwork
Consolidating all layers in a document into a single layer.

GIF
A standard file format for compressing images by lowering the number of colors available to the file.

Gradient / Gradient Fill
A graduated blend between two or more colors used to fill an object or multiple objects.

Graph
A diagram of data that shows relationships among a set of numbers.

Graph type
A dialog box that provides a variety of ways to change the look of an Illustrator graph.

Graphic Styles
Named sets of appearance attributes.

Harmony Rule
Sets of complimentary colors in the Color Guide, which work well together and help you choose colors for your illustration.

Highlight Intensity
Controls how intense a highlight appears.

Highlight Size
Controls how large the highlights appear on an object.

Hue
The name of a color, or its identity on a standard color wheel.

Image map
A graphic with areas defined as links for the Internet.

Imageable area
The area inside the dotted line on the artboard which represents the portion of the page that a standard printer can print.

Insertion mode
The drawing mode in Illustrator that allows you to add a new object to a live paint group. A gray rectangle surrounding a live paint group indicates Insertion mode is active.

Isolation Mode

A mode in which you work in Illustrator. In isolation mode, the selected group appears in full color, while all the remaining objects on the art board are dimmed and unable to be selected.

Joins

Define the appearance of the corner where two paths meet.

JPEG

A standard file format for compressing continuous tone images, gradients, and blends.

Kerning

Increasing or decreasing the horizontal space between any two text characters.

Keyboard increment

The distance that a single press of an arrow key moves a selected item; editable as a preference.

Layers

A solution for organizing and managing a complex illustration by segregating artwork.

Lighting Intensity

Controls the strength of the light on the object. The range for lighting intensity is 0-100, with 100 being the default.

Linear gradient

A gradient which can fill an object from left to right, top to bottom, or on any angle.

Live paint group

A live paint group is created when the Live Paint Bucket Tool is applied to selected objects. All of the resulting regions and edges are part of the live paint group and share a dynamic relationship.

Menu bar

At the top of the Illustrator window; a bar which includes all of the Illustrator menus.

Mesh lines

Paths that crisscross a mesh object, joined at their intersections by mesh points.

Mesh object

A single, multicolored object in which colors can flow in different directions and transition gradually from point to point.

Mesh patch

The area between four mesh points.

Mesh points

Diamond shaped points which function like anchor points, with the added ability of being able to be assigned a color.

Miter join

Produces stroked lines with pointed corners.

Miter limit

Determines when a Miter join will be squared off to a beveled edge.

Multiply

An essential blending mode in which the colors of overlapping objects create an effect that is similar to overlapping magic markers.

Non-process Inks

Special pre-mixed inks that are printed separately from process inks.

Offset

(noun) The distance that an object is moved from a starting location to a subsequent location.

Offset path

A command that creates a copy of a selected path repositioned at a specified distance.

Opacity

The degree to which an object is transparent.

Optimization

A process by which a file's size is reduced through standard color compression algorithms.

Outline stroke

A command that converts a stroked path into a closed path that is the same width as the original stroked path.

Outlined text

A command that changes text in a document to standard vector graphics.

Panels
Windows containing features for modifying and manipulating Illustrator objects.

PANTONE
The standard library of non-process inks.

Pathfinders
Preset operations that combine paths in a variety of ways; useful for creating complex or irregular shapes from basic shapes.

Pattern brushes
A brush style that repeats a pattern along a path.

Pattern fill
Multiple objects used as a fill for an object; the object is filled by repeating the artwork.

Pica
12 points, or $\frac{1}{6}$ of an inch.

Pixel
Picture element. Small, single-colored squares which compose a bitmap image.

Point
$\frac{1}{72}$ of an inch.

Point of origin
The point from which an object is transformed; by default, the center point of an object, unless another point is specified.

Process tints
Colors that can be printed by mixing varying percentages of CMYK inks.

Projecting cap
Produces a squared edge that extends the anchor point of a stroked path by a distance that is ½ the weight of the stroke.

Radial gradient
A gradient which fills an object as a series of concentric circles.

Recolor Artwork
An Illustrator utility that offers you the ability to affect color in an entire illustration dynamically—rather than fill objects with various colors individually.

Reflection
Occurs when light strikes an object and 'bounces' off the object.

Region
Similar to a fill, a region is a new shape or area created by the overlap of Illustrator objects. Regions are created when the Live Paint Bucket Tool is applied.

Resolution
The number of pixels in a given inch of a bitmap graphic.

Resolution-independent
Refers to a graphic which can be scaled with no impact on image quality.

Revolve
Another method that Illustrator CS4 provides for applying a 3D effect to a 2D object by "sweeping" a path in a circular direction around the Y axis of the object.

RGB
Red, Green and Blue; the additive primary colors of light.

Rich black
A process tint that is 100% Black plus 50% Cyan; used to print deep, dark black areas of a printed page.

Round cap
Produces a stroked path with rounded ends.

Round join
Produces stroked lines with rounded corners.

Saturation
The intensity of a hue.

Scatter brush
A brush style which disperses copies of an object along a path.

Scratch area
The area outside the artboard where objects may be stored for future use; objects on the scratch area will not print.

Slice
Divided artwork to be output as individual—and therefore smaller—files.

Smart guides
Non-printing words that appear on the artboard and identify visible or invisible objects, page boundaries, intersections, anchor points, etc.

Smooth points
Anchor points created by clicking and dragging the Pen Tool; the path continues uninterrupted through the anchor point.

Snap to point
Automatically aligns points when they get close together.

Stacking order
The hierarchy of objects on the artboard, from frontmost to backmost.

Status bar
A utility on the artboard that contains a list arrow menu from which you can choose a status line with information about the current tool, the date and time, the amount of free memory, or the number of undo operations.

Subtractive Primary Colors
Cyan, Magenta and Yellow; the term subtractive refers to the concept that each is produced by removing or subtracting one of the additive primary colors and that overlapping all three pigments would absorb all colors.

SWF
Macromedia Flash file format that supports vector graphics for the Web.

Symbol instance
A single usage of a symbol.

Symbol instance set
Symbol instances created with the Symbol Sprayer Tool.

Tick marks
Short lines that extend out from the value axis of a graph and aid viewers in interpreting the meaning of column height by indicating incremental values on the value axis.

Tile
Artwork, usually square, used repeatedly in a pattern fill.

Tiling
The process of repeating a tile as a fill for a pattern.

Title bar
At the top of the Illustrator window; contains the name of the document, magnification level, and color mode.

Tools panel
A panel containing Illustrator tools for creating, selecting, and manipulating objects in Illustrator.

Tracking
The process of inserting or removing uniform spaces between text characters to affect the width of selected words or entire blocks of text.

Transmission
Occurs when light strikes an object and passes through the object.

Trim marks
Like crop marks, define where a printed image should be trimmed; trim marks are used to create multiple marks for multiple objects on a page that are to be trimmed.

Trim size
The size to which artwork or a document is to be cut.

Tweaking
Making small, specific improvements to artwork or typography.

Type area select
An Illustrator preference which allows the user to select text simply by clicking anywhere on the text.

Variation
A group of swatches loaded by the Color Guide panel when you select an object on the artboard and then choose a harmony rule.

Vector graphics
Resolution-independent graphics created with lines, curves, and fills.

Visible light
Light waves that are visible to the human eye.

White light
Refers to the concept that natural light on Earth appears to people as not having any dominant hue.

Workspace
The positioning of panels on the artboard/computer monitor; Illustrator CS4 ships with preset workspaces targeted for specific types of work, like typography, painting, etc.

Zoom text box
A utility in the lower-left corner of the Illustrator window that displays the current magnification level.

Illustrator Art Credits

Chapter	Art credit for opening pages
Chapter 1	© David Newham/Alamy
Chapter 2	© Christopher Scott/Alamy
Chapter 3	© Radius Images/Alamy
Chapter 4	© Darryl Leniuk/Lifesize/Getty Images
Chapter 5	© Dimitri Vervitsiotis/Digital Vision/Getty Images
Chapter 6	© Veer
Chapter 7	© Barbara Peacock/Photodisc/Getty Images
Chapter 8	© Stuart Westmorland/Digital Vision/Getty Images
Chapter 9	© Nick Norman/National Geographic Image Collection/Getty Images
Chapter 10	© Georgette Douwma/Photodisc/Getty Images
Chapter 11	© Philip and Karen Smith/Digital Vision/Getty Images
Chapter 12	© Veer
Chapter 13	© Jeff Rotman/Digital Vision/Getty Images
Data Files/Glossary/Index	© Paul Souders/Photodisc/Getty Images